The New Lawyer

Law and Society Series
W. Wesley Pue, General Editor

The Law and Society Series explores law as a socially embedded phenomenon. It is premised on the understanding that the conventional division of law from society creates false dichotomies in thinking, scholarship, educational practice, and social life. Books in the series treat law and society as mutually constitutive and seek to bridge scholarship emerging from interdisciplinary engagement of law with disciplines such as politics, social theory, history, political economy, and gender studies.

A list of the titles in this series appears at the end of this book.

Julie Macfarlane

The New Lawyer: How Settlement Is Transforming the Practice of Law

To Emilia,
I hope this both
instruct & provokes —
enjoy!

Julie Macfarlane

UBC Press · Vancouver · Toronto

15   14   13   12   11   10   09   08   5   4   3   2   1

Printed in Canada on ancient-forest-free paper (100% post-consumer recycled) that is processed chlorine- and acid-free, with vegetable-based inks.

Library and Archives Canada Cataloguing in Publication

Macfarlane, Julie
    The new lawyer : how settlement is transforming the practice of law /
Julie Macfarlane.

(Law and society series, ISSN 1496-4953)
Includes bibliographical references and index.
ISBN 978-0-7748-1435-5 (bound); 978-0-7748-1436-2 (pbk.)

    1. Practice of law – Canada. 2. Practice of law – United States. 3. Dispute resolution (Law) – Canada. 4. Dispute resolution (Law) – United States.
I. Title. II. Series: Law and society series (Vancouver, B.C.)

K120.M33 2007   347.71′09   C2007-904426-3

Canadä

UBC Press gratefully acknowledges the financial support for our publishing program of the Government of Canada through the Book Publishing Industry Development Program (BPIDP), and of the Canada Council for the Arts, and the British Columbia Arts Council.

This book has been published with the help of a grant from the Canadian Federation for the Humanities and Social Sciences, through the Aid to Scholarly Publications Programme, using funds provided by the Social Sciences and Humanities Research Council of Canada.

UBC Press
The University of British Columbia
2029 West Mall
Vancouver, BC V6T 1Z2
604-822-5959 / Fax: 604-822-6083
www.ubcpress.ca

To Ellie,
whose energy and passion inspires and extends me

Contents

Preface

A 98 percent civil settlement rate and the increasing use of negotiation, mediation, and collaboration in resolving lawsuits have dramatically altered the role of the lawyer. The traditional conception of the lawyer as "rights warrior" no longer satisfies client expectations, which centre on value for money and practical problem solving rather than on expensive legal argument and arcane procedures. Based on my own empirical research, conducted over the past ten years with lawyers and their clients, this book explores changes that are taking place in legal practice as we enter the twenty-first century and prepare for the emergence of what I call "the new lawyer."

The book begins by examining and assessing the changes that have occurred within both the legal profession and the justice system over the past thirty years. In the profession, the business model has altered dramatically. Legal practice is now dominated by large firms and corporate customers. The economics of legal practice have been transformed by widespread reliance on billable hours, which reinforces both internal hierarchies and the traditional, time-consuming tasks of legal practice – the accumulation of vast amounts of information and procedural machinations – while litigation moves along at a sluggish pace.

Another significant change during this same period is in the demographic composition of the profession. There is a new diversity among entrants to the profession that holds out the prospect of change. However, evidence so far suggests that the strength of the profession to assimilate newcomers into its traditional norms and values is stronger than the means and will of new entrants to map out new pathways. This may change as a critical mass of lawyers develops who are other than white and male.

There are also signs that the patience and deference of the consumers of legal services is beginning to fray around the edges. Both corporate and personal customers appear increasingly unwilling to passively foot the bill for a traditional, litigation-centred approach to legal services, preferring a more pragmatic, cost-conscious, and time-efficient approach to resolving legal problems. A growing reluctance to spend very large amounts of time and money on litigation has provided an impetus for another highly significant change: justice reform. The most important of these reforms have introduced mandatory settlement processes into the civil courts, in the form of mediation and judicial settlement conferences. The same rationale – encouraging earlier settlement in as many cases as possible – has prompted the introduction of judge-directed case management in order to move cases along more efficiently. Similar changes are occurring in criminal law, with the introduction of diversion programming and restorative justice alternatives to incarceration, effectively institutionalizing plea bargaining and offering a range of new processes and sanctions. In family matters, the courts have often been more reluctant to press settlement procedures on parties because of obvious concerns (articulated by an effective lobby) about the potential for coercion and power abuse between spouses. Nonetheless, family courts across North America have been quietly developing diverse multi-service programs for the past twenty years, offering parties mediation, counselling, and sometimes a meeting with a family judge in an effort to resolve matters short of trial. As well, family law is an area in which voluntary participation in alternatives to litigation has grown exponentially, primarily in the form of family mediation or collaborative family lawyering. Finally, as the courts push mediation on recalcitrant parties and lawyers, many corporations and institutions have determined for themselves that they wish to adopt new voluntary policies and codes of practice that emphasize a problem-solving approach to conflict resolution, and aim to reduce their litigation budget.

For the last ten years, I have studied the ways in which lawyers are adjusting to changes in disputing processes. This book draws in particular on four major studies I completed during this time. Three of these four were concerned with the impact of the introduction of court-connected mediation on both lawyers and their clients. In 1995, I used surveys, interviews, and analysis of the court database to evaluate the Toronto ADR pilot *(Court-Based Mediation in Civil Cases: An Evaluation of the Toronto General Division ADR Centre)*. In 2000-01, I conducted in-depth interviews with a sample of commercial litigators in both Toronto and Ottawa who regularly participated in the court-connected mediation programs in each city *(Culture Change)*. In 2002-03, I evaluated the court-connected mediation program in the Saskatchewan Court of Queen's Bench (with Michaela Keet) and talked to lawyers and their clients in both focus groups and interviews as well as analyzing the court database *(Learning from Experience: An Evaluation of the Saskatchewan Queen's Bench Mandatory Mediation Program)*. Finally, from 2001-04, I studied the phenomenon of collaborative family lawyering by following cases in four cities (Vancouver, Medicine Hat, Minneapolis, and

San Francisco) and interviewing lawyers and their clients *(Collaborative Lawyering Research Project)*.

In addition, during this time, I evaluated the mediation programs offered by the Canadian Human Rights Tribunal (1999-2000) *(Systemic Change and Private Closure in Human Rights Mediation: An Evaluation of the Mediation Program at the Canadian Human Rights Tribunal)* and the Public Service Staff Relations Board (also 1999-2000) *(Negotiating Solutions to Workplace Conflict: An Evaluation of the Public Service Staff Relations Board Pilot Grievance Mediation Project)* (both projects undertaken with John Manwaring and Ellen Zweibel). Some of this data has also found its way into this book. Finally, during my year as Virtual Scholar-in-Residence at the Law Commission of Canada (2002-03), my work on the Commission's major policy paper on restorative justice *(Transforming Relationships Through Participatory Justice,* 2004) enabled me to talk with many lawyers and judges about their experiences of using restorative justice procedures and their impact on legal and judicial practice.

The hundreds of lawyers I have interviewed and observed throughout the course of these research projects have told me a great deal about the types of skills and knowledge they need in order to be effective in this new environment. Lawyers have many stories to tell about the adjustments in mindset and skills that are required by these new processes and the ways in which they have altered their relationship with their clients, whether commercial or personal. Further, their clients have given me insight into what clients – both corporate and personal – need and want from their lawyers, as well as into their own struggles with adjusting their image of a lawyer from that of a "warrior" to a "conflict resolver." Many other researchers also have explored the significance and impact of these new processes, building a body of empirical work that points to important patterns and themes in the changing nature of legal practice.

These lessons are consolidated and presented in this book. I argue that changes in procedure, voluntary initiatives, and changing client expectations are coming together to create a new role for counsel and a new model of client service. This role is moving away from the provision of narrow technical advice and strategies that centre on litigation and fighting toward a more holistic, practical, and efficient approach to conflict resolution.

The result is a new model of lawyering practice that builds on the skills and knowledge of traditional legal practice but is different in critical ways. The new lawyer is not completely unrelated or dissimilar to the "old lawyer." The new lawyer is an evolved, contemporary version of the old lawyer, and evolution and adjustment to change are the hallmarks of a vibrant profession. Both the old and the new lawyer offer legal expertise as their primary and unique skill. Both need client communication skills, good writing skills, and, sometimes, persuasive oral advocacy skills. Both frequently find themselves negotiating settlements. However, the new lawyer has discovered that she needs to utilize these skills in different ways and in new and different processes. The goals of these processes are almost always information exchange and the exploration of options. Sometimes they include the settlement of some peripheral issues, sometimes full resolution. The old lawyer is more familiar with processes that rehearse and replay rights-based arguments, look for holes in the other side's case, and give up as little information as possible. The new lawyer bases her practice on the undisputed fact that almost every contentious matter she handles will settle without a full trial and perhaps without a judicial hearing of any kind. She assumes that negotiation often directly involving her clients is feasible in all but the most exceptional cases and that in this capacity she is an important role model and coach for her clients. The new lawyer understands that not every conflict is really about rights and entitlements and that these are conventional disguises for anger, hurt feelings, and struggles over scarce resources. The new lawyer recognizes that part of her role is to assist her clients in identifying what they really need, while constantly assessing the likely risks and rewards as well as what they believe they "deserve" in some abstract sense. She also understands the purpose and potential of information in settlement processes. In adversarial processes, information is used to gain an advantage over the other side (information as "power over"); in settlement meetings, information is used as a valuable shared resource to broaden the range of possible solutions (information as "power with"). The types of outcomes that will be contemplated, discussed, and even promoted will also be different, including rights-based assessments that may be interim, long-term or short-term, relationship-centred, heavily pragmatic, or simply expedient. The practical and conceptual differences between the work of the old lawyer and the practice of the new lawyer are profound, and this book will present these using research data and many stories from the field.

At the heart of this new model is a concept I call conflict resolution advocacy. The new lawyer's advocacy role is focused on developing the best possible outcome – often in the form of a settlement – for her client, using communication, persuasion, and relationship building in contrast to positional argument and "puffing" up the case. This understanding of advocacy builds on traditional "zealous advocacy" but goes beyond the narrow articulation of partisan interests to the practical realization of a conflict specialist role for counsel.

At the same time, the lawyer-client relationship is fundamentally altered by the trend away from professional deference and the growing demands by clients of all types for value for money in legal services. Changes in the understanding of the lawyer-client "bargain" affect norms of decision making and control between lawyer and client, as clients participate more directly than before in settlement processes and determine how much time, money, and emotional energy to invest and in what type of resolution. In this book I explore the practical and conceptual dimensions of this new lawyer-client relationship, which I conceptualize as a working partnership. Some chapters tackle the question of the role of the law and legal advising in conflict resolution advocacy and the new ethical challenges faced by the new lawyer.

This book also argues that there are many aspects of legal practice – and its foundation in legal education – that have not yet caught up to the changing professional identity of the lawyer. Students are still graduating from law school imagining that their appellate moot court experience is representative of the work they will do in practice. Few schools offer negotiation and mediation advocacy courses. There is a misfit between the image projected by law school of legal practice and the reality. There is also a misfit between the core beliefs and values held by many lawyers, often unconsciously and uncritically, and the practical exigencies of the new disputing environment. These values and beliefs are first formed at law school and then challenged and refined in practice. They translate into what behaviours and practices are seen as professional, appropriate, and effective. I argue here that these beliefs and values need to be rethought in order to recognize changes in the disputing environment and in practice. Modifying these values and beliefs inevitably affects the behaviours and practices that are critical to the lawyer's professional identity, which is the core of how things get done in legal practice.

Some lawyers are already actively engaged in reshaping their professional role and identity. Disillusionment with the traditional "warrior" mentality has motivated some lawyers to initiate new ways of practising law that reflect a desire – both philosophical and pragmatic – to bring peace and resolution, rather than fight protracted court battles. These lawyers will welcome this book, and it will reflect much of what they already know and practice, albeit intuitively. I also hope that this book will be of interest to law professors and teachers, law students, members of bodies that regulate the legal profession, mediators, justice officials, and all others who work with and alongside lawyers in conflict resolution.

Lawyers who are more skeptical about the process of change, and those who are resistant to it, will also read this book, I hope. They may be surprised to find that it does not propose a rejection of traditional lawyering but, instead, presents an analysis of how many of the tools and skills of the zealous advocate can be melded with the new skills, knowledge, and sensitivities of conflict resolution advocacy. This book does not call for "paradigm change" but recognizes the reality of change and of a new approach to lawyering and client service that, while building on the old, is ready to meet the challenges of the new.

This book urges change, but it also offers an argument for the continued strength and vitality of the legal profession. Lawyers play a vital role in conflict resolution. They offer a unique form of client service. Lawyers are specialists in identifying legal issues and predicting legal outcomes. They should also offer their clients practical support, mentoring, counselling, risk assessment, and respect. The new lawyer will maintain and strengthen the place of the legal profession in our communities and allow lawyers and the public to again feel good about what they do.

Acknowledgments

This book is the culmination of ten years of research, teaching, and thinking, and there are many people who have played an important role in its development. My greatest debt of gratitude is owed to my hundreds of research subjects – lawyers, clients, judges, and others – who were generous and patient as they were subjected to my interrogations. Many of them told me that they hoped that describing their knowledge and experience would be valuable for others, and I hope they see that this goal was somewhat achieved in this book.

Over this period, I have received generous research funding for my various projects from the Social Science and Humanities Council of Canada, the Law Commission of Canada, and the Department of Justice, Canada. This financial support has been critical, and, as a researcher, I also appreciate the moral encouragement that this type of recognition brings.

A supportive yet always challenging professional community developed around me as I worked on these projects. I want to thank especially my dear friends and colleagues John Manwaring and Chris Honeyman, who along with Bernard Mayer and Gemma Smyth read and commented on earlier drafts of this book, and the "data chicks" for many instructive and inspiring conversations. I received terrific support and assistance from a galaxy of student researchers during both the gestation and the writing of this book. For helping me to cross the final finish line, I extend my grateful thanks to Hena Singh and Raong Phalavong.

We lost our dear friend and colleague Rose Voyvodic just as I was completing this book. Rose taught me better than any other person or any learned text that in facing new challenges and complexities, the touchstone for the new lawyer must be client-responsive service: practical, humane, and dignifying. Rose will forever epitomize the very best of the new lawyer for me.

Finally, I want to thank those who support and nurture me on a daily basis and make all things possible for me: at the barn, my wonderful coach and supporter Hilary, my faithful steed Houdini, and my new friend Louie; my constant doggie companion Lucy and her runaway sisters; my three beloved daughters, Sibyl, Ellie, and Hopey; and, with gratitude and love, my husband Bernie Mayer.

The New Lawyer

1
Changes in the Legal Profession and the Emergence of the New Lawyer

You're giving a speech about lawyers and *conflict resolution?*
Huh? I don't usually connect lawyers with conflict resolution.

– Waiter in Vancouver hotel

The disassociation between lawyers and conflict resolution expressed in this statement reflects the divide between the public image of what lawyers do and their perceived relevance to the practical solving of problems. This public image associates lawyers with conflict, not conflict resolution – whether as one's own advocate or as the agent of an adversary. This statement may also reflect the growing distance between private citizens and the delivery of legal services. Over the past thirty years, legal services have increasingly focused on corporate and institutional clients, diminishing their relevance for ordinary people with domestic disputes (and without the resources to pay for expert aggression or defence). The disassociation between lawyers and conflict resolution also does not work for commercial clients, who need to solve their business conflicts without unnecessary expense, delays, obfuscation, and posturing. The huge costs of protracted litigation and the delays in accessing judicial hearings increase a sense of profound disconnect between lawyers and attainable, expeditious conflict resolution.

If lawyers do not represent conflict resolution in our public culture, then what is their function? There is an urgent need for lawyers to modify and evolve their professional role consistent with changes in their professional environment. The most important of these changes are widespread public dissatisfaction with the delays and costs associated with traditional legal processes, and the disappearance of full trials in all but a fraction of cases – the so-called "vanishing trial."[1] Articulating a widespread experience, one Ontario lawyer points out, "It's considered exceptional now if we actually litigate something to a trial."[2] Despite the centrality of trial advocacy in the popular image of lawyering, it is now not uncommon for a partner in a law firm to have had little trial experience – and occasionally none.

While lawyers often assert that the declining trial rate demonstrates their ability to ultimately settle almost all their cases before trial, even beginning litigation may be an unattractive and unrealistic option for a client who wants an expeditious and practical solution at a reasonable cost. To be effective and successful in practice, the lawyers of the twenty-first century must find other ways to meet their clients' best aspirations – the achievement of effective, appropriate, and sustainable outcomes within a reasonable time frame rather than years tied up in legal procedures, draining their resources, and chasing an apparition of vindication and victory.

There is a growing realization among lawyers and their professional organizations that they are in danger of rendering themselves irrelevant to many ordinary people.[3] At the same time, they are concerned that the types of conflict resolution service that they have traditionally provided for commercial and institutional clients – specialized legal advice and file management through the shoals of litigation – often looks inappropriate and even irrelevant in the face of business realities. Spending vast sums of money and swatches of time on "fighting" is no longer acceptable to major corporations and institutions[4] and may never have been compatible with business culture.[5] The demand for value for money is coming through loud and clear from all client groups, probably accelerated by the phenomenal explosion of access to legal information facilitated by the World Wide Web.[6]

Governments and policy makers have already begun to act. Placing a high priority on cost-savings and efficiency, jurisdictions across North America have introduced earlier, informal, and simpler processes into civil and criminal justice systems, many focused on reaching an agreed bargain or resolution. Some of these new approaches have been forced on lawyers by policy makers who recognize the inefficiency of a conflict resolution model in which almost everything resolves before trial, but only after years of expending vast amounts of money on lawyers' fees and accumulating enormous amounts of paperwork, much of which is never used in the construction of a settlement.

The signs are clear and incontrovertible. Change is needed. And change is coming.

The Legal Profession and Change

The last thirty years have been a period of significant upheaval and reorganization within the legal profession. This chapter will analyze the most important of these changes and their impact on the role of the profession and the delivery of legal services. It will also offer an evaluation of the impact of these changes and begin to examine the complex relationship between the conservatism of the legal profession and the challenge of change. The contemporary profession reflects a classic tension between stasis (the tendency to resist change and hold tight to the status quo) and change. So much has changed, yet so much has stayed the same.

John Heinz and Edward Laumann characterize the legal profession as an "overdetermined social system,"[7] arguing that it is uniquely shaped by the changing social institutions of the external world. The legal profession is highly sensitive to economic change and developments in technology. The lawyer's role is continuously shaped and reshaped by the social and economic interests served by law. As agents for their clients' interests, lawyers must be responsive to changes in economic structures, political climates, social expectations, and disputing cultures. The same information drives a lawyer's self-interested response to changing market conditions. In other words, the profession is most responsive to those changing societal conditions that relate to its economic viability and wealth. Moreover, the historical development of the legal profession suggests that it is more concerned with following changes (particularly in the market) than with initiating change or with innovation. In this way, the profession is "more creature than creator of events and environment."[8]

While they must adapt in order to survive, lawyers also play a critical role in legitimizing new ideas and practices and in mediating between these ideas and their clients. Richard Abel notes that once new knowledge and skills are recognized as being legitimate and important, the profession will buy into what they regard as a significant means of ensuring their continued professional status – dominance even – in the field of dispute resolution.[9] The legal profession seems chameleon-like in its ability to mould itself to whatever current needs will sustain or extend its economic and social reach.[10] In studying the legal profession, we are, in effect, studying the changes in social institutions, relationships, and expectations that are relevant to law. Adjustments and reorientations in legal practice – whether administrative, procedural, philosophical, or strategic – are at least in part a response to changes in the environment.[11] The last thirty years offer numerous examples of this adaptive ability.

Economic, Structural, and Demographic Changes within the Profession

The structure of the profession – in particular, its economic focus and, hence, its practice emphasis – has altered dramatically over the final twenty-five years of the twentieth century. An obvious place to begin this analysis is the size of the bar. The number of lawyers has almost doubled in both Canada and the United States since the 1970s.[12] The size of the Canadian Bar has grown ten-fold since 1951, and it is estimated that the profession grows by 15,000 lawyers every five years.[13]

Major changes have taken place within the economic structure of the profession, with growing numbers of larger units or firms that reflect changes in client markets. The practice of law has become increasingly directed to the service of corporate and institutional clients, reflecting the expanding influence of increasingly large corporations, which are in turn impelled by the search for more efficient economic models in Western markets. The dispersion of lawyers among different sectors of the profession means that, while there are still sole practitioners entering the professional marketplace, the proportion of practice conducted in larger organizational groups has risen at a much sharper rate, often at the expense of sole practitioners who now face competition in their "core" areas – divorce, landlord and tenant issues, simple wills, and consumer bankruptcies – from a barely regulated market for para-legals and contract lawyers working for low salaries in larger firms.

While much of the data used as evidence of these changes originates in the United States, it is broadly applicable to other common law jurisdictions with similarly developed market models, legal professions, and legal systems. The profession in both Canada and the United Kingdom, for example, has experienced very similar patterns of economic restructuring over this period. Two studies that examined work patterns among lawyers in the Chicago Bar have been especially influential in highlighting these changes. The first Chicago study, published in 1975, suggested that two "hemispheres" of legal work were emerging, one related to delivering services to personal clients and the other dedicated to serving commercial clients.[14] A second study sponsored by the American Bar Foundation and published in 1995 found a similar separation between personal and commercial work although there was some overlap – for example, a tax lawyer might have both personal and corporate clients – and generally a much higher level of specialization among practitioners.[15] These conclusions were broadly accepted by Canadian researchers John Hagan and Fiona Kay, who recognized that the two hemispheres were typically represented by different models of a law firm, with larger firms representing commercial clients and smaller firms or sole practitioners representing personal clients.[16] Most significant, perhaps, is the fact that in the last quarter of the twentieth century the corporate sector grew at a far greater rate than the personal sector. In the second study, 61 percent of Chicago lawyers' time was spent on work for corporate clients compared with 53 percent in the first Chicago study, while the figures for personal client work dropped from 40 percent to 29 percent by 1995.

To meet the expanding demand from commercial and institutional clients, increasingly large firms (the so-called "mega firm") have begun to emerge. These firms can more effectively respond to corporate client needs by offering specialized departments and teams of lawyers dedicated to serving particular clients. The second Chicago study found that the average number of lawyers in a single law firm had rocketed from twenty-seven in 1975 to 141 in 1995. Ron Daniels and Hagan and Kay have found a similar trend toward larger firms and the absorption of sole practitioners in studying firms in Ontario in the early 1990s.[17] Firms that serve mostly commercial clients can now offer them a range of highly specialized legal services in new or emergent areas that were unheard of thirty years ago, including international trade law, e-law, and a range of intellectual property disciplines. Professional regulators increasingly offer specialist qualifications and designations that recognize areas of special expertise. Law school curricula also offer a larger range of subjects, representing many new specializations, especially in business law.

Unsurprisingly, the earnings of solo practitioners have declined significantly over the last thirty years, and the earnings of lawyers (and especially partners) in large firms have risen exponentially. The profitability of larger firms is maintained by the concept of the "billable hour"; as a result, targets are set for lawyers at all levels and younger associates, in particular, are required to work extremely long hours. Competition for the best young lawyers also means that in some cases earnings are rising at a faster rate than profits,[18] which simply increases the pressure to bill more hours to make up the shortfall.[19] The supremacy of the billable hour has other consequences too. By separating fee generation from salary calculation, the firm establishes and maintains a hierarchy within that is tightly controlled by the partners. Some firms now encourage consolidating the power of the partners by establishing two levels of partnership – one that enjoys only limited rights – in order to delay the achievement of full partnership status for associates.[20] Mobility within the firm is difficult other than by embracing the given criteria (not only the volume of billable hours but also the various social requirements such as client contact and networking). In order to be economically successful within this model, lawyers must also accept significant limitations on their personal autonomy and decision making.[21]

The dominance of the mega-firm market model within the professional culture has had a profound impact on professional identity. Law students quickly learn to regard articles on Bay Street or a job on Wall Street as the ultimate mark of status and success at law school. However, once they begin working within a large firm, their self-image may be challenged by the realization that the economic conditions of their labour constrain the types of professional autonomy and responsibility for decision making that they assumed would come with the "dream job" for which they have competed so fiercely.

Another consequence of the growth of corporatism in the second half of the twentieth century has been the establishment of corporate legal departments and the emergence of a new professional role: in-house corporate counsel. Almost unheard of prior to the 1950s, the number of in-house positions has grown rapidly and demonstrates the significance attached by large corporations to keeping a firm handle on their legal strategies and costs. Where litigation is still contracted outside the corporation, in-house counsel acts as a highly informed client asserting the company's interests. Robert Nelson found that the proportion of lawyers in corporate positions had risen from 4.4 percent in 1948 to 9.8 percent in 1988.[22] According to a survey conducted by the Association of Corporate Counsel in 2004, there were 71,702 corporate counsel working in 23,540 corporations in the United States. This number represents approximately 10 percent of the total number of practising lawyers in the United States.[23] In Canada, the Canadian Corporate Counsel Association was established as a conference of the Canadian Bar Association in 1998 and now has almost 9,000 members.[24]

As well as undergoing structural and economic changes, the demographic composition of the profession has also changed dramatically during this period, at least at the entry level. Women and minorities are entering law school and the profession in unprecedented numbers, and law school classrooms and associate levels in law firms have taken on a different gender and ethnic composition as a result. For example, in the 1950s, just 4 percent of law school entrants were female. By the 1990s, the numbers of men and women in law school classrooms had become virtually equal.[25] Lesser, but still significant, increases have also been recorded in the numbers of minority students attending law school, rising from 4.3 percent of enrolment in law schools approved by the American Bar Association in 1969 to 13.1 percent in 1990.[26]

However, it seems that previously excluded groups such as women and minorities have not yet acquired sufficient power to affect the organizational culture of the law firm. Research shows that these newer members of the profession also leave at higher rates than established white males and that, even when they stay, they rarely acquire the trappings of power and status their white male counterparts continue to enjoy. Fiona Kay and John Hagan's work has highlighted the marginalization of women in practice, even when they reach partner level.[27] The systemic barriers, including the lack of role models and mentors and unsocial working hours, were chronicled in the 1995 report *Touchstones for Change: Equality Diversity and Accountability*, which concluded that the consequence is a "glass ceiling" in the legal profession for women and minorities.[28] Women are also leaving the profession in greater numbers than men.[29]

This means that despite some efforts at diversification, especially at the level of law school recruitment, the legal profession in Canada continues to be overwhelmingly white and under-representative of minority groups. A 2004 survey sponsored by the Law Society of Upper Canada reported that less than 1 percent of the sample described themselves in one of the following categories: African-Canadian, South Asian-Canadian, or Aboriginal.[30] It is well known that minority law graduates face greater obstacles securing articles than Caucasians. Lawyers of colour face many barriers similar to those of women lawyers, including a lack of mentoring opportunities and difficulty achieving partnership status. Like their female colleagues, minority lawyers are often marginalized in particular roles within the profession, with an assumption that they will prefer and adopt certain positions.[31] The consequence is that minority lawyers are well represented in legal clinics and government positions, and under-represented in the larger law firms that represent the economic engine of the profession.[32]

The combined structural changes of the last thirty years have profoundly reshaped the business model of the profession. A market model of lawyering composed of large and very large firms, providing increasingly specialized services to primarily corporate and institutional clients, has become dominant. These changes have transformed the organizational and economic structure of the profession, although it is far from clear whether the profession's core values and practice norms have altered as a result. The limited impact, to date, of a new generation of women and minority lawyers should alert us to an apparent contrast between the relative ease with which the profession accommodates changes to its structure and organization, while resisting deeper changes to professional norms and values.

Changes in Dispute Resolution Processes

There is pressure all around for civil justice reform – from government, from policy makers, from the largely dissatisfied and often disenfranchised public, and from influential members of the bench and bar. The widespread introduction of court-connected and private mediation programs, case management, and judicial mediation is testament to concerns about costs and delays in justice. The rate of resolution before trial has risen to 98.2 percent.[33] All courts function differently than they did twenty years ago, with at least some shift toward the judicial management of cases and their settlement.

Some of the most significant innovations in developing an early and informal dispute resolution process have grown out of the dissatisfaction felt by some members of the profession with the limits of traditional litigation to bring peace and closure to their clients. Some sectors of the bar have started to experiment with practice models that focus on practical problem solving and have reduced their reliance on complex, expensive, and time-consuming procedures. A few initiatives – for example, collaborative law, where counsel is retained only to negotiate and is disqualified from litigating this case, in an effort to incentivize negotiation – have developed out of the frustration of lawyers who want to offer their clients a faster, less expensive, and more pragmatic, humane, and realistic approach to conflict resolution.

Far more frequently, however, the requirement of early settlement meetings is imposed by courts and legislators in response to the frustration of personal and commercial clients who, not unreasonably, want justice delivered in a timely and accessible forum. In Ontario, a 1994 civil justice review found that it cost each party an estimated $38,000 to take a case to a three-day trial. The average family income in the same year was $44,000.[34] Commercial clients have begun to turn in growing numbers to in-house counsel who are given strict budget parameters for litigation – and some corporations have started to cultivate a pragmatic, settlement-friendly approach to litigation.

The realization among policy makers of an acute need for change in public justice systems has been a watershed in many North American jurisdictions and has led to the initiation of dozens of programs that encourage and facilitate early negotiation and assessment of resolution possibilities. Civil justice innovations throughout North America, especially over the past twenty years, have focused on changing the procedural context within which settlement might occur, including case management programs (setting timelines, encouraging the early exchange of documents) and court-annexed mediation programs (assigning a neutral third party to facilitate settlement discussions and/or to evaluate potential legal outcomes).

Even before the initiation of major procedural reforms designed to divert civil cases into early settlement negotiations, the number of full trials had been steadily declining for at least three decades. Data collected by Marc Galanter show that, in spite of the growth of all aspects of the legal system (more law, more lawyers, more judges, more court personnel, and increased budgets), the absolute number of trials has declined significantly since 1962.[35] The phenomenon of the "vanishing trial" is probably not limited to the United States. The proportion of civil cases that proceed to full trial in Ontario has also been falling over the past twenty years. One study using a sample of approximately 600 cases a year shows that recourse to full or partial trials fell from 4.9 percent in 1973-74 to 3.2 percent in 1993-94.[36] Ironically, the decline in the number of full trials appears to have had little overall impact on the accumulation of cases on trial lists since, where trials do take place, they are often longer and more complex (using more expert witnesses and taking up more courtroom time).

The shift away from full trials – and the growing importance and credibility of processes designed to facilitate the settlement of issues that are unlikely ever to be argued in a courtroom – has many layers of significance for the legal profession. Recent scholarship examining the phenomenon of the "vanishing trial" has pulled back the curtain on the diminishing amount of time litigators now spend on trial work and asks what this means for how lawyers are trained and how they set realistic professional goals.[37] Lawyers (and judges) are increasingly involved in legal tasks that are not related to trials. This does not necessarily mean that the practice of law is focused exclusively on settlement activities, although such activities are increasingly important. In understanding the trend of declining trials, it is important to note the increase in pre-trial and motions activity, which is described by Gillian Hatfield and others in the United States.[38] Similarly, in Ontario, courtroom time attributed to motions and to pre-trials rose by 69 percent and 140 percent respectively between 1989-90 and 1993-94.[39]

Lawyers are playing a different role, offering different kinds of service to their clients and performing different tasks. Some of these tasks, such as negotiating with the other side or providing the written forms of advocacy required for pleadings and other litigation documents, are familiar but acquire a new significance in a legal culture that is increasingly conscious of the need to offer practical problem solving and resolution. Lawyers are also spending more time on newer and less familiar forms of advocacy such as judge-led settlement conferences and pre-trials as well as representation in mediation.

The combination of the decline of the full trial with the development of new processes (many of them mandatory) to facilitate dialogue about settlement has changed the environment within which civil litigation occurs. While the impact of these changes is greatest on civil litigators, it also reflects a new attitude toward the use of public adjudication – one that no longer assumes that this is the default dispute resolution. Also affected are lawyers who specialize in administrative law matters; most administrative tribunals now require or recommend an early settlement meeting, pre-trial, or mediation. Corporate lawyers are affected by a growing insistence among their clients on expeditious conflict resolution and a new focus on dispute resolution clauses and other planning devices to anticipate, and reduce the costs of, future conflict.

Reform is also taking place within the criminal justice system. Interaction between the public and the criminal justice system demonstrates similar patterns of dissatisfaction, diminishing trust, and a disconnect between the work of lawyers and the courts and the real-life solution of problems. Disillusionment with the effectiveness of the retributive model has led to legislative and programmatic initiatives to encourage restorative justice processes and outcomes that rest on the offender's acceptance of responsibility and agreement to cooperate with a sanctions regime. There is manifest evidence for the failure of the retributive model to reduce crime or increase public safety in light of recidivism rates.[40] Overcrowding in prisons and inadequate resources for rehabilitation programs mean that incarceration simply compounds tendencies toward crime and anti-social behaviours. The criminal justice system has also lost credibility as a fair and unbiased instrument of social control. In Canada, First Nations people make up 2 percent of the population of Canada but 10.6 percent of the prison population.[41] In the United States, blacks make up 12 percent of the population and 44 percent of the prison population.[42]

These startling social facts, along with the rise of victims' movements asking for greater involvement in the punishment process, have created a momentum to look beyond traditional models of crime and punishment to community panels, victim-offender mediation, and sentencing circles. In Canada, legislation now places a responsibility on criminal court judges to consider the possibilities of a restorative justice process for "all offenders, with particular attention to the circumstances of aboriginal offenders."[43] The 2002 *Youth and Criminal Justice Act* introduces a new regime described as "extra-judicial measures," which promotes the use of earlier and preventive alternatives to incarceration for juvenile offenders, where the offender pleads guilty and the victim is willing to participate in a dialogue.[44] Both of these innovations reflect the same trends seen in the civil courts, with an effort to reduce judicial time spent on hearing arguments and a corresponding emphasis on enlarging the responsibility of the parties, with the assistance of counsel, to negotiate an appropriate outcome. All of these processes are based on principles of dialogue, information exchange, and agreed outcomes, as are civil justice processes such as mediation and settlement conferencing. The universality of these norms is a reminder of just how closely related some types of criminal behaviour are to civil torts, especially where personal relationships are affected.[45] Just as civil litigators are having their legal practice changed by civil mediation and other settlement processes, so too are criminal lawyers seeing shifts in their work – their responsibilities, their relationship with client offenders or victims, and the strategies they may pursue – with the introduction of restorative justice measures.

How much impact have these procedural changes in dispute resolution processes had on the legal profession? Just as we saw in examining economic restructuring within the profession, there is plentiful evidence of significant external changes – in this case, in the ways in which contentious matters are managed by lawyers and by the courts. The sheer volume and extent of civil justice reforms suggest that a settlement orientation is here to stay. As well, some positive evaluation data[46] indicate deeper systemic changes measured by the acceptance of these new processes by both lawyers and their clients. While there is less clarity (and data) about the effectiveness of restorative justice programming (for example, in producing lower levels of recidivism), early experiments have produced good results.[47] Some (civil and criminal) programs have now been in existence for more than a decade, and we are beginning to see the mid-term impacts of an emphasis on facilitating early settlement wherever possible. A deeper level of acceptance and change may be a matter of time.

One conclusion drawn from studies of more established programs is that continued exposure to mediation and other settlement processes, even where these are strongly resisted at first (especially where they are mandatory), generally builds recognition of the usefulness of the process and commitment to its continued use. Several studies now demonstrate that the attitudes of counsel become more positive with time and as a result of repeated experiences with mediation, and they have even described themselves as "converts" or "believers."[48] As one lawyer put it:

> My experience has now belied my original idea that counsel can always do this themselves ... I recognize that in some cases what happens would never have happened that way without a mediator ... Without a mediator we often stop [negotiating] on hearing first offers.[49]

Another lawyer summed up what these studies are showing when he stated:

> I think it's fair to say that my experience with mediation has improved every time, and I suspect it will continue to improve.[50]

Similar changes over time are illustrated in data on changes in lawyer-client relationships in settlement processes. What is initially an unfamiliar and often uncomfortable shift in practice – working with the client present rather than holding him or her at arm's length from mediation – becomes more comfortable over time, and, as a result, lawyers can recognize and explore its potential benefits. Many find that their commercial clients welcome the opportunity to be more hands-on and active in the management of the file. Others point out that mediation can provide a welcome reality check for less experienced clients: "Mediation can ... put things into a different perspective, including seeing the shades of gray that were always apparent to the solicitors."[51]

While these findings suggest change not only in the structure of dispute resolution but also in its spirit and values, other data paint a far less rosy picture. Attitudes toward restorative justice and, hence, the actual use made of alternative measures in sentencing juveniles and other offenders varies widely between prosecutors and courts. Civil justice reform that does not capture the hearts and minds of the local bar is often reassimilated into more familiar process models and outcomes. Lawyers are critical in influencing the attitude their clients will take toward mediation or any other mandated settlement process and in determining the amount of effort and goodwill that is invested in the process.[52] Settlement efforts require good faith, given lawyers' influence over their clients, and it is easy to turn the claim that these processes are a waste of time into a self-fulfilling prophecy. Other strategies for resistance include belittling mediators and other "softies" (colleagues) who are supportive of mediation, using mediation and settlement conferencing to obtain a strategic advantage (such as informal discovery) rather than with an intention to settle, and "going through the motions" by showing up but being totally unprepared to negotiate. In Toronto, lawyers talk about the "twenty minute mediation," where they attend mandatory mediation without any preparation or intention of serious negotiation. The creative capacity of lawyers to find ways to frustrate the purpose of mandatory settlement procedures where they are convinced that mediation is unhelpful or useless is apparently boundless. Also in Toronto, lawyers boasted openly about defeating the random assignment case management system that existed in the mid-1990s by closing a file that was selected for case management and refiling it in the hope of escaping assignment. It is important to remember that formal procedural reforms are typically driven by legislators and policy makers and only rarely by lawyers themselves.[53] Unsurprisingly, imposed change, such as the introduction of case management or mandatory mediation, has not been welcomed by many bars, which regard such initiatives as an incursion on their professional autonomy.

Other lawyers accept the formal imposition of a mediation consideration but do not see this as having an impact on their practice.[54] There is a sense among some lawyers that these initiatives are a fad that will disappear, and they do not need to be concerned about any new knowledge or skills training that might equip them to function more effectively in some of these unfamiliar processes. Instead, lawyers can simply walk through new settlement-oriented processes in a mechanistic way, without making any commitment to the change or adjusting their norms and values or identifying or acquiring any new skills and knowledge. Other lawyers express open discomfort with processes that require a different approach to advocacy and negotiation, divergent from the traditional advocacy skills with which they are comfortable, and which are central to their self-image. As one lawyer put it:

> I mean, we're trained as pit bulls, I'm not kidding you, I mean we're trained pit bulls and pit bulls just don't naturally sit down and have a chat with a fellow pit bull, the instinct is to fight and you just get it from the first phone call. I'm bigger and tougher and strong and better than you are.[55]

Change – What Change?
This review invites the conclusion that the legal profession embraces some types of change and resists others. While historically adept in adapting to changing marketplace conditions, the core norms and values of the profession are much more resistant to change. Earlier in this chapter I suggested that the continuing difficulty faced by women and minorities in reaching

the same levels of status and influence as their white male peers is a good example of the ability of the profession to make structural adjustments without challenging or changing internal norms and values. The profession cannot resist the integration of women and minorities, but it can maintain its traditional systems of status, hierarchy, and evaluation in order to keep them "in their place."

A second example of the limits of structural change in changing deeper professional values is the entrenchment of traditional attitudes toward practice – for example, the image of the "pit bull" described in the earlier quote (or, as one female lawyer put it, "a bulldog with lipstick").[56] The types of strategies and attitudes implicated by the pit bull and bulldog analogies are still widely regarded as appropriate and even normative lawyering behaviour. This is despite the fact that justice reforms mean that lawyers are increasingly challenged to explore an early negotiated settlement via the intervention of a mediator or a judicial officer. It is certainly true that problem-solving styles of negotiation are more widely understood and utilized now than they were thirty years ago, the result of a growing market for continuing legal education programs and publications that teach models of problem solving and principled negotiation. However, there is also evidence that the traditional values of advocacy and adversarialism have, if anything, become more entrenched as a result of the increasingly competitive environment of the 1980s and 1990s. Extreme versions of these traditional values are common in larger firms in big cities, which promote competition and believe that they need to cultivate a macho image, particularly for their commercial clients.[57] The consequence is a noted decline in civility and the rise in adversarialism in civil litigation, exemplified by the increasing use of the unfortunately named "discovery" process to delay, obfuscate, obstruct, and badger.[58]

Possibly the most conclusive evidence for the assertion that despite sweeping structural changes, the profession's underlying norms and values remain relatively unchanged is to be found in our law school classrooms. While there have been important curriculum innovations – primarily the addition of specialized substantive courses, mostly in the business area but also in human rights, international law, and critical legal theory – the philosophy and substance of legal education, and, in particular, its implicit ideal of what makes a "good" or a "successful" lawyer, has been easily sustained without major challenge for the twenty-five years that I have taught in law schools. There have been some calls for a renewed commitment to professionalism[59] and some work on enhancing the practical nature of aspects of the law school curriculum.[60] However, legal education continues to be focused on the teaching of substantive knowledge, an adversarial normative framework, and the dominance of adjudicative decision making. Considerations that are not relevant to the making and proving of a legal case are ignored, and students are not taught how to assess or deal with such issues – the "client" is a purely metaphysical concept to most law students. The lawyer's "philosophical map" continues to include certain skills, knowledge, and values and to exclude others, and what is included and excluded remains largely static.[61] To be reminded of the entrench-ment of these principles, one need only refer to documents like the Arthur's Report,[62] which, while written in 1983, describes a reality that is little changed more than twenty years later, or to Brett Cotter's review of the historical and contemporary inadequacy of ethics teaching in law schools.[63] The practice values promoted by legal education in North Amer-ica continue to emphasize technical skills, client control models, and the irrelevance of non-legal and emotional considerations in disputing. These remain the dominant values of the profession.

It appears, therefore, that while significant changes have taken place in the structural, economic, and procedural character of legal practice, these have had far less impact than one might expect on the core practice norms and values or on the ways in which students are primed to enter prac-tice. On the one hand, one can see the impact of an increasing focus on corporate clients and the power of the "mega-firms" in the business orientation of many law school curricula, yet this shift in emphasis does not extend to a re-examination of the lawyer's role, and even further entrenches a traditional model of client advocacy founded on argument and assertion. There is a growing mismatch between traditional adversarial advocacy and the pressure to participate in early settlement processes – a tension experienced by many litigators and met with anything from out-right resistance to demands for an entirely different approach to legal train-ing. There is as yet no serious mainstream debate over what this means for the professional identity of the lawyer and the skills and services that she sells to clients. There is also little, if any, impact on the types of practice knowledge valued by larger and larger firms who serve an increasingly corporate-dominated client base; technical specialist knowledge is still widely regarded as many times more important than process experience or resolution expertise. At least at the point of hiring, there is little inter-est in other skills and qualities such as empathy, wise counsel, creativity, and conflict resolution. In this largely unaltered world, legal education continues to be functionally efficient – the image of lawyering promoted by the law schools fits with the qualities emphasized by many law firms at the entry level.

This apparent lack of interest in revisiting the profession's core beliefs and values in light of change is not, of course, universal. At senior levels of the bench and bar, there are individuals who increasingly recognize the need for adjustment and the acquisition of new skills for negotiation, consensus building, and settlement. In completing my research over the past ten years, I have heard and recorded these views, which usually emanate from the most senior and respected sources. However, these voices have not yet been able to challenge the traditional paradigm that law schools and the recruiters continue to use for what makes a "good" lawyer, namely, high grades awarded for memorization in technical courses and success in competitive mooting, rather than strong inter-personal and communication skills or successful clinical experience. At the critical point of entry to the profession, there is a continued failure to recognize the skills and qualities that are needed by a new generation of lawyers, in a new environment of dispute resolution, and facing a new generation of client expectations. The disconnect that occurs once these students become lawyers operating in the real world is plain to see.

The absence of real change in underlying values and norms should not really surprise us. Lawyers are an extraordinarily powerful professional group, whose clients hire them for their superior expertise and rarely question their judgment. Jokes denigrating the profession at large abound on the Internet, but how many clients – even sophisticated ones – can constructively and knowledgeably critique their lawyer's strategy and demand a specific alternative course? Like any professional field of practice sustained by its high social status, much of what lawyers do as a matter of course – that is, diagnosis, strategy, argument, and, eventually in most cases, settlement – has gone unquestioned and unchallenged for decades, despite the possibility of alternative approaches, potential efficiencies, and new ideas. Although there is evidence of increasingly negative public attitudes toward the legal profession as a whole, most clients report that they are satisfied with their own lawyers.[64] There is no apparent threat to the assumptive status of lawyers as the authoritative agents of conflict resolution in our communities.[65] Evidently, the public has enduring faith in the legal system and regard lawyers as the appropriate, if disliked, agents within this system.[66] Clients and potential consumers of legal services generally do not have an alternative model of lawyering that they will require or demand when they retain a lawyer. They just know that they want a speedy and inexpensive solution to their dispute. Unfortunately, the tools and skills of the old lawyer are often ill-suited to achieve these goals, but many clients – especially the "one-shotter"[67] – can only accept their lawyer's assurances that this is the "best course" of action and do not have the experience or knowledge to critique their lawyer's performance. Those who do are voting with their feet – for example, when corporate or institutional clients turn to their own in-house counsel to get the job done, or when middle-income clients decide to represent themselves in litigation.

Changing Professional Identity: The Evolution of the New Lawyer

What would it take for an evolved professional identity to emerge from the changes we are seeing in the structure of the legal profession and the practice of litigation? What would happen if, in addition to reorganizing the way it does business and manages client files, the profession also examined its professional identity – including its core values and skills – in light of the changes of the last thirty years?

Challenging Assumptive Practice Habits and Beliefs

The first step in any change process is a willingness to take a long hard look at cherished habits and modes of operation that may have become fossilized. There are many elements of the practice habits of lawyers – like any other professional – that are routine and go largely unquestioned. Every lawyer could identify some routinized habits in his or her particular practice. Some of these habits relate to negotiation, which is used as a detailed case study in Chapter 3.[68] There are also parallel sets of habits and routines for litigation drafting, courtroom advocacy, corporate deal making, and so on. Some of these habits are useful, important, and often successful. Others need revaluating in light of contemporary conditions. All need to be related to the needs of the individual client.

Practice habits arise from, and are sustained by, norms and values that form the ideological backbone of the lawyer's professional identity. These norms and values are sustained by beliefs, many adopted unconsciously and long ago. The evolution and modification of beliefs is an incremental process, which should continue over the course of an individual's professional life and over the centuries-long development of the legal profession. In order to challenge beliefs, it is necessary first to recognize and understand them, which may also mean challenging them. It is the hallmark of a vibrant and responsible profession that it can revaluate itself and its roles without fear and in anticipation of offering enhanced service.

Re-examining old habits does not mean starting again from scratch – far from it. While the skillful and effective representation of clients in settlement-oriented processes requires new "habits" of action and thought, these can be built on the traditional advocacy skills of lawyers. The discourse over just what needs to change – especially where this is led by lawyers who have personally embraced alternative approaches to practice – has sometimes been misleading and polarizing. Some loudly proclaim that the only acceptable change is one that amounts to the complete redrawing of the lawyer's professional role. An expression frequently heard in training sessions for new collaborative lawyers or aspiring lawyer mediators is "paradigm change." A call to lawyers to embrace "paradigm change" assumes that real change requires the elimination of the old "paradigm" (characterized by the old lawyer) and its replacement with a "new" paradigm (the new lawyer).[69]

This is an unhelpful and inaccurate characterization of what is happening and what is necessary for lawyers to challenge and to change their entrenched practice habits and beliefs. For example, the core value that lawyers should protect and advance their clients' interests is not changed by new dispute resolution processes that focus the parties on the potential for settlement. Many of the traditional tools that lawyers use to protect client interests remain important, for example, the evaluation of possible outcomes, the development of strategy, and the firm assertion of bottom lines (often supported by legal advice). The introduction of consensus-building processes into legal disputing structures does not mean an elimination of the "old" system of litigation. Rather, litigation continues to run alongside efforts to settle legal disputes using settlement processes. Although trial work makes up a much smaller part of legal practice than it has done in the past, many trial advocacy skills are similar to, or congruent with, the skills and techniques that the new lawyer needs to practice conflict resolution advocacy. For example, good litigators are extremely capable of assimilating large amounts of new information, analyzing and synthesizing data, and moving between strategies and options in order to maximize their clients' gains (often by providing expert legal advice). The new lawyer needs these same skills, albeit exactly how that information is used, and what types of strategy are most critical in building consensus, are quite different than presenting a winning argument to a judge.

Many lawyers feel justifiably offended by the implication that in order to move forward into a changed disputing environment they need to wipe out everything they ever learned and begin afresh with a transformed paradigm of practice. This assumption is overly simplistic and fails to capture the way in which change is actually occurring in this new environment. Instead of paradigm change and transformation, what is really happening is the evolution of a new form of lawyering, which is more effective and more realistic within a changed disputing landscape in which trials are a rarity and settlement procedures are taking on both a new formalism and a new vitality.

The profession needs to be willing to challenge the assumptive habits of practice and belief and consider whether they are a fit with the new contours of the disputing landscape. This includes a willingness to take some risks and to cautiously experiment with new dispute resolution processes. Experience in new processes and approaches will, in turn, lead to a demand for training in evolved or modified lawyering skills that meets the challenges of this new environment by addressing the "skills gap."

The "Skills Gap"

Some lawyers are coming to recognize that there is a range of effectiveness in relation to their participation in settlement processes. As their experience grows, they recognize that some of their peers are especially effective in these fora but that others are often ill prepared and, as a result, sometimes wrong footed. Consequently, lawyers are beginning to identify special new skills and knowledge – albeit often built on more familiar practices – as valuable and relevant to them and their clients. Many of these skills and tools have developed on a "need-to-know" basis. Having been "thrown into" mediation or similar processes, and discovering that these processes often offer a genuine opportunity for advancing client interests, these lawyers have found that they need to develop different types of approaches in order to do an effective job for their client. For example, one lawyer explained:

> My role has significantly changed and now I don't think a litigator can be a litigator without also being a ... person who has advocacy skills relevant to conducting the process of mediation ... How do you do an opening statement? How do you identify issues? How do you know to prepare yourself for what issues you want to give up? What issues do you want to hold on to? How do you best present your client's case? *All of those things are done quite differently at the mediation.*[70]

Despite there being an increased number of alternative dispute resolution training courses for lawyers, judges, and third parties, these courses – offered both in law schools and commercially in continuing legal education programs – tend to be general in nature and often include only a secondary focus on the role of the lawyer as a representative in mediation and other settlement processes. There have been a few books published over the last ten years on "mediation advocacy," but the dearth of writing and training in this area speaks for itself.[71] There are complex and sophisticated skills involved in acting as a lawyer advocate in a settlement-oriented process, and our current state of knowledge about these skills and how to enhance them is as yet quite underdeveloped. This may explain why even lawyers who are positive about mediation often fail to recognize that they may require any new strategies, tools, or skills. A surprising number appear to believe that assuming the persona of "Miss Helpful," who takes on a friendly and helpful facade in mediation, will be sufficient.[72] However, as settlement processes become more mainstream and accepted, the expectation of skillful performance, and its market value, rises. Firms and individual lawyers begin to market themselves as mediation or alternative dispute resolution "specialists" as this expertise becomes a valuable commodity.[73] Once the skills associated with effective settlement advocacy become recognized as a commodity that has economic and reputational consequences, the profession will buy into what they regard as a significant means of ensuring their continued professional status.[74]

Changing the Norms of Legitimacy

The ultimate step in any change process is altering the norms of legitimacy. In this case, it means determining what good lawyers do. Are they classic zealous advocates, who leave negotiation until the last minute, advocate positionally as long as possible, and assert rights-based arguments until a final "compromise" is reached on the courthouse steps? Are they the "good lawyers" of law school mythology, who spend every day in appeals court arguing obscure points of law? Or are good lawyers those who see themselves as conflict resolvers, providing efficient, realistic, principled, and humane dispute resolution with constructive and practicable results? A personal reputation for collaboration becomes a valuable resource where a critical mass within the community has embraced consensus building as being reflective of "good" lawyering. The following statement makes this point perfectly:

> Good lawyers, in this town, understand what mediation's about ... I think that's what is accepted in the system, so lawyers have made the change.[75]

The challenge is to create credibility and legitimacy for new conflict processes within the profession itself. The norms that will be changed as a result encompass both community and personal values. Lawyers who choose to practise in a settlement advocacy model need a supportive community within which to work. One indicator of "real" change would be the point at which lawyers in a community find themselves regularly facing opponents who have a similar level of skill and commitment to engaging in serious settlement processes. Many lawyers describe the frustration they experience when a negotiation or mediation meeting reverts to the lowest common denominator – when the lawyer on the other side is poorly prepared, or unskilled, and/or unwilling to take the negotiation process seriously, they cannot gain traction. Exasperation with the predominance of settlement-averse lawyers in their community has led collaborative family lawyers to form their own networks that over time have provided critical mass for their alternative process.

Outside the voluntary networks of like-minded lawyers, a "critical mass" of support for settlement processes can only be achieved by changing the norms of legitimacy and the types of practice that are associated with "good lawyering." This shift may be accomplished faster in smaller communities where the legal culture is more cohesive with stronger prevailing norms and a relatively homogeneous client base.[76] In larger communities, the role of the most influential players in the wider legal community – and their leadership role in encouraging innovation and change – is critical. Local professional leaders include not only members of the judiciary[77] but also seasoned litigators. The experience of Ottawa and Toronto with mandatory mediation provide for an interesting comparison. In Toronto, there are some professional leaders committed to mediation, but these individuals are fewer and less powerful than their compatriots in Ottawa. This contrast is reflected in the peer group norms in Toronto. It is still not fashionable for top-flight Toronto litigators to be vocally supportive of mediation and certainly not of the mandatory mediation program. In contrast, the widespread acceptance of mandatory mediation in Ottawa is such that lawyers wish to be seen as supportive of such a positively regarded development. This is a strong indicator of change at a deep level – at the level of the norms of legitimacy.

The Myth of "Paradigm Change" and the Reality of "Convergence"

I have argued above that calls for "paradigm change," which would transform the role of lawyers and, in particular, diminish the significance of their specialist expertise and partisan advocacy, fail to understand the evolutionary process occurring within the profession. This is not to say that the evolution of the new lawyer does not bring substantial challenges to old ways of thinking and behaving, including challenges to the three key beliefs I articulate and set out in Chapter 2. Chapters 3, 4, and 5 highlight many new or modified attitudes and practices, which are in relation to the conduct of legal negotiations, client advocacy, and working with the client.

However, insisting on "paradigm change," which in Thomas Kuhn's original thesis means the elimination of the old and its replacement with something entirely new, is throwing out the baby with the bathwater.[78] Lawyers will continue to use and build on their foundational skills of negotiation, information assimilation and analysis, advocacy, and advice giving. Rather than eliminating the old paradigm and substituting a new one, the better analogy for the evolution of the new lawyer is a *convergence* between litigation and consensus building, representing both the old and new approaches to dispute resolution. What is meant by convergence is mutual influence and cross-fertilization, whereby the old informs the new and the new builds on the old. The new lawyer is evolving from the traditional paradigm rather than offering a new, transformative substitute paradigm.

The changes that we are seeing in legal practice represent the convergence of two quite different cultures of conflict resolution: adjudication and consensus building. Many of the growing pains of the changing disputing culture – the taking of positions or sides by lawyers who identify exclusively or strongly with one of these two cultures, the stop and start of civil justice reforms – reflect the sometimes uncomfortable readjustment that is necessary to effect convergence between two such different cultures. At the extremes of each culture – those few lawyers who regard adversarialism as a credo and those equally few who would eschew law and legal advice as "contaminating" their settlement-only practice[79] – there will be no such adjustment but, rather, a hardening of commitment and eventual isolation from the mainstream of legal practice.

However, these are the exceptions. Most lawyers will experience some type of convergence. What happens in the process of convergence is that each culture takes on some of the ideas, values, and practices of the other, and there is an intertwining of cultural norms and traditions. Even the traditional zealous advocate, who finds herself in disagreement with many of the arguments in this book, will find her practice and, over time, her thinking to be affected by changes in procedure to encourage settlement, changing client expectations, and the increasing redundancy of protracted litigation to solve practical problems. At the same time, the committed proponent of collaboration and consensus building carries with her at least some of the assumptions and beliefs of the traditional practitioner. The convergence of different cultures, despite falling short of the creation of a "new" something, might be compared to a genetic combination, where the essential properties of each process or culture are significantly changed as a result. Of course, the convergence that I am describing does not take place in a single moment, and the mutual influence of the two cultures will develop and evolve over time. The process of convergence is also affected by ongoing environmental factors, such as the market for legal services, the efficiency of the courts, and continuing civil justice reforms.[80]

There is plenty of room for skepticism about both the authenticity and the desirability of "convergence." Is convergence really a cover for the assimilation of one culture or model within the dominant one, a way of satisfying calls for change while maintaining the dominance of the old system? There are certainly precedents for this – for example, the ways in which Western legal adjudicative culture has swallowed up others (for example, Aboriginal conflict resolution traditions) by imposing its own criteria of substance and process.[81] Similar concerns are sometimes expressed that mediation and settlement processes may be co-opted back into an adjudicative mode by the widespread use of evaluative mediators, whose often-pressured approach focuses on the legal merits of the dispute. In processes that continue to be dominated by lawyers and legal discourse, clients will attend (satisfying the call for greater client participation) but often remain silent. Another potentially assimilative use of mediation is the instrumental use of mandatory mediation as an early, cheap discovery process. Nancy Welsh has used research data to persuasively argue that there is significant evidence of the assimilation of mediation into a model of adversarial litigation practice.[82] On the other side, those who strongly oppose any "dilution" of the traditional adjudicative model see mediated outcomes as "a watered down legal system."[83] They express alarm that mediation, which is seen as the "soft" approach to conflict resolution, could take over and all but wipe out adjudication.[84]

It is premature to judge the likelihood or extent of assimilation between the two cultures of conflict resolution – adjudication and consensus building. However, convergence seems the most probable outcome in the absence of one or another model being roundly rejected, culturally and institutionally. Most lawyers who have become familiar with mediation and other settlement procedures already recognize the phenomenon of convergence at some level, even if they are not yet clear what particular new skills and knowledge these changes imply. Convergence also offers the best choices to the consumers of legal services. Consciously or not, lawyers are developing some skill in determining when each approach – adjudication or consensus building – would be appropriate. As lawyers blend the concepts of fighting and settling, what is increasingly common is a perspective on mediation and other fora that explores settlement as a process that not only recognizes serious differences between the parties, framed by the threat of legal norms and sanctions, but is also conscientious in its effort to find common ground:

> Some mediators ... say: "Can't we settle this, isn't there a way that we can all just kiss and make up and go home?" ... that type of mediation ... is the antithesis of the old "take no prisoners" style of litigation. I like to think that myself and most mainstream litigators are *somewhere in between now*.[85]

The New Lawyer

My contention that what we are witnessing is "convergence" between two cultures of disputing practice does not mean that the legal profession can or should be passive in the face of these changes. Lawyers and their professional organizations should take a proactive approach to managing the new disputing environment and continuously assessing the need for new skills and knowledge. The profession needs to apply the same agility and responsiveness that characterizes its approach to changing market conditions to changing procedures and processes and to client expectations for faster, less costly, and more effective conflict resolution strategies.

Within a convergent or blended model of legal services, law and legal advice continue to play a critical role – and not only in adjudication. There are many new alternatives for directions in legal practice, options that lie within the choice of individual practitioners and depend on how they wish to practise law. If they are not to be left behind in the change process, the legal profession as a whole needs to take seriously the changing expectations of service, especially demands for value for money, the open provision of information, and timelines that keep pace with real-life needs and deadlines, which are replacing traditional assumptions of deference to a professional advisor.

If lawyers are to rise to the challenge of moving with the times, they must be willing to open up and reappraise some of the "sacred texts" of lawyering, including the devotion to zealous advocacy, the drift toward adversarialism, and the primacy of rights-based dispute resolution processes. It is not enough to change the structure of conflict resolution processes nor to reorganize the business of lawyering to protect profits and growth. There is a need for a "new lawyer" with evolved beliefs and new habits of practice.

This book will focus on three core dimensions of new lawyering that distinguish the new lawyer from the old lawyer. The first is the elevation of negotiation skills. Lawyers have always negotiated on behalf of their clients, but they have done so in a model that favours arm's-length communication between agents and a bargaining dynamic framed by legal positions. Despite the regularity with which negotiation closes a dispute, negotiation has not been regarded as a primary area of expertise for lawyers. Negotiation skills are critical to the effectiveness of the new lawyer, and she will place a far greater emphasis than her predecessors on becoming an effective negotiator. The old tools of positional bargaining, which are often a ritual bluff and bluster represented by a terse exchange of offers, do not serve her or her client well in consensus building. They are being replaced by greater reliance on problem-solving strategies and more effort to directly include the client in face-to-face negotiation.

Second, communication skills, such as listening, explaining, questioning, and establishing rapport and trust, have always been important for lawyers who work directly with clients or as oral advocates. Yet in the litigation model, effective communication is an adjunct to the content of substantive and procedural arguments. In the hierarchy of effective communication skills, the pinnacle has traditionally been courtroom eloquence – the persuasive making of substantive legal arguments. For the new lawyer, a different type of eloquence is necessary. Communication becomes the primary vehicle for the resolution of conflict and not only the making of arguments, whether via negotiation, mediation, or another settlement process. The importance of interpersonal communication skills, and the potential for these to set one lawyer apart as being particularly skillful and ultimately successful, rises as a consequence. So does the significance of so-called emotional, as well as legal, intelligence, including attributes such as empathy, self-awareness, optimism, and impulse control, which are important qualities for an effective negotiator.[86] Recognizing the importance of persuasive communication in conflict resolution also means a greater concentration on what the other side in a dispute needs and wants. Reaching a good agreement is not achievable using the old tools of assertion and reassertion. Other types of information and tactic are required. One experienced litigator describes this as follows:

> I call it the new lawyering role. You do have to be in tune to the other side's interests. For instance, I've seen counsel do it for a plaintiff in a personal injury action, a lot of it is they just want to be able to look at my insurance client and vent, and money is not always what they want they just want the other side to feel their pain and to understand what they've gone through. You start thinking about what their interests are, and what they really need out of this mediation and a lot of times it's just that, in order for them to understand or for them or your client just to see the other side and hear their side of story and see what's driving them and their personality. You have to be more attuned to the interests of the parties and what's going on between them, I think.[87]

Third, the new lawyer's relationship with her client is different from the traditional paradigm. She considers her client a partner in problem solving, at least to the extent that it is feasible and desirable (for the client) in any one case. Ideally, there is a new mutuality of both purpose and action between lawyer and client. The client will participate more actively in planning and decision making and perhaps in the conduct of negotiations with the other side. The new lawyer offers a participatory model of compassionate, client-centred, professional service instead of the traditional "trust me" detachment of the old lawyer. Conflict resolution advocacy accepts the potential for human connection in lawyer-client relationships and needs counsel to be self-aware and transparent about their personal values and biases, lest these unknowingly interfere with their judgment.

The legal profession needs to pay urgent attention to an evolving model of legal practice and client service that will enable lawyers to practise as conflict resolvers in the twenty-first century. This is the challenge. Can the profession make itself invaluable to its existing clients and relevant to a more complete constituency? Can lawyers really be conflict resolvers despite the skepticism of the waiter whose quote opened this chapter? The next chapter opens this discussion with an examination of the status quo – the traditional core beliefs and values that presently impede or constrain the emergence of the new lawyer.

2
Constructing Professional Identity

The sweeping structural and procedural changes described in Chapter 1 have given rise to debate, analysis, and some controversy within the legal profession. In contrast, the core beliefs and values of the profession, which are the foundation of the professional identity, role, and purpose of lawyers, have remained remarkably constant and insulated from serious challenge. Although well aware of the structural and procedural changes occurring around them, lawyers seem to be quite unreflective about the deeper impact of these changes on their professional role and practice values. Despite a current interest in renewing "professionalism" in law (usually understood as referring to appropriate professional behaviours), this has not extended to a serious dialogue over the values and norms that must underlie any sense of professionalism. This chapter examines the origins of professional identity for lawyers and suggests an existing set of core beliefs and assumptions, which, in turn, drive the norms of acceptable "professional" behaviour. The static nature of these beliefs, which are reinforced by a number of sources of influence for lawyers, stands in sharp contrast with the external changes in lawyering structures and systems described in Chapter 1.

A sense of professional identity, however established, is critical to establishing motivation and giving purpose to one's work. Professional identity is constructed from many sources, some of which are personal in origin (for example, the influence of family members, life experiences, and role models outside one's chosen profession) and some of which are professional (for example, working in particular practice contexts, professional mentors, and education and training). As law students are socialized into the legal profession, and as lawyers construct some sense of role identity, they are subject to multiple sources of influence.

Beginning with the Adversarial Stereotype

Almost anyone you ask – whether a law student, a member of the public, or a practising lawyer – is familiar with the widespread stereotype of the lawyer's professional identity. These characterizations are seldom flattering, especially when members of the public describe them. In general, public opinion on the subject of lawyers is fairly or highly negative; lawyers are frequently characterized as greedy, self-interested, aggressive, and even dishonest.[1] The general dislike that the public seems to feel toward lawyers as a "class," however, is not reflected in individual lawyer-client relationships. Evaluations of personal experiences with legal representatives tend to be somewhat more positive.[2] Yet such personal considerations do not apparently enhance the public's low level of respect for lawyers in general, who are the subjects of ever enlarging collections of "lawyer jokes."[3] Whether or not such stereotypes are accurate or fair, they are unquestionably universal. Those outside the profession of law evidently have access to ample information about lawyers, generated and fed by popular culture, on which to base their assumptions and opinions, even when they have never had professional contact with a lawyer themselves.

Judging by the attention paid to lawyers in media and popular culture, the general public has an apparently endless fascination with the profession of law. James Elkins, who teaches one of the first law school courses devoted to studying lawyers and film, observes that the media portrayal of lawyers is a "cultural phenomenon – lawyers and law have never been more prominently featured in popular culture (television, movies, novels, journalistic accounts in newspapers, and radio talk-shows) than they are today."[4] Some scholars draw a strong correlation between public opinion and public culture, seeing the media as expressing views that are deeply held within the community's psyche.[5] The contrary argument is that media portrayals themselves establish certain stereotypes in the public's mind.[6] In either case, stereotypical images, once solidified by constant media images, are highly resistant to change.[7]

Whereas earlier movie and television images of lawyers were more often positive – for example, Atticus Finch,[8] Clarence Darrow,[9] and Henry Drummond[10] – portrayals of lawyers in contemporary popular culture are predominantly negative. These often portray lawyers as greedy, mean-spirited, self-interested, incompetent, and dishonest.[11] They are rarely "ordinary" people but are extraordinary in some way, including frequent recourse to substance abuse and susceptibility to depression. These negative pictures of lawyers also signal that this is the type of behaviour that one should *expect* from a lawyer. Such expectations of adversarial and highly partisan behaviour may contribute to the disparity between popular contempt for lawyers and positive individual appraisals of personal legal representation.

As Elkins wryly comments, "The negative public opinion of lawyers does not seem to have resulted in the kind of suspicion that keeps anyone from filing a lawsuit or hiring a lawyer to do their legal work."[12] Instead, the stereotype is exactly what many members of the public believe they want when they ask a lawyer to assist them in a conflict. It is human nature to want to win over one's adversary and not to accommodate or compromise, and the adversarial stereotype satisfies this basic need. It may not, however, meet other equally basic needs – for cost-effective and expeditious dispute resolution, for example.

Students entering law school develop their initial ideas about practising law from many of the same stereotypes. The difference is that their image of the adversarial lawyer is the glamorized image of the courtroom lawyer battling for individual rights. The negative stereotype presented by popular culture is open to a more positive interpretation by those who believe they understand the "special" role of lawyers. Hence, law students tend to see assertiveness rather than aggression, determination and tenacity rather than closed-mindedness, entrepreneurial values rather than money grabbing, and zealous advocacy for their client rather than unethical or even illegal conduct. Positive images of lawyers focus on the determined pursuit of "justice" by all available means and uncompromising attitudes. These people are rarely "good" (in the sense of being well adjusted). Indeed, they are often pictured making "wrong" choices about family and career. However, their drive, tenacity, and determination are depicted as being admirable. This line of characters, beginning with John Mortimer's "Rumpole of the Bailey," continues today with the media portrayals of real-life lawyers like Gareth Pierce[13] and paralegals like Erin Brockovich[14] as well as fictional "superheroes" from the pages of John Grisham novels.[15] Positive images emphasize the "special" nature of lawyering as a tough career that requires a strong personality in order to succeed. These assumptions are evident in legal education where students are inculcated from the outset with a sense of elitism and encouraged to be highly competitive.

Lawyers themselves are naturally aware of the prevalence of negative public opinion and the highly adversarial stereotypes that are attached to their cultural image. While rejecting any implications of dishonesty or corruption, some lawyers embrace the adversarial stereotypes with relish, taking delight in describing themselves as a "barracuda," a "bad ass," or a "shark" (or, in the words of the lawyers quoted in Chapter 1, a "bulldog" or a "pit bull"). Others knowingly point out that clients seem less offended by aggressive and borderline unethical practices when their own interests are being promoted. A few actively reject any association with the stereotypes by committing themselves explicitly to non-adversarial forms of legal practice.

Unpacking the Stereotype: Values and Norms

A great deal lies beneath the adversarial stereotype that requires examination and evaluation. Some of its worst excesses may have limited practical significance in a profession where the exercise of personal judgment is a constant requirement and where a reputation for unpleasant and uncooperative behaviour, once made, is difficult to shake off. It may be self-perpetuating and difficult to step away from. A reputation for highly adversarial practice affects professional relationships with other lawyers and has more negative than positive consequences. In other words, there are many quite effective social pressures against the most extreme adversarial behaviours. This suggests that the colour and glamour of the adversarial stereotype owe more to the demands of popular entertainment than to the reality of legal practice.

Nonetheless, the stereotype also reflects a reality that most practising lawyers both recognize and acknowledge: that lawyers are expected to be argumentative, pedantic, and unyielding and that many lawyers believe themselves to be well suited to legal practice if they possess these qualities (and, conversely, ill-suited if they do not).[16] I am exasperated by the number of applications to law school that I have read over the years that assert that "because" this candidate is aggressively argumentative and opinionated he or she must be a natural fit for the legal profession. Certainly, these qualities are strongly associated in the public culture with the meaning of "advocacy." It seems to be impossible to entirely separate public culture from the professional identity of lawyers because each sustains and is reinforced by the other.

The Elements of Professional Identity

Whatever the impact of public expectations, lawyers construct a sense of professional identity from their beliefs about the proper role of the profession and client service. The elements of professional identity are embedded values and norms that, while they may be affected by popular culture, also reflect the deeper practical experience of practising law and serving clients. This experience provides many sources of influence, each of which has the potential to shape beliefs and values and, hence, norms.

I use the term "values" here to refer to those underlying beliefs that guide behaviour, and "norms" to refer to the standards that govern behaviour, either explicit or intuitive.[17] There is an important functional relationship between norms and values. Norms, or standards of behaviour, are inevitably derived from values or beliefs, which are, in turn, shaped by personal, professional, or societal culture. As one writer puts it, "Norms tell the actor how to play the scene, culture tells the actor how the scene is set and what it all means."[18] An examination of professional identity requires mining professional legal culture for those dominant values and beliefs that determine (rationalize, justify, and enable) certain types of behaviour.

The populist adversarial stereotype of lawyers focuses on behaviours: aggressive argument, positional bargaining, formalistic rituals and procedures, and the conduct of a single strategy (to win). More elusive but equally important to the formation of professional identity are the values and beliefs about law and legal practice that underpin and motivate such behaviours, whether these are excessive or somewhat moderated by practical exigencies. These include beliefs about the purposes of law, the role of the lawyer, the value of argument and assertion in the resolution of conflict, the potential for interest-based solution, the role and value of precedent, the extent to which conflict resolution is a public or private process, the responsibility of the individual for the collective good versus individual self-maximization, and many other issues close to the heart of legal practice.

Beliefs and values are often formed early in personal development, absorbed at an unconscious or semi-conscious level from the professional (or family or societal) milieu or "culture." For this reason, they often go unchallenged and largely unexamined. For many lawyers, their value system is implicit, buried beneath the assumptive decision making of their busy practices. Nonetheless, personal and professional values operate as an invisible and unarticulated driver for their practice behaviours and choices. Whether explicit or implicit, beliefs and values guide lawyers in how to play their role as the "servant" of the client and justify and rationalize practice and conduct choices.

A tendency to assume that "all the members of the club know the rules" becomes especially prevalent in elite groups where insider status depends on familiarity and comfort with the (often unwritten and unspoken) rules. An overt challenge to the rules always raises questions about membership. In this way, the legal profession assumes that with membership comes an understanding of an appropriate professional identity rather than needing a discussion or debate. Instead, the profession relies on rule-based approaches (via codes) to educate young lawyers about appropriate behaviours rather than encouraging a curious exploration of professional identity.

Recent discussion regarding lawyers' "professionalism," which has generally focused on standards of civility, collegiality, and commitment to public service within the profession,[19] touches on important issues that fall within the constellation of professional identity. Certainly, these issues implicate deeper values and beliefs. However, much of the debate over fostering a stronger sense of professionalism has chosen to focus on particular behaviours (such as courtesy and decency) and character attributes (such as honesty and integrity) rather than probing core beliefs and attitudes or the origins of established practices. This approach carries with it the danger that "professionalism" will be defined as those behaviours and attributes that reflect the status quo as understood by the most powerful groups within the legal profession.

The discussion over "professionalism" is just one aspect of a much larger debate over the role, purpose, and meaning of legal practice. This debate needs to consider more than just behaviours and preferred innate qualities. It needs to critically examine the beliefs systems that are core to the professional identity of the lawyer. If this is done thoroughly, it will be possible to evaluate the relationship between the traditional beliefs and values widely held among lawyers and the new realities and exigencies of legal practice. How well do the traditional beliefs reflect the new culture of dispute resolution, for example? How far do they reflect the increasing diversity of the profession rather than the particular assumptions of previous generations of lawyers? How far does the adversarial – argumentative, positional, rigid, rule-focused – stereotype reflect the reality of legal practice today, and, more importantly, just how relevant and effective is it?

A first step in deepening a discussion over professionalism and adversarialism is to consider how lawyers form their values and norms. What are the influences, aside from the admitted influence of popular culture, on their understanding of their role and their sense of professional identity?

Where Do Lawyers' Values and Norms Come From?

The conventional answer to this question is that lawyers are required to adhere to a code of conduct. Sometimes described as the "bargain of self-regulation," the strictures of codes are assumed to provide the foundation of professional values. What little teaching on professional values does take place, either in law school or at the professional stage of legal education, tends to focus on the jurisdictional code as the source of principles and general guidance on standards of behaviour. The actual impact and influence of codes of conduct is discussed later in this chapter. It is evident, however, that there are a number of other important influences on the socialization of young lawyers, each of which contributes to a set of core values and norms that become "essential" and "basic" to the lawyer's craft. Many of these beliefs are first developed long before a law student or young lawyer becomes familiar, in any practical sense, with the relevant code of conduct. For this reason, these other sources of influence are considered first.

Legal Education

The impact of the experience of law school on the original aspirations of students and their images of lawyering practice has been documented in many research studies. Some of the most interesting of these studies also show the before-and-after effects of legal education. Typically, students enter law school with idealistic visions of what they might do as a lawyer. Many have altruistic motivations. This idealism and altruism declines rapidly during law school.[20] Susan Daicoff reports that personal characteristics that appear to be developed or amplified in law school include a decrease in altruism and an increase in interest in private practice with a firm (coupled with a decrease in interest in public service); an increase in cynicism about the legal profession; and an increase in insecurity, defensiveness, anxiety, and sometimes psychological distress.[21]

Law school, with its overriding curricular emphasis on appellate advocacy and legal argument, does little to correct the images of lawyers presented in popular media. If anything, it revels in the stereotype of the tough, aggressive, single-minded litigator. Legal education seldom raises issues of professional norms and values in anything other than a formalistic positivistic frame (that is, by teaching the rules of professional conduct). Despite talk of the "pervasive approach" to integrating professional ethical values into the curriculum, few if any schools have been able to achieve this ideal.[22] It is unclear whether this is because of a lack of commitment or a lack of faculty expertise (of course, these two are related). In the hierarchy of knowledge presented by legal education, a low score is placed on professional ethical awareness and sensitivity (compared with, for example, knowledge of substantive law and procedure or mooting skills). Consequently, students are rarely motivated to concern themselves with these questions beyond a formal analysis and what their individual professors are interested in teaching them.

As a result, the beliefs and values that lie behind the role played by the glamorized courtroom advocate, and their implications for behaviour toward clients and other lawyers, are rarely discussed or held up for scrutiny. There is no real debate in legal education over whether the courtroom advocate is the appropriate role model for young lawyers. For decades, there has been a complacent assumption – questioned now in the increasingly concerned tone of debates over "rekindling professionalism"[23] – that young lawyers will absorb the "correct" norms and values by a process of osmosis as they progress through law school and into practice. Just what are the "correct" values can only be discerned by observing what types of law student behaviour bring rewards from the professoriate: evidently hard work, strong and well-researched assertions of positions, a willingness to jump into an argument, deference for professorial opinions, and an appetite for the cut-and-thrust of student mooting.

The seemingly unitary character of these norms appears paradoxical given that many members of the academy strongly reject the assumption that the legal profession rests on a set of universally shared norms and values that must be promulgated by them at law school. The recruitment of feminist, critical race, and other critical legal scholars into the law schools over the past fifteen years has had a noticeable impact on law school curricula, including the introduction of both courses and teaching methods that critique notions of universal norms and values. Yet these important hirings and critical curriculum additions do not seem to present a serious challenge to the norms of "good law student" behaviour described above – indeed, they absorb and reflect many of the same norms. Their focus of critique is generally on the state and society rather than on legal education or the practice of adversarial advocacy. Invaluable though these courses are in broadening the intellectual foundation of the law school curriculum, their critique is often highly abstract and rarely applied to the practice of law itself. The intellectual critique thus continues to co-exist with an uncritical acceptance of adversarialism as the best approach to conflict resolution. There is also a pervasive disinterest, or perhaps a lack of awareness that failing to offer an alternative continuously reinforces the status quo.

Professional educators have long cautioned that a belief in universally shared norms is a dangerous assumption. The absence of discussion of ethical questions sets up implicit values and norms. By presuming that ethical decision making is "obvious" and "simple," this ideology leaves law students and new lawyers with nowhere to go when they encounter a personal dilemma or moral quandary. Educators also caution against the assumption that professional values can be simply taught and imposed on personal values without any regard for integration and coherence, especially in a professional environment where the exercise of personal discretion is so central. The nurturing of professional attitudes and behaviours is a matter of individual developmental maturity, not group think. Leaving out a discussion of personal mores from the development of individual professional attitudes renders any teaching of "ethics" that does take place more fragile and superficial.[24]

Not only does law school neglect open discussions about individual values and beliefs about legal practice, but it also implicitly pushes a set of beliefs and norms that encompasses both educational and social dimensions. The intensity of the law school experience permeates all dimensions of student life, both inside and outside the classroom, and is highly effective in solidifying adversarial norms as future professional values. Systems of hierarchy among persons and ideas flourish in an environment that constantly "grades." Law school students learn, for example, that it is important to be competitive, even aggressively so, since they are regularly – some would say continuously – judged against one another. The bell curve ranks students in relation to one another, not in relation to what they have achieved.[25] Judgment and evaluation is a constant in the law school experience, both formal and informal, which is apparent even in "academic street-corner talk at which one is informally tracked as excellent, good, fair, poor or terrible."[26] As one law student put it, "There are a lot of judgements passed around in the law school, [law school] is a capital for that."[27] Law students quickly assimilate this judgmental norm. One student who was surprised at how guarded her peers were about asking questions or offering answers in class commented that "other students ... told me that in law school you don't let anyone know how intelligent or stupid you are." Any sign of weakness often results in cruel nicknames and teasing or banishment to the "retard room." While one might assume (and studies show) that many students who make it into law school are likely to be highly individualistic and competitive, the passive acceptance of competition as "inevitable" means that these values become strongly reinforced in the course of law school and solidified as future professional norms.

Instrumental and often condescending attitudes toward clients are also promoted by law school teaching and learning methods. Students rarely discuss conflicts in terms of real people but, rather, in terms of rules and principles. They are seldom if ever asked to imagine what the clients' goals might be but, instead, to develop a strong legal theory for their case. Law students learn that facts are more important than emotions and that emotions are, in fact, a distraction from real lawyering work. They also absorb the message that what is most important about clients is their potential to provide facts that will fit a theory of the case. The other parts of what they need or may have to say are less significant and may be an unwelcome distraction from the real work of arguing cases.

This analysis also demonstrates that legal education is highly efficient at doing what many would argue is its core function – teaching the intellectual values that are congruent with a traditional approach to professional advising and decision making in law. The structure of legal education and, in particular, its approach to "legal reasoning" whose internal definition of "relevancy" excludes certain types of argument and includes others, reflects the traditional values of rights-based expertise and a complete deference to this approach.[28] The "adversary method" of argument,[29] in which positions have more significance than interests or needs, is pervasive throughout legal education. In this way, the intellectual focus of legal education once again entrenches a particular system of values and beliefs – one that holds that there will inevitably be winners and losers in conflict and that a good lawyer is always on the winning side – which are largely unquestioned and unchallenged.[30]

The assessment model that has been widely adopted throughout legal education reinforces these values.[31] The most prevalent assessment model in law school is still the "unseen" examination, in which students regurgitate information and sometimes take a position on a hypothetical situation or issue. In line with the dominant values, grading rewards comprehensiveness and persuasiveness (with good reason) but fails to reward an

analysis of the causes of conflict, meeting non-legal needs, the consideration of negotiation strategies, or any other analysis that fails to adopt the
adversaries model. Further examples include the differential valuation of
student contributions to class discussion (for instance, "emotional/intuitive"
input usually carries far less weight than the "rational/logical" comment)
and standards for research papers (valuing the descriptive/analytic over the
narrative/discursive). In this way, the culture of legal education emphasizes
a particular form of technical knowledge above all other learning goals.

How much choice do law students have in either avoiding or modifying these norms and values? Law students are rapidly assimiliated into the
culture of law school. The norms are reinforced by upper-year students
who quickly "initiate" first-year students into the appropriate expectations
and modes of behaviour. Unless students participate in the assimilative
process, they will remain "an out-law, an outsider, a victim until s/he becomes assimilated into the genre."[32] There is extensive documentation of
the high levels of stress experienced by law students.[33] High levels of stress
make fighting the "system" even more difficult. Resistance to assimilation
may be further weakened in a recessionary period as law students experience intense competition in the job market. Whatever their personal
distaste for it, standing apart from the competitive culture becomes very
difficult when it excludes one from not only the most prized social and
economic rewards but perhaps also from any employment at all.[34]

Communities of Practice

Once out in practice, there are many influences on the young lawyer's
professional identity. The first of these is the culture of her own firm or
practice environment, described by Lynn Mather, Craig McEwen, and
Richard Maiman as "communities of practice."[35] The increase in specialization and the growing differences between urban and rural practices and
big firms and solo practices gives rise to myriad subcultures and "communities within communities." Each of these subcultures has its own norms
and values, which are sometimes described as "local legal culture."[36] Local
legal culture is more than simply differences in formal rules or practices.
It reflects a "how we do things here" perception in relation to particular
rules and practices. These perceptions arise from local expectations and
assumptions – for example, an expectation of usually dealing with counsel with whom one has worked before (or not), an assumption that a particular judge will be flexible on a particular issue (or not), shared mores
on the timing and type of exchange of information, and so on. Knowledge
of local legal culture, whether it is based on a firm, a practice area, or a
geographic region, is what distinguishes an "insider" from an "outsider"
and, hence, is a source of power.

In most law firms, practice bars, and geographic legal communities, the norms of behaviour are fairly clear (though often implicit), and most lawyers adopt them without question. Where these norms are sufficiently developed and widely accepted, they become a powerful form of professional socialization. For young lawyers in particular, there are costs associated with not following the local norms because more experienced lawyers often act as gatekeepers to more interesting and profitable types of work. Acquiring knowledge about one's local legal culture is more important for a junior lawyer than challenging or questioning it.

McEwen, Mather, and Maiman build on the idea of local legal culture in their concept of "communities of practice." They argue that such communities play a critical role in defining professional norms and values via the mediated influence of collegiality.[37] Membership in any one or more of these multiple worlds – for example, in a law firm, a practice group within a firm, or the local family/employment/personal injuries bar – contributes directly to professional development "by translating the general and often contradictory professional identities and norms into guiding principles for daily application."[38] McEwen, Mather, and Maiman argue that "communities of practice" are as or more significant in the development of lawyers' professional identity as codes of conduct. These communities, which are sometimes self-consciously selected but more often are simply a matter of chance, determine the acceptable and unacceptable ways to practise, the appropriate professional goals, the ways of relating to clients, fee levels and billing practices, and so on. Any one lawyer may be a member of more than one community, but she will probably establish a primary loyalty to one that enables the resolution of sometimes contradictory instincts and reactions – in other words, the community in which she operates most comfortably and naturally. A lawyer operates comfortably within her primary community because she knows the "rules" of conduct and there is a predictable nature to professional interactions. In many ways, this is a substitute for the more abstract exhortations of codes of conduct and a means of staying "between the lines" in the routine of practice.

Particular community characteristics are often associated with a tendency toward greater or lesser degrees of cooperation/adversarialism and degrees of informality and formality. For example, in smaller communities, litigators sometimes establish conventions that allow for the sharing of information without unnecessary procedural formalities that may be routinely expected in larger and more competitive bars.[39] The social networking that tends to follow professional relationships in smaller communities provides an incentive to adopt and follow the community norms and may allow them to become rapidly stable and predictable. Even in larger legal communities, norms can be established among lawyers who work regularly with one another, although these may be more difficult to establish and more subject to change.[40]

When a lawyer representing one party arrives from "out of town" or a new lawyer joins the local bar, the community may take on the role of educating the newcomer in "the ways we do things here." The concept of "outsider" serves the purpose of alerting lawyers that they should be ready for different and less predictable behaviour – for example, a different approach to negotiation – if the lawyer they are dealing with is from another professional "community" with different norms and values. For example, Ottawa lawyers often comment on the different approach to mandatory mediation they see when they work with Toronto lawyers:

> Certainly in the Ottawa area I would say that lawyers are much more amenable to mediation and non-traditional court methodology of settling cases now ... I find that the Toronto lawyers in general are resistant – even if you ask the mediators they'll tell you that. They're resistant to mediations, they feel that they can't settle them, and they feel they're unable to put their skills forward and properly advise their clients.[41]

> Lawyers in Toronto ... are still under the impression that ... I can't even give my client a legal opinion until we've been through discoveries and done all the nine yards – I mean come on.[42]

Clients also have an impact on the internal culture of a community of practice. The orientation and outlook of family lawyers are affected by the high levels of emotion and anger experienced by their clients. As one family lawyer bleakly put it, "You're seeing people at their absolute worst."[43] Constant dealings with highly emotional and angry clients take their toll on family practitioners and result in many "community" strategies to blunt the impact, including an emphasis on remaining detached, the use of (often sardonic) humour, and sometimes a cynical attitude toward marriage and family life. Lawyers who serve particular constituencies, especially when these represent a significant proportion of one counsel's work, recognize that this may place them under particular constraints or expectations. For example, lawyers working for corporations will be obliged to adopt the "company line" on negotiation and settlement. Some organizations intentionally foster a reputation for being tough and unwilling to negotiate and expect their legal counsel to embrace this approach.[44] Lawyers project an image that – rightly or wrongly – they believe fits with the expectations of appropriate behaviour from their main client group. For example, as one lawyer expressed,

> in my community I see my role as a lawyer as just being a hired gun to take a fight.[45]

Other corporations want legal agents who will embrace a settlement orientation. So in contrast, as another lawyer explains:

> A lot of my clients want to settle. They're business people, they're not litigators ... they didn't choose my profession, they chose theirs. So they want an excuse to settle and if you have mandatory mediation it gives them a reason to continue talking.[46]

In Chapter 4 I present a case study of dominant values and norms in the context of legal negotiations. Like every other aspect of the lawyer's role, negotiation behaviours are tempered by the conventions that exist within immediate communities of practice. For example, is negotiation in this community usually hardball or co-operative, is information routinely disclosed or withheld, is aggressive behaviour tolerated or not? Is it expected that one will generally contact the other side and propose informal negotiations or would this action be considered a sign of weakness? Does counsel habitually speak privately and frankly with counsel for the other side and, if so, in what setting, business or social? (Community norms might even extend to attending a particular pub or restaurant favoured by the local bar assocation.) Are local judicial settlement conferences, mediations, or pre-trials seen as an important resolution opportunity, or do counsel attend simply in order to "go through the motions"? Can discoveries *de rigueur* before settlement become a subject of serious discussion, or can negotiations proceed earlier? These and many other dimensions of negotiation practice will reflect the values and norms of the local legal culture and relevant community of practice.

Personal Experiences

Many aspects of our personal value systems derive from our membership in particular cultural groups and communities of practice. We also gravitate toward assumptions and tendencies that reflect our generation and times. For example, baby boomers work hard and are competitive and applied in their work ethic, whereas "Generation X'ers" are more interested in work and life balance and in having fun. However, our generational, familial, cultural, and ethnic roots, while significant, do not account for all of our values. Much of the remainder of what we believe and our assumptions about right and wrong behaviours can be explained by our life experiences, both positive and negative. Exposure to different personal experiences – in particular, clients, cases, colleagues, opponents, and judges – inevitably shapes individual values and norms. The range and variety of our personal experiences and the opportunities we take and those we do not take mean that we do not all understand the world in the same way. Instead, we make meaning as we "connect" experiences to what we already know in a process of implicit comparison.[47]

The values and norms of young lawyers, as well as of more experienced counsel, are inevitably shaped by their personal experiences, both inside and outside the practice of law. Some lawyers can still recount a life event that took place before they started law school – typically, an experience of a family member with the legal system – that provided the original inspiration for their decision to enter the field. This particular event, while followed by many subsequent experiences (perhaps quite different) as well as the development of actual knowledge about law, may continue to affect their deepest attitudes toward law and legal practice, evidenced by the fact that it is still recalled as a formative experience. For others, more recent events may have shaped their approach to practice. For example, a surprisingly large number of lawyers who practise collaborative family law (where the parties retain counsel for the negotiation only and are disqualified from continuing with the same lawyer into litigation) have been through a messy divorce themselves. As a result, they have become motivated to ensure that the experience is less distressing for their clients. As one lawyer explains:

> I went through a divorce myself several years ago, well four years ago, and I just thought it's such an emotional time and I'm suffering so much and I wish that this process [collaborative family law] was available to me ... because I thought this is perfect. Because people are already just hemorrhaging with their emotions and we're flipping from anger to guilt to sorrow to all kinds of emotions – and I thought why should attorneys get involved and turn these parties into war people, instead of just getting them through the process and the transition period?[48]

The range of procedural alternatives facing both civil and criminal lawyers today adds another layer of potential experience to the development of beliefs and attitudes regarding appropriate professional behaviours. Different processes and procedures raise different expectations about how the lawyer should play her role and offer different models of effective client service. For example, when a lawyer meets with her client in order to obtain instructions to file a statement of claim or defence, her goal is to secure sufficient information to make an arguable case. She also needs to know about any potentially prejudicial information. In a traditional litigation frame, absent a mandatory mediation or settlement conferencing regime, it is unlikely that this client (unless she is perhaps an experienced commercial client) will take part directly in negotiations or that there will be any face-to-face discussion involving the client and the other party along with a third party. The lawyer may discuss possible settlement options (although probably not at the pleadings stage), but the assumption is that any negotiations will be handled directly by the lawyer herself. The lawyer can be confident that her relationship with the client is a privileged one, in which she will take information and use it to make decisions in her client's best interests. In contrast, if the lawyer is preparing to involve her client in direct negotiations, mediation, or a judicial settlement conference, her goals and consequently her interaction with her client will be quite different. In working with the client to prepare her to participate in one of these processes, she adopts a different agenda. The lawyer needs to ask sufficient questions to gain a broader picture of her client's understanding of the conflict, including issues that may not bear directly on the strength of the legal case but that are important considerations for her client when considering settlement. The lawyer and client should review what the client will say in the meeting, what they will not talk about, consider any background information about the personal relationship or past experience this client has had with the client on the other side, and so on. Lawyers experienced in preparing clients for mediation characterize this dialogue as deeper and broader than the discussion that would precede either the planning of a litigation strategy or preparing the lawyer to negotiate on the client's behalf. The experience of preparing a client for mediation, negotiation, or another type of settlement discussion is quite different for a lawyer than preparing a client to give an affidavit or to present testimony in a trial. Exposure to different experiences – including how positive or negative these are – inevitably affect the development of professional values and norms in legal practice.

Social psychologists have long posited a dynamic relationship between changing behaviours – for example, by exposing lawyers to new procedures – and changing attitudes.[49] It seems reasonable to assert that changing behavioural practices, even by dictat, allows for new and different experiences, which, if positive, may change lawyers' attitudes. This remains the strongest argument in support of mandatory mediation processes.[50] Recent research studies on settlement processes bear this out, suggesting that personal experience can make a measurable difference to lawyers' attitudes. Lawyers who have had significant exposure to court-connected mediation (for example, in Ottawa, Regina, and Saskatoon or in the United States within the Florida and California state court systems),[51] or family lawyers practising in jurisdictions where family mediation is a regular occurrence, are generally more positive about it than their counterparts with less experience.[52] An evaluation of the Saskatchewan program uncovered many accounts from lawyers who described themselves as being resistant to the legislature's introduction to mandatory mediation in 1994, but whose views have changed over time. As one senior practitioner put it, "After ten years [since the introduction of the mandatory mediation program in the Queen's Bench], mediation is no longer a dirty word."[53] As one Ottawa lawyer acknowledged:

> We've had it [mandatory mediation] 100 percent now since 1 January 1997 so we've been three years into this. So ... a lot of us who do a lot of work have done literally hundreds of mediations ... It's a learning curve about the value of this process.[54]

Adjustments based on experience are also evident in the data on changes in lawyer-client relationships in settlement processes. While lawyers new to settlement processes tend to focus on minimizing client participation,[55] those who are more experienced recognize the dynamics of client involvement and its potential benefits. The inclusion of clients in mediation and settlement conferences (especially early on in the process) represents a significant change in the balance of power:

> I couldn't believe my clients sold out on me the way they did. I was concerned that I had a serious client control problem.[56]

Personal experience is especially critical to the development of professional values and norms when there is a great deal of diversity and variety in the practice approaches. The emergence of many new and varied dispute resolution options over the last thirty years means that individual lawyers will have many different types and levels of experience with new processes and procedures, depending on the type of work they do and the attitudes within their community of practice. These experiences are reflected in different attitudes toward the lawyer's role in dispute resolution and working relationships with clients and have a cumulative impact on understandings of role and professional identity.

Mentors

All professions need inspirational role models who can draw in new recruits and motivate those who are already insiders. Individuals seek sources of socialization – they are not purely passive – and this fact is especially true for those contemplating joining an elite profession. For many, the influences they gravitate toward, for instance, a particular mentor, cultural icon, or law school professor, entice them toward a developing set of practice goals and values. In his book *The Lawyer's Myth: Reviving the Ideals of the Legal Profession,* Walter Bennett laments the demise of powerful role models in the legal profession, such as the "lawyer-statesman," the lawyer as a "champion of the people and causes," and the lawyer as a "paragon of virtue."[57] These old-fashioned archetypes are barely recognizable to us today, and what has taken their place are mostly negative stereotypes. Bennett argues that without modern heroes, both archetypes and living images, the profession is doomed to drift without direction. He encourages us to take seriously the task of identifying new hero models and actual mentors who possess these qualities. Mentors can provide advice, encouragement, and motivation. They establish important relationships between senior and junior colleagues. They also offer stories, which maintain an essential narrative that passes on professional ideals to the next generation.

Bennett's premise is that relationships with particular colleagues who act as personal mentors – or with those admired from afar as role models – are an important source of influence in the development of role identity. Young lawyers may use these models to identify both the qualities they wish to emulate and those they wish to avoid. Some, for example, would be inspired by Alan Dershowitz, who urges young lawyers to consider that "if everybody likes you ... you're not being tough enough" (from his book *Letter to a Young Lawyer*).[58] For others, their choice might be the late Johnnie Cochrane, whose high-profile defence practice made him instantly recognizable as a wealthy and influential lawyer. Other law students and young lawyers are looking for a different, more low-key type of role model, someone who encompasses their values. Here is one student's description of a person who represented an important role model for their future practice:

> She is compassionate, understanding and objective. She is a person who I could trust with personal issues but whom I could equally rely on to handle professional problems in a holistic and professional way.

Others go outside the legal profession for their heroes and role models, finding no one inside the profession who meets their ideals.[59]

Mentoring has always taken place informally within the legal profession, often with an emphasis on social events and guidance regarding professional behaviours. Several law societies offer volunteer mentoring programs, but these focus on providing advice on substantive issues. Some young lawyers have wonderful mentoring relationships with more experienced lawyers, finding encouragement, guidance, and motivation. Some law firms adopt strong mentoring systems and systematically pair young lawyers with associates or partner mentors. In other cases, mentoring is an informal system and can be pretty "hit or miss." At worst, it can be a damaging or disillusioning experience for the mentee. Sometimes a mentoring relationship is little more than a front for exploitation of the junior's work by the senior colleague.[60] Sometimes, the "wisdom" that is passed along to the mentee does not seem to meet any standards of professional integrity or respect and does not invite comment or discussion. A student summering in a large city firm described the most significant moment of his experience as a conversation with his mentor about the fact that a young associate was intending to take paternity leave when his partner's baby was born. The mentor commented that this would be the end of this person's career prospects at the firm. The message to the summering student was clear and chilling. There was no further discussion because the student felt that he could not question or challenge this statement.

Growing concern has been expressed in the last decade over the difficulty experienced by women and minority lawyers in finding mentors. As a result, these groups may be seriously disadvantaged in terms of patronage and promotion within their firm.[61] This situation may partly reflect the association of mentoring with social settings, which those with family responsibilities or those less comfortable with the particular setting may prefer to avoid.[62] Shortage of peer mentors for these groups is also a reflection of the limited number of senior female and minority lawyers available to mentor their younger colleagues. These groups are already experiencing the pressures of a marginal group in a workplace (typically, to perform better and conform completely) and, hence, have little time or energy left for mentoring younger peers.[63] If mentoring is to maximize its potential to motivate and guide the development of professional identity for young lawyers, it is important to ensure that opportunities for relationship mentoring – and not only for social patronage – exist for as many lawyers as want them. The profession could also consider a threshold qualification for mentors and, generally, a guide on how to promote mentorship in a way that is altruistic rather than self-serving.

So far, this chapter has considered a range of informal sources that are influential in the professional socialization of lawyers. I have intentionally left until last an examination of the influence of codes of conduct. What part can and do codes of conduct play in the construction of professional identity for lawyers?

Professional Codes of Conduct

There is a broad similarity among the various codes of conduct for legal professionals operating in common law jurisdictions. The codes that operate in the United States and Canada are similar in language and tone, and, as a matter of historical development, they have in most respects paralleled the conduct rules promulgated by the Law Society of England and Wales.[64]

Lawyers' codes of conduct are underpinned by a set of fundamental and fairly consistent moral values, including the importance of upholding the rule of law, a commitment to integrity in relationships with other lawyers and the courts, and the central value of dedication to realizing the clients' interests. For example, each of the many codes that exist in North America includes a statement about advocacy and uses a variety of adjectives that are broadly descriptive of the principled stance taken by the lawyer toward the promotion of her clients' interests, such as zealous, resolute, fearless, dedicated, loyal, and partisan. In the Law Society of Upper Canada's *Rules of Professional Conduct,* Rule 4.01 reads:

> When acting as an advocate, a lawyer shall represent the client resolutely and honourably within the limits of the law while treating the tribunal with candour, fairness, courtesy, and respect.[65]

An excerpt from the original *Canon of Professional Ethics* set down by the American Bar Association in 1908 states that

> [a] lawyer should represent a client zealously within the bounds of the law.[66]

In practice, such general statements of principle are interpreted in different ways by different practitioners and are always affected by context. Once the codes try to make their advice more concrete and less generic, some differences of nuance and emphasis begin to emerge. For example, the Ontario code tries to provide further specific guidance on the application of Rule 4.01 in its commentary section, stating:

> The lawyer has a duty to the client to raise fearlessly every issue, advance every argument, and ask every question, however distasteful, which the lawyer thinks will help the client's case and to endeavour to obtain for the client the benefit of every remedy and defence authorized by law.[67]

The American Bar Association (ABA)'s *1908 Canons of Professional Ethics* has been revised many times over the past century and, in each case, has become more detailed and specific. In the *2007 Model Rules of Professional Conduct,* there is an entire section devoted to an elaboration of the advocacy role:

> A lawyer shall not bring or defend a proceeding, or assert or controvert an issue therein, unless there is a basis in law and fact for doing so that is not frivolous, which includes a good faith argument for an extension, modification or reversal of existing law.[68]

A student comparing the Ontario and the ABA codes might understandably ask: When does the responsibility to "advance every argument ... which the lawyer thinks will advance the client's case" (Ontario) become a "frivolous" argument *(Model Rules)*? Could one make an argument that is in "good faith" *(Model Rules)* but subsequently turns out to be "frivolous"

(Ontario), or does one preclude the other? Further, when the law itself is uncertain, how can one know that one is making an argument "authorized by law" (Ontario) or for which there is "a basis in law and fact" *(Model Rules)*? We can speculate but in practice the lines are not clear.

Let's add one further example. The Law Society of British Colombia's *Canon of Legal Ethics* offers the following language to describe and explain the parameters of the advocacy responsibility:

> A lawyer should endeavour by all fair and honourable means to obtain for a client the benefit of any and every remedy and defence that is authorized by law. The lawyer must, however, steadfastly bear in mind that this great trust is to be performed within and not without the bounds of the law.[69]

This approach is a little less strident and sets a more positive tone than the earlier examples. However, is it really saying anything substantively different than the other two provisions?

These examples illustrate both the usefulness and the limitations of codes of conduct in identifying and sustaining professional values and norms. The appeal of codes is that they can and do establish some core principles for the profession, and the similarity between general statements to be found in each code setting out the advocacy obligation of counsel is a good example of the consensus that can be achieved around this core principle. However, the diversity of individuals who make up the legal profession, and the diversity of the work that they do, means that this language needs to be very general to facilitate broad agreement. When codes start to become more concrete, as in the explanatory provisions quoted above, and articulate the practical application of the rules as specific norms of behaviour, they inevitably become less consistent and are more likely to raise objections or controversy. The examples quoted above from the Ontario commentary on Rule 4.01, the British Columbia *Canon of Legal Ethics*, and the ABA's *Model Rules of Professional Conduct* demonstrate that, without any direct contradiction between the texts, each reflects somewhat different approaches to advocacy. There are, of course, innumerable further articulations and permutations possible within the general framework of client advocacy.

Furthermore, each practitioner will also have her own interpretation of how the text relates to her own work. This distinction relates to what the anthropologist Clifford Geertz describes as the "material" elements of a practice culture, contrasted with the "immaterial" elements – the precise meanings and interpretation given to the norms by the individual players.[70] The individual lawyer understands her advocacy role within the context of her particular clients, work, and the forum – an administrative tribunal, a motions hearing, a mediation, or negotiation for example – in which she acts as an advocate. There is real difficulty in distilling general principles for advocacy into a simple, consistent practice instruction.

The ability to use personal (informed, educated) judgment is a core principle or value for non-routinized professions such as medicine, engineering, and law. "Good judgment" is a frequently cited characteristic of those lawyers who are widely admired by their peers. The exercise of discretion itself rests on often-tacit norms and values about appropriate professional behaviour. However, most codes of conduct for lawyers ignore the role of discretion in professional decision making.[71] A code of conduct may articulate a procedural basis for the exercise of discretion regarding ethical choices – for example, when to terminate a relationship with a client – but rarely identifies the choices between actions that are possible or their differing value implications. These limitations are especially noticeable when – as in the legal profession – ethical dilemmas characteristically arise from the management of human relationships rather than from procedures (for example, accounts auditing) or events (for example, trading in insider information). The types of ethical dilemmas that arise in the course of managing client relationships are often difficult to anticipate and are subject to numerous contextual variables. General rules are not especially helpful in these types of situations.

Moreoever, knowledge of the rules contained in codes of conduct does not of course guarantee good behaviour. Donald Schon warns about the distinction between "given" or stated norms of conduct and how lawyers actually behave.[72] There is a further risk that knowledge of a generalized formal rule may replace the process of individual reasoning and the weighing of alternatives until the moment when an intuitive and immediate response is demanded. Research suggests that the existence of ethical codes serves to limit or inhibit individual reflection and reasoning about moral problems by limiting assessment to whether or not a formal rule has been broken.[73]

Codes are an important but insufficient element in the construction of professional identity, values, and norms. Codes provide an important symbolic means of setting benchmarks and parameters for appropriate conduct and may allow for the identification of potential areas of difficulty or dilemma. At best, they can provide a common set of values and a starting point for thinking about ethical choices. Yet codes can offer little by way of the operationalization of these values as norms or standards of behaviour. Since codes must describe absolutist rather than contextualized standards, they tend to be highly non-specific and subject to multiple interpretations. Codes also provide little or no guidance on how to resolve tensions or conflicts between different rules (for example, the rule on confidentiality and the duty to the court). Codes are also limited in how far they can assist the identification of new and emerging dilemmas for the profession as a result of changes in practice. This is in part because by their very nature codes must assume a more heterogeneous culture of values and norms than may in fact be the case. Codes are an inadequate means of understanding the complex blend of sameness and difference in the way that law is practised. In essence, codes are more significant in theory than in practice and may be a substitute for "real thinking" about the development of professional roles and identity.

All of the influences described in this chapter on the socialization of young lawyers deserve to be taken seriously if the evolving professional identity for lawyers is to be taken seriously by the bar and the law schools. In legal education, this means confronting the more damaging and inaccurate stereotypes of so-called "good" lawyering, and providing alternatives. Instead of allowing law students and young lawyers to unconsciously absorb any number of influences, there should be an effort to assist them with the conscious development of role identity, including a discussion of how this can continue after they have completed their formal training. The impact of communities of practice and varieties of personal experience are often highly significant in the professional development of a young lawyer. The more structured and integrated opportunities there are for reflecting on these influences and culling the lessons for future practice, the more self-aware, open-minded, and ultimately sophisticated we become about professional identity, role, and purpose. An important means of encouraging such reflection is mentoring. Mentoring is taken very seriously in some firms, and higher standards should be expected throughout the profession. Taking a hard look at the sources of lawyer socialization is critical to the future of the legal profession and should be a subject that concerns law schools, bar associations, and lawyers' organizations, rather than simply being left to chance.

Reflection and discussion about the formation of professional identity among young lawyers offers a chance to identify and evaluate core beliefs and attitudes for lawyers and to appraise these in relation to changes in legal practice and contemporary client needs and demands. The next chapter describes three key beliefs that presently sustain an often uncritical and assumed professional identity for lawyers – one that needs to be reevaluated in light of the contemporary conditions of legal practice and client expectations and needs.

3
Three Key Professional Beliefs

What core beliefs and values do the sources of socialization for young lawyers promote and sustain? In order to be a legal profession "insider," what norms of behaviour are expected? Even as we observe significant changes in the structural and procedural environment of legal practice, there are widely recognized and broadly accepted values that continue to dominate lawyering, regardless of context. The collective impact of the sources of professional identity described in the last chapter is a set of core beliefs about the practice of law that continue to enjoy widespread acceptance among lawyers and appear well defended against revision and renewal. This chapter identifies and elaborates on these core beliefs – a default to rights-based dispute resolution, justice as process, and the expertise/ control nexus in client relations – which flow fairly naturally from the structure of our legal system.

The articulation of these values also throws into sharp relief some of the challenges that confront young lawyers in managing changes in the structure and environment of legal practice while meeting the real needs of clients. The core beliefs were established long before the recent changes described in Chapter 1 and appear in some respects to be out of step with the new disputing environment. Despite this disjuction, the core beliefs are well entrenched and rarely questioned. They are sometimes reinforced and sometimes contradicted by personal experience. Some communities of practice explicitly offer an alternative view of the core values and beliefs. Regardless of these minor rebellions, a set of foundational beliefs rests at the heart of the legal profession, beliefs that express the purpose of the practice of law and against which all other beliefs and practices are set in contrast or comparison.

Making an argument for a set of dominant contemporary values for legal practice is a controversial and inevitably somewhat generalist exercise. I do not assume that each and every member of the legal profession subscribes to these beliefs to the same degree or holds them with the same depth of conviction. Just as we saw in the discussion of codes of conduct, for any set of beliefs and values there is individual interpretation and application as well as the context to consider. An attempt to extrapolate core beliefs must acknowledge, but cannot account for, the multiple variations in the way in which they may be interpreted and played out by individual practitioners and applied by their communities of practice. The discussion in Chapter 2 demonstrates how individual professional values and norms are created and reinforced by a variety of factors. This range of influences inevitably produces nuanced individual "takes" on the core mission of the profession.

However, individual idiosyncrasies and variations among local legal cultures cannot obscure the common threads that link different communities of practice and the lawyers within them. The result is less than universalism, but neither is it a diffuse collection of unrelated values and norms. Identifiable differences between "arenas of professionalism" such as substantive specialization, client base, firm culture, and the culture of the local bar association are generally maintained within a limited spectrum of alternatives.[1] This means that the extent of digression from the core beliefs is carefully contained. The core beliefs represent the mainstream and determine what is an "outlying" position.

This level of coherence may be essential to maintaining a unified profession. It is also borne out by research on legal cultures. For example, Thomas Church found significant agreement among prosecutors and public defenders over case disposition (whether or not a trial was necessary), which indicated shared norms over the pace of criminal cases.[2] Church also found disagreement between these groups in sentencing norms, but these differences can be accommodated and explained within the pattern of role and traditional adversary theory – that is, prosecutors ask for harsher sentences than defence lawyers.[3] Church's work shows that disagreement over substantive issues and consensus over procedural fairness are in themselves critical norms for the profession and therefore do not threaten a sense of cohesion and shared "mission." Widely understood and shared beliefs about the function of law – in this case, the criminal justice system – enable lawyers to "make sense" of their disagreements (with the other side, with judges, and with their client) and justify and reinforce position taking. Different actors within the legal system have different and complementary roles to play, but they share a basic moral and practical commitment to the system of justice itself.

Core beliefs and values about the role of the lawyer are found in the most common, oft-repeated mantras of legal practice and legal education. These values also represent a force for stability. To a large extent, they have been barely revised or challenged since the formal establishment of the profession almost two centuries ago.[4] Within a hierarchy of beliefs, the most important and fundamental is, unsurprisingly, a belief in a default to rights-based processes of dispute resolution.

The Default to Rights

A belief in the primacy and superiority of rights-based conflict resolution is introduced by legal education, reinforced by communities of practice, and memorialized in professional codes of conduct. Rights strategies are characteristically presented as the default or sometimes the only appropriate approach for a lawyer to take to conflict resolution. The practical consequence of this belief is that the basis of the lawyer's role is rights-based advocacy. Although such a belief is critical to the function of a legal professional, adherence to this model often means that other forms and styles of advocacy and the promotion of client goals and interests are overlooked or rejected. This section will identify some of the consequences of a default to rights-based advocacy strategies and the resulting limitations on practical dispute resolution.

The philosophic and structural nature of the North American legal system creates the conditions for the assumptions of a default to rights, and it is hard to imagine a more functional core belief for lawyers than this system. Western justice systems emphasize an individualist approach, in which the rights of the individual will be recognized and upheld, or the converse, in which the individual will be protected against the oppressive assertion of the rights of others (including the state).[5] This commitment to individual rights means that the primary responsibility of the lawyer is the furtherance of her clients' goals framed as legal ends. These legal goals are understood as principled and legitimate and sustained by moral rationalizations. Strong advocacy is therefore equated almost exclusively with a strong assertion of positional arguments over rights claims. This belief, which is highly logical and functional, flows from, and sustains, the substantive knowledge base of legal training and practice. An emphasis on rights is also key to the unique technical expertise that lawyers offer their clients.

Rights claims are essentially the assertion of moral arguments previously designated in law as superior – for example, the right of a property owner to enjoy possession of his land over the right of a hiker to walk across it, or the right of a custodial parent to make and carry out decisions that the non-custodial parent opposes. The winner will be the party whose arguments are judged to be the most compelling via the application of legal principles. Put another way, for an advocate to function effectively within a rule-based system of dispute resolution, she must focus her energies and talents on convincing decision makers – real or imagined – that she has the stronger rights-based argument. There is no need to convince the other side or to propose mutually agreeable solutions. The value of argument lies in its appeal to rights rather than to any other persuasive force. One side will carry the day. In a final judgment, the inevitable outcome is a winner and a loser. The appeal to rights lies at the heart of the lawyer's craft and drives much of her education and training.

The rights-based model assumes that the source of conflict is in all circumstances an uncompromisable moral principle or an indivisible good. Once the conflict becomes "objectified" in this way (sustained by an appeal to allegedly objective moral standards and beyond merely partisan preferences), it becomes inevitable that the aggrieved party will press her moral claim.[6] In this way, the rights model, while effective in protecting and advancing critical aspects of personal rights, sometimes gets extended into areas that are really more about communication breakdown, personal losses or gains, or simple incompetence than about the denial of rights. When the moral language of legal arguments becomes attached to a conflict and transformed into a fight over rights, it may obscure or even belie the underlying issues. While any particular outcome can always be advocated as the most expedient, the most logical, or even the most fair, not every conflict can plausibly assert the moral superiority of a particular resolution. As one scholar notes, "When IBM and Xerox square off against each other in court over the issue of controlling shares of some market in computer hardware, the issue of justice may be very remote. The battle is a cold-blooded struggle over resources."[7]

While functionally logical – assuming the intervention of an adjudicative decision maker – building values about the lawyer's role exclusively on a rights discourse carries limitations that are both conceptual and practical. Focusing only on a rights-based analysis assumes the essential moral basis of any conflict, since rights arguments are couched in terms of right and wrong rather than in terms of what is expedient, feasible, or wise. This is one of the most seductive aspects of legal services for clients, who want nothing more than to be told that they are wholly "right" and that the other side is wholly "wrong." A natural tendency to elevate our conflicts to the level of "a matter of principle" – an intellectualized justification that "trumps" the other side while largely ignoring the more practical and emotional aspects of the dispute – is further aggravated in a model that sets up opposing rights-based arguments on either side.[8] A system that holds out the potential of moral victory to every disputant reinforces our tendency to presume the moral basis of claims and assertions.

Focusing on rights raises the stakes for clients by offering only two possible outcomes: winning or losing. Since a 100-percent loss must be avoided at all costs, the practical consequences of a rights-based approach are mitigated by lawyers who will negotiate a settlement in most cases. This likely outcome sets up the client for future disappointment when their "strong case" (as originally appraised by their counsel) is almost always ultimately compromised in a negotiated settlement. Since a default to rights tends to sustain a continuing belief in the possibility of a "win" for as long as possible, the basis of this compromise will often be an eleventh-hour analysis of risk or alternatives and transaction costs, rather than a measured analysis of how to address the problem in a way that satisfies the interests of all parties to some extent.

The default to rights-based dispute resolution and the (often explicit) claim that this is what "real" lawyering is all about is only rarely challenged, either in law school or in legal practice. Indeed, alternative formulations – for example, the use of mediation and collaborative lawyering – are sometimes virulently derided as "a soft, lovey dovey approach to the world." This tension is undoubtedly exacerbated by the tendency of some who support alternative approaches to conflict resolution to deny or exclude the importance of technical legal advice. Yet it is also an expression of the machismo and bravado sometimes associated with right-based advocacy and the belief that this particular type of challenge represents "real" lawyering. For example, as one lawyer asserts:

> There are a lot of lawyers who probably shouldn't be litigators because they don't grow up before they get to court and they get too nervous, they don't like it, they don't want to put in the time because going to court takes up a tremendous amount of time – you work night and day when you're in trial.[9]

Many practitioners are well aware of the tendency of "rights-talk" to transform a dispute that is initially over resources – a dispute over turf between two corporations or an argument over price and payment – into a conflict over "principle." They also understand that resources matter. Having the best and the most costly legal counsel and the means to conduct extensive investigation and discoveries could make a difference to one's chances of success in presenting a supposedly "moral" claim. The navigation of a rule-based system requires substantial expertise and is inevitably vulnerable to subversion by a more powerful and better-resourced party. This party may choose to use their resources to purchase superior legal expertise, which will enable them to impose their will (via negotiation) on the other party. Many lawyers are painfully aware of the subsequent disassociation of "rights" from "justice" or "fairness" (see the discussion later in this chapter). As Richard Bell points out in drawing a contrast between Western and African justice models, "To have bought into rights language is to believe that power can be counterbalanced by power."[10] This reality is echoed in the following statement by a litigator:

Remember our job, our duty is to our individual clients to fearlessly assert the clients' rights and if we have a client where they have more economic might or other weapons in their arsenal, they maybe ought to win or prevail just as they do in the business world, over people with less weapons and a smaller arsenal.[11]

For the most sophisticated and experienced counsel, the deployment of a rights-based approach is simply a front for the advancement of the most aggressive case, with a view to an ultimate settlement. However, for many lawyers, a rights-based approach is less of a strategy and more of an ideology. Counsel frequently assume and assimilate the merit-based arguments that they can advance on behalf of their clients into their own moral universe. Some regard this as an important dimension of demonstrating their loyalty to their client. This can blind them to the poor "fit" that often occurs between the legal or moral claims advanced and the clients' underlying motives and goals. As one senior litigator reflected:

There's a tendency in our profession to go from step to step without standing back, taking an overall look at what's this all about, and what does the client hope to get? One of the single biggest criticisms of lawyers that I would make as a result of that is that they have not been realistic with their client as to what their client is going to get out of this litigation.[12]

This ideological rather than practical component of a belief in the primacy of rights means that many lawyers feel little discomfort in moving into a highly adversarial model. After all, it is what lawyers are trained to do, and it is the currency of their expertise. As one lawyer put it, "It's just brain power in a particular niche, in our case it's litigation ... we're just salesmen, in our case, brain salesmen."[13] Over-reliance on and dedication to a rights-based approach carries the risk of blindness to alternative strategies or the dismissal of these as being less than "real" lawyering strategies. In the characteristic single-mindedness of adversarial rights talk, there is no midway point in the making of arguments. Rights claims are never asserted as "maybe" or "perhaps" but are always put forward with unwavering certainty, even when counsel knows better. This (public) commitment to one's asserted position is a core, unshakable belief for many lawyers. More troubling still, it generally overwhelms a consideration of other sometimes more appropriate ideologies of practice (such as business or commercial considerations). In contrast to rights-based advocacy, every other approach is "soft," leading this commercial lawyer to demean his own business knowledge:

I'm the softy of our litigation group. I think it may be because I've got more of a business-type background.[14]

In reality, many disputes are brought to lawyers that simply do not require, and are not suitable for, a rights-based argument or solution, and they may escalate unnecessarily if viewed exclusively through this prism. They may also become significantly more difficult to resolve once entrenched rights positions have been traded back and forth. This is a profound limitation for rights-based dispute resolution and exposes the weaknesses of a belief in a default to rights. Once made, positional statements are hard to take back without appearing weak. Compromise and accommodation become harder to achieve. Many conflicts that turn into lawsuits do not originate in value differences or moral outrage. Instead, they are usually precipitated by incompatible aspirations involving access to finite resources, principally money. Other types of resource-based conflict, common in commercial, workplace, and even family contexts, include disputes over non-monetary resources such as relative status or spheres of influence – for example access to and competition within markets, status and reputation, and issues of personal control.[15]

Understood in this way, resources encompass psychological and emotional needs (for power, control, and influence) as well as the material means (usually money) to achieve personal goals. Addressing emotional needs may take a very different form from a contested distribution of rights. Bargaining over these goals looks different than asserting rights and justifications for entitlement (although rights claims may still provide an important set of criteria or alternatives if bargaining fails). Resource-based disputes characteristically enable outcomes in which the resource "pie" (for example, money, influence, status, and market control) can be divided among the parties. This allows for solutions that "expand the pie"[16] – for example, by generating solutions that have value to one or both sides but that fall outside what is formally claimed, such as future business arrangements, apology and acknowledgments, or the bestowal of some other valued outcome by one party on the other. It also encourages parties to make explicit their priorities rather than claiming an entitlement to absolute victory, thus enabling both sides to achieve some of their objectives.

Despite the limitations on problem solving in a rights-based model, the danger of exploitation of superior resources, and the risks of over-commitment, a rights-based approach to legal disputing remains essential to the rule of law. It is an appropriate approach for dispute resolution over "public goods"[17] and a critical means of reinforcing and extending principled protections and entitlements. Lawyers work within a system of rule-based adjudication, and they are charged with the stewardship of rights by their education and training. Lawyers must understand, respect, and promote rights entitlements. In some cases that implicate rights, negotiation or compromise may be a sign of failure or an unjustified or coerced accommodation.

The problem lies in the belief in the universal application and superiority of rule-based adjudication, which makes advocacy via rights claims a dominant value for lawyering practice. Introduced first in law school by a focus on technical knowledge and the study of appellate decisions, this model is reinforced in legal practice by the constant association of "rights talk" with "tough talk." This default means that counsel believes that their responsibility to their client is best met via the pursuit of a rights-based strategy, which values "winning outcomes" above "winning solutions." There is a reliance on rights-based strategies in virtually every aspect of contentious legal work (except for those cases that are too small or unprofitable to be concerned about). This assumption is dangerous, shortsighted, and increasingly outmoded in an era in which very few cases are ultimately adjudicated. Instead of assuming that disputes will be resolved by an argument over rights before a third-party decision maker or judge, lawyers should recognize that they will usually be resolved through negotiation, which will take place in the shadow of the law and rights entitlements but not be determined by it.

While rights-based processes will continue to be crucial to the conflict resolution approaches offered by lawyers, they should not, and in practice cannot, be the only approach, nor should they be the default. In many cases, wise and transparent bargaining – with a keen appreciation of the legal parameters – toward the best possible settlement is a better strategy and one that more directly addresses clients' needs, both legal and non-legal. Where rights become an ideology rather than a strategy, it is difficult for many lawyers – and especially young lawyers with less practical experience – to draw this important distinction.

Justice as Process

Sustaining and reinforcing the dominance of rights-based approaches to conflict is a second value set regarding the authority and respect that attaches to the formal legal process. Some of these values directly reflect the structure of the adjudicative system. There are detailed procedural rules and regulations (civil, criminal procedure), which require each and every disputant to follow the same steps in pursuing or defending a claim. This notion of procedural equality is sacred to the adjudicative system, which assumes that a significant component of fair process is the sameness of procedures for each disputant, including filing requirements, timelines, and appearances.

Of course, formal equality in legal procedure does have its limitations as a means of ensuring fairness. In practice, procedure can be used to great advantage by those with greater knowledge and staying power, and defendants represented by superb criminal lawyers may be acquitted more often than those defended by duty counsel. Apparently fair and reasonable procedural rules raise a risk of exploitation by those with greater power and resources, just as substantive rules raise the risk of manipulation.

A belief in the inherent fairness of the legal-judicial process is widely shared among lawyers. This is in contrast to law students whose naivety is manifest in their commitment to a model of *substantive* or outcome justice, an outlook that they likely will adjust to meet the reality of practice. At law school, what seems important is that the final result is "fair," which is generally presented in the form of an appellate court decision. In practice, most cases do not end up in appellate court. Most do not end up before a decision maker at all. Further, the uncertainty and ambiguity that characterizes adjudication, especially at the lower court levels, makes a reliance on outcomes as a measure of justice a risky proposition for lawyers to sell to their clients.

In contrast, and perhaps as a substitute for a certain outcome, lawyers' belief in the justice of the legal process takes on some of the qualities of "reification." That is, the inherent justice of legal procedures is considered an objective and unassailable truth that is not directly related to outcomes at all (where justice may "fall short") and is generally above criticism. For many lawyers, it is their commitment to legitimate (recognized, fair, and consistent) procedures that is the practical realization of claims of "justice" rather than the actual outcomes of legal action. In this way, process is reified and made the central public good of the legal system. For example, one lawyer explains:

> I really believe in justice. I think it's an indispensable part of the process, but I don't think of results as justice. I think of process as being a just process. If somebody wants to settle a case for a five-year deal in carrots, then so be it. If that's what they wanted I can't say that that's not just, if they've had a fair hearing or they've had a fair mediation if the process is just. That's where I attach the word justice.[18]

Practitioners know that the "best" arguments do not always succeed, and they are candid about this reality. There are many ways in which even the best legal arguments can be defeated or an unforeseen challenge made. Some individuals are even more cynical about the elusiveness of "justice," as illustrated in the following quotes and exchanges:

> Justice has nothing to do with it. I'm sorry that may sound very jaded,

but in my view, as I say to my clients, there's only one person who dispenses justice, he doesn't live on this earth.[19]

Interviewer: Is there a difference between a good outcome and a just outcome in commercial litigation?
Interviewee: It's only money. Justice has nothing to do with it.[20]

Given these realities, commitment to good process (that is, a process that follows the given rules) is a more attainable and sustainable belief for lawyers than an abstract commitment to "justice." It is also less likely to disappoint clients. Clients often come to lawyers with a focus on achieving a substantive "justice" that will enable them to feel vindicated – they want the lawyer to fight for this version of "justice" on their behalf. So lawyers must play down the potential for the legal system to offer "real" or "ultimate" justice.[21] As Austin Sarat and William Felstiner write in their study of interactions between divorce lawyers and their clients, "There is, if you will, a particular kind of justice that the law provides, but it is not broad enough to include the kind that the client seeks."[22] In the alternative, lawyers often try to manage their clients' expectations by replacing hopes for a particular definitive outcome with a guarantee of a just process. In this way, lawyers project their own commitment to process, rather than certain outcomes, onto their clients:

> I attempt to find a way of developing a person's expectations, so that they will in the end feel that they've got justice. Usually when I do that, I achieve those expectations, and once they achieve those expectations then I think they feel they've received justice.[23]

A belief in justice as process does not preclude – indeed, it may sustain – the widespread use of procedural tactics. Procedural rules and regulations set the scene for many skirmishes as each side struggles to use the process to their tactical advantage. In fact, such games are embraced as a necessary and valuable means of ensuring fairness. Using a process in an instrumental or even mean-spirited way to get a step up on the other side – for example, using mediation as "a fishing expedition,"[24] taking advantage of an expired time limit for filing, or moving to strike a claim before critical information can be obtained – does not appear to affect counsel's belief in procedure. It is simply normative to use it to one's advantage wherever possible. Evidently, there is a broad tolerance for procedural games as long as they fall within the given norms of the community of practice or broader culture and they are not seen as a challenge to the fundamental legitimacy of the system.

The strong consensus around legal process, both civil and criminal, which has been established over centuries, may be why so many lawyers feel threatened by and sometimes strenuously resist procedural reforms. They may be even more resistant to procedural innovations that offer flexibility without clearly stipulated "rules" and steps (for example, private mediation). Whatever arguments might be made for new and different approaches, lawyers remain heavily invested in the legal processes and procedures they use every day. They are familiar and comfortable with them and can confidently counsel their clients over the procedural steps that lie ahead of them.

A default to rights and a belief in justice as process – rather than as outcomes – appears at first glance to be contradictory. However, these two beliefs are fully reconcilable. Lawyers' faith in justice as process is faith in a rights-driven, truth-seeking model of process, which, though not perfect, is "the best that we have" in pursuit of an honorable ideal. Faith in justice as process, rather than justice as a particular substantive outcome, is an extension of their belief in rights as a means to resolve human conflict, but it also represents a more pragmatic and ultimately credible belief. Justice via outcomes is abstract, fickle, and subject to uncontrolled variables. Justice via process is a concrete, rational, and "sensible" means of advancing or defending a claim:

> I think it's an enormous mistake to confuse a procedurally sensible, reasonable, system with a fair system of justice. Justice is not a concept that can be measured by meanings ... to measure justice you must take certain values and apply them to ... the procedural system. You may well have a system that leads to a result quite appropriately but that is not just according to the abstract criteria of justice.[25]

The conclusions of research on procedural justice, which examines how process affects perceptions of outcomes, especially in terms of fairness and inclusivity, are highly congruent with lawyers' belief in justice as process. These results suggest that in emphasizing justice as process rather than as outcomes, lawyers are in tune with many of their clients' needs and priorities. This is especially interesting since procedural justice is rarely if ever alluded to in law school, despite its potential relevance for the future stewards of legal process. This corpus of work suggests that the process by which a result is reached is often as, or even more, important than the substantive "rightness" of the outcome itself in fostering a sense of fairness or justice among participants. In particular, the work of John Thibaut and Laurens Walker has established (and later studies have confirmed) that perceptions of fair treatment are as important as outcome when disputants come to appraise dispute resolution processes.[26] While there is an obvious relationship between a sense of fair process and a favourable outcome, this work indicates that these judgments are substantially independent.[27] One study even suggests that procedural fairness is *more* significant than distributive fairness (that is, outcomes) in determining the attitudes of litigants toward the courts.[28]

Procedural justice research also explores what factors are seen by process participants as being critical to fairness. These include a belief that one's issues are being given serious consideration; a feeling that one has been listened to and that the listener, even if she ultimately rejects one's arguments, can explain how she took account of these factors in any final judgment;[29] a minimal level of comfort with one's own role in the process that unfolds; and some type of control over the process. What procedural justice theorists term "decision control" translates, in dispute resolution, into some level of direct client involvement – for example, planning, anticipating, strategizing, or reviewing options, whether or not actual participation is desired.

It is noteworthy that these elements of process are generally more characteristic of less formal settlement-orientated processes – such as mediation or judge-led settlement conferences that include clients directly, address them specifically, and solicit their input and other process alternatives that encourage more face-to-face interaction at an early stage – than formal adjudicative approaches. At the same time, procedural justice research also suggests the need for dispute resolution processes to be dignified and associated with a sense of order and gravitas, including the need for third parties to be both trustworthy and authoritative, which suggests that traditional adjudication may sometimes appear more appropriate than more informal procedures such as mediation or pre-trial.[30] If lawyers were to consider the procedural values of disputant voice and control as a part of justice as process, one would expect it to lead them to embrace new settlement processes (albeit those that proceed with some "dignity" and gravitas), which are generally better placed than adjudication to incorporate these elements.

Procedural justice research appears to reinforce the faith of many lawyers in justice as process. However, many lawyers who are committed to justice as process are less than supportive of client participation in settlement processes. This is because their belief in justice as process is conceptualized as a commitment to the formal legal system, rather than to fair process as a value made practical in participatory processes. It is a commitment to justice as a reified abstract value rather than as a concrete, present experience. The lawyers quoted earlier in this chapter appear to be saying to their clients that they should trust the capacity of the process to produce fair results. This is an externalized value, which is not dependent on their experience of being listened to and taken seriously. Its potency – at least for the lawyers themselves – derives from the universalism of procedural rules and their historical place in their profession (including their legal training). However, as client participation in settlement increases and clients themselves become increasingly accustomed to taking a more active role in negotiations, lawyers might expect their somewhat abstract version of justice as process to be transformed into a more concrete set of positive process values, including those described by procedural justice researchers.

The process of justice itself is the only aspect of litigation that lawyers can control and predict (although even this control is being reduced by the introduction of mandatory case management and mediation). Lawyers can offer the certainty of how the process will unfold as a compensation for the other aspects of the system that cannot be controlled, such as a loss at trial or a compromise in settlement. In this way, the lawyer's obligation to seek "justice" is met by the application of the formal adjudicative system and its procedural rules, which are widely regarded as being inherently fair and equal or, more simply, tried and tested and the best that we have.

Lawyers in Charge

> Look, we're big people and we can settle the darn thing, what do we need a third party for and why do our clients have to be there?[31]

This statement reflects a frequently expressed frustration among some lawyers that their training and expertise should entitle them to assume authority and autonomy in decision making. In this particular quote, a third-party mediator and her clients are regarded as being unnecessary, irrelevant, and possibly obstructive to her task. A third area of fundamental beliefs and values for lawyers relates to the relationship of lawyer and client. Assumptions about the appropriate balance of power between lawyer and client are originally developed in law school and reinforced in practice. The established norms of the decision-making process, while occasionally negotiable, still generally assume that the lawyer manages the file and steers in whatever direction she considers appropriate. Douglas Rosenthal's now classic work on the dynamics of lawyer-client decision making suggests two models of lawyer-client relations. These are the "traditional," in which the client is passive and the lawyer is fairly autonomous, and the "participatory," in which the client plays a more active role. Rosenthal's analysis suggests that the passive client, the one who follows the lawyer's instructions and is detached from the problem-solving process, is the conventional model, and that departures from this norm – for instance, clients who want to participate actively in anything other than the established areas of client input – are seen as aberrant and even disruptive by many lawyers.[32] While sophisticated commercial clients, especially repeat players, may now be less prepared to be passive and more inclined to assert their wishes,[33] historically, most clients have appeared to have chosen to nominate their legal representatives as both managers and agents in disputing.[34] This is especially the case with domestic or "one-shot" clients.[35]

The roots of such assumptions over power and control in the lawyer-client relationship lie in the epistemology of law school and professional legal training. These emphasize a model of professional expertise that elevates technical know-how, the model described earlier as "brain salesman." Legal education, in common with most other professional disciplines, has an entrenched bias in favour of what Donald Schon calls a "technical-rational" model of knowledge.[36] To be an "expert" in a technical-rational model requires technical competence but not intuition, emotional intelligence, or interpersonal skills. While the ability to work constructively with one's client and to build rapport with the other side are skills often recognized and appreciated by lawyers within their own communities of practice, the public face of the profession continues to elevate the importance of legal knowledge as the primary indicator of expertise. The expertise of the lawyer lies in her ability to implement the goals of the client via a legal strategy, as determined by the application of her legal knowledge to her client's "story."[37] In this way, her primary function is as a technician rather than as a counsellor or, to use Anthony Kronman's analogy, as the predictor of weather patterns.[38] The extent of commitment to this model of expertise is reflected in attitudes toward other tasks and skills. For example, an emphasis on the lawyer's counselling role almost always provokes the comment, "But we're lawyers, not therapists." Partnering with and referrals to other professionals are at best regarded as secondary to a focus on technical advice giving and at worst an inappropriate extension of the lawyer's role.

The adoption of a rights-based strategy endows the lawyer with the power of expertise no matter how powerful or wealthy her client or how knowledgable the client may be in another area. The lawyer's power rests on her possession of the necessary technical knowledge. In some lawyer-client relationships, this expertise is all that enables the lawyer to retain any status and authority within the relationship. High profile and high billing client accounts assert their own form of social power, and this further exemplifies the traditional lawyer-client hierarchy. In relationships with commercial clients – in particular, clients who account for a significant percentage of the lawyer or firm's business – lawyers often feel less than powerful – for example in exercising personal judgment or discretion or in making decisions about whether to take on a file. In the first Chicago study, discussed in Chapter 1, John Heinz and Edward Laumann asserted that there was an inverse relationship between the status of clients and lawyer autonomy.[39] Robert Nelson and others have since shown that lawyers working for big clients frequently experience a reduced sense of personal autonomy and decision making. Nelson's study of corporate lawyers in four large Chicago firms found that lawyers rarely refused a client assignment, and even smaller numbers of individuals turned down a file because of personal values or principles – for example, refusing a client assignment for personal reasons. Many lawyers felt that they had little or no control or influence over the choice between different strategies on a client file.[40] Robert Nelson and Rebecca Sandefur's later study bears out this phenomenon, tying it directly to organizational structure (lawyers working in large corporate firms and government departments) as well as to client groups.[41] The antidote to this loss of autonomy and prestige is the assertion of superior legal knowledge, namely, that lawyers will always remain "in charge" in key areas of substantive (if not tactical) decision making.

A rights-based model of dispute resolution assumes that lawyers acquire some form of ownership – and not simply stewardship – of their clients' conflicts as a consequence of their professional expertise. This is especially apparent where the relationship is understood as being one of expert/naïf, which is usually the case for a first-time client. There is little for the client to do other than place herself in the hands of her lawyer. An exclusive emphasis on a rights-based paradigm reinforces this attitude because it identifies the lawyer as a technician "fixing" the problem by applying the law.[42] As William Simon describes this model of advocacy, "the litigants are not the subject of the ceremony, but rather the pretext for it."[43]

The consequence is that many litigants feel that their original problem becomes transformed into something they do not readily recognize, moulded into a "stock story" via a statement of claim or defence.[44] The burning issue that originally belonged to the disputants, both intellectually and emotionally, becomes detached from them on both levels when it is placed in the hands of a legal representative. Client goals are reframed where necessary to fit a theory of rights. A theory of rights leads to a different framing of the conflict than, for example, a theory of the public good or a theory of power. Since legal remedies are primarily monetarized, self-interested economic maximization[45] is the "imputed end"[46] of most if not all clients within the traditional model of rights-based advocacy, where counsel's job is to achieve it as literally as possible, often unmoderated by other (non-legal) consequences or opportunities. This is despite overwhelming evidence to suggest that both commercial and domestic clients of legal services identify supplementary and even alternative goals and strategies for themselves. The disconnect can be only partly explained by the fact that few law firms have a system for systematically gathering and channelling client feedback to lawyers. Yet even if regular client feedback were built into the process of file management, the nature of expert advising in a rights-based model makes questioning or challenging the lawyer's assumed strategy extremely difficult. As well, the inevitable risks and uncertainties of litigation (which only the lawyer can really assess) make it possible for the lawyer to justify almost any decision or choice of tactic.

This assumption of ownership by lawyers is both practical and emotional. Only certain types of client input, which are deemed to be relevant to building a strong legal argument, are sought. Where other issues such as a client's emotionality or sense of urgency intrude, the message is that these fears should be assuaged and controlled in order that the lawyer can get back on track. The widespread resistance to the intervention of emotional issues into the management of a file is epitomized by the quip, "The only thing I don't love about legal practice is the clients." Like the most enduring jokes, this comment is not without truth. By the time young lawyers enter practice, they have spent three to four years being educated in law without the intervention of clients, either physically (unless they work in a legal clinic, but even in this case the environment is artificially focused on litigation in order to provide "exciting" and "action-based" training) or intellectually (clients are rarely if ever mentioned in law school classrooms). It is not surprising then that the arrival of real-life clients who are experiencing the anxiety, uncertainty, and fear of conflict is an unwelcome intrusion for many. Even for those lawyers who are more interested in the real people behind the story, they have few, if any, tools to deal with especially difficult or high maintenance clients and quickly become burned out. In a law school class, I once sent a group of students to interview a "client" actor, whom they came upon sitting weeping in an office. The students immediately returned to me, horrified, saying that they had no idea what to do. At this point, the detached "lawyer-in-charge" model looks much more attractive than trying to be a "counsellor," as does buying into the dominant belief that clients are secondary to and ultimately detached from their legal problem.

A traditional adversarial model of legal services that centres on technical advice – "taking instructions," which in effect means telling the clients what is best for them – allows lawyers to control the relationship between themselves and their clients. It limits their professional role to that of technical expert (with which they are generally comfortable) and at the same time limits the intrusion of emotional and other less predictable dimensions of conflict resolution. Yet this traditional model may be losing its appeal and strength. As litigation wanes in its attraction to commercial clients and is replaced with strategic approaches to negotiating resolution, and as personal clients feel increasingly empowered by greater access to legal information via the World Wide Web, lawyers can no longer assume the traditional relationship of expert/naïf. Increasingly, both commercial and personal clients are coming to expect not only technical legal advice but also assistance with negotiation, strategic appraisal of options, and practical problem solving. These same clients also expect more involvement in the progress and perhaps the conduct of their case and are far less content to hand over control to the lawyer and sit on the sidelines than in the past. Some clients will always prefer to have their lawyer take on their problem for them, but increasingly the new lawyer is finding herself negotiating a partnership instead of being able to simply assume the traditional lawyer-in-charge arrangement.

Role, Values, and Resistance

However much comfort lawyers find in the perpetuation of these three key beliefs, without re-examination and some modification they seem inadequate to meet the challenges of legal practice in the twenty-first century. There are many signs of pressure on the traditional role identity of lawyers, evidenced by the changes described in Chapter 1. Yet the core values and norms of the profession described here – beliefs that, while not uniformly accepted, are widespread in their influence – appear to be entrenched and quite resistant to change. This is plain if one attends a handful of law school classes, observes a series of client consultations, sits in on a partners meeting in a law firm, or observes a pre-trial hearing or settlement conference or even a mediation. The three beliefs described in this chapter are much in evidence in each of these settings.

Another sign of the pressure to review and reformulate these key beliefs is the increasing number of lawyers who are beginning to speak out about the mismatch they experience between the contemporary culture of the legal system and their personal beliefs. Legal education and the traditional values of legal practice have conventionally forced a separation of personal and professional values, such that personal beliefs are usually required to be subsumed within overriding professional duties (such as the right of representation, the obligation to follow client instructions, and so on). Law school has traditionally discouraged students from concerning themselves with the relationship between their personal moral values and those they adopt in pursuit of justice for their clients.[47] Personal moral scruples are discouraged or even derided as being "soft," which is a message reinforced by the adversarial culture of legal practice. Instead, the moral bargain is that lawyers are excused from any feeling of moral responsibility because their choices and actions are necessary to "play the system" for their clients.[48]

More lawyers are starting to question the assumption that they must acquiesce in this moral bargain. A desire for the realignment of these personal values with their professional ones is a constant theme in research conducted with lawyers who decide to move to a collaborative model of family practice.[49] Many collaborative lawyers are highly reflective about what they see as the inevitability of adversarial behaviour and hurtful consequences in the traditional litigation model and their discomfort with being drawn into this situation. These lawyers admit that they have found the adversarial system highly seductive but ultimately dissatisfying because it constrains and even distorts their personal value system. For example, one lawyer explains:

> It's about winning. And you don't care. I'm a pretty moral person but in the old system you want to win for your client and that's it.[50]

> I would find myself encouraging ... grossly inflated and unrealistic expectations on the part of the client as you prepare for trial. You file settlement conference statements that ask for the moon and stars because you know you're only going to get a half to a third of what you ask for so you have to do that ... You're taking a complex life situation and you're reducing it to cartoon characters of black and white.[51]

A sense of lack of purpose and dissatisfaction may also be exacerbated by the organizational structure of large firms. Increasing numbers of law school graduates work for corporate clients in large firms. The emphasis on a narrow technical role, while still appealing to some, and the diminution of autonomy undermine the potential for fulfilment and satisfaction and may account for disillusionment among some lawyers who find that the expectations of practice that were encouraged in law school are not realized within these professional structures.[52] More and more lawyers are actively seeking alternative ways to practise law, whether in corporate or personal practice, that are more congruent with their personal values and original goals. This is evident in networks of lawyers considering holistic practice, the application of therapeutic jurisprudence, and other non-adversarial approaches to the practice of law.[53] Others are choosing to leave the profession altogether.[54]

In the face of public dissatisfaction with justice systems and tensions within the profession itself, do the traditional values and beliefs of the profession stand up to scrutiny? Are they realistic in the era of the "vanishing trial" and in the face of growing client empowerment and demands for value for money? Is there a mismatch between the professions' core beliefs and the changes in the external environment? At a minimum, the profession must confront the widely recognized problem of a diminishing sense of pride and purpose.[55] This situation is merely a symptom of a wider malaise – a concept of professional identity that is at best frozen in time and at worst increasingly inchoate. Lawyers need to be able to make sense of change in a way that is congruent with their perception of their skills and expertise and that enables them to establish a sense of purpose. They also need to identify and develop new areas of skill and knowledge that build on the old, just as the evolution of the modern legal profession builds on 150 years of legal practice.

The next chapter offers one such appraisal in the form of a case study of the conduct of legal negotiations. It describes how the three key beliefs interact with the traditional structures of legal negotiations to produce remarkably consistent but highly inefficient norms of behaviour for lawyers as they negotiate. And it asks how the three key beliefs need to be modified in order to better engage the realities of twenty-first-century legal practice.

4
Translating the Beliefs into Practice: The Norms of Legal Negotiations

How are the beliefs and values of the profession described in the last chapter operationalized in the negotiation and settlement of lawsuits? Legal negotiation provides an example of how the key beliefs – a default to rights-based conflict resolution, justice as process, and the assumption that lawyers are "in charge" in the lawyer-client relationship – get translated into everyday choices about behaviour and practice. Put another way, what norms of practice flow from the dominant values when lawyers negotiate?

Legal negotiations also provide an important insight into the significance of the structure within which lawyers perform their tasks. This structure includes timing, the sequence of tasks undertaken, and the context for bargaining – usually a parallel activity to litigation – as well as the roles played by the various actors (lawyers, clients) in the bargaining process. There is an obvious interdependence between the structure of legal negotiation and the three key beliefs. These structural characteristics, which research consistently describes as predictable and highly stylized,[1] have evolved from and sustain the dominant values. Therefore, the adoption of a rights-based approach to negotiation flows from the assumption that lawsuits will be resolved through an adjudicative paradigm. Equally, the tendency to delay serious negotiation until the closing stages of litigation, when legal arguments have been deepened and formalized, further enables and makes logical a rights-based approach to negotiation. As we shall see, the interdependence of values and structure means that challenge to traditional bargaining practices is both difficult and complex.

The Structure of Legal Negotiations

Preparing for Trial
Marc Galanter memorably described negotiations over litigation as "litigotiation."[2] In other words, it is a structural and conceptual creation of the litigation model. The anticipation of future (both intermediate and ultimate)

steps in litigation determines the manner in which lawyers approach the negotiation of lawsuits on their clients' behalf. This anticipation drives not only decisions about potential settlements, measured against the likely legal outcome at trial, but also decisions over the disclosure of information, requests for information, the framing of arguments, the strategic use of delay, and all communications with the other side. In this way, the strategic framework for legal negotiations is dominated by the anticipation of an event – a full trial – that will almost never occur.

Given this paradigm of bargaining dynamics and, in particular, its constraints on the exchange of information and an emphasis on rights-based arguments, it is surprising just how many lawsuits are settled by negotiation. We have already noted that the number of civil trials is falling – down to 1.8 percent of United States federal courts filings in 2002[3] – and the assumption that follows is that these cases are being settled by negotiation. It is true that these 98.2 percent of cases are resolved outside a trial but the complete story is more complex. Cases settled by negotiation do not necessarily reach a result independently of the courts. Growing attention is being paid to the significant increases in motions activity and other forms of pre-trial adjudication. Full trial adjudication may be being displaced by non-trial adjudication. In these ways, lawyers are still using the litigation process and the authority of judges to settle cases, but they just do fewer trials.

This insight underscores a fundamental characteristic of lawyer-to-lawyer negotiation. While negotiated or non-tried outcomes are the overwhelming norm in civil litigation, the practice of negotiation is an adjunct to the practice of litigation. Lawyers spend far more time preparing for litigation than they do preparing for or holding negotiation sessions. Some would argue that this is precisely because negotiation is simply an extension of a litigation strategy. Studies consistently show that negotiation is a low intensity activity for most lawyers who devote significantly more time to the procedural aspects of litigation (drafting court documents, preparing motions, and conducting discoveries) than they do to negotiating settlements.[4] The amount of dollars that clients invest in settlement preparation and negotiation, compared to what they expend in taking procedural steps in litigation, seems disproportionately small for such a significant, almost inevitable, event. The settlements appear as if by magic once the parties have exhausted (and perhaps bankrupted) themselves with the legal process. Researchers have found that most settlements result from one or two exchanges of offers only.[5] Further, this exchange is usually done at arm's length, not by face-to-face contact, and is almost always a monetarized solution reflecting the anticipation of likely legal outcomes (consisting of primarily monetary remedies) rather than creative or original solutions or outcomes (see the discussion later in this chapter).[6] This means that there is a limited role for the client, who must defer to the lawyer in matters of legal knowledge. It also maintains the primacy of rights-based conflict resolution and preserves the technical control of the lawyer whose specialist knowledge is the sole or dominant currency of the settlement process.

This conceptual framework for legal negotiation raises a number of client service issues. The first is that if negotiation is treated simply as an adjunct to litigation, with preparation for negotiation regarded as virtually identical to the preparation of a strong litigation file, clients are not being offered specialized negotiation techniques and strategies that could heighten their chances of a good settlement and expand the range of available outcomes. Instead, negotiation proceeds along a fairly predictable and unimaginative path of an exchange of inflated offers and counter-offers, until the distance is broken down to a meeting point. This helps explain why negotiated outcomes seem to fall within such a narrow range and focus so heavily on monetarized compromises without the "value-added" components that would require a more creative approach to negotiation.

Second, this approach to settlement negotiation often leaves clients facing an unexpected collapse in their expectations when settlement offers do not match up with the initial claims and demands made by their counsel. Whereas lawyers are accustomed to reducing expectations in order to find a deal that will avert the costly and uncertain possibility of a trial, their clients are usually less knowledgeable about this dynamic. Since the strength of a negotiating position in litigation is characterized almost entirely by its appeal to legal principles and assertions of convincing legal argument, the eventual compromise, which probably abandons at least some legal arguments, is for many clients wholly incommensurate with earlier assertions of confidence by their counsel. Especially when the client has been only minimally involved in any strategic dimensions of the negotiation, the presentation of a settlement proposal may come as something of an unpleasant shock. Having been initially advised that they have a good case that counsel will vigorously pursue for them, clients are now told that they should face the reality of the costs and uncertainty of trial and settle for something less than their original claim. Some counsel do a better job than others of preparing their client for the almost inevitable compromise.

A third problem for the client is that the difference between the original offer of settlement and the final agreement is often negligible, especially when legal costs are factored in.[7] While lawyers feel compelled to spend time gathering information and building a theory of the case, the eventual payoff for their clients in settlement dollars may be less than the costs of this work. The calculation of value to the client may be further complicated by counsel's perception that he needs to protect himself against professional negligence claims. If counsel is motivated by this concern, it becomes even more difficult to determine whether an investment of significant resources in steps taken before serious negotiations provides good value for the client. Experienced litigators are better positioned to make good judgments about the relative value of the expenditure of resources (on witness affidavits, on discoveries) on the chances of improving the eventual settlement. A further problem is that such judgments may be compromised by the fact that pre-settlement expenditures also directly benefit counsel. As one senior litigator put it:

> My radar is very much in tune to a deal that I think accords with the clients' wishes ... what fits with the client, and is probably pretty close to what I would have otherwise got two years hence, after thousands of dollars of money down the toilet in litigation. By the way, that toilet is my pocket.[8]

Sometimes work preceding the opening of negotiations genuinely strengthens the client's case and puts them in a superior bargaining position; in other cases it may be simply a matter of habit (for example, a reluctance to open negotiations before discoveries, whether or not that information is actually utilized in effecting a better settlement). The difficulty of appraising the usefulness of pre-settlement work is heightened by custom and practice surrounding the timing of negotiations in a legal model.

The Timing of Negotiations

A second critical, and often overlooked, structural characteristic of legal negotiations is the timing of discussions leading up to settlement. We know that the actual back-and-forth pattern of bargaining tends to be of low intensity and fairly short.[9] The contested point is when bargaining should commence. Counsel generally resist opening negotiations until a point at which they feel they have collected sufficient information to be able to make a strong legal case. In larger civil cases, this point almost always comes after examination for discovery:

> I think that a lot of lawyers just react as a knee jerk reaction [saying], how the hell can you mediate something when you haven't even had discovery?[10]

As mentioned above, there is a built-in economic incentive to prefer this approach and to be disinclined toward any dispute resolution model that settles before the real billings come through. One Toronto counsel commented:

> At times, you see a file that was going to keep you into discoveries for three months and it just got settled on very good terms for the client and you kind of go: "Wait a minute, is that the wildest thing I ever did?" I

think there's a certain tone of that, especially among senior partners that goes: "Wait a minute." Then there's a tension there. You can't deny that there's tension there.[11]

One of the strongest sources of resistance to the introduction of mandatory mediation in Saskatchewan and Ontario in the 1990s came from lawyers who felt that the timing of mediation was premature. These programs were designed with the intent that most cases would go to mediation before discoveries. The adjudicative model, and the dominant adversarial style of lawyering, assumes that the function of information and fact gathering is to strengthen rights-based arguments (and conversely to repudiate those of the other side). Only after significant investment, and the satisfaction of "due diligence," can a file be ready for negotiation discussions. However, information deemed pertinent to this end may or may not be relevant and useful in the negotiation of a pragmatic solution.

There is some evidence that the presumption of a need for certain types and depth of information changes as lawyers gain more experience with early negotiation and mediation. Lawyers have begun to question the assumption that particular types of detailed information are really necessary in order to negotiate responsibly and effectively. They note that at least some of the information they have assumed is essential to the initiation of serious settlement discussions might not in fact be relevant to the type of solution that could emerge, and sometimes has emerged, from these very early negotiations.[12] One lawyer characterized the current norm in the following way:

There is an almost fetishistic obsession with knowing everything about a file before you can say anything about it.[13]

Another made this remarkably frank comment:

I personally am concerned that if only 3 percent of the cases actually go to trial, that means 97 percent of the time all the pre-trial stuff is wasted to a large extent, so therefore 97 percent of money I make is from wasted time.[14]

The assumption that negotiations are best left until a later stage in the case is reflected in data on the timing of settlement. Studies of the Ontario program using control groups demonstrate that requiring early negotiation has a significant impact on the timing of settlement. A study by the author in 1995 contrasted the mean number of days from filing to settlement for both mediated cases and a matched control group of litigation cases, and found that cases that were mediated were consistently settled in a shorter period of time than those without any mediation intervention.[15]

A study of the same program found that a substantially higher proportion of cases that went through mediation resolved within three, six, nine,
and twelve months of those that did not use mediation.[16] Despite these
figures and success elsewhere in early mediation programs,[17] many counsel, in the absence of compulsion to early negotiation, continue to insist
that they generally cannot be "ready" to negotiate until close to the time
of trial. Without mandatory mediation, case management, or settlement
conferencing, lawyers often control the timing of negotiation and generally prefer to "wait" until discoveries are concluded or even later.

Bargaining by Agents

> We decided the lawyers could settle this easier. So every two months, I
> took them to Canoe [an upscale Toronto restaurant] upstairs for drinks,
> or they would take me, and we would try to settle. We're getting close,
> we're now extremely close, but we're not there yet.[18]

Many lawyers argue that they are better able to accommodate and resolve
differences between disputing parties than the clients themselves. After
all, this argument goes, the lawyers can remain emotionally detached from
the burning issues and understand what is and is not relevant as a matter
of law. The earlier quote illustrates this assumption and also its social-
professional context. The implication is that in a comfortable environment,
such as an expensive restaurant, the lawyers can have a civilized, rational
negotiation in language and terms they all understand. Just how efficient
regular meetings over drinks are for the resolution of the clients' problem
is of course less clear. Thus, a third structural characteristic of legal negotiations that has an important impact on the dynamic of bargaining is the
general exclusion of clients from the negotiation process. While some experienced commercial clients may occasionally wish to be included in formal face-to-face discussions, the vast majority of such meetings take place
between lawyers in the absence of their clients. Austin Sarat and William
Felstiner make the following observation on settlement work in divorce
cases: "The major ingredient of this settlement system is the primacy of
the lawyers. They produce the deals, while the clients are limited to initial instructions and the after-the-fact ratification."[19] Indeed, the inclusion
of clients in mediation is viewed with considerable apprehension by many
lawyers. For example, one lawyer had this response to a question:

> *Interviewer:* Is there anything different that you're doing in terms of prepar-
> ing the client or anything that you can think that affects your relationship
> with the client when you are preparing for mediation?
> *Interviewee:* I teach them to "shut-up."[20]

A model of representation by agents is entrenched in legal culture and reflected in assumptions about decision making and control between lawyer and client. We have already considered the continued dominance of a "lawyer-in-charge" model. Even where alternative paradigms are emerging – where there is an intention of "client-centredness"[21] or where commercial clients rein in the independent decision making of their lawyers – clients are rarely immune to the influence and paternalism of their professional advisors. This effect is further heightened by the relatively passive role of the client and the active role of the agent in legal representation. Agency representation in negotiation has two significant and interrelated effects on clients. First, it is harder for the client to assert a position independent of or contrary to the lawyer's advice since she can always be told that she cannot fully appreciate or comprehend the dynamics, context, personalities, or other factors at play. For example, a lawyer may also be using what she knows about the negotiation reputation of the other counsel to formulate a strategy and a set of predictions.[22] This information is rarely accessible to clients. Even when a lawyer mentions the reputation of opposite counsel in explaining her recommendations, this information is usually intended to remind clients that they cannot be as well informed as their counsel is in this situation. The same applies to proposals presented by the agent as a result of a meeting in which she participated without her client present. The presentation by counsel of both offers and options inevitably affects her client's perception since she is the sole source of this information and can frame it in multiple ways.

Second, the very act of transmission of instructions from client to lawyer to the other side inevitably changes the message and places the instructing client at arm's length from its ultimate final presentation. Once a position or proposal is filtered through the agent, delivered by the agent to the other side, and then passed on by opposing counsel to their client, its tone, while not its content, may have been altered quite significantly. Moreover, this tone is often a part of the discretion that a client allows (or resigns) to counsel to reflect the fact that she is dealing face to face with the other side, whereas the client is not. Where there are, as Jeffrey Rubin and Frank Sander put it, "extra moving parts" in a negotiation, there is less control and more uncertainty for a principal.[23] The net result is often heavier reliance by the client on the agent than they might have originally wished or intended (although some clients are only too happy to hand over management of their case to their lawyer).

Agency representation extends the time it takes to effect a settlement. It is more time-consuming for an agent to go back and forth between principals, especially when there are agents on both or all sides, than it is to undertake direct negotiations. A contrary perspective sometimes taken (and another version of the emotional detachment argument) is that excluding the individuals who are in conflict enables counsel to discuss the options more frankly and to move the dialogue forward more efficiently. This may sometimes be the case, and it is one of the better arguments for using agency representation in some types of bargaining. However, the transmission of instructions, options, and proposals via agents almost always seems bound to increase the time taken from initiation to settlement or closure, even if this communication is as clear as possible.

Finally, bargaining by agents in the absence of clients may exclude some of the potential creative energy that clients can bring to the negotiation process by their direct involvement. Ontario litigators who were questioned about the types of solution reached in mediation of commercial cases frequently described business solutions that could be hashed out in mediation with the clients present. Such solutions are less likely to be forthcoming from traditional lawyer-to-lawyer negotiations. Sometimes these lawyers heard their business clients proposing new and innovative solutions for the first time at mediation, as they worked with their counterpart on solutions that matched the business context. Beyond the settlement of the particular dispute, other types of business outcomes that counsel have described as being the result of mediation include the continuation of a commercial relationship, a new commercial relationship such as trade partners or joint venturing, the completion of a (disputed) sale and purchase agreement, access to the preferred terms of a new supplier, agreement to a forbearance period, consent to judgment for a lesser sum, agreement to vacate in order to avoid eviction proceedings, and a settlement structured to maximize tax advantages for the parties.[24] These examples demonstrate that it is critical to have the client present in order to ensure that the full range of operative interests are brought to the table and not just those that are easily translated into rights-based arguments. Creative agreements, which maximize the integrative potential, are more likely to be achieved on the basis of this richer range of interests.

Many counsel recognize that these types of solutions require that their commercial clients participate directly in mediation. As one lawyer put it, "The clients take much more of an active role because they understand their business better than I do. I understand it the least."[25] Deals between business people often seem to be much simpler and straightforward than anything the litigation lawyer can offer. For example, one lawyer explained:

> I mean, you have to have like a 27 page settlement with all the ye'old and releases and stuff, with all that language that you know no one understands, because you're afraid that the guy is going to try to pull a fast one

because they're not happy, they've been forced to sign a deal. Whereas business people who do it voluntarily can do it in four paragraphs in that agreement.[26]

In addition, having the clients present sometimes motivates them to create immediate closure. For example, as one individual stated:

Both of them can end it that day. No letters going back and forth, that you receive five days after you sent something to some other lawyer, then the other lawyer goes to somebody else and gets back two weeks after ... On that day, this whole thing can be over with. That day you don't have to talk to your lawyer anymore if you're the client. That day you can easily walk out of there with this problem over.[27]

Movement toward the inclusion of clients in negotiation, which is a hallmark of collaborative law as well as some court-connected mediation programs, challenges the primacy of legal agents in the bargaining process. For now, client participation in dispute resolution bargaining remains relatively limited. Not all court programs require clients to attend, and lawyers often control what participation does occur.[28] In judicial settlement conferencing, the degree to which clients are expected to participate depends on the approach of the individual judge, although there are signs that as experience grows with this forum, judicial attitudes may be changing. In family matters, in particular, judges are increasingly convinced of the value of having the client speak up and be spoken to.[29]

The structural characteristics of legal negotiation – the low intensity of legal negotiations and the dominance of litigation preparation, the timing of settlement discussions, the agency role of counsel, and the limited direct participation of clients – are consistent both with one another and with the structure and values of an adjudicative system. One must behave as if one is going to trial even though one will almost always negotiate a settlement. Thus, settlement can only be considered when substantial resources have been directed to preparing the best possible legal arguments, and the final discussions are assumed to be most effective and efficient if lawyers act on behalf of their clients, focus on the likely legal outcomes, and minimize the potential emotional dimensions of the conflict. There are some obvious deficiencies with this model of negotiation. Its focus on preparation for trial when trial is extremely unlikely is often inefficient. It exacerbates a divergence of lawyer and client interests in the pursuit of settlement since lawyers can bill for each hour they spend on the file, while clients want to minimize expenses in pursuit of settlement, and there is little accountability for the relationship between expenditure and eventual settlement. This approach to legal negotiations often produces mediocre and unimaginative settlements at a point at which the parties are exhausted, embittered, and settle in order to avoid further expense, not because they are satisfied with the outcome.

The structural characteristics of legal negotiations are consistent with the assumptions of an adjudicative system in which everything is a rehearsal for trial. They also support and reinforce the three key beliefs described in the last chapter. How is the widespread commitment to rights, justice as process, and lawyer control operationalized in the context of "typical" legal negotiations? How are the beliefs manifest in how lawyers behave in bargaining?

The Norms of Legal Negotiations

When lawyers negotiate, they consciously or unconsciously use their dominant values and beliefs to navigate their way through the process. These beliefs drive their choice of strategy and behaviour, often at an unconscious level. While this approach is typical of any professional task, it is especially fascinating to examine legal negotiations as an example of a task undertaken in a professional capacity for which the professional has often not been formally trained. Since relatively few lawyers presently in practice have received any specialized training in negotiation, considered the various theories and models of negotiations in law or any other context, or practised negotiation in an educational setting where they can receive feedback, in negotiating counsel depends to a large extent on her instincts in making choices over appropriate actions and decisions. These instincts are directed by the given structure of legal negotiations and are critically, if unconsciously, shaped by the three key beliefs.

The norms of legal negotiation described below take some of their shape and form from the context in which they are applied. There are numerous minor conventions of bargaining that appear to be specific to practice areas, such as those described by Hazel Genn in her work on personal injuries litigation[30] or by John Baldwin and Michael McConville in their work on plea bargaining.[31] There have been some attempts to identify particular norms of bargaining with practice areas. For example, the work of Lynn Mather, Craig McEwen, and Richard Maiman suggests that the norms of "reasonableness" in negotiation are more strongly established in the family bar than in other areas of practice such as commercial litigation.[32] Other research, however, suggests that family lawyers are more adversarial and less committed to problem solving than other practice groups.[33] However, associating particular practice characteristics with particular groups is a tricky business. There are always exceptions.

What is less contentious is that the broader culture of legal negotiations encompasses both structural conventions and constraints and a set of dominant behaviourial norms. The behaviourial norms of legal negotiation are principally driven by the key beliefs. Such is their strength that practice variations generally take place within rather than in opposition to the spectrum of behaviours described next.

Play to Win (Legal Negotiations Are a Zero-Sum Game)

The following is a description by a lawyer of his client's approach to negotiation. It is a perfect description of the moral force of "playing to win," the techniques involved, and the ultimate goal. Despite the fact that it is a description of the behaviour of a "non-lawyer," the very same techniques are commonly used by lawyers in legal negotiations with the same eventual goal.

> She uses the blunt force of her own power, ... her disapproval and the word "no" as tools to get what she wants as she goes for the win, that is, capitulation.[34]

Legal negotiations are about winning and playing to win. Of course, lawyers also know that they will eventually compromise to some degree and settle. At the same time, many lawyers assume that the harder they play to win, the better the settlement they will eventually achieve. Whether or not this is true, and there is plenty of evidence that it is not, it supports the fiction that one can, indeed – one must – "win" at legal negotiations. Playing to win means regarding negotiation as a zero-sum game.

A zero-sum game is a conception of bargaining in which one side's loss is the other side's gain. This approach to negotiation means that all or both parties are assumed to want the same thing and that the only way to settle is to divide up this so-called "fixed pie" (money, market share, intellectual property rights, child custody, and so on) in some acceptable way. In legal negotiations such shares are usually pegged to an anticipation of likely legal outcomes – that is, the more one can credibly advance an argument of likely success at trial, the larger the slice of the pie one credibly claims (and vice versa). Because settlements tend to mimic likely legal outcomes, this means an almost exclusive reliance on monetary remedies and little creativity or diversity.[35]

In this classic distributive model of negotiation, where negotiations take place along a single continuum representing monetary value, the goal of every competent professional is to take as much as they can, thereby increasing their share of the pie and reducing their opponent's share. This goal lies in contrast to the exploitation of potential for benefits on all sides and the maximization of mutual gains.

Lawyers understand legal negotiations as zero-sum because they approach negotiation as an adjunct of litigation, usually preparing in the same way for each. This means that their conception of the outcome of negotiation is the same as their conception of the outcome of adjudication: that there will be a single winner who takes all and that the rest will be losers. The norms surrounding a zero-sum approach to bargaining fit perfectly with the belief in a default to a rights-based approach, driven by legal expertise. Expert knowledge of the law becomes critical to developing a so-called "winning" strategy. Assuming that legal negotiation is a zero-sum game privileges substantive legal expertise as a predictor of likely victory and, therefore, of strength. In this model, negotiation strength means confidently asserting the strongest arguments to place oneself as the victor in a legal adjudication.

Just how plausible is the argument that legal negotiations should be played to win, as zero-sum negotiations, as if all parties want the same things and for the same reasons? In many legal disputes, the parties want different things, in different ways, and for different reasons, and there is plenty of potential for intelligent and strategic bargaining that recognizes the differing priorities and goals of the parties. In reality, the substance of and issues at stake in legal disputes are rarely zero-sum, just as few disputes, or few elements of some disputes, are truly about indivisible values.[36] For example, disputes over commercial influence and market share, or the co-parenting of children, or the ending of an employment relationship, are not zero-sum. Each of these examples admits many possible creative outcomes in which giving one side some of what it wants does not *have* to mean less for the other.

Instead of arguing "for" or "against" certain outcomes, lawyers provide better service to their clients when they examine the various possible benefits that they could negotiate on their behalf. This is sometimes described as exploring the "integrative potential" of a deal,[37] such that negotiators review all the options, ideally to the point of "Pareto optimality."[38] There is usually a point in every negotiation at which the expansion of the "pie" of possible benefits has been taken as far as is practical, and this "expanded pie" now needs to be divided up in some way that makes sense to each side's sense of fairness. At this final stage in bargaining, even in the most collaborative negotiation, priorities need to be set and choices made. However, where the earlier discussion between the parties assumes the potential for joint outcomes that can be attractive to all sides and are not necessarily zero-sum, the result is more choices, a better and more complete understanding of how to meet both sides' needs, and a more constructive and creative bargaining climate.

Nonetheless, impelled by the belief in the primacy of rights (and reinforced by the commitment to rights processes as a means of establishing justice), legal negotiations are usually played *as if* they are zero-sum, in which there will be a winner and a loser. This means that the benchmark for transition to a settlement mentality is whether or not enough work has been done on maximizing the chances of "winning." Whether it is the client who raises settlement, suggesting that there may be room to make a deal or that it may be time to make a deal, or the lawyer who broaches this topic with her client, the assessment that the lawyer makes is "have I played hard enough at winning now to be able to make a good deal?" This means factoring in how much time and work has gone into the file, as it is even harder for lawyers to imagine a "win" that happens within the early stages of a file, perhaps even before the development of a ("winning") theory of the case or a disclosure and document exchange.

The most adversarial lawyers are so focused on working for a win that they do not regard deal making as being part of their job, as this next lawyer explains:

> *Interviewer:* What if the client starts for whatever reason to get cold feet and says to you: "I want you to go to them and ask them if they'll talk settlement," how might you respond to that?
> *Interviewee:* Very badly!
> *Interviewer:* What would you say to the client?
> *Interviewee:* I would say to the client: "If you're interested in settlement, you go and talk to the other side about it, I'm very bad at it, my job is to manage a war, not to manage a peace."[39]

This war metaphor is frequently used by lawyers to describe legal negotiations. While not all lawyers would feel comfortable describing litigation as a "war" (this particular lawyer goes on to explain that "the objective is to destroy the opponent"[40]), many use metaphors of "fighting" and, most tellingly, will describe settlement as "giving up on fighting."[41] Such vocabulary reveals the underlying ideology of negotiations – often right up to the point of settlement – as playing to win.

Information Is for Winning

The zero-sum assumptions of legal negotiations have many implications for the way in which information is understood and valued in legal negotiations. The acquisition and development of information is regarded as being primarily about winning rather than about understanding and elaborating the clients' needs, developing shared facts, or understanding more about the other side and possible mutual gains. When information is only about winning, a culture of secrecy and non-disclosure develops in legal negotiations that borders on the paranoid. Disclosure of almost any information is assumed to give an advantage to the other side. As a consequence, "litigotiation" is conducted on the basis of very limited information being available about the other side's motivations, goals, or priorities. In the absence of any knowledge to the contrary, counsel naturally acts to protect herself and her client against the possibility of adversarial or unhelpful behaviour by the other side, often assuming the worst. Sometimes this protective-defensive stance means making a pre-emptive strike as a demonstration of strength without waiting to observe how the other side conducts itself.

The tendency toward this type of defensive entrenchment or, worse, aggressive hostility is noted by game theorists in numerous iterations of the Prisoner's Dilemma game and is classically analyzed by Robert Axelrod in *The Evolution of Co-operation*.[42] In the Prisoner's Dilemma game, two friends are held in adjacent cells and questioned separately about an alleged crime in which they both participated. Each has to decide whether to confess and turn in the other or deny their involvement and hope that the other does the same. They are dependent on one another for determining the best strategy but ignorant of the other's decisions to confess or deny. The game illustrates the difficulty of interdependent decision making, or negotiating, when there is little or no information about the other's motivations, goals, priorities, and so on. The ensuing dynamic is generally defensive-reactive because without information to the contrary, each prisoner must assume that the other side will do likewise.[43]

In the same way and for the same reasons, the norms of the bargaining process in legal negotiations are pre-emptively competitive rather than presumptively co-operative. In deciding whether to share information in litigation, the choices are the same as in the Prisoner's Dilemma game. If both sides share information, more mutual benefit can accrue. If both sides refuse to share information, negative results ensue. If one side shares information but it is not reciprocated, it gives a real advantage to the receiving side. Assuming the worst and protecting oneself perpetuates a culture of secrecy in which even apparently innocuous information – for example, about goals and motivations – is routinely withheld.

Instead of information being used collectively to develop an understanding between the parties – for example, exchanging ideas and information regarding how bargaining will be conducted, or setting out party priorities – information is regarded as most potent in legal negotiations when it is concealed from the other side. This is sometimes described as using information for "power over," rather than for "power with," the other side.[44] The value placed on secrecy here highlights the function of information in legal negotiations: to ambush the other side with a brilliant legal argument, relevant precedent, or startling new fact, in order to maximize the chances of a "win." In preparing a case for trial, counsel must collect information that makes the rights-based case, and this information (aces up the sleeve) becomes relatively less valuable if it is shared with the other side.[45]

This approach to the function and use of information is perfectly illustrated by the discovery process, which is principally concerned with what information can be dragged from the other side and what can continue to be concealed (often leading to endless motions), rendering the term "discovery" something of a misnomer. Litigation requires the collection of information – large amounts of it. Plaintiffs drive their case forward by collecting as much data as possible that are advantageous to them. Defendants stall the process – and any possible judgment against them – by requesting further and better information from the plaintiff.[46] The emphasis on rights-oriented case development encourages the collection and concealment of as much information as possible, and discourages the early exchange of information about needs and interests.

Playing out legal negotiations as if they are a zero-sum game obviously privileges certain types of information deemed to be "relevant" to making the legal argument, and diminishes other types of "irrelevant" (also described as non-legal) information. Because the information sought and collected is limited to what strengthens the clients' rights-based case, it rarely includes information about what either side really wants and needs in order to settle. Instead, information (evidence) is gathered in order to assert or defend a particular version of events. Any other "irrelevant" information is routinely discarded or ignored. This includes information that has no legal implications (but may be extremely significant as emotional context or reflecting important commercial needs and interests) and information about strategies and bargaining context (for example, the culture of bargaining in a corporation or the conventions of settlement for a particular insurer). These types of data are not identified with building a "winning" case and, hence, are frequently overlooked and under-utilized in making a settlement.

The zero-sum assumption also requires that information be presented as "fact" and requires the denial of any ambiguity, circumstances, or context (unless it is self-serving). Any acknowledgment of uncertainty in relation to a given fact or theory or the possibility of multiple understandings and interpretation immediately undermines an assertion of a "winning argument." Conversely, this requires the exploitation of any ambiguity in the "facts" as presented by the other side. Thus, when one side or the other presents information, it is routinely attacked by the other. It also makes the presentation of ideas as simply "options" for consideration in an effort to enlarge the creative scope of bargaining practically impossible, since the introduction of any information is assumed to be decisive, and not exploratory.

A focus on the strategic uses of information excludes the possibility of using information to develop a shared understanding of priorities and issues among the disputants, to clarify goals and motivations, to enlarge the scope of settlement alternatives, or to explore further tentative options. Information is for winning, not for sharing, and certainly not for enhancing the possible options that are available to the parties. This perspective on the function of information in legal negotiations, and the zero-sum analogy that underlies it, is strikingly at odds with the reality of accommodation and settlement that is the end result of most cases. It is likely to delay the development of solutions that almost always require better information – that is, information used other than as assertion and that focuses on much more than alleged "facts" and applicable legal theory – about party needs and interests.

A commitment to the making of zero-sum arguments and the use of information for winning is not always shared by the client. However, this deep commitment makes it difficult, sometimes, for counsel to move on and embrace their client's preferred practical solution. Even where the client is satisfied with the outcome, it may be hard for their counsel to derive satisfaction from a settlement they do not think was a legal "win." For example, as one lawyer explains:

> We settled it for $165,000. $165,000 more than I thought the case was worth, so justice was not done. These people who sued picked up $165,000 that they weren't entitled to. Was it a good settlement? My client was delighted ... [T]hey're delighted with my handling of it. I'm not, I think I lost. I don't think we won, we lost. Justice was not done there.[47]

The zero-sum fiction of legal negotiations and the ways in which information is understood and used also affect tactics and behaviours seen as legitimate in legal negotiations in order to secure a "win."

Stick to Your Position

There is an obvious relationship between a win/lose approach to dispute resolution and the tendency to deploy the tactics of positional bargaining. If one is playing to win, the rules of this shadow adjudication game require the articulation of a strong, unyielding position based on the best legal arguments. In order to demonstrate strength, lawyers adopt a stance of conviction that their arguments are certain to succeed at trial. A certain amount of hardball tactics and failure to cooperate with the other side is *de rigueur*. Acknowledging weakness on any issue or even articulating a priority from among a list of demands is widely regarded as "soft" advocacy. Hence, counsel quickly defaults to a positional approach to bargaining.

Positional bargaining is somewhat like the communication between two people who do not share a common language but who believe that by constantly restating their needs in an increasingly loud voice they will eventually get what they want. There is no effort to go behind the demand by obtaining more information about the needs of the other side or about what type of accommodation (perhaps expanding the pie of potential solutions) would satisfy them. Instead, there is simply an increasingly insistent and repetitive restating of one's own position. As one lawyer put it,

"You can posture and advocate until you're green in the face, but unless you're trying to solve the other person's legitimate issues, you're not going to succeed."[48]

Threats, bluffs, and posturing, although common in legal negotiations, are just one manifestation of positional bargaining. There is also a "soft" version of positional bargaining, which is characterized by less posturing but no more concern about the outcome and no less neglect of underlying interests and needs. The core problem with positional bargaining is less about the manner in which positions are presented and more about the narrowing of the scope of bargaining that always follows – that is, limiting the discussion to justifications rather than exploring motivations and goals.

Many lawyers acknowledge that the positions they take at the beginning of negotiations with the other side are inflated. They are conforming to the ritual dance of legal negotiations, when each side gradually evolves their opening position toward something more reasonable and realistic. However, there is always the risk that a positional approach may drive the dynamics of legal negotiations toward an impasse or, at best, a lengthy period of negotiation and the significant adjustment of expectations. This potential is well illustrated in the following quote, in which a lawyer contrasts positional bargaining with a more open, mutual gains approach in which information is exchanged and expectations clarified:

> In a traditional litigation file, if I thought my client's claim was worth $50,000, I'd ask for $100,000. If the other lawyer thought the claim was worth $30,000, they would say it's worth zero. In a collaborative law file, I have the confidence to say to my client: "Let's not talk about the 50 to 100, it's a waste of your time, it's not going to happen. Let's concentrate on the 30 to 50 that we all can agree on and make some creative options that suit you both within that 30 to 50."[49]

A "dance" toward an acceptable proposal, beginning with extreme positions from both sides, can be inefficient and time-consuming. It may be further impeded by the need of one lawyer or the other to show strength by holding tenaciously to her original position. Less experienced counsel are especially susceptible to this concern. Tenacity over a legal position, which often means resistance to any movement away from a winner-take-all result, is seen by many lawyers as an important aspect of their advocacy role. As the lawyer quoted in Chapter 2 said, "remember our job, our duty is to our individual clients to fearlessly assert the clients' rights."[50] Since in legal negotiations there is as yet no third party available to rule on the reasonableness of arguments or proposals, the best way to assert them is assumed to be total confidence, which sometimes borders on aggression.

Nonetheless, legal negotiations see a broad spectrum of positional behaviours and not all of these are "aggressive" in nature. Just how aggressive one might be in advancing a position in legal negotiations may depend in part on who you are dealing with. One lawyer, who was describing a case with an experienced counsel on the other side, anticipated position taking in the following way:

> I know them, and they're going to put every obstacle in my path. It's going to be obstructive, difficult, cranky. You know, a joyless, lifeless, adversarial, somebody's got to win, somebody's got to lose type situation.[51]

However the widespread norm of ulitizing varying degrees of confidence/aggression in defence of one's position in legal negotiations means that lawyers fear that they – and their case – will appear weak if they do not adopt this approach. This dynamic drives even those lawyers who know better, or who would prefer to behave differently, toward positional bargaining:

> I struggled to get that adversarial model to begin with. It never felt right. I always felt that I wasn't giving as good service to my clients as I could be giving, but I was forced into it because [that] is what the system required.[52]

Positional bargaining appears to be the inevitable consequence of the structure and beliefs that shape legal negotiations. As a tactic, it is consistent with the belief in legal negotiations as a zero-sum game and uses (particular types of) information as "power over" rather than "power with." Positional bargaining may be conducted as a "soft" tactic or as "hardball," but in either case it can be inefficient, unrealistic, and blind to the clients' underlying goals and needs. In a similar way as the selective, appropriate use of rights-based approaches described in Chapter 3, positional bargaining may be the best and most appropriate choice of strategy in some circumstances and at some (usually later) stages of a negotiation, but it should not be an unconsciously applied default tactic.

There is another problem with the widespread use of positional bargaining in legal negotiations. In another parallel with the default to rights-based approaches, there is a tendency for positional bargaining to become an ideological rather than a strategic commitment. The deficiencies of positional bargaining are further exacerbated when the use of this tactic becomes highly adversarial. Despite the small number of cases that proceed to a full trial, there is a widespread sense that a culture of adversarialism is on the rise. By "adversarialism," I mean the adoption of an aggressively confident, "take-no-prisoners," uncooperative, and secretive attitude toward negotiations with the other side. This goes well beyond the conventional rigidity and somewhat pedantic assertion of positions which are so characteristic of legal negotiations. An adversarial attitude may be played out in formal correspondence, in lengthy and convoluted discovery processes, in the aggressive use of other legal procedures (for example, requiring your opponent to bring a motion to compel disclosure of relevant information), or even in social settings. Adversarialism transforms the characteristic withholding of information frequently seen in positional bargaining into the disclosure of deliberately misleading information. It turns "stick to your position" into "defeat the other side at all costs."

Despite their prevalence in popular culture, extremely adversarial attitudes and behaviours are not generally expected in smaller centres with small bar associations and may be socially discouraged. An adversarial self-image seems more common in larger and more competitive bars and then is often explained as being a response to client expectations:

> Mainly people come to me because I'm known as a son of bitch. I'm not afraid to go to trial. I won't cave in and go and settle. I have clients who know that and don't mind losing. They want to fight, so they expect me to be a son of a bitch.[53]

Legal practice in urban settings is increasingly competitive and has been described as "a nasty business" that is "no longer fun."[54] This competition extends into law school where students vie for the best-paid and highest status jobs. A more competitive environment persuades many lawyers that they need to be mean to survive and meaner still to do well. Andrea Schneider's recreation of Gerald Williams' pioneering research on how lawyers negotiate suggests that both the number and the "nastiness" of "adversarial"[55] lawyers in the sample had increased.[56] She attributes this increase at least in part to the culture of competition in law school and in legal practice. She bluntly describes the reality: "Given the choice between being too soft and too hard, most lawyers would opt for too hard."[57]

An attitude of adversarialism among lawyers may be part of a wider shift in the West toward a disputing and argumentative culture. In her book *The Argument Culture,* linguist Deborah Tannen discusses the pervasiveness throughout our culture – whether in law, sport, media, or business – of language and metaphor that adopt extreme and polarized perspectives and understand issues in terms of the conflict between opposing positions.[58] Tannen is not the only contemporary linguist to draw our attention to the power of metaphors to act on our conceptual frameworks and entrench assumptions about how we understand what we are doing, for example, when we are arguing. George Lakoff and Mark Johnson describe the dominant metaphor for argument in our culture as "war." In other words, "argument is war." This assumption makes our approach to arguing in this way appear "normal" or "ordinary."[59] As Tannen points out, this tendency to understand every issue as a battle between opposing views "limits our imaginations when we consider what we can do about situations we would like to understand or change."[60]

Signs of Change

The structure of legal negotiations, combined with the dominant values of legal practice, result in fairly ritualized and predictable norms of bargaining behaviour between lawyers. The status quo may be comfortable for lawyers, as long as they remain in control of this format, but it is less popular with their clients. The sensitivity of the consuming public (especially institutional and corporate clients) to exponentially rising legal costs has led to demands for less costly and more efficient methods of dispute resolution, demands that policy makers have begun to respond to via procedural reforms. An increasing appetite for early reporting, strategic settlement planning, and early dispute resolution is noted in relationships between commercial lawyers and their institutional clients (for example, financial institutions and insurance companies).[61] Sometimes this shift in expectations is attributed to the increasing influence of in-house counsel who are obliged to account for and justify all litigation expenditure to their managers.[62] Litigators themselves are noticing the change in approach among many of their commercial clients. As one individual expressed, "The old 'just fight-at-all-costs' and don't look at it [the legal bill], don't even think about an approach [opening negotiations], [that attitude] just doesn't seem to exist anymore."[63]

The relationship between the structure of legal bargaining and the norms that sustain it is less the creation of a self-interested profession and more the result of a conflict resolution model in which the slightest possibility of adjudication overshadows every activity and decision. Just how much of the blame for the inefficiencies, expense, and limited creativity of outcomes in legal negotiations can we lay at the feet of the profession itself? Lawyers, of course, often exacerbate and sometimes exploit the worst excesses of the dominant model. They do this through unnecessary and prolonged delay, protracted time and dollars spent on discoveries, failing to read and digest material in a timely manner with a view to settlement,[64] and self-important posturing as an alternative to working at settlement. As well, there are certainly obvious financial advantages to the profession of settling after, rather than before, the most costly steps in litigation (usually discoveries). However, legal negotiations are not inefficient and expensive because lawyers plan them this way. They proceed in this way because there is a functional congruence between the way that legal negotiations are usually structured and the three key beliefs. It is easy, therefore, for lawyers to continue to operate in this way, despite the impoverishment of the process and its outcomes and the many disadvantages of this approach for their clients. The question this raises is whether their clients will continue to accept the deficiencies of this approach. There are some signs that they may not.

The conclusion that the structure of legal negotiations perpetuates systemic problems of inefficiency and lack of creativity is reached by Milton Heumann and Jonathan Hyman in a study of legal negotiations among New Jersey litigators.[65] Heumann and Hyman observe that while positional bargaining is the dominant model of legal negotiations, lawyers state a clear preference for problem-solving approaches that expand the pie and seek out mutual gains. The question then is: Why do lawyers not change their approach? Heumann and Hyman suggest that it is due to a number of factors, principally the "habits" that are formed around negotiation behaviours, such as the focus on entitlement assertions rather than real-life events, and the control exerted by lawyers over their client and the negotiation process. This drives the way in which narratives are developed and presented in negotiation settings. The way in which the researchers observed the telling of "stories" in negotiations and settlement conferences was to facilitate the taking and making of positions and positional arguments rather than problem solving. Finally, they point to the reality that changing the dominant ethos of legal negotiations would take time and effort, whereas resorting to the status quo is much easier. Especially in larger bar associations where lawyers may not encounter their opponent again, there is little incentive to "change the rules" of legal negotiations.[66]

A further disincentive to changing the habits of practice in legal negotiations are attitudes toward principled or problem-solving bargaining. It is widely assumed that when counsel proposes a problem-solving approach (for example the early mutual exchange of information) and/or the use of principled bargaining looking at satisfying interest as well as rights claims, this is because of deficiencies in their case, or, worse still, deficiencies in their backbone as an advocate. The conflation of "good" advocacy with positional bargaining means that adopting a settlement-friendly approach may reduce one's personal reputation as a "good" advocate. Lawyers who propose negotiations with a view to settlement are often perceived as being "weak" or assumed to have a poor legal case. Lawyers who like mediation are described by their peers as being "gun shy."[67] As one lawyer attending mediation training put it, "All the other lawyers I see here are wimps – that's why they're here." Within this framework of values, taking risks (by going to trial) fits best with the populist image of the strongest advocates. The prevalence of the assumption that going to trial is the "way of the warrior," while negotiation or mediation is for the risk-averse, is, however, at odds with what we learn about negotiation from the Prisoner's Dilemma game. The Prisoner's Dilemma game suggests that proposing settlement negotiations – offering to cooperate without any certainty regarding the other side's good faith – is the riskier strategy, and that going to trial – assuming the worst about the other side yet not rejecting serious efforts to negotiate – is in fact the safer, more conventional option.

The advent of mandatory mediation has enabled some lawyers to overcome this bias against negotiation as a sign of weakness. For example, one lawyer explains:

> I think what mediation has done is made it easier to try and negotiate a settlement or discuss settlement without doing so from a point of view or giving the perception that you're doing so because you're worried about your case, or it comes from a point of weakness because you can just say everybody does it, so you want to do it.[68]

However, for many lawyers, stepping up the timing of negotiation and adopting strategies (like the exchange of information) to facilitate settlement remain both counter-intuitive to their mindset and habits of practice, and are regarded as "soft":

> I think that listening to the more senior people the whole concept of litigation is the more comfortable forum. They're used to fighting and taking things to trial and often mediation seems like a soft lovey, dovey approach to the world that they are not accustomed to.[69]

Despite these disincentives, some lawyers are questioning the prevailing model of legal negotiations and are beginning to develop alternative ways of approaching settlement negotiations. Len Riskin writes about the importance of escaping the constraints of the lawyer's "philosophical map" in order to move toward non-judgmental perspectives that enable real insight into people and situations.[70] There are examples of emerging practitioner organizations that aim to develop an entirely new philosophy toward the practice of law, emphasizing therapeutic interventions and healing as an alternative to fighting litigation "battles."[71] Others have developed specific strategies for reinventing the ritual of legal negotiations, with the goal of including clients, creating space for creative solutions to emerge, and reducing hostility and negativity. Strategies include the development of a general firm-wide reputation for settlement expertise (for example, the establishment of an alternative dispute resolution department within a firm) or membership in a formal group seeking to promote a more collaborative approach to negotiations (such as those corporations that have

signed on to the CPR Pledge).[72] Another strategy is to separate the litigation and the negotiation function by formally designating certain lawyers
as specialist "settlement counsel." Working alongside litigation counsel on
the same file, settlement counsel can offer clients special expertise in the
negotiation of early settlements and can conduct negotiations, represent
clients at mediation, and generally offer assistance in relation to the development of consensual solutions at an early stage in the litigation.[73] If their
best efforts fail, their place is taken by "litigation counsel" who would
proceed to trial.[74]

Despite scholarly interest[75] and experimentation within larger law firms
with the creation of alternative dispute resolution departments composed
of specialist settlement counsel, the culture of adversarial litigation has
remained remarkably impervious to change. Even within law firms with
alternative dispute resolution departments and a stated commitment to
embracing settlement processes, the development of specialist settlement
expertise has been largely limited to the work of one or two individuals
rather than affecting the broader culture of the firm.[76] Settlement counsel are usually only retained on very large files when it is possible to fund
both settlement and litigation counsel. This reality limits the range of
cases in which specialist settlement counsel is available. Paradoxically, separating the settlement and litigation functions may, to a degree, reduce
the pressure to settle since a litigation strategy is being developed in parallel with settlement efforts.

One approach to changing the culture of legal negotiations is to ask lawyers
to make an advance commitment to the principles of co-operative bargaining. Instead of having to guess at and assume the worst about one's
opponent's negotiation style, there is a shared commitment to the disclosure of information, a respectful and timely response to communications, and an effort to build rapport and trust. This approach reduces
the unknowns of the Prisoner's Dilemma game and allows lawyers to negotiate on the basis of shared understandings about process. It institu-
tionalizes the assumption of beginning co-operatively, which Axelrod
proposes,[77] and changing this approach only if there is bad faith. The
growth of co-operative lawyering groups promotes this approach, which
conceives of co-operative tactics in negotiation as an overall mindset and
a professional commitment rather than something that requires formalizing in a contract.[78]

Others argue that in order to change the norms of bargaining, it is necessary to go further in altering the fundamental structure of legal negotiations. For this reason, the collaborative lawyering movement has focused
its attention on removing the spectre of litigation – and the zero-sum set-
up – from bargaining. In a collaborative law case, the responsibility of
counsel to facilitate settlement is directly traded for the traditional core

responsibility to win in litigation, a trade that is undertaken by all lawyers participating on a single file. The basis of the retainer agreement in a collaborative law file is a contractual commitment between lawyer and client *not* to resort to litigation to resolve the client's problem. The legal services provided by counsel are limited to advice and representation regarding the non-litigious resolution of the conflict, and the focus is on developing a negotiated, consensual outcome. There is no parallel litigation strategy. If the client does decide that legal action is ultimately necessary in order to resolve the dispute, the retainer stipulates that the collaborative lawyer (along with any other collaborative professionals, such as divorce coaches or financial planners) must withdraw and receive no further remuneration for work on the case.[79] This device is described as the "disqualification clause/agreement."

Rather than develop a settlement strategy once litigation has commenced, collaborative lawyering proposes that the lawyer-client relationship be confined to circumstances prior to the commencement of a legal suit. Without the possibility of litigation in the background, lawyers will take different steps and adopt different strategies in negotiation. For example, in anticipating negotiation, counsel will not need to be "papering" the file as they would approaching litigation. The argument is that once a legal action has been commenced, the temptation to use a legal discourse and paradigm for analyzing and resolving disputes is irresistible – first with threats and then with action.[80] Instead, the objectives of collaborative lawyering are to change the context for negotiation itself and to provide a strong incentive for early, collaborative, negotiated settlement without resorting to litigation.[81] One of the earliest proponents of collaborative retainer agreements (often described as a "participation agreement" because of the emphasis placed on client participation) argues that it changes the context for negotiations by enabling "a way to approach a person with whom one has a perceived conflict with a request for an honest and detailed examination of the problem in a way that also offer[s] an absolute and irrevocable commitment to do so in a non-adversarial manner."[82]

The participation agreement further stipulates that all relevant information must be disclosed voluntarily and that, when a client resists disclosing information, the other side should know that the lawyer may withdraw from the case. By their own account, it is rare for collaborative lawyers to experience situations in which either their client will not disclose relevant information or they suspect the other side of not meeting their obligations.[83] If this perception is accurate, the exchange of information facilitates both substantive discussions and the development of some trust in the negotiation process.

Some lawyers, including but not limited to the co-operative lawyering groups, see the approach of the collaborative lawyers as overly formalistic and process-oriented. The disqualification agreement, they argue, is unnecessarily constraining where the client and the lawyer can simply agree to use a co-operative approach.[84] This claim has not yet been tested by research comparing the two models. An examination of the collaborative lawyering process provides some evidence to support collaborative lawyers' claim that the use of a formal collaborative retainer agreement including a disqualification clause reduces posturing and gamesmanship of traditional lawyer-to-lawyer negotiation, including highly inflated and low-ball opening proposals. Whereas most lawyer-to-lawyer negotiations begin with a ritual of unrealistic opening offers, the first one to three meetings among lawyers (and other participating professionals) and clients are generally spent reviewing the commitments of the participation agreement, followed by a process of information gathering. Usually no proposals are tabled until these stages are completed, often to the frustration of the clients. After these initial meetings, there is a much clearer sense of what each party wants and expects than when opening shots are fired. There is also an awareness among collaborative lawyers that they are responsible for modelling co-operative behaviour to their clients. Unlike conventional lawyer-to-lawyer negotiation, clients are observing counsel's negotiating behaviour first hand and minute to minute in a four-way conference.

Despite the quasi-religious and ideological language used by some collaborative law proponents, a significant part of the intellectual and moral weight behind the commitment to co-operative bargaining is practical. As one lawyer explains:

> The reason why we don't do positional bargaining is it doesn't work, not that it's morally reprehensible but that it doesn't work in a consensual process.[85]

Given the training and past experiences of lawyers within the dominant norms of legal practice and legal negotiations, it seems unlikely that either collaborative or co-operative law processes will eliminate positional bargaining or posturing. One collaborative lawyer acknowledges:

> Sometimes we catch ourselves. It's hard not to [engage in positional bargaining] because we have done it for a long time. We are used to it. That's what we learned at law school from day one. It's really hard work.[86]

Changing the norms of legal negotiations requires not only challenging the way things are "usually" done – the mindset of zero-sum negotiations and the habits of positional bargaining – but also developing a community that can support and nurture a different type of bargaining culture.

In both collaborative and co-operative lawyering groups, the commitment to co-operative negotiation is strengthened by the "club" culture of the groups or networks and a sense of shared values. The collaborative group, for example, becomes a critical "community of practice" for individual collaborative lawyers, which is highly influential in shaping and maintaining informal practice norms and behaviours.[87] Belonging to a collaborative community of practice seems to demand that the collaborative lawyer place this allegiance first among competing demands and norms of other communities of practice. Furthermore, a collaborative lawyer who is deemed to have taken an unnecessarily adversarial approach to negotiations will be monitored by his or her collaborative law community. This monitoring may take place informally – for example, "the lawyers watch one another and we will catch ourselves doing it [positional bargaining]"[88] – or it may gradually take on a more formal, regulatory character.[89]

A supportive culture has also developed in centres where the bar and the bench have embraced mandatory civil mediation. Reputation in negotiation is an extremely important resource given the degree of strategic uncertainty and lack of information that accompanies classic legal negotiations. This reputation includes not only behaviour during the actual negotiations but also related qualities and abilities, including honesty, competence, ability to manage one's own client and reach a firm decision, and follow-through in drafting a memorandum of agreement and meeting subsequent obligations. Expectations of the behaviour of the other side, along a continuum from highly adversarial to highly co-operative, are critical to the dynamics and, hence, the outcome of negotiations.[90] A personal reputation for collaboration becomes a valuable resource when a critical mass within the community has embraced mediation and settlement processes as mainstream and reflective of "good' lawyering. One would expect that once the skills associated with effective settlement advocacy have become recognized as a commodity that carries positive consequences – for reputation and for earnings – the profession will buy into what they regard as a significant means of ensuring their continued professional status.[91]

Presently limited almost entirely to the family law field, the collaborative lawyering model – and to a lesser degree, the growth of alternative co-operative lawyering groups – raises many important questions that go to the heart of the debate over the role of lawyers in dispute settlement processes and, in particular, in negotiation within an adjudicative paradigm.[92] Along with efforts to introduce early mediation, co-operative protocols, and settlement-only counsel, the development of collaborative lawyering represents a major effort to change the dominant structural model of legal negotiations and the norms that flow from these.

Changing the Culture of Legal Negotiations: Revisiting the Three Key Beliefs

Changing the culture of legal negotiations, by questioning its assumptions and developing alternative behaviours and practices, presents the same difficulties as changing any other aspect of legal practice based on the key beliefs described in Chapter 3. The way in which they conduct legal negotiations represents a way for lawyers to demonstrate to their colleagues that they understand and accept "the way things are done." There are many disincentives to challenging "the way things are done," particularly for those new to the profession. Becoming part of a profession brings with it implicit obligations to maintain the central claims of that vocation to professionalism and expertise. For lawyers, this means a commitment to defining disputes through the lenses of "rights," believing in the "justice" of legal process and taking ownership of clients' conflicts. Challenging these values may be seen as disloyal to the profession – a betrayal of the claims that sustain the self-image as well as the economics of legal practice. In reality, of course, there are many ways to practise law and provide legal services and many individuated approaches and commitments. Nonetheless, every member of a bar association is aware of the pressures to conform at least in part to the dominant norms that the profession has established for clients and for collegial relationships. Noisy and public departures from these norms usually attract disapproval and even censoring from other parts of the profession.

While it is difficult to challenge core practice beliefs and values in the short term, one strategy adopted by public policy-makers, and now by some practitioner groups such as the collaborative lawyers, is to change the structures, or the procedures, of legal disputing. As people become more familiar and comfortable with new structures and procedures, normative change will follow. While changing the process does not in itself change attitudes, there may be a longer-term relationship between process and attitude change.[93] Although mandatory mediation may secure lawyers' obedient conduct without necessarily changing their minds and hearts, the changed conduct may, with further practice and exposure, affect a lawyer's normative values and attitudes toward mediation.[94] The use of the disqualification clause in collaborative practice may appear to some as an overzealous imposition of a collaborative commitment, but it also normalizes and supports behaviours that historically have not been habitual in legal negotiations. Social psychologists have long posited a dynamic relationship between changing behaviours and changing attitudes. This approach assumes a relationship between changing behaviours and changing attitudes. For example, if management and labour representatives agree to a set process for consultation and issue raising and carry it out consistently, communication will likely increase and improve over time. In the family context, if co-parents agree not to speak poorly of one another in front of the children and if each keeps their word, doing anything other than this may in time begin to appear inappropriate. Thus, engaging in a particular, well-defined mode of behaviour can normalize this mode and enable those affected to experience a different and hopefully constructive alternative to the old behaviours.[95]

Changing the culture of legal negotiations means putting in place coherent and thoughtful alternatives to conventional practices. These alternatives must have a conceptual and practical structure that is as complex and rigorous as the prevailing values and norms. It is critical that alternative strategies do not reject the expertise that lawyers have developed over generations in negotiating their clients' conflicts but, rather, build on existing skills, knowledge, and attitudes. Lawyers spend a lot of time negotiating and whatever the deficiencies of the structure and norms of "litigotiation," they have much practice wisdom. As well, their legal knowledge is vital in providing an assessment of the "shadow of the law," which is sometimes a decisive influence on the outcome of bargaining. However, as the discussion above makes clear, the development of alternative strategies for legal negotiations must revisit the three key beliefs and the resulting norms of behaviour if legal negotiations are to move to a higher level of sophistication and provide clients with the creative, practical, and fair outcomes they want.

A first step is questioning the assumption that all conflicts necessarily implicate rights. Many do, and it is a critical underpinning of the principles of social democracy and respect for equality to deal with these within an adjudicative framework. Saying that not all conflicts implicate rights does not mean that none do. Interests-based bargaining and negotiation over rights entitlements can and must coexist. Adopting an interests-based approach to finding a feasible long-term solution does not exclude bargaining for a clear rights-based threshold (for example, payments in line with or above child support guidelines or structured settlement payments for breach of contract). The key to effective lawyering lies in discriminating between different types of conflicts and what are the appropriate means of addressing and resolving them in ways that meet both the needs of the disputants and society's interest in fairness.

Lawyers should be able to apply their professional judgment to this question rather than adopting without question the nomenclature of every client who describes their conflict as "a matter of principle." The claim of "principle" is attached to many disputes that, in their origins at least, appear to be wholly or primarily attached to the sharing of resources, including property, business interests, or time with children, and implicate power, status, material wealth, reputation, and other desired social symbols. While a principled argument can be, and usually is, constructed for each side's "moral" position, this analysis may miss both the core of what the conflict is and the potential solutions or accommodations. Even when the conflict is over a moral difference – for example, the custody of children or decisions over their schooling – determining who is "right" via the application of legal principle may not address the core needs of the parties. An exclusive or overwhelming focus on a rights-based model is an inadequate, inappropriate, and simply impracticable means of resolving every type of dispute. The further implication of this argument is that if lawyers were to limit their caseload to only those cases requiring an exclusively rights-based approach, their practice would shrink dramatically. It is time for lawyers to learn how to handle other types of conflict resolution.

Few cases merit the singular application of either interests-based bargaining or negotiation over rights entitlements. Lawyers need to utilize both approaches to negotiation – in many different forms – in as many cases as possible. Effective bargaining on behalf of the client requires the identification of those issues that require a rights-based benchmark to ensure that power does not violate rights or overwhelm interests; what elements of a deal require distributive (dividing up the pie) bargaining; what extra value can be created for both sides; and what aspects of a conflict can be resolved using principles developed and embraced by the parties themselves.[96]

Second, in the context of negotiation, lawyers' belief in justice as process may be more concerned with justifying professional legal services than understanding and meeting client needs. Lawyers are right to discourage their clients from assuming that they have a lock on judge-dispensed "justice," but their habits of discouraging an early exchange of information – even innocuous information about motivations and priorities – delaying serious negotiations until after discoveries, and behaving as if the final outcome will be adjudicated even when it almost certainly will not, cannot feel satisfactory for many clients, especially when instead of directly participating in these decisions themselves, clients are presented with these strategies as "the way we do legal negotiations." Procedural justice research suggests not only that participation in decision making over negotiation strategies is important, but also that there are important values surrounding the way in which the negotiation process unfolds – did the other side listen and take their concerns seriously? Were they civil and polite? Did they acknowledge some fault or ambiguity? – which have an eventual bearing on a sense of "justice" having been done.

The bottom line for many clients is a practical solution rather than an elusive and abstract sense of "justice." In these cases, it may be important for the clients themselves to create their own sense of "justice," which enables them to live with the outcomes they choose, both practically and emotionally. They may need to participate in shaping different processes that give them a voice and the chance to be listened to and taken seriously. These same clients may also be unprepared or unwilling to hand over control and ownership of their dispute to their lawyer, as the third key belief expects. They may want a discussion over how and when negotiations are opened that does not assume the given structure of legal bargaining.

As well as refining and modifying the key beliefs, changing the· professional identity of the legal profession also requires the thoughtful and skillful development of new behaviours and practices that reflect and enable new norms. In legal negotiations, this means creating a model for strong co-operative bargaining and conventions on disclosure and information exchange. It also may mean the creation of many different modes and structures of negotiation practice that relate to, for example, the timing of negotiations, conventions on disclosure, and the roles played by the various actors (lawyers and clients). The new lawyer needs a new road map for making practice choices for negotiation. She may not have taken any courses on negotiation at law school and, in practice, has been confronted with an entrenched model that seems unassailable.

Adjusting the values and norms of legal negotiations to acknowledge· the altered conditions of legal practice and client service is not the only challenge facing the new lawyer. She must re-examine myriad other practice tasks and professional responsibilities in light of an emerging professional identity that once again associates lawyers with conflict resolution in the public consciousness. The new lawyer needs help in developing a model of advocacy that can meet her clients' goals for effective conflict resolution rather than for absolute "victory." Her relationship with her client will be profoundly altered by a reconfiguration of roles and expertise such that each contributes expertise and each takes responsibility for planning, negotiation, and decision making. Her legal knowledge and expertise is no less significant in this model, but the way that law is applied to conflict resolution will be different. Finally, a new road map for values and norms sets up a new set of questions for ethical professional conduct, challenging the stability of conventional lawyer-client expectations and introducing new dilemmas in identifying appropriate professional conduct. The remainder of this book will examine each of these challenges in turn and will propose a model for the new lawyer to adopt, adapt, and apply in developing a conflict resolution approach to legal practice.

5
The New Advocacy

Advocacy is at the heart of how lawyers understand their role and of what is different for the new lawyer. In its broadest sense, advocacy suggests dedication to clients' goals and ends and strength in both expert knowledge and moral commitment to the clients' cause. These ideals are essential to any notion of advocacy and are important to the new lawyer too. However, the style of advocacy that we associate with lawyers in the twenty-first century is more needlessly adversarial and somehow less noble and dignified than this ideal. It even sometimes veers into a wild caricature in which the lawyer is prepared to behave in uncivil, immoral, even barely legal ways in order to achieve client goals, however questionable these goals might be. In these instances the core principle of dedication and strength morphs into blinkered single-mindedness and sometimes aggressive defensiveness.

In this chapter, I shall argue that the central role of an advocate in a system of conflict resolution is to assist the client in continuously reassessing what he needs and wants in light of what is possible and what the costs may be, and then to advance that goal. This role includes regularly assessing the potential for resolution, which means that the advocate must draw on the qualities of the effective negotiator, including listening to what the client really wants and prizes and what he is prepared to give up in order to achieve resolution, being firm about bottom lines, and being creative about negotiable issues. It does not mean giving up or throwing away the traditions of dedication and strength in advocacy. It means retooling these principles for a different type of engagement with the problem and the possible solutions.

In a pluralist social and legal culture, the role of an adversarial advocate is extremely limited. However single-minded and aggressive, the advocate cannot guarantee his client any particular outcome and may end up getting his client less rather than more – for example, permanently ending a relationship or running up costs that cancel out or seriously offset the monetary gains. Despite this risk, which is not always well understood by clients, many people continue to want and need a strong advocate. What is it they need an advocate for? They want someone to help them find and articulate their voice, to validate their concerns, and to protect them and their interests, perhaps because they are fearful and/or vulnerable. A good advocate has a number of choices for how to meet these fundamental needs in ways that are different from and ultimately more effective than adversarial bargaining.

It seems important to reclaim and redefine what we mean by "advocacy" in conflict resolution. Advocacy is considered by some to be a dirty word in conflict resolution as it seems that we have largely surrendered our populist cultural sense of "advocacy" to an adversarial frame. We associate it with noisy argumentation and table banging. We are also unused to making alternative associations with the concept of "advocacy," for example, that it is possible to be philosophically committed to the service of a single client – "on their side" or "in their team" – and also committed to promoting peace and resolution in a way that meets their interests. Instead, we often assume that "standing up for your client" is incompatible with and disables us from acting as promoters of peace and consensus builders. There are many examples of the power of this assumption in the field of social justice, where activist advocacy is often framed as being at odds with efforts to promote peace. We seem stuck with the idea that only neutrals can be "real" conflict resolvers.[1]

In fact, if we go back several decades we discover that this assumption of polarization between conflict resolution and advocacy has not always existed. The earliest community-based conflict resolution initiatives – in areas such as policing, racial conflict, and public policy – were seen as forms of social activism that involved promoting awareness and progress on important issues, while, at the same time, modelling non-violent resistance.[2] Traditional notions of lawyer advocacy among small-town general practitioners have not assumed, and, perhaps, still do not assume, that having a single client's interests at heart – transparently, *not* being neutral – precluded lawyers from the promotion of peace and understanding.[3] Nonetheless, the last thirty years have seen mainstream professional values and norms, driven by large firms in city settings, evolve to reflect a more "zealous" version of advocacy, which in some cases is plainly adversarial. This conception of advocacy sets the promotion of peaceful resolution at odds with many widely expected behaviours and attitudes.[4]

"Zealous Advocacy"

The description of the lawyer's duty to the client as one of "zealous advocacy" has been the subject of intense debate ever since its original articulation in the American Bar Association's *Model Rules of Professional Conduct.*[5] The most traditional, literal formulation of zealous advocacy has come to mean doing anything and everything that is lawful in order to advance the clients' interests. Described by William Simon as the "dominant view," this understanding of advocacy assumes that "the only ethical duty distinctive to the lawyer's role is loyalty to the client."[6] The interests of the other side, third parties, or public interests are extraneous to this loyalty, and the client's position must be asserted unambiguously.[7] In fact, any sense of these outside interests may distract or undermine the lawyer's focus. This perspective on advocacy also implies that the time for talking is past. There is no suggestion in this model that the lawyer-advocate should be scrutinizing, questioning, or reassessing the client's goals or positions but, rather, focused on acting as her instrument in furthering these (legal) goals. Legal negotiations again provide a useful illustration. Zealous advocacy in this context means, at best, positional bargaining that repeats rather than discusses the clients' "entitlement" and, at worst, the types of adversarial tactics and techniques described in the last chapter.

In practice, few lawyers understand their advocacy responsibilities as narrowly or as unambiguously as Simon's dominant view posits. Grounded advocacy must also comprehend information gathering, appraisal and evaluation, and advice giving. Most lawyers would regard counselling and weighing options as being an important part of their role rather than simply as the blind adoption and pursuit of client goals. Zealous advocacy understood in this practical framework means commitment to the clients' legal goals but includes other responsibilities for counselling and realistic appraisal of all options.

Nonetheless, the appealing clarity and apparent simplicity of the "dominant view" continues to be enormously influential, especially for law students and new entrants to the profession. A literal, uncontextualized version of zealous advocacy may seem divorced from the reality of most legal practice, but its clarity and simplicity are attractive. It includes the assumption among some lawyers and educators that zealous advocacy is a synonym for the whole of lawyering, minimizing the constant need for dialogue with the client, reappraisal, and adjustment. Zealous advocacy has historically assumed that the sole focus of advocacy is the pursuit of rights and it generally does not contemplate other types of goals or strategies. The zealous advocacy model allows for apparently uncontested control over strategy and decision making by counsel, who alone are regarded as having the necessary (legal) expertise to succeed in this system. The model is sustained by the continued commitment of legal education to a model of lawyer dominance through substantive expertise. The zealous advocacy model is plainly compatible with the three key beliefs. In the last chapter, a drift toward adversarialism in legal negotiations was explained by its highly functional role in an adjudicative model of dispute resolution. The zealous advocacy model is closely associated with a win/lose outcome in conflict.

Another aspect of the appeal of the zealous advocacy concept is the idea of aggressive strength and the power that the literal model has come to exemplify. Students entering law school are commonly fixated on the idea of acting in this way on behalf of a deserving client, perhaps a vulnerable party facing a wealthy corporation or state authority.[8] They are highly susceptible to the position taking of competitive mooting as they focus, often intensely, on this rite-of-passage experience. The acceptance and adoption of some adversarial behaviours is also a part of the socialization of young lawyers in larger firms that operate within a highly competitive culture. In these environments, the demonstration of commitment and dedication is associated with behaviours such as advancing positional arguments, disinterest in the issues raised by the other side, minimal communication, and the withholding or obstruction of any information that may be useful to the other side. Under such conditions, and without clear guidance on the limits of zealotry or alternative conceptions of advocacy, zealous advocacy can easily morph into adversarial advocacy.

The adversarial delivery of zealous advocacy is also prominent in media portrayals of lawyers. Whether presented as being selfish or selfless, lawyers are almost always portrayed as aggressively adversarial, at least in interactions with peers and sometimes also with judges and clients. In these narratives there is often a focus on interactions with other lawyers and justice officials in which the lawyer acts in a very self-confident, adversarial, and even macho fashion, and there is relatively less attention paid to interaction with clients illustrating advice giving or counselling or evaluation of options. This showcases zealous advocacy in dealings with the other side, and minimizes the time counsel will spend in a consultative role with his client where he is also acting as an advocate, but perhaps in a less exciting and aggressive manner.

Some consumers of legal services consider that a significant part of what they are paying for is the confident assertiveness of an adversarial advocate who will "stand up to" the other side. This expectation may be transferred to their lawyers, who believe that for their client to see them as a zealous advocate they should behave in an adversarial manner. It is often associated with machismo attitudes about engagement in conflict. For example:

> In the construction industry you have to be known to be tough ... All of the most successful construction firms have good lawyers who fight, and you know if you're going to fool around with these boys, you're going to have to fight.[9]

This expectation continues in relationships with other lawyers, perhaps especially in urban centres where there is greater competition for clients, and between lawyers of different levels of experience (for example, a new associate dealing with a senior lawyer in another firm). Gaining credibility with another lawyer is associated with adopting the norms of that legal community, which, in some instances, means adversarial advocacy.[10] One lawyer previously quoted in Chapter 1 described how this attitude seeps into any and all communications with other lawyers:

> I mean we're trained as pit bulls, I'm not kidding you, I mean we're trained pit bulls and pit bulls just don't naturally sit down and have a chat with a fellow pit bull, the instinct is to fight and you just get it from the first phone call. I'm bigger and tougher and strong and better than you are.[11]

In this model of advocacy, the end goal – achieving the clients' legal goals – is disassociated from "justice." Hardly surprising, then, that when asked about their conceptions of justice in civil litigation, commercial litigators are consistently dismissive. For example, one lawyer states:

> Justice is too deep for me. I'd be wrong working as if I knew what justice was. Justice for me is what makes people happy ... I get into some obscure area of ... law ... and, believe me, justice plays a little role and the client just wants to know, will I win or will I lose? And I say you will win and the other lawyer says [to their own client] you will win.[12]

Where zealous advocacy focuses only on the achievement of expressed client goals, absent any other consideration either toward the client or the broader collective good, it seems able to justify almost any behaviour as a means to this end. Many types of otherwise intolerable and unreasonable behaviour appear rational and morally justified. Whereas popular culture often depicts this behaviour as the result of the lawyer's search for "truth," the closer reality is that it is usually associated with the blind pursuit of client goals. What lawyers describe suggests that "truth," and its sister value "justice," are far less important as motivations for zealous advocacy than total commitment to furthering client interests. As David Luban points out, a professional obligation to present facts selectively in accordance with advancing a client's position is unlikely to be an effective means of uncovering "truth."[13] Instead, the emphasis is on "winning advocacy" that achieves victory by position taking, supplemented, if necessary, by intimidation and bluffing, rather than by "winning outcomes," which are enabled by skillful negotiation, creative problem solving, and the development of fair and reasonable solutions.

A Historical Perspective

How did the legal profession come to embrace a notion of advocacy that sees justice as being so marginal and adversarial tactics in pursuit of client goals as being so normative? The social history of the lawyering profession offers some insights into the evolution of zealous advocacy. Although extreme adversarialism among some lawyers may be a fairly recent phenomenon, some of the clues to its genesis lie in the historical development of law as a profession. The hallowed expert status of the lawyer is derived from eighteenth-century notions of "professionalism," which regarded law as a "gentlemanly" profession and a vocation or higher calling. The apparent selflessness with which the lawyer devotes himself to the client's cause is what legitimizes his unquestioned authority and expertise and sets him apart from others who sell services with a lower social cachet. The lawyer's own gain or advantage must be secondary to furthering the clients' goals. In the words of Lord Brougham:

> An advocate, in the discharge of his duty, knows but one person in all the world, and that person is his client. To save that client by all means and expedients, and at all hazards and costs to other persons, *and amongst them to himself,* is his first and only duty.[14]

The tacit exchange between lawyer and client is that this single-minded devotion to the service of the clients' interests is rewarded by unquestioned social status and professional autonomy. In this exchange, the lawyer acts as his clients' honorable alter ego, reframing the facts of the conflict as suits the legal arguments, and presupposing his or her imputed goals (which, in a legal equation, are always monetarized). Apparent liberties with the construction (or reconstruction) of the client's conflict, and assumptions about his needs and motivations, are justified by the superior technical knowledge of the lawyer working in a dispute resolution system in which the ability to anticipate legal outcomes is the currency of expertise. Along with the other major professions, law has come to increasingly promote a culture of competence centred on technical rationality, in which specialist knowledge – the ability to predict legal outcomes – is prized above all other skills and aptitudes.[15] In another element of the bargain, the lawyer will be unemotional and objective in reaching decisions about appropriate actions, and, in exchange, the client will grant him complete or relative autonomy in the management of his case.

It is important to recognize that this exchange transaction was formulated at a time when lawyers were foreclosed, at least in principle, from a profit motive.[16] Eighteenth-century legal practice was socially constructed as a "gentleman's calling," and, as such, personal gain was seen as being antithetical to a principle of selfless professionalism. The clients of English barristers were expected to offer "honoraria" in "gratitude" rather than being formally charged fees.[17] Of course, there were some fairly clear social expectations, and a failure to remunerate would rarely be tolerated. Yet the principle was that lawyers served only at their clients' pleasure and should be rewarded in a way that reflected their success in achieving their clients' goals.

No one would expect today that lawyers should be motivated entirely by considerations of "service" in the absence of remuneration, and their eighteenth-century colleagues were likely not so disinterested in personal gain either. The notion of being paid only if you were successful in achieving the clients' goals is reminiscent of today's contingency fee arrangements. However, the business conditions of legal practice have changed fundamentally since client service principles of following the clients' instructions and achieving his goals were first developed for the exchange transaction between lawyer and client.

Yet despite the changed environment, these client service principles, which translate into various different versions of zealous advocacy, ranging from moderate to adversarial, remain largely unmodified. And zealous advocacy takes on a very different character when a profit motive is introduced. The populist conception is now more "hired gun" than alter ego. In the reformulated (monetarized) bargain of twentieth- and twenty-first-century lawyering, the lawyer will "prove" his value to the client by (more or less) aggressively asserting his chosen legal strategy right up to the boundaries of the law, complete, in some cases, with dirty tricks and adversarial behaviours. Far from using dispassionate objectivity, the lawyer may on occasion make an investment in winning the conflict that is as great as or greater than that of their clients.

The old-fashioned virtues of client loyalty and commitment take on a new face in this economic environment. They have survived so well because they fit well with the win/lose, either for us/or against us, morally righteous ideology of the adjudicative system. Adversarial notions of zealous advocacy offer a highly efficient strategy for lawyers working in a fee-for-service capacity within the modern-day legal system. The dominant view simplifies the lawyer's role by setting clear role expectations. It carries a clear social status. To be a good lawyer one needs to be confident, assertive, and unafraid to take advantage of the other side. One must act as if every case is to be tried by a judge, and remain defiant about settlement until the last possible moment. In the meantime, all hours spent gathering more information toward the file are billable. If lawyers are to advance their clients' interests within this model, they are expected to play this game to some degree and to use it to justify whatever unreasonable behaviours and incivilities may result.

In the eighteenth century the notion of the lawyer as the (in theory) unpaid servant of the client proposed an honorable rationale for zealous advocacy motivated by a desire to achieve justice for the client. The contemporary culture of economic competition and individual wealth maximization inevitably changes the nature of the lawyer-client transaction. The manifestations of zealotry are now less about a commitment to justice and more a marker of economic success. Attracting and retaining clients is now critical to a lawyer's personal advancement and economic well-being. In the cut-and-thrust nature of urban practice, it is, as Andrea Schneider reminds us, easier to err on the side of being too hard – aggressive, competitive, and overzealous – than too soft, and the culture of big firm practice expects this sort of behaviour.[18] As a result, contemporary zealous advocacy is often more adversarial and less interested in "justice" than earlier models – perhaps even more than the original drafters of the *Model Rules of Professional Conduct* intended or anticipated.

Tensions within Zealous Advocacy

Despite its functional efficiency and apparent clarity in delineating a narrow role for counsel, the traditional zealous advocacy model is associated with a number of tensions and strains. It has already been pointed out that for many small-town lawyers a literal version of zealous advocacy has always been an inadequate description of the complexity of their role as advisor, counsellor, reality-tester, and so on, especially with clients with whom they have lifelong relationships. Today growing numbers of lawyers in all practice settings are finding that traditional strategies of pressure and intimidation associated with zealous advocacy are less useful in trying to settle lawsuits than in trying to win them. As the collaborative lawyer quoted in Chapter 4 pointed out, positional bargaining simply does not work when you are trying to persuade the other side to settle with you. Similarly, aggressive argumentation, withholding information, and an unwillingness to acknowledge any weaknesses in the clients' cases are seldom effective strategies to achieving a good deal in either negotiation or mediation. This lawyer tellingly talks about the difference in the way that an advocate approaches "the other side" in mediation compared with trial advocacy:

> You don't worry about the other side as much at a trial because *they're the other side*. When you're working towards a consensus – then it matters.[19]

The move toward the increasing use of settlement processes, many of them mandatory, means that lawyers are being asked to plan and act in ways that are at odds with their formal training. As one explains:

First and foremost our training is in rights-based advocacy, that's first and
foremost and that creates the tension because you're saying settlement,
they say why? You sort of feel like why do I have the right training, maybe
... I should just have the training in problem solving. We do have that
training and it's there and you still have to use it and so the compromise
is always cut against your training to a certain extent.[20]

As more and more work is done in settlement meetings, lawyers are finding that some of the "habits" of positionality assumed by zealous advocacy impede problem solving, and that they need to find a new approach.
As this lawyer describes it:

Less and less do I find that I have to take positions that are very black and
white and simply advocate that position and put blinders on and go straight
ahead and say there's an offer, take it or leave it – and maybe that's partly
caused by repetitively being put in a room with a bunch of people and a
mediator and sitting down to try and work out solutions to the problems.[21]

The impact of court-mandated settlement regimes is just one of the signs
of strain on the traditional zealous advocacy model. Another tension
comes from the new economic climate of legal practice and changes in
expectations of the lawyer-client relationship. Part of the original exchange
transaction between lawyer and client was that in return for his commitment to the clients' service, the lawyer was afforded significant professional autonomy to use his judgment in the clients' best interests
– judgment that is based substantially on his knowledge and appraisal of
the relevant law. Zealous advocacy – for example, how he communicated
and dealt with the other side – was his chosen expression of this judgment,
and it was rarely challenged or questioned by the client. In some lawyer-
client relationships, this exchange is still an important though unarticulated
part of the bargain. Yet in other contemporary lawyer-client relationships,
especially those with corporate and institutional clients, the reality of the
lawyer's autonomous judgment is undermined by the business model of
legal practice. The business of one large client may be fundamental to the
economic viability of a practice. In this case, the notion that the lawyer
should use her independent judgment in pursuing the clients' goals by
the best possible means is severely limited by an obligation to a primary
client whose business is critical. As they charted the changes in firm size
and structure that characterized the 1970s and 1980s, John Heinz and
Edward Laumann noted that the prized notion of autonomy was probably far less eroded for personal services lawyers with a large and changing client base than for corporate-commercial lawyers working with large

institutional clients.[22] Similarly, Robert Nelson's research suggests that associates in larger firms perceive very little autonomy.[23]

In practice, the assumption of autonomy and the central importance of technical legal expertise – the give and take of the exchange transaction between lawyer and client – fits uneasily with a blanket commitment to furthering client wishes. What if the instructions the client gives are simply not in his or her best interests? Should the lawyer assume that he knows best and persuade his client of this? How far should counsel press the client to hold out for a better deal when the client is ready to settle? There is a risk of paternalism, such that counsel assumes she "knows best" within the narrow scope of the particular expertise that she offers. Conversely, there is a risk the client will be so influenced by the lawyer's opinion that they cannot make a personal decision.[24] Many lawyers find the balance between client decision making and lawyer expertise a difficult one to strike, especially within the context of a primarily adversarial system that assumes fighting is "more" and settling is "less." It is difficult for lawyers to know how to manage a conflict between their rights-based advice and a client's desire for resolution based on other factors. Lawyers are not trained to recognize these tensions – other than intuitively – much less to balance them. The seductive simplicity of the zealous advocacy model provides them with little guidance on how to conduct these negotiations with their own client. How does counsel discuss this issue with his client and how does he give appropriate advice? Resolving tension between what the lawyer is trained to do and what the client wants to do is uncharted territory that most lawyers can only respond to instinctively. For example, as one lawyer explains:

> I've (sometimes) found it harder to take off the advocate hat and see clients coming in prepared to settle. I can think of one mediation with a number of different parties where once again, we were acting for a bank as a plaintiff in this case, and the bank's claim was $4,000,000. There were a number of parties including two insurers on the other side and the merits of the case I thought justified a pretty high settlement ... In this case a new account manager comes in and was about to retire and wanted to get a win on his docket before he retired. He just ended up settling for 20 or 30 cents on the dollar in order to avoid going to trial, and more importantly to wrap it all up before he retired. In that case I found myself in caucus saying to the client: "This is obviously your decision, this is a business decision and I will respect your decision but, I think the case is worth a lot more than 20 or 30 cents on the dollar." I have found it difficult at times to take off the advocate hat and to be sensitive to the client's business objectives.[25]

The zealous advocacy model assumes the lawyer-in-charge model in which the client will always accede to the lawyer's advice. The above example illustrates the difficulties that arise when this does not happen, which is not uncommon with sophisticated business clients (or highly invested personal clients). When the client does not defer to the lawyer's rights-based advice, zealous advocacy runs into the practical problem of how to balance client interests and professional judgment. Since the zealous advocacy model assumes that lawyering is about providing technical legal advice in order to achieve the clients' best legal outcome, the lawyer's relationship with other dimensions of conflict resolution – business goals, psychological interests – is ambiguous and undetermined. Most lawyers would agree that client goals and preferences must ultimately trump the lawyer's judgment, but how far does the zealous advocate press the rights-based case? How much weight should a lawyer give to the clients' non-legal goals? As a result of its focus on entitlements, the zealous advocacy model has no tools to analyze this problem, and instead lawyers rely on their own best judgment. Experienced counsel have developed their own, often highly sophisticated, approach to this issue over the years, but young lawyers are left with little or no guidelines.

Even where the lawyer's advice is taken, simplifying the relationship between lawyer and client and removing this particular tension, other tensions arise. Some would argue that the zealous advocacy model, and especially the more adversarial version that characterizes contemporary big firm/big town practices, is open to moral challenge. Murray Schwartz has observed that some lawyers believe they operate under a principle of moral non-accountability in order they can be unrestrained in the zealous pursuit of their clients' goals.[26] This perspective suggests there is little or no need to maintain a clear line between zealous and immoral forms of advocacy. Maintaining these lines is of course much more difficult and subject to far more pressure, with the added responsibility of ensuring that you or your firm retains a particular client, expecially when that client measures the lawyer's loyalty and commitment by the extent of his adversarial behaviours. Significant economic rewards, or losses, may be at stake, which serves to further exacerbate competitive pressure.[27] The dramatic rise in executive salaries over the past ten years inevitably leads to an ever more cutthroat practice environment.

Some types of adversarial behaviour condoned by the principle of moral non-accountability, and encouraged by client expectations, are highly seductive. This lawyer reflects on just how easy it is to become engrossed in this world of winners and losers:

> I'd come back from court and I'd say: "I'm a winner! I'm a winner!" Or,
> I'd come back from court saying: "Can you believe what that damn judge

did?" It's about winning ... So what if the court agreed with your sub-
mission that was a little goofy and gives you $2,000 more per month that
you shouldn't have gotten? You are a winner, and you did good for your
client. So what if you took advantage of some other lawyer's stupidity? I
don't care – I'm a winner![28]

This quote again illustrates the deceptive simplicity of this approach. However, for other lawyers, rather than reducing or eliminating tension, the
principle of non-accountability heightens the conflict they experience
between their own values and those of their client or the adversary system itself. For example, one lawyer explains:

My nature, my personality has always been much more collaborative. I
struggled to get that adversarial model to begin with. It never felt right.
I always felt that I wasn't giving as good service to my clients as I could
be giving but I was forced into it because that is what the system
required.[29]

Anthony Kronman has pointed out that morally "blind" adherence to
the clients' goals is not the way law was traditionally practised or the way
that lawyers in smaller communities – who often play a more general role
in the community as a wise advisor – understand their role.[30] Kronman
argues that a more appropriate approach, and one that is more faithful to
the professional identity of lawyers, mediates the zealous advocacy approach
with the responsibility of lawyers to enable the client to evaluate and appraise
their goals and options and to offer judgment or "deliberative wisdom."
Deliberative wisdom is more than simply a legal evaluation or the advice
of a technical specialist. It also includes considering other non-legal implications of the decision to act.[31] It might also include advice on the dilemmas inherent to bargaining described earlier, which are always present in
the space between the lawyer's legal appraisal of the value of a case and
the client's expectations or settlement goals. Kronman's position is that
offering deliberative wisdom on how a client might achieve his goals is
an honorable and valuable role, which much contemporary legal practice,
especially corporate commercial practice, inadequately recognizes and
affords space for.[32]

Whether or not Kronman is accurate in his image of a bygone profession,[33] the deliberative wisdom model deepens and complexifies the idea
of zealous advocacy by assuming that the lawyer has something useful to
say to clients about their moral and legal choices. For the new lawyer, it
means inviting discussion of client goals that goes beyond the information deemed necessary to formulate a rights-based approach in order to
produce a more complex, multi-layered version – for example, considering

business goals and priorities, weighing the needs of the client for closure, and re-emphasizing the needs and interests that lie behind the asserted positions. Translating this additional information into client advocacy and pursuing the clients' core needs and interests, whatever these might be, looks quite different than advocating only for the goals framed through the lens of legal rights.

Problems with and tensions within the zealous advocacy model open up the possibility of developing a modified notion of conflict resolution advocacy. Further pressures for adjusting our conception of advocacy to meet new realities are coming from an emerging culture that promotes settlement, both in the courts and in business. Both internal tensions and external pressures are indicative of a need for debate, clarification, and perhaps some change in notions of zealous and now adversarial advocacy. Crises over identity and role conflicts are often seen as presaging fundamental change in professions because there is pressure to adjust to resolve or reduce the conflict. Even minor adjustments in practice routines – for example, those associated with court-mandated settlement processes – are critical to the construction of professional identity for lawyers where they impact, as these do, on notions of role and purpose.

However, the apparent clarity and simplicity that is part of the appeal of literal notions of zealous advocacy and especially adversarialism is also a real obstacle to change. Central to the "hang tough" values of the adversarial model are the rigidity and inflexibility of its strategies, making it especially difficult to adjust to a "new," or at least changing, set of cultural and procedural circumstances. There is little space in the traditional model for counsel to negotiate with her client or internally with herself. Instead, there is certainty and resolution of purpose, which is seen as strength. The traditional model does not come with a companion road map for flexibility, detours, or innovations.

Despite these challenges and limitations, the zealous advocacy model, and especially its most adversarial manifestations, fails to offer a complete or even adequate conceptualization of the lawyer's role in the twenty-first century. The evolution of advocacy values and strategies to meet changing conditions of practice and client expectations is increasingly imaginable. What would a new model of conflict resolution advocacy look like?

An Alternative Conception of Advocacy

If an alternative conception of advocacy is emerging, it is as a result of the cultural and institutional changes taking place in legal practice because of the widespread introduction of court-connected and private mediation programs, case management, judicial mediation, and the "vanishing trial."[34] Just as adversarial advocacy has evolved out of earlier notions of zealous advocacy, we can imagine a new conception of advocacy evolving out of

·current practice in response to the changing conditions of legal practice. I shall call this "advocacy as conflict resolution" or conflict resolution advocacy. This does not mean that resolution is the only outcome, but, rather, that the goal is fair and just resolution wherever possible. Conflict resolution advocacy is at the core of the professional identity of the new lawyer.

The new lawyer will conceive of her advocacy role more deeply and broadly than simply fighting on her clients' behalf. This role comprehends both a different relationship with the client – closer to a working partnership and described in Chapter 6 – and a different orientation toward conflict. The new lawyer must help her client *engage* with the conflict, confronting the strategic and practical realities as well as making a game plan for victory. The new lawyer offers her client skills and tools for conflict analysis, an understanding of how conflict develops and evolves over time, and the experience of working continually with disputants on (perhaps similar) disputes. Conflict resolution advocacy means working with clients to anticipate, raise, strategize, and negotiate over conflict and, if possible, to implement jointly agreed outcomes. If jointly agreed outcomes are not possible or if they fall short of client goals, there are other, familiar rights-based strategies available that can be pursued either simultaneously or alternatively. In this conception of conflict resolution advocacy, there is no diminishing of the lawyer's responsibility to achieve the best possible outcome for his client. In fact, advocacy as conflict resolution places the constructive and creative promotion of partisan outcomes at the centre of the advocate's role and sees this goal as entirely compatible with working with the other side – in fact, this goal can be achieved *only* by working with the other side.

Conflict resolution advocacy requires lawyers to modify two of their three key beliefs, and to extend the third. It challenges the automatic and "obvious" primacy of rights-based dispute resolution, preferring a more nuanced, multi-pronged strategic approach to both fighting and settling. Conflict resolution advocacy regards rights-based strategies as important and useful but rarely exclusive tools for engaging with conflict and seeking solutions. As a result of broadening discussions to include non-legal issues and potential solutions, the role of the client in conflict resolution advocacy becomes more significant in both planning and decision making, modifying the simple notion of the lawyer as the expert "in charge." Finally, conflict resolution advocacy does not deny or contradict justice as process, but it takes what lawyers already know about the importance of integrity in the processes and procedures of conflict resolution and applies this awareness to private ordering outside the legal system. As a consequence, the new lawyer will be deeply involved in and knowledgeable about the design of processes and procedures of negotiation, mediation, and other collaborative processes that protect clients' interests and promotes trust in the development of solutions.

The principal conceptual difference between zealous advocacy and conflict resolution advocacy is that the former is organized around a system of adjudication and the latter around a system of conflict resolution that includes but is not limited to adjudication. This sounds like a simple, realistic adjustment, but it has many implications for both the way lawyers understand their role and the way in which they carry it out. What type of professional commitments and practical skills does this conceptual shift translate into – what stays the same, recognizable as part of the traditional zealous advocacy concept, and what is different?

First, let us examine what remains the same or at least familiar and recognizable. A common fallacy is that in the pursuit of settlement, the commitment to one's client, which represents the very nature of advocacy, must somehow be compromised. The new lawyer remains just as dedicated to achieving her clients' goals as the zealous or adversarial advocate. What changes is that her primary skills become her effectiveness and ability to achieve the best possible negotiated settlement, while she remains prepared to litigate if necessary. There is no contradiction between a commitment to explore every possibility of facilitating an agreement with the other side and a strong primary loyalty to one's own client. One very experienced lawyer describes this loyalty in a very practical way as follows:

> I think, to be honest, it's natural for an attorney ... that my best friend in the room is always going to be my client.[35]

Counsel's loyalty and focus should be on achieving the client's best possible outcomes. As a result, effective collaborative family lawyers can assure their clients: "I shall still get the best result for you."[36] Or as a commercial litigator put it, "I see a completely different form of adversary process. You can call it a mediation because we're working together to come up with a deal, but we're still adversaries – I'm still trying to get the best possible deal I can."[37] A contradiction between client loyalty and creative consensus building only exists if counsel is convinced that the only effective way to advance the clients wishes is by aggressive position taking or by pressing rights-based processes to their final conclusion. Aside from these fairly exceptional cases, the goal of the conflict resolution advocate is to persuade the other side to settle – on her clients' best possible terms.

In a model of conflict resolution advocacy, lawyers continue to encounter many of the same tensions and dilemmas as they do as zealous advocates – for example, when and how to settle, how to balance their judgment with the clients' aspirations, and how to balance what has been gained with what will be lost in settlement. However, as we have seen, zealous advocacy has no frameworks for resolving these dilemmas because admitting a need to compromise undermines the core of zealous advocacy. Conflict resolution advocacy both anticipates them and makes them resolvable on a clearly principled basis. Whereas adversarial advocacy tends to see settlement as capitulation, conflict resolution advocacy is committed to evaluating the pros, cons, and the alternatives of any settlement option, which includes an evaluation of the legal, cognitive, and emotional dimensions because all of these are part of how clients appraise settlement.[38]

So what is different about conflict resolution advocacy? Instead of behaving as if constantly preparing for a courtroom battle – but, in practice, almost always negotiating to a settlement – conflict resolution advocates do not base their strategy on an assumption of an adjudicated outcome. While standing ready and able to move to an adjudicated determination of their case, conflict resolution advocates plan their approach based on one simple and undisputed fact: that most cases settle. This recognition opens up the unpredictable and flexible dimensions of strategic bargaining, focusing counsel less on gamesmanship around the rules of engagement (the rules of civil procedure) and more on the management and tactics of negotiation.

A New Focus on Negotiation

The relationship between time spent on procedural steps such as drafting and filing pleadings, preparing and bringing motions, and developing negotiation strategy and actual negotiation is reversed in a model of conflict resolution advocacy. Since lawyers conventionally spend little time on negotiation compared to taking procedural steps,[39] this reversal represents a significant shift of time and energy. Some lawyers already see the time they spend on procedural matters as an aspect of negotiation – in effect, softening up and checking out the other side in preparation for bargaining – but, in this approach, negotiation is a mere subset of procedural manoeuvers and not an explicit tactic. In conflict resolution advocacy, the development and implementation of effective negotiation strategies is moved to the centre of what advocates offer their clients.

This shift transforms how we think about negotiation as a discrete skill rather than as a subsidiary of other traditional lawyering practices. It catapults the self-conscious development of negotiation skills, which are evaluated by their effectiveness rather than justified by their habitual character, up the hierarchy of lawyerly skills and capacities. Taking negotiation strategy seriously makes the routine dynamic of exchanging written offers before "sawing it off in the middle" appear inadequate and gauche. Instead, conflict resolution advocacy demands that negotiation planning be addressed even in the earliest stages of file development as a part of the process of canvassing with the client about their goals, priorities, and alternatives. An early and explicit focus on the negotiation potential requires the holistic framing of the problem rather than the selective use of information in a way that narrows the case to its generic legal issues. This may also shift the planning focus away from procedural steps and deadlines and toward the development of a complete strategy for file management, which is perhaps worked out within a team or between those in a firm's litigation and corporate departments.[40] As one lawyer, whose practice was dramatically altered by the introduction of mandatory civil mediation, reflected:

> My practice is more and more on the phone talking about *strategy*. Less and less do I ever mention the words *civil procedure*.[41]

Recognizing the central role of negotiation for the conflict resolution advocate means a new emphasis on skills that have often seemed to be peripheral for zealous advocates. Intimidation, aggressive positionality, and secrecy are not helpful in trying to build consensus. Summarized by one lawyer as "lose the bark, keep the bite,"[42] strategies which persuade the other side first to listen to you and then to (hopefully) accede or agree with you implicate both oral and written advocacy. Effective negotiators ask questions that reveal information rather than holding forth themselves. They have a sense not only of when to be accommodating but also of when to be tough in order to protect their clients' interests, working incrementally to create trust and enhanced solutions. They understand and develop norms of reciprocity with the other side, beginning with establishing comfort and rapport. This process requires good interpersonal and communication skills, including the ability to put the other side at ease, demonstrate respect and perhaps even empathy, and, most challengingly, create a shared sense of trust. The development of trust is key to exploring enhanced mutual solutions, and it requires effective explanation, persuasion, and personal authenticity:

> I want to persuade and get the other party to understand what my client wants, so there's that part of the persuasion, but it's more based on building a foundation first, the more they understand, the more they trust then the more likely they are able to understand why we think we want a certain thing.[43]

Conflict resolution advocacy also requires a certain amount of new knowledge, which can enhance the breadth and depth of the negotiator's skills. For example, skillful negotiators understand the distinctive dynamics of both distributive (divide up the pie) and integrative (expand the pie, then divide it) negotiations as well as the need to move between these two modes depending on the type and stage of negotiation. Understanding the dynamics in negotiation of both value claiming, whereby one establishes and holds to a "bottom line" or core components of an acceptable solution, and value creating, whereby one explores the additional benefits that the parties might jointly develop and distribute, creates balance and provides alternatives when one strategy gets "stuck." Lawyers who understand different bargaining strategies can move with ease between them and are proactive in shaping negotiation outcomes. They use an expanded range of options to identify priorities and negotiate trade-offs. Experienced negotiators are also sensitive to the importance of identifying and allowing for cultural differences in both the framing and the resolution of conflict, recognizing that disputants often need to relate the process and the outcome to their cultural (familial, community, organizational, ethnic) expectations and preferences.

Lawyers who are experienced in settlement advocacy identify a number of discrete negotiation skills – implicating both cognitive and emotional abilities and qualities – that enable them to be most effective. These include preparing an effective opening statement in negotiation or mediation, which adopts a firm yet not overly positional tone; matching the appropriate informal process to the case; displaying confidence and openness; and thinking outside the "box" of conventional, legal solutions in developing creative problem-solving skills. One frequently voiced observation is the importance of being able to conceptualize and understand the dispute from the perspective of the other side. Critical to being able to persuade the other side to settle on your client's best terms – the goal of conflict resolution advocacy – is an understanding of what the other side needs in order to be able to settle.

This is not a new idea. Good negotiators have always operated with an awareness of the interests of the other side, and these lawyers already take the interests of the other side into consideration in order to enlarge the co-operative space in which negotiations can take place.[44] The belief that the clients' best interests can only be achieved if the interests of the other side are taken into account is a central premise of the principled bargaining approach popularized by Roger Fisher and Bill Ury.[45] Moving negotiation to the centre of the advocate's role makes this common sense even for those who have previously been wedded to zealous advocacy models. One experienced litigator provides the following description:

> Probably the biggest change I made was really thinking about ... the opposing party's profile and really making an effort to put myself in his/her shoes ... I do that principally as I strategize the case.[46]

Gathering and Using Information

Another way in which conflict resolution advocacy differs significantly from the zealous advocacy model is in its approach to fact gathering and information in the development of a legal case. In Chapter 4, I described the dominant epistemology of litigation in which knowledge and information have the sole purpose of advancing the clients' legal case. This approach means that only information that fits the legal argument is either sought or utilized, leaving aside significant information that may be important to realizing the clients' goals. The zealous advocacy approach to information is highly competitive, with information withheld even when it may be of little or no consequence and often when it would be beneficial in clarifying the goals of each side. The nature and uses of information in a conflict resolution model are distinctively different from the zealous advocacy model. First, the type of information that may be important is expanded. The involvement of clients in negotiation and mediation and in planning for these processes allows for the discussion of different types of information – for example, business issues or personal issues – that may have an important impact on the resolution of the conflict but would not ordinarily be a part of discussions between counsel. If counsel takes seriously her responsibility to engage the client in the resolution of the conflict, she will seek out information that might formerly have been considered irrelevant or marginal but that could be key to understanding how to advance the clients' interests and needs as well as legal entitlements.

Second, conflict resolution advocacy regards information as a shared resource that may advance all party interests. This approach to information sharing requires significant reorientation, both conceptual and collegial. For a less aggressive and more collaborative approach to information sharing to work, lawyers need to be able to build trusting relationships with other counsel and other professionals. There is an obvious need for norms of reciprocity. Such norms have always existed in smaller communities where lawyers are accustomed to providing information as requested without forcing their opponent through procedural hoops. Even when reciprocity is not clearly established, there may be other strategic reasons to send information to the other side. Counsel have always had to consider what information they want from the other side, and what information they are willing to provide on request. Effective conflict resolution advocates must also consider what information they believe the other side must have, in order to persuade them that they should settle on their best possible terms.

Judicial centres with long-running mandatory mediation programs have begun to evolve conventions to enable the mediation process to be maximally effective in terms of information exchange. In Saskatchewan and Ottawa, mediation generally takes place before discoveries.[47] In the absence of formal requirements over documentary exchange, many counsel adopt

a practice in which they exchange affidavits of documents before mediation and agree to honour subsequent requests.[48] There are still concerns
expressed by some over this strategy – it is not applied in every case and
will depend on the level of trust and comfort[49] – but it is a significant
recognition of the positive value of exchanging information, and a radical departure from the zealous advocacy norm.

Re-Envisioning Outcomes

Another important and potentially profound difference between conflict
resolution advocacy and zealous advocacy lies in how counsel imagines
and appraises what she understands as the "best outcome" in any case.
This dilemma often arises in the context of when to advise the client to
settle, discussed earlier in this chapter. In zealous advocacy, the best outcome anticipated by counsel is always a victory on the legal arguments,
which usually means a monetary judgment. Therefore all potential negotiated outcomes are measured by how close they come to the original legal
goals. Of course, experienced counsel know that in practice this is not the
only measure of success, or even necessarily "success" as the client sees
it. Even if "winning" is ultimately achieved, it may not be all that was
hoped for. Emotional closure or business viability and recovery are often
pushed further away in litigation. In civil trials, the process of resolution
may be further prolonged by the need for enforcement steps after securing a favourable judgment, which may partly explain why in my 1995
Ontario study (matching a control group of litigants who went to trial
with those who mediated their dispute), only 8.5 percent of trial group
litigants described themselves as completely satisfied with the outcome of
their case (either settled between the lawyers or adjudicated). The most
frequently given reason for a negative or partly negative assessment of
outcome in the remaining 91.5 percent (obviously including some litigants who won their cases at trial) was the length of time and the emotional energy consumed.[50]

In envisioning and evaluating potential outcomes, conflict resolution
advocacy will certainly include a measures-based proximity to an "ideal"
(i.e., successful) legal outcome, but many other factors will also be important. For example, responsible counsel will always consider the issue of
costs in planning a conflict resolution strategy. Conflict resolution advocates should consider how far any one outcome will meet client interests.
Aside from "winning," these might include, for example, recognition and
acknowledgment, business expansion or solvency, future relationships both
domestic and commercial, vindication and justice, emotional closure, and
reputation. These interests have both short-term and long-term elements.
They reflect not only outcome goals but also the importance of procedural justice – feeling listened to, being taken seriously, and being fairly

treated. In a conflict resolution model of advocacy, it is not only the final deal that matters but also how the client feels about how it was reached, which includes a sense that the outcome is fair and wise in light of the clients' interests, and a recognition of the limits of the system to offer alternative, better solutions.

In some disputes, it is important for the outcome to be responsive to a sense of systemic and underlying issues. This may come at the urging of one party or another – for example, the employee claiming discrimination who wants to see future procedures changed to avoid the problem re-occurring, or the manager who sees the need for a new set of procedures and protocols to enhance clarity and fairness in decision making. In some conflicts, it may also be important to set the stage for future re-engagements, which may be inevitable – for example, in disputes over land use between municipalities and communities or between parents sharing custody of children. By stepping outside the limits of remedying the immediate problem, the conflict resolution advocate takes a proactive approach to averting future conflicts. Rather than thinking "solutionally" (a "rewind" approach), she is thinking "preventively" (a "fast-forward" approach).[51] Conceived of in this wider frame, conflict resolution advocacy sometimes requires lawyers to adopt a systems approach to future, anticipated problem solving.

In order to develop effective processes and systems for clients who anticipate future conflict, it is extremely helpful for counsel to understand the basic characteristics of systems, including the tendency for systems to create their own internal culture, the risk of systems functioning differently than intended (for example, to suppress conflict), and the need to ensure that there is buy-in from not only the parties but also from other potential disputants who will use the system. It is also helpful for counsel to be aware of some basic system tools for planning, which, in this case, might include a spectrum of dispute resolution processes, some process precedents, tools for monitoring system processes and outcomes, and so on. Not every outcome will include these dimensions of future problem solving, but in conflict resolution advocacy they should at least be on the table for consideration.

Conflict resolution advocacy is about focusing more of counsel's energy on the creation of good settlements rather than good positions, and developing new knowledge and skills to support this new and enhanced focus of their work. Conflict resolution advocacy is less about aggressive posturing and game playing and more about working with the client to diagnose their needs and priorities, and staying open to the creation of new pathways to meet these. It does not mean abandoning rights-based advocacy and even trial work in appropriate cases. In fact, conflict resolution advocacy builds on some traditional skills and knowledge, notably information assimilation, legal research, effective oral communication, strategic planning, and insider knowledge, which are core elements of effective trial advocacy. Conflict resolution advocacy takes these familiar tools and applies them to a new challenge: the pursuit of reasonable and acceptable settlements.

New Tensions in Conflict Resolution Advocacy

The Dilemma of the Two Hats

Lawyers who are now regularly required, or who choose, to participate in processes focused on settlement such as negotiation and mediation are beginning to experience changes in their professional identity that flow from the adjustment from adversarial to conflict resolution advocacy. Unless they have eschewed litigation as a dispute resolution tool altogether, as a small minority have, lawyers who practise conflict resolution advocacy need to constantly "switch hats" between a negotiation and a litigation mode. To a lesser extent, zealous advocates face this same dilemma when they deal with the question of whether or not to recommend a settlement offer to their client. However, lawyers who have embraced conflict resolution advocacy probably experience a more acute tension between a "fighting" and a "settling" role. Furthermore, in conflict resolution advocacy the role tension is caused by participation in parallel processes – one that attempts negotiation and the other that presses ahead with litigation. This tension is also likely to occur much earlier (especially in court-mandated programs where participation in settlement meetings is often required before discoveries) than when the zealous advocate customarily faces the comparable dilemma of whether to recommend a settlement offer (often made on the courtroom steps). In a model of conflict resolution advocacy, the lawyer will often be expected to participate simultaneously in both rights-based and settlement processes. This creates a new set of tensions and challenges for the new lawyer.

Some lawyers describe this tension in an instrumental, matter-of-fact way:

> In drafting a mediation brief, for example, I'll often try and use plain language rather than inflammatory language simply because if you want to achieve the settlement it may not be in your interest to get the other side going, and so you have to be a little cautious in terms of how you approach things. That's if you really do want to reach a resolution of the case that applies after the mediation – whereas if the case goes to trial, then I'll be as aggressive as I think necessary.[52]

> I think in a mediation process I attempt as much as possible to be conciliatory and look for opportunities for resolution. Try to understand what

might make the person on the other side of it tick. What would interest them in terms of a resolution. If I get in a courtroom I'm quite different. I think people all of a sudden see a different person, but that's just the nature of the business.[53]

Another lawyer accepted the role switch and dealt with it by "acting" conciliatory in mediation. While on one hand she had no problem justifying such "acting" as a highly functional tactic, on the other hand, she conceded that it made her uncomfortable on an "ethical" level:

[The two roles] are completely separate. It feels kind of slimy doing it, from an ethical point of view. It feels slimy, it's a complete act and usually the clients on the other side are so naive as to buy into the act and from an ethical point of view that doesn't feel that great, but it's what we do.[54]

Counsel whose commitment to conflict resolution advocacy is deeper – for example, where it is reflected in their choice of strategies and tactics rather than a superficial veneer – find switching between these two approaches to advocacy quite disorienting, and prefer to find a means to avoid it, focusing exclusively on one strategy or another. Generally, these are lawyers who take the differences between the two "hats" more seriously. Two groups, in particular, experience a strong feeling of tension between their adversarial and their settlement roles. The first group comprises those lawyers who have the greatest experience in mediation and other settlement-oriented processes and who now (if not initially) enthusiastically support the use of mediation – the so-called "true believers."[55] Many in this group are working toward developing a settlement-only practice in order to avoid the role conflict, but, as yet, only a limited (although growing) number of lawyers have found this economically viable. The second group, which is highly sensitive to tension between settlement work and traditional advocacy roles, comprises those lawyers who are most negative toward mediation and other settlement processes. These lawyers see settlement advocacy as a dilution – a sell-out – of the lawyer's traditional adversarial role and do not regard the two approaches as in any way complementary or commensurable. As one lawyer expressed, "Inevitably you have to stop one part of your role [the settlement-seeking part] in order to preserve the other part."[56] The preferred course of these so-called "oppositionists" is the rejection of any developed role for lawyers in settlement advocacy.

Most lawyers, however, neither reject this tension nor find it especially difficult to manage, but they do struggle at some level with the misfit between their traditional advocacy identity and the role they realize they need to play in order to be most effective in settlement processes. This is sometimes expressed as a sense that they are not doing what they were trained to do, and are doing something else that they also were not trained to do.[57] This awareness is most common for lawyers practising civil litigation or family law since their involvement in institutionalized and often mandatory settlement processes increases. Moving between two different roles – for example, appearing in motions court in the morning, and participating in mediation or a settlement conference in the afternoon – can be confusing for both lawyers and clients. Some lawyers speculate about whether "over time" they will become less like "traditional barristers" and more like "social workers, counselors."[58] The opposite and equally pressing dilemma is how to meet high expectations on the part of clients, especially "one-shotters," who often assume that the best advocacy must be adversarial:

> Some clients come to a litigator and expect a bulldog who believes in their case, believes in their defence and isn't going to compromise and is going to go in there and fight for them – and what do they think if the second question out of the lawyer's mouth is, what are you prepared to pay or what are you prepared to settle for?[59]

Can the two roles fighter and settler be reconciled? Does resolving the tension between fighter and settler require a commitment to one perspective or another or can counsel prepare for war and peace at the same time? And, if so, how is this balance to be achieved?

Here is the heart of all the tensions that arise in a model of conflict resolution advocacy. The new lawyer must learn how to wear the two hats of fighter and settler, and understand when to take one off and put the other on. She must evaluate when one approach should be preferred over the other, when one approach should be entirely set aside or suspended, and even when both hats need to be worn at the same time (for example, a last-ditch settlement meeting before initiating litigation, or proceeding to trial).

The tension between fighting and settling takes on a special challenge and nuance within collaborative lawyering. As a result of its unique structure, collaborative law offers a fascinating case study of the most difficult tensions that potentially arise in a model of advocacy as conflict resolution. Lawyers who practise conflict resolution advocacy must continuously assess the balance they strike between the counselling role – offering the client Kronman's "deliberative wisdom" in private[60] – and the advocacy role – making the public case for the client's position. How much time and energy should counsel give to each of these functions? How important is each? While establishing this balance is a challenge for all conflict resolution advocates, collaborative law is especially interesting because its structure effectively eliminates the conventional distinction between these two functions, such that counselling occurs as a private conversation between lawyer and client and advocacy takes place as the public manifestation of decisions taken in private. Instead, counselling may sometimes still take place in private, but it will probably also occur in the four-way meetings (including both lawyers and both clients). Many conventions surrounding the style and delivery of advocacy, especially the most adversarial advocacy, assume that the audience is limited to counsel for the other party and only occasionally for the client himself or herself. In a four-way gathering, such as a mediation with clients present or a settlement conference, the other side is always present to hear and perhaps to directly respond. In traditional processes, the opportunity to separate the functions of counselling and advocacy have allowed lawyers to adopt a confident and even aggressive attitude in public and a more cautious tone in private consultations, to present certain information in private but not in public, and so on. In collaborative law and client-attended mediation, counsel needs to choose a place to stand on the fighter-settler continuum that not only works for the facts of the case and for the client and also maintains consistency both in public and in private.

Client Autonomy and Lawyer Direction

A related dilemma for advocacy in consensus-building processes such as collaborative law and mediation is how to find a balance between client autonomy and lawyer control of overall direction and strategy. How this dilemma is resolved will have a significant impact on the basis of the lawyer-client relationship, which is the subject of the next chapter. It is difficult for lawyers to relinquish their traditional control over decision making. As one lawyer comments:

> Lawyers often don't want clients settling unless there is a rationale (as defined by a lawyer) for the settlement. So some lawyers find it hard to understand why [for example] their clients might be willing to pay more than they might.[61]

While striking a balance between client autonomy and lawyer control is a dilemma for all advocates, it becomes especially complex in conflict resolution advocacy where the ultimate goal is to empower the client to make their own best, informed decisions. While almost every lawyer will, if asked, agree that their client is the ultimate decision maker, in practice a shadow negotiation takes place between lawyer and client as they develop strategy and tactics that are both both procedural (do we negotiate, what do we offer, do we play hardball?) and substantive (what is a good outcome, what is a just outcome?).

At a general level, this debate is often characterized as a contrast between client autonomy and lawyer paternalism. The autonomy approach emphasizes the personal goals and interests of the individual client as well as attention to factors other than the legal appraisal by expert counsel, which are perhaps known only to the client. The premise of the autonomy approach is that the lawyer's primary responsibility as an advocate is to enable her client, by not only providing legal advice but also by asking questions and canvassing options, to assess her own situation in a manner that enables him to determine the best possible course of action for himself. The paternalistic view places a stronger emphasis on the expert judgment of the lawyer, which, combined with the emotional distance possible for a professional, enables the lawyer to be the better judge of the "right" outcome for this client, no matter how removed are their own circumstances. The paternalistic approach is also more in line with the traditional bargain of zealous advocacy described earlier in this chapter. This approach acknowledges that at least some clients expect counsel to tell them what to do and to advocate for them on the basis of the counsel's expert opinion.

In practice, there is an obvious overlap or blurring between the autonomy and paternalist positions.[62] Some clients require significant input from their lawyers in order to reach an "independent" evaluation and decision. Given their power in the relationship, lawyers still heavily influence not only client decision making but also the appraisal of just how much clients need to know in order to function "autonomously." The lawyer often (and with one-shot litigants such as divorce clients, usually) controls what information will and will not be presented for the client's consideration. What about situations in which the client's capacity for making an unemotional and rational decision appears to be impaired: In such situations should the lawyer press his advice more assertively?

In a classic example of the blurring of the lines between autonomy and paternalism, some collaborative lawyers go further still and hold their client to the decisions that represent his "highest functioning self." In other words, the client is "forced" (paternalistically) to act as "his best self" (autonomously). A few collaborative retainer agreements include clauses that commit the client to act as his "highest functioning self" and allow his lawyer to pull him back from selfish or destructive behaviours.[63] Advocacy in this formulation becomes "trying to achieve what the client has identified as their highest functioning goals."[64]

With neither a "pure" paternalist nor autonomous position likely to occur in practice, the essence of this debate becomes the balance of power between counsel and client over determining the direction of the case, including decisions regarding both negotiation strategy and eventual outcomes. Any amount of lawyer paternalism – whether or not it is presented as being for the client's own good – cannot exclude the influence of extra-legal considerations such as the psychological state or economic conditions that may mean that counsel is unable to persuade his client to take his advice. Whatever the reason for a client refusing advice, this probability is heightened when the client is the more powerful (social, economic) player in the lawyer-client relationship. The next chapter discusses the power that experienced commercial clients bring to the lawyer-client relationship and the ways in which this dynamic transforms the paternalist paradigm.

Personal Values and Professional Service

Even lawyers who regard client autonomy as being critical to conflict resolution advocacy must accept that the values as well as the substantive expertise of the individual lawyer are never irrelevant to the process of reflection and deliberation. In conflict resolution advocacy, the lawyer often brings a personal commitment to the pursuit of settlement via advocacy. While counsel must negotiate with each client the degree to which settlement is pursued relative to rights-based or even adversarial tactics, this personal commitment may be difficult for counsel to set entirely to one side. A client who instructs her divorce lawyer to "sue their lying lips off" may be unable to successfully work with a settlement-oriented lawyer, and vice versa. Even when both lawyer and client have committed to a conflict resolution approach (for example, by signing a collaborative retainer agreement), each probably adopts this strategy for quite different reasons. Lawyers are often motivated by deeply held values and beliefs about appropriate approaches to conflict resolution, while their clients are usually motivated by far more pragmatic considerations like minimizing the expenditure of time and money. Collaborative lawyers are sometimes set back when they find that their clients are less committed than they had hoped to consensus building, and, at this point, they may press them to accept their own values about "healthy family transitions" with minimal acrimony.[65]

The autonomy/paternalism debate highlights the ways in which the lawyer's own values and beliefs will inevitably influence their judgments over the best approach to client advocacy. This is another dilemma that conflict resolution advocacy, unlike zealous advocacy, can recognize and thus can develop ways to address. The traditional zealous advocacy model, in contrast, would have us believe that lawyers have no normative position of their own or little emotional attachment to the resolution of the issues in any particular way. Instead, they adopt the norms and values of whatever rights-based position they argue for. In practice, it is sometimes difficult to distinguish between the zealous advocate's own position (and their moral beliefs about the resolution of the conflict) and the one that he is arguing for on his client's behalf. These lines are especially blurred in adversarial forms of advocacy, when the lawyer sometimes appears to be as or even more morally committed to fighting than their client.

Lawyers who work as conflict resolution advocates need to be aware of the values they bring to the processes that they promote and use. While rights-based bargaining explicitly describes the normative basis for a position, interest-based bargaining, by focusing on a non-evaluative articulation of needs and priorities, can disguise the underlying normative assumptions of these interests (for example, if I want to return to school after my divorce to further my education, my normative assumption is that good parents can combine child-rearing with furthering their own education). Creating a set of outcomes – for divorce, for a commercial dispute, or for a response to an environmental disaster or a labour-management conflict – based on negotiated needs and interests rather than legal entitlements implicates no more or less normative judgments. The tendency of interests to be presented as "just" an expression of what the client wants contributes to a misplaced assumption among consensus builders that while rights-based negotiation is value-based, interests-based bargaining is somehow "neutral."

In contrast to the traditional paradigm, conflict resolution advocates should be willingly transparent about the values they bring to conflict resolution. This transparency includes where they lie on the fighter-settler continuum, whether they are committed to resolving matters by negotiation in every case or to trying to settle only to a certain point or for certain cases, and how comfortable they are accepting and working with client values and priorities. Attitudes toward these and other issues that implicate their personal values are an important part of the advocacy that lawyers offer their clients, and clients need to know what they are buying.

The Future of Advocacy

Reclaiming advocacy, and changing the historic assumptions, however intellectually questionable, about what makes for effective advocacy, requires the creation of new meta-principles that transcend the old. Such meta-principles include a new emphasis on the importance of negotiation in legal practice, the acquisition of new knowledge and skills in process design and the conduct of negotiations, an ability to switch hats or tracks between fighting and settling, and a recognition of the value of non-legal, preventive, or systems-based solutions. A new model of conflict resolution advocacy should be alive to the many tensions that exist between the lawyer's aspirations and his clients' interests, between the long-term and short-term consequences of conflict resolution, between individual and community or systems interests, and between what disputants want and what they need. Into this fluidity and uncertainty, we should also be willing to introduce an examination of the ways in which the advocate's own values and beliefs inevitably shape his or her participation in the bargaining process. Ignoring these or assuming that they have no place in legal advocacy obscures the reality of how individuals both conceptualize and implement advocacy behaviours.

The promotion of an alternative model of conflict resolution advocacy requires the thoughtful and skillful development of new behaviours, skills, and practices that reflect and enable these meta-principles. Some of these skills have been described in this book, but we have much more work to do on identifying and then teaching them. Some grow out of more traditional legal skills, while others are less familiar. As ever, the role of the law schools in encouraging or neglecting the development of these skills will be critical. The most significant challenge, however, is a conceptual one. It requires us to be imaginative and flexible in contemplating the extent to which a partisan role can be effective in promoting problem solving. It is a major challenge for the new lawyer and one that, if met, will profoundly change the goals and practice of legal advocacy in the next fifty years.

6
The Lawyer-Client Relationship

Practising conflict resolution advocacy changes many aspects of the traditional lawyer-client relationship. The stable assumptions of the traditional model, where the client "instructs" the lawyer by accepting her expert advice, are challenged by a conflict resolution model that seeks to build consensus by drawing on the knowledge and ideas of all sides and all parties. In working toward consensus, whether using negotiation, mediation, collaborative law, or any other facilitated and non-facilitated settlement processes, clients play a very different role than the traditional lawyer-in-charge model allows. The voluntary and institutionalized conflict resolution processes that we see emerging in the twenty-first century require collaboration not only between the sides to the dispute but also between the lawyer and her client. This collaboration offers the client the potential for a more active role than ever before, which at its best is a working partnership in both substance and effect.

The traditional paradigm of the lawyer-client relationship and its assumptions about decision making and client participation are not easily replaced by a partnership. Many lawyers find it hard to intentionally cede this amount of power to their clients unless faced with client demands to do so. Even then, some lawyers struggle with the expectation of their experienced commercial clients that they should participate in all decision making. Clients are virtually "invisible" in law school, and legal education does almost nothing to prepare prospective lawyers to "relate" to the client, as clients are sometimes painfully aware:

> Let's face it, what in law school teaches a lawyer how to read the needs of the client? Nothing.[1]

On the rare occasions that clients are mentioned in law classrooms, their position is understood and framed through the prism of the lawyer in charge, as a set of legal strategies directed by counsel. In some law school classrooms, clients are described either explicitly or by inference as "the enemy," as minor irritations or at worst as impeding the lawyer's pursuit of a rational legal strategy. This patronizing attitude is reflected in the origins of the word "client," which can be traced back to a Latin verb that refers to the right of a Roman aristocrat to impose his own name on his slaves.[2] These perspectives make the prospects for a genuine lawyer-client partnership, at first glance, look unpromising.

Traditional Conceptions of the Lawyer-Client Relationship

The idealizing of lawyer-client relationships in a predictive, adjudicative frame implicates a particular understanding of lawyer-client relations, one that is focused on the technical knowledge required to achieve "best results" in adjudication. In this framework, the relationship of lawyer to client is inevitably one of (substantive) expert to naïf, and this relationship is reflected in assumptions about decision making, judgment, and autonomy.[3] Predictive negotiations have focused on legal rules, and principles "both grow from and reinforce the professional expertise of lawyers."[4] Since only lawyers have the skill and knowledge to engage in this type of negotiation, their clients have little choice but to trust them to take control. In common with other professions whose expertise gives rise to a claim to autonomy, lawyers are accustomed to their clients giving up their own judgment and handing the decision making over to them.[5]

Douglas Rosenthal's classic work on the dynamics of lawyer-client decision making proposes two models of lawyer-client relations: the "traditional" model in which the client is passive and the lawyer fairly autonomous, "assuming broad control over the solutions to the problems brought by the client;"[6] and the "participatory" approach in which the client plays a more active role. Rosenthal's analysis suggests that the passive client, who follows the lawyer's advice and is detached from the problem-solving process, operates as the conventional model and that those who depart from the norm, namely, clients who want to actively participate in anything other than the established areas of client input, are seen as being aberrant and even disruptive by many lawyers.[7]

While there is both structural and anecdotal evidence to support Rosenthal's model, especially in personal legal services, it is important to recognize that not all lawyer-client relationships are the same. The relative power and status of the client will impact the extent to which counsel can assert her traditional control, both explicit and implicit, over the management of the case. Commercial clients have historically assumed a larger role in decision making, especially where they were regular customers and where they considered their own "business savvy" to be critical to developing an effective strategy. When these types of clients represent a significant portion of a counsel's work, they will inevitably diminish her autonomy.[8]

There are more recent signs that areas of decision making that have been previously left to counsel are being affected by the introduction of settlement processes that explicitly include clients, as well as by the growth of in-house counsel. There are of course many other variables, including how much an individual business client wishes to be closely involved with litigation or corporate contracting, and the nature of the personal relationship that develops between the chief executive officer and counsel (including how much trust exists). Other research suggests that there is an important difference between one-shot clients and clients bringing regular business; the former are more likely to fit the model of the "passive" client and the latter more "active." For the purposes of the discussion that follows, it is useful to remember that lawyer-client relations in commercial contexts probably begin from a somewhat modified status quo compared with the model of subordination dominant in personal legal services.

Evidence of the control exerted by lawyers with their one-shot (personal) clients, and even with some more passive business clients, is substantial. Lawyers themselves are frank about the power and control they are accustomed to having in their client relationships, and the "rush" that this brings:

> You basically call the shots when ... client[s] entrust their case to you. A good litigator runs the show. The clients always say, do [what] you want to do ... It's kind of like a director of a play, and when you're in court the biggest CEO is a witness and he's in your world – and you ... direct this play to hopefully a good result at the end of the day in front of a judge.[9]

Lynn Mather, Craig McEwen, and Richard Maiman's study of divorce lawyers in Maine noted that "lawyers have considerable leverage in their relationships with clients that enables them to bring pressure to bear in aligning their clients' perspectives with their own."[10] William Simon argues that lawyers cannot avoid influencing their clients' decisions, whether or not they intend to be controlling and paternalistic.[11] This influence includes reshaping and even transforming the clients' expectations and objectives until they are more in line with those of the lawyer – for example, moving from repairing a business relationship to obtaining a court order, from impoverishing an ex-spouse to proposing a settlement within the likely legal parameters, and from focusing on relationships to focusing on compensation. As Austin Sarat and William Felstiner remark in their study of divorce lawyers, "time and again we observed lawyers attempting to focus their clients' attention on the issues the lawyers thought to be major while the clients often concentrated on matters that the lawyer considered secondary."[12] The lawyer usually wins out in this struggle over framing. While some negotiation over roles and status takes place within most professional relationships, it is generally assumed that the client will cede control to the lawyer.

This conception of lawyer-client relations brings with it a set of parallel assumptions about appropriate professional behaviours. Counsel demonstrates her professional effectiveness by behaving in a way that shows that she knows exactly what to do and how. "Taking instructions" from the client often amounts to telling the client what the lawyer will do, and perhaps asking if there are any questions. As one lawyer frankly admitted:

> I think that ... as advocates ... we had a bad tendency – notwithstanding that we would say: "It's on instructions from my client" or "It's our client's wishes" – that we would really be telling the clients what they *should* do.[13]

Just as we saw in the case of legal negotiations, the location of lawyer-client relations within an adjudicative model of conflict resolution makes many of the resulting values and norms logical and, to some degree, inevitable. In order to advance his case, the client must allow the lawyer to transform his "story" into something that fits a legal frame of reference, which is often making it fit into a "stock story."[14] This means that the lawyer assumes the client's permission to refashion the story in a way that makes it more likely to be successful in a legal-adjudicative framework, emphasizing certain details and overlooking others.[15] Anything that is irrelevant to a legal problem-solving approach – for example, hurt feelings, business practices, or future business dealings – is set to one side.[16] This transformation distances the client even further from being able to actively participate in and contribute to the resolution of their conflict.

Rosenthal argues that the traditional assumption of lawyer control and client passivity is strengthened by an underlying norm that has competent lawyers managing cases using routinized and "closed" systems of analysis and solution seeking. The default to a rights-based approach means that the client's narrative must be framed in a way that best advances rights-based arguments, and that this system or mode of analysis is self-contained, controlled by the lawyer, and closed to other perspectives, including that of the client naïf. The projection onto the client's problem of a rights entitlement (or, from the defence, of disentitlement), which is presented as both "obvious" in light of legal principles and achievable, is understood as a means of removing the uncertainty that otherwise causes clients so much anxiety. The development of "stock stories" is an example of this approach, and it illustrates the minimal practical contribution that clients can make once the problem has been framed in this way (that is, in legal discourse rather than in terms to which they can relate). In contrast, lawyers who invite clients to participate – the "participationists" in Rosenthal's study – frame client problems as "difficulties,"[17] which are open to multiple analyses and possible solutions. Many of these difficulties require input from the client and admit far more ambiguity than traditional "problems."

The final building block of the traditional lawyer-client relationship is also a consequence of the belief in the primacy of rights in legal problem solving. The assumption is that only the professional herself can be the judge of whether or not her work on the client's behalf was effective. If problems are solved by expert knowledge that only the lawyer is privy to, how can her client evaluate his performance? Professionals, including not only lawyers but also doctors, engineers, architects, and others, have long assumed that their autonomy in decision making rests on their unique expertise. Historically, this expertise has been a hallmark of a "profession." As this lawyer puts it:

> The way you treat your doctor, who says your child has a cold and you say: "Yes, thank you for helping me doctor." I assume people come to their lawyer, take their advice, and say thank you.[18]

In this traditional model, clients are expected to defer to their lawyer's expertise: "Since they are presumed to be the only judges of how good their work is, no layman or other outsider can make a judgment of what they can do."[19] Scrutiny by outside bodies and evaluation by clients themselves sit uneasily with these assumptions of power and control. While there are procedures available to clients who wish to lodge a formal complaint against their lawyer, which are administered by law societies, these tend to focus on complaints about lack of communication skills or the costs of legal services rather than on areas of judgment that are difficult for the client to second-guess. Recently, a few law firms serving primarily commercial clients have begun to experiment with client evaluations of lawyers, but there is no data yet available on these.[20] However, both complaints and evaluation occur only after the lawyer-client relationship has ended and are mere scratches on the surface of the control exerted by lawyers in most client relationships. While the client always has the power to fire the lawyer, it is difficult for the client to appraise when such action is the right course to take, and the consquences are potentially costly. There is a clear power imbalance in many lawyer-client relationships, especially those involving lawyers and personal clients, and this stems from a continued reliance on a particular model of expertise, which, absent egregious neglect or error, is virtually unassailable by lay persons.

Changing Conditions of a Changing Relationship

Despite the entrenchment of the traditional model, there are signs that these comfortable and well-established expectations may be changing. In the twenty-first century, deference of clients to professionals seems to be eroding. There are more tools for self-help and access to knowledge that support a stronger culture of self-empowerment among consumers. The World Wide Web facilitates access to information that was previously available only from professional sources, and has fed an appetite for consumer self-help and a sense that consumers should be less deferential and demand value for money from service professionals.[21] In what Bill Ury calls "the age of knowledge," the Internet represents the potency of access to knowledge and global communication, which empowers consumers and revolutionaries alike.[22]

It is instructive to compare the changes occurring within the legal profession with similar developments within the medical profession. Much of the earliest research on professional relationships was conducted in the context of medical services. Just as in law, changing client expectations in medicine affect the relationship between medical doctors and their patients. Like lawyers, doctors are accustomed to using their special expertise to identify and define the problems – in their case, the health problems – and to determine how they should be addressed. Early writing on doctor-patient relationships emphasized the role of the doctor in "fixing" the "problem" of sickness, which (somewhat like conflict) was considered a deviance from normality.[23] In an echo of Rosenthal, passive patients who accept their doctors' advice without question and follow instructions are seen as easier to work with. In this traditional model, the doctor's expertise goes virtually unquestioned: "Professionalization grants physicians a monopoly on the definition of health and illness, and they use this power over diagnosis to extend their control."[24]

The push against the assumption of professional control and expertise began with the work of Thomas Szasz and Marc Hollender in the 1950s, who argued that "a relationship of mutual participation" in medicine would produce better therapeutic outcomes.[25] The patient must be enabled to participate in both raising and managing issues of their care. Over the past decade, the increasing availability of medical information on numerous websites has contributed to this trend – indeed, many such websites promote self-diagnosis. Patients are now more likely to feel that they have access to an alternative "viewpoint," if not a medical opinion. Medical malpractice litigation and the publicity that some cases attract have further fed a sense that doctors need to be carefully monitored by their patients, who may not always trust their judgment. The important point here is not whether patients really do know and understand more about their health care options than they used to but, rather, that they believe that they do. This belief undermines the historical sense of professional deference and status inequality between doctor and patient.

In law, too, the traditional relationship of expert/novice in which the client is very, or somewhat, passive is increasingly challenged on both philosophical and practical grounds. In this area also, the growth of the Internet has led to a proliferation of legal advice sites, which are the legal equivalent to self-diagnosis sites for health issues.[26] Just like doctors in relation to their patients, lawyers now need to be conscious that the consumers of legal services are likely to either have or believe that they have more knowledge than previous generations of clients. The consequence is a diminishing of professional deference and an increased demand among clients for what they see as value for money in legal services. Clients in all areas of practice – but especially corporate and institutional repeat players in the legal system – are looking for increased involvement in decision making and empowerment in relation to issues that are important to them, whether it is a business decision or the negotiation of a family con-flict. Certainly, some clients still and always will prefer to delegate their problem to their lawyer and may even regard this as the essence of what they pay their lawyer to do – relieve them of responsibility for problem solving. Nonetheless, there is mounting evidence that more and more clients prefer greater responsibility and the ability to exercise more control than simply handing over the matter to counsel for transformation into a legal dispute with its own mysterious narrative. They are less inclined to accept that their professional adviser always "knows best" and should function autonomously and without limits. On a practical level, both commercial and personal clients are racketing up expectations of value for money, which often means faster, more immediate results. Pragmatic problem solving is more likely than protracted legal procedures to achieve this result (for example, there is a difference between obtaining a judgment and collecting one's payment, and between engaging in litigation and negotiating a resolution that enables or even secures a future business relationship). Personal clients often have less experience than commercial repeat players to enable them to translate a goal of value for money into specific instructions on how to manage their case. As we shall see later in this chapter, this predicament is changing with the introduction of procedural reforms and increasing awareness among consumers of other process options that are intended to both reduce costs and give clients more active responsibility for problem solving, should they choose.

Pressure to rethink the traditional hierarchy of control within the lawyer-client relationship is also increasing from access to justice advocates, who argue that more people would use the legal system if it were less intimidating and formalistic in its approach to conflict resolution. Traditional legal culture (re)constructs client narratives of need and entitlement into the speech forms of legal culture. Many people are excluded from legal processes because they have neither the skills (vocabulary or knowledge about access) nor the social power to participate in them in any meaningful way (they can see no relationship between going to a lawyer and solving their immediate problem). These constraints "undermine the capacity of many people in our society to use the procedural rituals that are formally available to them" and thereby undermine participation in a democratic society.[27] At the same time, there is a growing recognition of the need for public participation in dialogue where decision making affects them.[28]

The weakness of the access to justice argument lies in the fact that, as we have seen, corporate and institutional clients have over the past thirty years become far more economically significant for the profession than the provision of personal legal services. What will carry the argument forward now are changes in expectations and demands from the most lucrative sector of legal services, namely, corporate and institutional clients.

Corporate and Institutional Clients

Signs of change in client expectations are most evident in corporate and institutional practice. Like personal clients, corporate and institutional clients have historically chosen to nominate their legal representatives to be both managers and agents in disputing.[29] In this traditional paradigm, the expertise of the lawyer was seen as being sufficient and appropriate to resolve the problem, requiring minimal input from the business client. This assumption has been changing over the past thirty years, as corporate clients have shed the deference traditionally afforded to counsel in favour of a more "business-like" and hands-on approach to legal services.

This lawyer describes an incident earlier in his career when he realized that business clients saw themselves as "customers" rather than as people hostage to the authority and prestige of their lawyer:

> It was a very difficult realization for me when I watched a client walk all over a senior partner when I was a very junior associate. I was watching how a person I revered, as one of the smartest people I had ever seen in my life, was selling shoes, in effect, to a customer. This "customer" should have been holding the senior partner in reverence because he was such a brilliant, capable man but we're just shoe salesmen ... or dispute resolution salesmen. That's the basic underlying ... relationship with a client – I'm selling service and I want them to buy it ... It's not that I don't want to be a grand professional, or hold some 100 year old notion of a superior profession. But the reality is if the clients don't believe it, then it's not real anymore ... [M]y illusion in growing up and through law school was that you approach your professionals with a degree of respect and reverence ... I learned quickly that we are selling a service.[30]

The sensitivity of institutional and corporate clients to rising legal costs has led to demands for less costly and more efficient methods of dispute resolution and, specifically, to an increasing appetite for early reporting, strategic settlement planning, and early dispute resolution.[31] Maintaining competitiveness in the business world means avoiding the absorption of corporate energy and monies in litigation and instead finding a smart route to settlement. An enlarging role for business clients is thus a natural consequence of exponentially rising legal costs and the increasing scrutiny of costs by clients.

The ballooning costs of litigation mean that experienced commercial clients are less prepared to be passive and more inclined to assert their expectations for the efficient management of conflict. Business managers are showing an increased interest in participation and control, which has coincided with (or led to) the erosion of some of the traditional barriers of deference and autonomy around the role of the legal professional. Some clients feel that they can do better in moving toward a business solution if they participate more actively and directly in the discussions and welcome – and even create – opportunities to participate more directly. Even though their role in planning and process may be limited (for example, giving depositions, appearing at pre-trial conferences, or, more recently, participating in mediation), some corporate representatives build up considerable experience in litigation and some justifiably feel that they have more to contribute to the resolution of a business dispute than counsel might recognize. Some are not diffident in bringing this opinion to counsel's attention.

This shift in client expectations is widely noted by commercial litigators, sometimes with a note of ruefulness over the loss of control. The following quotations offer just a few examples of counsel's recognition of this change:

> When I started practising back in the mid 60s there was a terrible arrogance in our profession. We thought all clients were not necessarily idiots but didn't know what was best for them, and the client had no idea what was going on in the legal system. People are 100 percent more sophisticated now, know what goes on in the system generally, and are much more conscious of where their buck is going than they used to be.[32]

> The old "just fight-at-all-costs" and don't look at it [the legal bill], don't even think about an approach [opening negotiations], [that attitude] just doesn't seem to exist anymore.[33]

> Now more and more clients are asking for an assessment right at the top from a timing stand point, and asking you to analyze what's the best time

to get a resolution of the thing and especially with in-house counsel involved. They are very conscious of the costs and they want to know up front where the thing is going.[34]

Another significant factor in tracking the movement toward greater client involvement in file management is the growth of in-house or "inside" counsel.[35] Many commercial lawyers now work directly with "inside" counsel. In many ways, corporate counsel inhabits a parallel universe to private practice. Unlike his private practice colleague, inside counsel is obliged to account for and justify all litigation expenditure to his or her manager.[36] Unlike their peers in private practice, corporate counsel are generally valued and rewarded for their abilities to resolve disputes efficiently in a manner that allows the organization to continue to be productive. For example, the successful candidate for chief counsel with one of the world's major corporations gave an interview presentation that consisted of a single PowerPoint slide reading "it's time to stop fighting."[37]

This approach to conflict resolution stands in curious contrast to attitudes within private practice, perhaps explaining why more and more commercial organizations prefer to control litigation via their own legal counsel. In-house counsel are oriented toward the overall business efficiency of their organization in a way that outside litigators are not. Some litigators describe having to work closely with in-house counsel in a manner that limits their accustomed autonomy and makes them more accountable for any decisions that extend litigation. The gap between the two worlds of business and law is further exacerbated by the tendency among private commercial litigators to regard the work of inside counsel as lower in status – less autonomous or, perhaps, simply less macho because of a reduced focus on litigation strategies – than their own. The extent of this divide is well captured in John Lande's 1998 study, which compared attitudes toward litigation between outside counsel, inside counsel, and executives. The "faith" of lawyers in litigation vastly outweighed that of business executives. One business executive quoted by Lande comments:

> We are so anti-litigation that [someone in the company who would commence litigation] would get their hand slapped if they bring in the lawyers.[38]

Many experienced business people find it hard to embrace a fixed and potentially constraining system of precedent or rules (such as the legal system). Another business executive interviewed for Lande's study remarks:

> As I look back at my business career, I have an antipathy for precedent at times because I find it constraining in terms of the ability to break new ground. So I don't necessarily always look for "Well, how was it done

before? Or what did some previous court decide? Or what did some previous regulatory body conclude on this?" as opposed to "Give me the facts and circumstances today and where we want to go in the future. Try to define a problem or the opportunity in terms of the visions of the future as opposed to the precedent in the past."[39]

The growth of a new professional culture of corporate counsel is just one of the ways in which traditional relationships between lawyers and their corporate and institutional clients are being widely renegotiated.

Personal Clients

Personal clients begin from a position that is generally far less powerful than that of commercial clients in attempting to renegotiate the lawyer-client relationship. Nonetheless, the advent of new processes and procedures, some of which are voluntary and some mandatory, has allowed for a bigger role and greater involvement for some personal clients than in the past. These new processes include contracting with their lawyer to use particular procedures that give them a clear role and set of responsibilities (such as collaborative family law) or procedural rules that require their attendance at mediation or case settlement.[40]

Collaborative law clients are often attracted to the idea that they will have more power and control in the negotiation process (for instance, they will participate along with their lawyers in four-way meetings) than in a traditional litigation file. For example, as one client explains,

> I do need to have a sense of control ... This [collaborative law] is the process that is much more likely to give you that sense of control, the lawyers are much less likely just to say "we're doing this."[41]

> It gives you a sense of control. You are controlling your own destiny.[42]

Making a deliberate decision to work with their lawyer – emphasizing negotiation rather than confrontation and remaining involved – rather than simply handing the "problem" (the messy divorce) over to her is also reflected in the objectives of collaborative law clients. By limiting the lawyer's retainer agreement to negotiation not litigation, these clients are able to set out a direction and a strategy for handling their case from the beginning, and they do not risk their lawyer adopting a different approach. For example, as two clients state:

> I don't want this to make me bitter. So I think this is the best process so that you don't become bitter. I don't want to be an angry person and I think this will be helpful.[43]

I like the idea of no fighting. Bypass the fighting and let's get to it. It's going to happen anyway, you know. It's not a nice process but it's happened, so let's get to the other side where I can heal.[44]

Collaborative law also provides examples where moving to "mutual participation" raises new questions over the division of responsibility between lawyer and client, for example, when clients grumble that their lawyers sit back and now expect them to do all the work.[45] Ironically, these comments serve only to underline the emergence of a more empowered, self-confident consumer who asks more questions than ever before and sets higher standards for competence and efficiency.[46]

The advent of mandatory mediation programming in the courts has created a growing group of personal clients who are asking questions about the traditional parameters of the lawyer-client relationship. Mandatory mediation means that clients who have no knowledge or experience of mediation are finding themselves attending sessions with a mediator, along with their lawyers, early on in their file. Studies have consistently demonstrated that the vast majority of clients welcome the chance for mediation and see it as a valuable opportunity, whether or not settlement follows.[47] Further, there is no significant difference in satisfaction levels, which remain consistently high, between clients mandated into mediation and those who chose the process voluntarily.[48] Some recognize the opportunity for them to become more actively involved and to express their views directly to the other side. One client described the experience in the following way:

[The process] gave me a chance to express my complaints ... I felt quite at ease and was able to express what I wanted to express, and the [other party] was able to express their concerns. We were both listening and talking. It had a good feeling in that respect.[49]

Some personal clients maintain that the mediation process is useful for them even in the face of discouragement from their lawyer and a lack of evident anticipation or preparation for a session. In such cases clients sometimes suggest a complete reversal of the traditional hierarchy in lawyer-client relationship: that if their lawyers don't want to "get with the program," they might be better off without them. One client expressed this as follows:

If I could have sat down with the other person, and no lawyer, we would have settled.[50]

Resentment and frustration is sometimes expressed by personal clients about what they see as their counsel's inappropriate use of mediation – for example:

[My lawyer told me before mediation] you can't say this, this, and this. Because we're holding that as a secret weapon if we go to trial.[51]

This client went on to point out that this made the mediation process far less useful than it could have been. This is just one example of an increasingly typical phenomenon: a client developing his own views on how to utilize mediation regardless of his counsel's advice and attitudes. Assumptions of control and hierarchy are challenged when counsel and client are obliged to participate together in settlement-oriented processes.

Following Rosenthal's work, a whole literature has developed on client-centred legal services that envisage greater equality and more of a working partnership between lawyers and their personal clients.[52] The gap between legal framing (by lawyers) and original client narratives means that many personal services clients are unable to construct their needs in legally recognizable norms and speech forms – nor would they choose to do so. In order to really hear the client's story, counsel needs to listen carefully to how her client presents her story, without assuming to impose the structure of any particular legal narrative on it.[53] Particularly in relation to services for vulnerable clients (for example, mental heath patients, HIV-AIDS patients, and young offenders), some scholars now advocate a model of lawyer-client relations in which all the clients' particular needs and interests are carefully identified and included in the planning strategy.[54]

This method necessarily implicates a more holistic approach to the clients' issues, looking, for example, at how to transition a family through divorce rather than simply dealing with the legal issues of custody and property. This is sometimes described as attention to "non-legal consequences."[55] Lawyers have an obligation to review the clients' legal needs within the context of a larger picture of the conflict and its consequences and, where appropriate, to refer their clients to other professionals to address psychological, financial, and other needs outside the ambit of the lawyer's expertise. Therapeutic jurisprudence scholars describe this analysis as the identification of "psycho-legal soft spots," wherein lawyer and client identify sources of anxiety, depression, hurt feelings, and so on, that may be the unintended consequences of a particular legal action or strategy.[56] The premise is that a cookie-cutter approach is both inappropriate and inadequate in addressing underlying client needs (especially where these flow from systemic inequities or disadvantages) or in ensuring that more harm is not done by formalistic legal interventions. By working from the client's own narrative rather than imposing an external framing of the issues, one is able to draw the client into a closer working relationship with both his counsel and his own problem.

To sum up, changes in client expectations for shared responsibility and participation in legal problem solving appear to reflect underlying changes in public attitudes toward professional autonomy and control as well as a general decline in professional deference. Participation and empowerment, rather than expressing the unquestioning acceptance of professional advice on what to do and how to do it, are increasingly seen as important aspects of a democratic, participatory culture. Moreover, the high and rising costs of legal services mean that all clients, whether personal or commercial, need to ensure that they achieve value for money. However, these changing expectations may have had little impact on legal services – other than a declining use of legal professionals by personal clients – if it were not for further changes in the disputing environment, offering personal clients the opportunity to participate in new types of dispute resolution process. Even when processes do not require the attendance of the client, the change in culture means that judges increasingly ask lawyers to bring clients with them to settlement conferences. The introduction of dispute resolution processes that mandate or encourage client participation – for example, mandatory mediation and collaborative law – has positioned even one-shotter and inexperienced personal clients to evaluate their lawyers' attitude toward what appear to be common-sense procedures to encourage settlement, and enables them to draw their own conclusions (which may be at odds with those of their counsel) from their first-hand experience of such processes.

These changing conditions demand the development of a new model for a working partnership between lawyer and client, which is appropriate for the conditions of twenty-first-century consumer needs and demands. The traditional assumptions of the lawyer-client relationship, including ownership of the conflict, control and decision making, and responsibility and participation, are under scrutiny. The days of handing over a file to a lawyer who makes the assurance "trust me, I'll handle it" appear to be significantly over, for both personal and corporate clients.

Three areas of lawyer-client relations highlight the impact of these changes and serve to illustrate some of the philosophical and practical "terms" of a new relationship. These are the negotiation of decision making and control between lawyer and client; the impact of client participation in settlement processes; and the personal or affective[57] dimensions of the new working partnership between lawyer and client.

Decision Making and Control
Whereas clients once told their lawyers "I trust you, you go ahead and decide," now more and more want in on the process of decision making – as one client put it, "[I want to be] in the mix at all times."[58] Reframing the lawyer-client relationship as a working partnership has profound implications for the balance of power in lawyer-client relationships. A partnership gives the client far greater power not only to review and critique

decisions but also to participate in making them. This shift of power also requires clients to take greater responsibility for choices and outcomes. An explicit transfer of responsibility is especially marked where clients directly participate in process and decision making as they do, for example, in collaborative lawyering:

> The overall responsibility has shifted to the clients. We tell the clients they are responsible for the problem. We are going to help you to fix it. We will give you the mechanism, the procedure for resolving it. But it's not our problem. Before, I think too many lawyers would make their clients' problems their own.[59]

In collaborative law, clients are expected to take an active part in planning, analysis, and the formulation of strategy. Collaborative lawyers expect to have frank conversations with their clients about choices of approach, tactics, and options. Obviously some are more effective than others at including their clients in these discussions, but the intent is clear and genuine. Similar adjustments in the participation of the client in planning and decision making occur when lawyers find themselves in mandatory settlement processes that require the participation of their client. The contrast with the "old style" is made clear in this interview with a younger lawyer:

> *Interviewee:* Counsel who practised for many years under the old style ... I think that they had a stronger sense of their lead role ... of their role in making all decisions on how a case should be managed.
> *Interviewer:* Rather than sharing those decisions with the client?
> *Interviewee:* Rather than getting the client as involved as they are involved under mandatory mediation.[60]

When the development of strategy and the conduct of negotiations are no longer under the sole control of the lawyer, the extent and type of information that counsel needs from her client are also quite different than in the traditional paradigm. Instead of filing the pleadings and waiting for the legal process to grind along, mandatory settlement meetings force lawyers to ready their case for negotiation at an early stage. Practically speaking, they need significant input from their clients in order to do this effectively. In anticipation of early mediation, there are many questions that the lawyer now needs to ask at the planning stage, questions that only the client can answer and that are not necessarily related to making the legal case. Gathering and analyzing this information may even enable counsel to make an early offer to the other side to settle the case; where cases are referred to mandatory mediation, there is a demonstrable tendency for them to settle before mediation.[61] Above all, if decision making is to be undertaken jointly, there should be no surprises for the lawyer in a future meeting, collaborative negotiation, or mediation:

> I ask them [the client] "what's *really* going on in the dispute?" If they're the defendant, what they really think the reason for the dispute is? If they're the plaintiff, what they think the reason is that the defendant isn't doing what they want them to do? What's the real reason behind it – do they have financial difficulties, that type of thing.[62]

> For instance, in commercial areas you want to know about the business relationship between the two parties – how long it's been going on, what future opportunities there are together, whether there is an interest in keeping the relationship together for long-term purposes or other business opportunities and so you want to know a lot more about that than you would if you were strictly looking at that case at hand and the legal rights in the dispute issue.[63]

The different type and volume of information shared between lawyer and client in this model is not only the result of the lawyer needing more information and asking more questions. It is also a natural consequence of engaging the client more completely in the development of the case and a dispute resolution strategy is to expand the issues that will be considered and taken into account. If he is directly involved in planning for mediation, for example, a business client is likely to provide additional information on business needs and goals, both long-term and short-term, which can be effectively incorporated into planning a strategy for negotiation. Issues that would not otherwise surface may do so – for example, a manager may introduce a discussion of systemic issues relating to workforce management that will affect her willingness to settle. Instead of removing emotional and psychological issues from the negotiation, the inclusion of clients in planning may mean that important and otherwise unspoken barriers to settlement can be raised and discussed.

Not only does counsel need different and expanded information from her client in order to make effective use of early settlement processes, she may also find herself relying to a far greater degree on what her client tells her. Whereas discoveries and subsequent lawyer-to-lawyer negotiation allow counsel to verify what she has been told by her client and gather appropriate supporting evidence for a claim, early negotiation or mediation implies a greater degree of reliance on the clients' information and a relatively lesser degree of reliance on legal arguments in the preparation of the case.

In short, the greater involvement of clients in planning and decision making opens up the menu of possible topics and options for resolution and enables a different type of dialogue to occur in the settlement process itself. One writer neatly encapsulates this shift in the agenda for lawyer-client discussions as enabling "more space for human agency within [the] lawyering project."[64]

Reconceiving lawyer-client relations in this way means that much of the weight of both moral and practical responsibility shifts from the lawyer to her client. Depending on the extent to which counsel embraces a working partnership with her client, this shift may be a significant one or it may be more marginal, but it will occur in some way. This rebalancing relieves a significant source of stress for many lawyers, who testify to the impact of stress in their working lives and, in particular, to the toll exacted by litigation:

> I hated taking these things home with me. I really worried about the outcomes. I would be up to 2 a.m. preparing.[65]

While some revel in the drama and excitement of litigation, others complain that litigation produces a sense of anomie and disconnect, which undermines their feeling of purpose and satisfaction in their work:

> The stress and anxiety of being a litigator (means that I am in) ... a place of being detached, really disconnected from my clients, disconnected from the other lawyer, and not feeling connected with the process either.[66]

Not all lawyers welcome the opportunity to relinquish their customary approach to file management. Some find setting aside their conventional assumptions about control an unsettling and disconcerting experience. Relying on the client for information prior to a collaborative negotiation or mediation may be nerve-racking and is certainly counterintuitive for lawyers accustomed to the lawyer-in-charge model. The extent of this anxiety among lawyers is illustrated by its prevalence among even those collaborative lawyers who have explicitly opted for a settlement-only approach. Although collaborative lawyers believe in empowering their clients to participate in a working partnership, they acknowledge that some of the consequences are less than welcome – for example, when their clients become sufficiently self-confident that they meet without their lawyers and make a "kitchen-table agreement" or when the client is so "empowered" that she questions the final bill.[67] Similarly, collaborative lawyers often offer their family clients additional choices such as working with a therapist or financial specialist, but may then feel excluded and strangely powerless if the client likes this approach so much that they spend more time with the other professional than with their lawyer.[68] Some collaborative lawyers acknowledge that one way to resolve these anxieties is to place some practical limits on power sharing:

Let me go back to the control thing just for a minute if I may ... I think its very clear, we still have a ton of control ... in fact, more control maybe than we had, in a sense, before. Not of the outcome, necessarily, [but] over process and over behaviour in the meeting and so on.[69]

A similar ambivalence over the reality of sharing control is sometimes voiced by collaborative clients. Some embrace a partnership approach in principle yet express resentment that they are paying a lawyer as well as being asked to carry out many of the functions themselves (for example, gathering documents and preparing plans before meetings). Some clients resist participating in planning or implementing joint strategies, preferring to hand over their dispute to their lawyer in a more traditional fashion and to give him or her control over the file.

Even when both lawyer and client are committed to this approach, practising shared decision making and responsibility has a number of important prerequisites if it is to be workable in practice. It often requires the lawyer to first educate her client to ensure she has sufficient information on which to base any decision. A good example of this is the degree to which previously financially inexperienced partners in divorce (often the wife) are asked to consider the data and make their own decisions about financial support. One collaborative client described a conversation in which her lawyer explained a financial issue and then asked her if she understood:

I said no, [I don't], but I trust you.

Her lawyer was not willing to accept this role and pressed her further.

He replied "No, K., you need to understand this issue to make a decision about it." So he explained it again and asked me what I thought.[70]

Another example of circumstances in which the lawyer is responsible for educating the client to enable them to make an informed decision is in relation to choosing to invest (or not) in a dispute resolution process. In an authentic working partnership between lawyer and client, consideration of dispute resolution options must go further than the lawyer simply recommending her preference for one particular course. Counsel should present a range of options to her client rather than proposing one approach – her favourite or the preferred process – as a *fait accompli*. A willingness to expose the client to the possibility of a range of dispute resolution options is especially important given the weight that clients often attach to their lawyer's personal opinions. When a lawyer is positive or negative about a particular procedure, this is extremely influential in determining the clients' own views. If a process option is either not discussed, or dismissed with minimal explanation, personal clients and one-shotters in particular may not have the experience to press further or ask questions and are likely to simply accede to their lawyer's preference. Research shows that lawyers who are positive about mediation seem to have clients who feel positive about mediation, and, similarly, lawyers who are negative and dismissive about mediation tend to engender the same attitude in their clients.[71] This research suggests that the new lawyer should be transparent about her process preferences, but avoid advocating for a single course and placing perhaps unintended yet significant pressure on the client.

This example illustrates the dangers implicit in the need to educate the client.[72] Counsel still has access to more reliable, technical information than her client and can present it in such a way as to make the client's decision inevitable. One of the ways to safeguard against this resurgence of lawyer paternalism is to ensure that, once informed, the client understands that they must take responsibility in making a final decision. The balance between client autonomy and lawyer judgment (or paternalism) is a delicate and difficult one, as the discussion in Chapter 5 demonstrates. It must always depend on the needs of the individual client.[73]

Collaborative law provides an interesting example of the difficulties of striking an appropriate balance between autonomy and paternalism, particularly when lawyers bring to the relationship not only technical knowledge but also personal ideological views about what comprises the "best outcomes." Collaborative law claims to "liberate" clients and give them the freedom of autonomous decision making by assuming that a particular set of substantive and procedural values is what is best for them.[74] The procedural dimension is the collaborative commitment itself, which assumes that a better outcome for the whole family will be achieved by negotiation toward consensus. The collaborative retainer further complicates client autonomy in decision making by introducing some significant pre-existing constraints. Certain decisions – for example, the decision to litigate or to refuse to disclose information for any reason – would risk ending the lawyer-client relationship. While the premise of pressing for negotiation is compelling, and strongly reinforced by research on the impact of acrimonious divorce on families, especially families with children,[75] the consequence may be to impose on the client a strategic path to decision making that is more than simply procedural (avoiding litigation) and includes a set of implicated values about the family's "best interests." This makes it more important than ever that the client understands that these values are implicated when he is offered collaborative law as a process choice, and he should make that choice with as much information as possible and without pressure or obfuscation.

If a client is to participate authentically in decision making, the choices open to her ought not to be limited without her explicit and informed consent. This does not preclude the lawyer from making a recommendation or stating a preference – far from it. However, such a recommendation must be fully explained and some alternatives canvassed at least as thoroughly. Clearly, offering the client a single option or course of action and asking them to "decide" is not authentic shared decision making, whether this is rights-based adjudication or collaborative law. The fact that all but one member of the family bar in Medicine Hat, Alberta, have adopted a collaborative approach to family law raises a question over genuine client choices.[76] In a working partnership, the choices made by the client may not always jibe perfectly with the lawyer's own preferences, but without real choices it cannot be a real partnership. Once the client is offered choices and has been fully briefed on both their implications and the counsel's own preferences, the lawyer needs to be able to step back and let the client decide.

The interaction of information and choice goes to the heart of the adjustment we are considering in the lawyer-client relationship. One lawyer described the difference between a partnership approach and traditional representation as the need to be able to suspend her own judgment and let the client make her own decision: "To step away from finding the solutions for the clients. They have to find it for themselves."[77] This can be a difficult transition for both lawyers and clients habituated to the "old" approach. From law school on, lawyers are trained to take responsibility for directing their clients toward what they believe is "best" for them – in this way the lawyer-in-charge belief is seeded and sustained. Engaging in an authentic and open-ended dialogue both at the planning stage and throughout the implementation of a strategy runs against many of these instincts. Finding the balance between continuing to offer expertise – after all, this is what the client is paying for – and respecting the autonomy of clients in setting their goals and determining their best interests is complex and challenging, but it is key to successful lawyer-client relationships for the new lawyer.

Client Participation

> It completely caught me off guard at first. The first few mediations, I hadn't had any mediation training. My only training was the general attitude in the profession that this is a lot of horse crap and I had settlements hit me between the eyes and I couldn't believe my clients sold out on me the way they did. I was concerned that I had a serious client-control problem.[78]

This lawyer is describing his early experiences with bringing a client to a mediation session. Having his clients present redirected the locus of control in a way he did not expect and did not plan for. In informal settlement procedures, lawyers have far less control over the proceedings and need to be able to understand how their client will behave and how to relate to him throughout the process. The new lawyer needs to be able not only to minimize any negative consequences of the client being present but also to maximize the benefits.

So far this chapter has described the impact of lawyer and client working together on planning and strategizing more generally. The dynamics of control and decision making within the lawyer-client relationship are further and sometimes dramatically altered when clients attend settlement meetings with their lawyers. Whether in collaborative four-way, a mandatory mediation, or a judge-directed settlement conference, the presence of the client changes the practical dynamics of decision making. Instead of the lawyer bringing back a proposal to the client from the other side and presenting it to the client with her own overlay of analysis and recommendations, decisions in mediation may be made on the spot as new offers emerge or solutions develop.

The past thirty years have seen the introduction of a range of dispute resolution processes that either mandate or strongly encourage client participation. Jacquie Nolan-Haley suggests that the strength of the trend toward client participation changes the questions about the involvement of clients from "whether" to "how." She writes, "The critical decision-making questions in mediation are concerned not with the extent to which clients should be allowed to participate, but rather the manner in which lawyers should be involved."[79] Some might see such an assessment as premature, especially in light of the tactics adopted by some lawyers aimed at ensuring that the participation of their clients remains minimal and tightly controlled (see the discussion below), but it presages the significance of a change in practice that has fundamental implications for the balance of power between lawyer and client.

The particular nature of client participation has differing implications for the preparatory work that lawyer and client must undertake together, over and above the more general analysis and strategizing described in the first section. When lawyers are obliged to take their clients with them to mandatory mediation, for example, they must spend at least some time readying the client if only to ensure that the process does not come "off the rails." However minimal the client's role may be in practice,[80] the willing or reluctant cooptation of the client as a player in negotiations constrains the lawyer's autonomy to play out the conflict relying solely on his own strategies. Similarly, collaborative and co-operative lawyering protocols promote negotiation in four-way gatherings that include the clients.

Once counsel has recovered from the culture shock (described in the first quotation in this section) of sharing space in a negotiation setting with his client, the results can be very positive. One lawyer described the contribution made to negotiation by clients as

the intangibles that a lawyer can't bring. Like what was said at a particular meeting when the deal was done or what everybody's perceptions were of what was going to transpire. So that you can sort of retrace the chain of events that lead to the dispute and see where everybody's expectations have fallen short, not just the claimants expectations.[81]

Another lawyer told the following story to illustrate the way in which these particular clients reframed the conflict through their own prism of conflict analysis (which appears to be more about interests than rights):

In this particular case we were done by noon. I thought we were going to go all day because this particular person was ready for blood. She hated everybody ... then we get into the room and somebody just magically says something along these lines ...

Client 1: "Well, why didn't you say that before? And why didn't anybody call me? And why didn't anybody come to see my basement?"
Client 2: "Well, we did come to see it."
Client 1: "Well sure you did, you came a year afterwards, after I already sent a nasty letter to you" ...

We're lawyers, not psychologists, and we don't always know what's going on. The interesting part is, it comes up in commercial litigation and yet you think these are all rough, tough people, business people. You know, that's where it comes up because that's where the feelings get hurt, that's where it's personal, it's about an ability to run or operate a business, and that's personal. It may be about money but it's personal.[82]

Lawyers' attitudes toward preparing for and encouraging client participation in dispute processes are in many ways a litmus test for how far they are willing to share control and decision making more broadly in a partnership, or whether the old hierarchy will reassert itself. Inevitably, this is at least partly a matter of learning from experience. This means more than a brief conversation outside the settlement conference room or mediation venue (which is still typical).[83] Counsel experienced in mediation and other convened settlement processes have learned that bringing a client with them who is not prepared and has not agreed in advance on how to present the issues (for example, how much and what information to disclose, or what options to canvass) may be a recipe for disaster. As this lawyer reflected:

I am much more involved with the client in terms of what we're going to say and what we're not going to say in a mediation case as opposed to a standard litigation, because you just have to micro-manage what your client's saying in a mediation because if it doesn't settle, you've let time bombs loose.[84]

The uneasiness with which inexperienced lawyers often approach the participation of clients in settlement processes speaks volumes about how much it challenges conventional lawyer-client norms. Many lawyers, like the one whose quotation opens this section, fear that client participation will result in their loss of control. Sometimes the anxiety of inexperienced lawyers who are required to take their clients to settlement meetings is so overwhelming that they use their control to ensure that their client's participation is minimal and that the discussion remains dominated by the lawyers, with the goal that the lawyers will dominate the proceedings and their clients will simply be "wallflowers." Some lawyers are candid about the fact that they use this strategy. In the following examples, "them" refers to clients in general:

I'll warn them – I say if you're saying stuff and I can't tell you in a quiet way I will kick you – so they know it's coming.[85]

I teach them to "shut-up."[86]

Nancy Welsh argues that there is significant evidence of the assimilation of court-connected mediation (where lawyers are customarily required to attend with their clients) into a model of adversarial litigation practice. She writes that "court-connected mediation of non-family civil cases is developing an uncanny resemblance to the judicially-hosted settlement conference," hallmarks of which are a lack of direct client involvement and a focus on the legal arguments and their relative merits.[87] Whereas clients increasingly accompany lawyers to settlement discussions (either because they are required to under the rules of civil procedure or have voluntarily agreed to protocols such as collaborative law), many clients complain that their lawyers often fail to fully prepare them or to consult them on how to effectively use the process. In reflecting on the disparity between advocates for mediation (who emphasize "decision control" by clients who must consent to any agreement) and disputants themselves (who present more mixed assessments of their actual control), Welsh also argues that while lawyers assume their clients understand that their consent is required before an agreement is made, clients themselves may neither fully understand this condition nor be likely to experience a lawyer-dominated negotiation as being under their own "control."[88] This data underscores the fact that unless both lawyer and client embrace a new partnership model, new processes that are inclusive of clients will actually look and function in a very similar manner to traditional ones.

The efforts of lawyers to maintain complete control over their clients in mediation and similar processes has not gone unnoticed by their clients. There is some evidence that clients are often extremely dissatisfied with being excluded or silenced by their lawyers in mediation:

> In the first few mediations, our lawyer told me to speak only when I was asked a question, and the mediation was mostly an exchange between the lawyers. Then the city solicitor changed. He told me that mediation was really for the clients to talk, not the lawyers – that we can use it to do the [public relations] thing and if it's a legitimate case say sorry – and that he would take care of the legal issues. Now my feeling about mediation has totally changed.[89]

In some instances, exposure to mediation leaves clients feeling frustrated by their lawyer's unconstructive attitudes. Client participants sometimes note that they are more solution focused and less emotional and rigid than their lawyers. For example, as one client expressed:

> The lawyers' egos got in the way of the discussions ... it may have worked better without the lawyers being there.

> It seemed like the lawyers came in with more of a chip on their shoulders than the parties.[90]

The greater the experience of counsel with settlement processes that include the client, the more open (or resigned) they appear to be to accepting client participation. More experienced counsel come to regard efforts to exclude or silence clients as counterproductive:

> You can see some lawyers come in and they don't let the clients talk, they read the brief, they dominate the discussion, they're trying to push the mediator. And when that happens I go okay, we're not going anywhere, fine ... I think it's too bad generally because it robs the process of much of its practical value when you do that, because it controls the understanding of the clients too heavily.[91]

Counsel may even become sanguine about the potential risks of the client "speaking out of turn":

> I don't see the harm in it, if my client says off the record: "So you think

those things we delivered didn't work?" I don't really see that as really hurting me because probably my client's going to have to say that on discovery, or it's going to be proven out one way or another. So if my client says that in those circumstances, I don't think you're giving much away. It's going to come out anyway and, quite frankly, sometimes showing that bit of weakness is worthwhile if the object is to settle this. Somebody's got to give something.[92]

There is also a clear shift among this group toward identifying ways in which client participation can be used strategically and to effect in negotiations. These lawyers see the potential for the client to play a very practical role in proposing and testing possible solutions. A working partnership between lawyer and client aims to produce superior solutions – that is, superior to those solutions negotiated privately by lawyers or imposed by a judge. Involving clients in negotiation and mediation processes can significantly advance this goal.[93] Face-to-face interaction allows parties in both domestic and commercial disputes to explore their understanding of what feels fair and realistic and to refine details that might otherwise follow a standard or assumed path. There is room for "honest assessments of the big picture."[94] There is the potential for value-added outcomes that include creative substantive dimensions not forthcoming in other fora as well as secondary benefits such as enhanced communication and relationships.

Collaborative law provides a useful example of this phenomenon. While the substantive outcomes in collaborative cases do not diverge far from cases that are negotiated between lawyers, collaborative lawyers often point to aspects of a final settlement that are "value added" and context specific and that are unlikely to have been negotiated between lawyers alone in the absence of their clients (nor would such remedies have been available to a court). Examples include creative alternatives to support (such as paying for school fees or paying for a particular time period subject to given conditions) and custody and access arrangements (such as special oversight arrangements), which only this type of direct negotiation can really produce. Such alternatives may even include the negotiation of outcomes that exceed the legal requirement – sometimes described by family lawyers as "leaving money on the table" – which is generally discouraged by lawyers in traditional negotiations.

When clients participate in negotiation or mediation, the role of their agents in filtering and framing information is diminished. A settlement proposal can be presented directly to a client, instead of the agent presenting it to the client following the meeting. The client can consider the proposal on the spot, ask questions, or press for further enhancements rather than managing this follow-up via their counsel. Face-to-face communication between the parties is often critical to gaining sufficient momentum and trust to enable an interim, or "trial," solution. In arm's-length negotiation, lawyers may be anxious about committing to an interim solution in case of jeopardizing future claims, and clients may be less trusting about such an experiment if they have not been a part of the dialogue. Experience in mediation and collaborative processes suggests that including clients in the discussions opens up the possibility of exploring a temporary solution, which can then be reviewed by the parties after an agreed period of time.

Simply bringing the clients into the room to haggle over a proposal appears to have a significant impact on deal making – on its scope, its procedure, its timing, and its overall viability. This growing realization means that the new lawyer needs to take seriously the participation of their clients in dispute resolution processes and to work on constructively managing the consequences of this change, as well as their anxiety about it.

Affective Lawyering

The affective or emotional dimension of a working partnership between lawyer and client provides another important insight into the role and identity of the new lawyer. By the affective dimension, I mean the emotions – both positive and negative – that are created in the lawyer-client relationship. The traditional paradigm denies any emotions on the part of the lawyer, assuming that if she is acting "professionally" she will not be affected by any emotional response of her own. Similarly, any emotions manifest by the client are treated as something to be controlled and suppressed, lest they derail the lawyer's legal strategy.

Over the past thirty years, some scholars in the field of skills development and, more recently, therapeutic jurisprudence have worked to raise awareness of the usefulness of the psychological dimensions of the lawyer-client relationship (for example, the work of the late Andrew Watson and, more recently, of David Wexler and Bruce Winick).[95] However, this fascinating work has received little attention in legal education where it has been pushed to the margins. From law school on, young lawyers are taught to devalue emotional responses – both their own and those of their clients – and usually respond to a discussion of emotions with discomfort, followed by a chorus of "but we're not social workers!"

For these reasons, even opening a discussion of the emotional dimensions of the lawyer-client relationship might seem irrelevant, and perhaps inappropriate, from the perspective of a traditional lawyer-client relationship. In the traditional model, personal (emotional) and professional (knowledge) aspects of the relationship are clearly separated. The claim is that the lawyer can and should keep her emotions out of practice choices and decisions. Yet some type of human connection is part of every encounter, whether informal or planned, whether brief (buying candy from a store clerk) or protracted (making and closing a complex real estate deal). The same is true of every lawyer-client relationship, whether that connection is weak or strong, positive or negative.

Moreover, the emotional dimensions of the lawyer-client connection are in so many ways more complex and significant than the purchase of a candy bar from a store clerk. Numerous emotions, both positive and negative, are implicated in the way in which a professional advisor – whether a lawyer, a doctor, a therapist, or other – relates to her client at a time of crisis. These are what Marjorie Silver calls "intense, non-reciprocal relationships involving power imbalances."[96] Lawyers and their clients often work together at times of great stress in the client's life, and, for short periods, they may spend many hours together. This proximity produces an emotional intensity, yet the lawyer and client, at least in the traditional paradigm, are not "friends." After all, one is being paid to work for the other. In practice, many lawyers become emotionally invested in their cases, whether in the position taken by their own client, in the client personally, or in opposing the position of the other side.[97]

The rights-based approach to dispute resolution establishes clear boundaries between a technical-rational analysis (appropriate and relevant) and an analysis influenced by emotions or intuition (inappropriate and irrelevant). This distinction is maintained by the lawyer-in-charge, whose expertise is sustained by his superior legal knowledge (what one writer once called "legal pharmaceutics"[98]) and the exclusion of other forms of problem solving. In the traditional paradigm, the lawyer keeps the interactions between lawyer and client focused on law and legal solutions, conveying the message that emotional reactions to conflict are at best irrelevant and at worst an indication of embarrassing weakness. Lawyers who subscribe to this belief will resist being drawn into discussions that appear to have little legal relevance but that offer the client psychological support or encouragement. Instead, they model for the client the importance of separating emotional from legal considerations and not letting emotions direct legal strategy.[99]

The new lawyer's working partnership with her client cannot function effectively within such rigid parameters. A partnership requires a certain degree of mutuality – in goals, in power, and in action. The new lawyer must seek to reconcile her goals with those of the client and to make decisions jointly. Each must have some measure of power in the relationship – the lawyer will have superior knowledge and the client will have ownership of the conflict – and they each must understand how they will share this power in developing and implementing a strategy for problem solving. When lawyer and client "meet" in the space between their different worlds, there should be a mutuality between them. Both will experience some emotion, and this emotion will be another aspect of their mutuality.

Since legal education neglects to teach young lawyers about the affective dimension of lawyering, many lawyers describe their first encounters with live clients, either in the law school clinic or in a firm, as something of a seismic shock. They are meeting with a real human being who brings emotion, either under control or not, and who raises an emotional response in the lawyer. Naturally, there will be some type of human connection, good or bad, weak or strong, with each client. Affective lawyering looks at the meaning and impact of what happens in the affective dimension between lawyer and client. As Linda Mills explains, "This [the affective] method acknowledges that clients demand an emotional response, explicitly or implicitly, and that lawyers must have the skills to address the anger, frustration, despair or even indifference that legal interactions evoke."[100] Rather than denying the reality of human connection, the new lawyer aspires to understand how she responds to her client – with like or dislike, belief or mistrust, affection or repulsion – because this response inevitably affects how they will work together in a partnership. To avoid emotional responses that are unconscious and uncontrolled – for example, feeling dislike for a client, which affects negotiations on his behalf, or feeling strongly protective of a vulnerable client – the new lawyer needs to be highly conscious of her emotional response to each client and to identify her personal biases.

The relationship between the new lawyer and her client is based on a greater openness as they jointly plan their strategy based on a wider range of data that is both legal and non-legal and related to both rational and emotional needs. This approach reduces the formality and distance of traditional lawyer-client interactions and often results in a more personal, informal, and compassionate connection with the client. It also blurs the supposedly bright lines of the traditional lawyer-client relationship. Having let emotions out of the box, what should the lawyer do with them? Just how far should the personal connection go? The client relationships sought by some lawyers who embrace consensus building and settlement work may be unrecognizable to more traditional practitioners. Consider the following descriptions:

I open a dialogue with the client on a more interpersonal level – the connection is different.[101]

I am becoming much less of a traditional lawyer and much more of a coach. So the language that I'm using with you is language of connection, it's the language of support.[102]

I prefer the intimacy of client relationships that collaborative law allows ... I am no longer a lawyer to my clients, I am a friend.[103]

While this last comment was made by a collaborative lawyer, its description of personal friendship may resonate for many small-town lawyers whose practices sometimes focus on the personal affairs of several generations of the same families. Donald Landon has explored the relationship between country lawyers and their clients in his study of rural legal practice. Landon quotes one country lawyer as follows:

> Here in the country most clients are acquaintances. They come to you as friends. We've met most of them someplace before they come to the office – in the lodge, at a school or church function, or in the Christmas parade.[104]

Landon recognizes the complexities of "intimacy" between lawyers and clients in a country setting where most lawyer-client relationships are "multiplex" – that is, they coexist in other forms outside the law office. His conclusion is that this dynamic has tended to enlarge the lawyers' conception of their role and that they have frequently understood themselves as being "helpers" rather than simply technical advisors.[105] Landon also notes that closer personal relationships seem to result in a heightened sense of accountability on the lawyers' part, raising client expectations regarding easy access and loyalty.[106]

Long before the emergence of collaborative law or mandatory mediation, there has been extensive debate over the role of the lawyer as the client's "friend." Charles Fried first developed a notion of "lawyer as friend," emphasizing the role of a friend as a positional ally who fights ruthlessly for the advancement of his "friend's" legal position.[107] Those more skeptical of the notion of "friend" in a professional context have since pointed out that the lawyer-as-friend analogy works only if it is regarded as an "advantage-friendship" – that is, one in which the client pays the lawyer to adopt his goals and the lawyer adopts them because he is getting paid.[108]

Nonetheless many writers have pursued the notion of the lawyer working with his client in a supportive role that might be described in some way as a "friend." It is interesting to contrast Anthony Kronman's more recent model of supportive counselling with Fried's understanding of the lawyer's professional "friendship." Kronman does not reject the notion of the lawyer acting as a friend/supporter so much as the notion that a friend is always morally committed to fighting for their client-friend's position. Kronman's more nuanced idea of the lawyer as friend is reminiscent of earlier work by Thomas Shaffer and Robert Cochran, who advance a notion of "lawyer as friend" that represents the Aristotelian "moral virtues" of friendship. This assumes that friends take responsibility for raising questions of morality, integrity, and fairness with one another, motivated by both respect for the friendship and respect for the values of the wider community.[109] In short, their relationship is more complex and multi-dimensional than simply "fighting on the side of" the client, and may include giving the client-friend advice they do not like. This contention led Shaffer and Cochran into a debate with Jack Sammons over the dangers of "moral imperialism" by lawyers acting as know-it-all friends and assuming shared moral values with the client.[110]

None of these writers really imagined the scope and focus of the therapeutic relationship that some collaborative lawyers and others now see as a natural evolution of their new intimacy with their clients. While a desire for an explicitly therapeutic relationship is not universally or even widely shared by collaborative lawyers, some of them have dramatically and explicitly redefined their role in this way. These lawyers regard the provision of a supportive and healing environment for their clients as a central and perhaps primary aspect of their expertise. Understanding their role in this way raises obvious dangers of "moral imperialism" since these lawyers bring their own values and beliefs to the client relationship. These collaborative family lawyers often present divorce as a journey of personal growth. When they meet privately with their clients, they may offer diagnoses of relationship dynamics as well as coaching the client in how to be more effective in negotiation. They understand the lawyer's role as assisting clients in realizing their personal and emotional goals as well as their legal and problem-solving goals.[111] Consider this description by one lawyer:

> A part of my goal for them is to try to leave their dysfunctional communications systems behind and replace them, basically from the ground up, starting with baby steps, medium steps, and then larger steps, with the goal being that they replace the old system with a new communicative system [and do not] lapse back into the old dysfunctionality.[112]

The obvious danger is that lawyers are generally neither authorized nor qualified to undertake a therapeutic role. Some collaborative law clients, whose lawyers regarded their role as highly therapeutic, have pointed to a general lack of training to equip lawyers to offer this type of service (and often noting that mental health professionals are not only generally more competent than lawyers in this capacity but usually less expensive). Some describe their lawyers as being unable to cope with highly volatile emotions in four-way meetings other than by taking an ineffectual "please behave" approach.[113] Another problem is that clients go to lawyers expecting them to provide them with legal advice and, to some degree, to adopt an advocacy perspective on "their" position, and they are discomfited to find their expectation replaced with counselling, succour, and relationship advice.

Some mental health professionals who work with collaborative lawyers are even more skeptical, expressing concerns that there may be a blurring of the boundaries between their role – for which, they point out, they have been professionally trained and qualified – and that of a lawyer who assumes a more therapeutic relationship with the client:

> When lawyers begin to cross into the therapy role, there is a wobble there. Lawyers are not accountable about how they understand family systems theory, they can just wing it any way they want it.[114]

This focus on the lawyer as therapist has been prompted by the emergence of practice models such as collaborative and holistic lawyering. For most lawyers who are exploring new forms of working partnerships with their clients in negotiation and mediation processes, managing new challenges in their affective relationships with clients is less likely to concern their therapeutic expertise (which most lawyers safely assume they do not possess or, at least, are not licensed to practise) and more likely to relate to how to establish an appropriate personal relationship with the client in a power-sharing partnership. The challenge is how to act as the client's "friend" in some sense without creating emotional or psychological attachments and/or dependence. In a working partnership, lawyer and client are likely to have different types of conversations in which they touch on personal motivations and psychological pressures and which are often unrelated to proving the legal issues in the file. Naturally, it is almost always easier to advocate for someone one likes and trusts, and correspondingly more difficult to do the same for someone one finds less attractive and credible. Within the affective dimension of the lawyer-client relationship, there are many examples of transference (when the client projects onto counsel her emotions of rage, fear, or bitterness) and counter-transference (when the lawyer assumes some of these emotions as her own).[115] Some clients may want their lawyer to act as their alter ego, acting out their anxieties and concerns for them or bolstering the client to act tough. One client describes litigation as the means whereby "the lawyer becomes your surrogate angry person."[116] This lawyer describes one such client in the following way:

> The client has been giving me all this information and now he wants me to be out there, not only as his gladiator, but he actually wants me to build up his confidence about going forward. He's spending money and he's an individual, he doesn't have money to be able to pay the ridiculous fees that we charge him here, and yet he wants me to keep him driving along there ... there's a funny role you play in that process.[117]

Rejecting the traditional assumption that emotions and feelings can somehow be excluded from the lawyer-client relationship, the new lawyer should accept that it is inevitable that her personal feelings and biases will become woven into her lawyering practice. Most importantly, she needs to be able to recognize the most extreme cases when this involvement interferes with her ability to provide the most effective service – for example, when she has over-identified with a client's goals, or conversely when she cannot offer loyalty and commitment to a client because of personal feelings. It may sometimes mean that she cannot work comfortably with a particular client on a particular file.

This level of self-awareness can deepen the lawyer-client relationship in many positive ways. As well, there are dangers in the lawyer-client relationship becoming overly personalized. Some difficulties are practical – for instance, how do you bill a friend? Do you expect a friend to bill you? What are the boundaries of the lawyer's "friendship"? Other issues echo the Shaffer-Cochran/Sammons debate over the philosophical basis of friendship. Friends often believe they know what is best for many aspects of our lives that we would prefer them to stay out of, and the boundaries are sometimes less than clear. What are the boundaries of appropriate lawyer influence and when should they be crossed? Is there a risk that working partnerships could morph back into lawyer-controlled models of decision making by creating dependency relationships with clients? Does an overly "zealous friend" risk overwhelming her client with "the moral paternalism of the guru lawyer"?[118]

In these and other ways, the new lawyer faces both conceptual and practical challenges in recognizing and managing the affective dimensions of the lawyer-client relationship. Removing the traditional assumption of emotional distance and detachment on both sides casts the new lawyer into new and unfamiliar territory. Acknowledging the existence of personal connection – whether positive or negative, weak or strong – gives up the comfort of the (albeit artificial) boundaries between the lawyer's professional and personal reactions to a file, and between the client's rational and emotional response to their problem, and forces lawyers to think about how they should handle this aspect of their relationship with their client. There are many choices here and they do not require a lawyer to take sides in the debate over the therapeutic nature of the lawyer-client relationship – much will depend on the individual client and his or her needs, the experience and expertise of the lawyer over time, and in each case how her technical assistance relates to a potential role as a trusted supporter or friend.

As we begin to learn more about this and other aspects of a new working partnership between lawyer and client – in which "no one person is in control"[119] – we see that there is no rule book for how to conduct this relationship and, as yet, little in the way of role models for lawyers to follow. There is little or no effort to teach these ideas to law students and allow them to think about how the dynamics of a partnership might be managed. Instead, we are right at the beginning of thinking about what this means for the lawyer's professional role.

Challenges of a Working Partnership

The re-envisaged partnership between lawyer and client described in this chapter is different, but it evolves from earlier iterations of the lawyer-client relationship. A partnership model does not resolve all of the challenges inherent in the traditional paradigm, and, in fact, it creates some new ones. The continuity between the old and the new is exemplified by a classic dilemma that is common to both. When should counsel advise a client to accept terms offered in settlement and when should she resist and continue to fight? This is a dilemma that may be made more acute by a converse reaction between lawyer and client – that is, when the lawyer thinks the client should settle and the client does not want to, or when the client wants to settle and the lawyer thinks that he or she should hold out for more. The conditions and circumstances will vary widely, from a lawyer advising a commercial client who wants to settle as a result of internal operational pressures, even if not for top dollar, to a lawyer working with an Aboriginal band whose values and norms about fairness may be different from those of the Western legal system, to a client whose expectations continue to outpace what the lawyer believes is realistic in terms of settlement. However, the moral and practice dilemma comes down to the same question: How much pressure and what type of pressure should the lawyer put on her client? This dilemma is a useful motif for the lawyer-client relationship, in part because it is so common, but especially because it implicates so many of the choices and actions this chapter has discussed: Who participates in settlement discussions and in what capacity? Who controls the choice of strategy and outcome? Who ultimately makes a decision and on what basis? And what feelings does this process generate on both sides?

The impact of adopting the working partnership model proposed in this chapter is less on the substantive outcome of such cases and more on how counsel and client together analyze, reason, debate, and ultimately choose an outcome. For lawyers, the more specific challenge is how to move through this process of analysis and decision making in a role that offers their clients the best of their professional advice without imposing a paternalistic outcome.

When asked about how they resolve this dilemma, most lawyers in practice quickly acknowledge that the ultimate decision maker is the client. I have consistently heard this response in my research, regardless of whether the interviewee works in collaborative law or mediation, as a traditional litigator, or on non-contentious work for corporate clients. For many lawyers, their major concern is ensuring that they have performed sufficient due diligence in warning the client about the consequences of their decision to avoid a future malpractice suit.

What would be different about the process of counselling the client in this situation for the new lawyer, who aspires to a working partnership, compared with the old lawyer who holds to the three key beliefs? A lawyer who is heavily committed to rights-based dispute resolution will often feel that her advocacy role is compromised when her client says he is ready to stop fighting. She is also likely to feel that the client is "wrong" not to accept her advice, which is, of course, almost always superior to the client's own knowledge of the legal probabilities. She may also feel that an early settlement offer should naturally be resisted because the client has not yet had "their day in court" or the equivalent thereof in other formal and costly procedures such as discoveries or pre-trial. A lawyer who is less than comfortable acknowledging and probing the affective dimensions of the relationship and their own and their clients' emotional reactions to a settlement offer may be baffled by what appears to be a capitulation – or stubborn resistance – by the client in response to the settlement offer. This lawyer may be unaware of the emotional or psychological reasons that make it difficult for the client to accept the offer or impossible for her to refuse it. She may also be unaware of how much pressure she is placing on her client, or that this may be unconsciously fuelled by her belief that cases are best resolved by rights-based outcomes (which will affect her assessment of the offer – how close is it to an adjudicated outcome?).

The new lawyer should not let the three beliefs get in the way of a thorough and open discussion with the client that fully appraises each serious settlement offer. Her assessment of the offer will not be exclusively about its proximity to an adjudicated outcome, *if* the offer meets the client's needs. Equally, the timing of the offer – however close to the beginning of the litigation process – should not be an issue *if* the offer meets the client's needs. She may feel that the client could do better by pursuing further rights-based processes, but she will also help the client consider what the real costs of continuing litigation might be. When an offer appears unreasonable, unfair, or unlikely to achieve the clients' goals, the new lawyer will of course protect her clients – especially her most vulnerable clients – from exploitation. However, her professional identity is not dependent on fighting. She will regard the negotiation of a settlement – and providing subsequent advice on offers – as a central aspect of her professional role and not as a diminution of her advocacy. On the contrary, this process of discussing and assessing an offer to settle, both with the client and with the other side, is exactly where her advocacy skills are important. She must appraise what may be lost and what may be gained and assist the client to clarify her needs and goals. Recognizing that there are emotional dimensions to fighting or settling, she must also accept and incorporate the client's own data on the emotional and other non-legal consequences of either course.

In short, while the answers to this classic dilemma come no more easily for the new lawyer than for the old, the new lawyer has some new tools with which to undertake this analysis. The most important of these is a commitment to good outcomes that are not measured exclusively by the benchmark of adjudication. This means the new lawyer relies on a broader knowledge and understanding of the clients' goals and motivations, perhaps an established rapport with the other side and an insight into their goals and an acceptance of the potential significance of emotional factors for her clients. Moreover, in a working partnership, there will already be a prior history of working with the clients to resolve issues of choice before the question of a settlement offer is first faced.

The following two stories are based on real-life descriptions given by lawyers and their clients. The first is an account of a settlement negotiation told to me by a commercial litigator and presented here in his own words. The second is my summary of a story told to me in seperate interviews by a client and her lawyer on a collaborative case. The two cases turn on similar issues of decisions over settlement offers but in very different contexts. The additional contrast is that the first involves a fairly traditional commercial litigator and the second a committed (and trained) collaborative lawyer.

A Business Settlement

I acted for the defendant. We had a huge case in dollars and cents of sure business. I had what I considered to be a 100 percent case. You don't often get those. I know people have accused me of being a little bit opinionated sometimes in the worth of my case, but this was a good one.

My client did not want to litigate [earlier in the interview, this lawyer had said that he was aware that his client was approaching retirement and that he was very motivated to clear up this dispute before he left the company, and to leave without any "blemish" on his record]. I had $250,000 in my pocket to settle. This case wasn't worth $25,000 and wouldn't have cost more than $70,000, worse case scenario to litigate, but they wanted to settle. For the other side, it was a stab for some easy money.

I knew they would back off, but my instructions from my client were to settle this thing and do not leave that mediation without a settlement. I've got $250,000 of the clients' money in my pocket and every instinct in my body says: "This is stupid."

My client was sophisticated. My client was giving me instructions, obviously I have to follow my client's instructions. There's nothing immoral about them, nothing unlawful about them. So I have to follow them.

We went down there and we settled it for $165,000. $165,000 more than I thought the case was worth, so justice was not done. These people who sued picked up $165,000 that they weren't entitled to.

Was it a good settlement? My client was delighted. They had $250,000 in their pocket and they got out of there with $165,000 and one of the two people I was getting the instructions from thought we had won because he was able to go back and say I still have $85,000.

My job was to save as much of the $250,000 as I could. If I had to pay the whole $250,000, then I would have been really browned off. I was disappointed – but the client is as happy as hell and they're sending me something else. They're delighted with my handling of it. I'm not, I think I lost. I don't think we won, we lost. Justice was not done there.[120]

A Divorce Negotiation

A and B are negotiating their divorce using the collaborative law process. They have been married for twenty years and have three children, aged nineteen, sixteen, and ten. A, the wife, graduated high school but has not completed college – she has taken courses part-time on and off for years but finds it is always too much to juggle with child care and her job as a telemarketer. Her husband, B, has a college education and is a member of the Canadian Armed Forces. He has been offered a promotion and relocation to another city, which he intends to take once the divorce is finalized.

The main issue here is money – there is not a lot to go around. A and B want to sell their house and believe they will realize about $10,000 after the mortgage is paid off. A will remain in the town with the children and rent a home. The rental housing market is presently very expensive, and she is concerned about making ends meet. She makes $1,000 a month at her job.

Early on in the negotiations, before the first four-way, B begins to press for A to give up her share of his pension. A feels that this is unfair – and she is worried about money – but also wants to get the matter resolved. She wants B out of the matrimonial home and is afraid he will not leave until the deal is done.

A is worried that B will tell different stories to different people to satisfy them but ultimately will not be straight in the negotiations. She is beginning to feel that she needs to do the best she can and get it over with. She muses, "I could walk away with just nothing, I could say, 'Fine, you want it, take it.'"[121]

The two lawyers on the file agree that B needs a reality check on the question of the pension, and he is told that his wife has a legal right to share his pension. At first, B seems to accept this, but the issue comes up again once the four-way meetings begin. This becomes an impediment to a final settlement.

Between the four-way meetings, A discloses to her lawyer that her middle son – aged sixteen – is skipping school, and the school principal has called her expressing concern. She has not shared this information with B because she is worried that he may become very angry with his son. A's lawyer puts some pressure on her to put this information on the table in a four-way meeting. With some misgivings, A does so. At the meeting, B responds calmly enough. However, when he gets home after the meeting, he is very angry with their son, and A regrets revealing this information.

At the end of the collaborative process, A agrees to take 30 percent of B's pension. They make an agreement for monthly support. A remains in the matrimonial home paying the mortgage and the equity is to be shared once it is sold. A feels mostly positive about this agreement. She is relieved that she kept some of her pension entitlement and attributes this to the combined pressure of the two lawyers on her ex-spouse: "With both lawyers showing him what was fair it was not like me and my lawyer against him and his lawyer."[122] However, there is no doubt that A concluded the agreement partly because of a need for closure and partly because of a fear of emotional abuse from B, who was still residing in the home up to the point of the agreement. Her own lawyer was aware of these fears, but the other lawyer was not.

Analysis: What Would the New Lawyer Do?

In the business law story, the lawyer was extremely discomfited because he felt that he had not seen "justice" done. Nonetheless, his client was telling him that he was perfectly happy with the outcome. While the lawyer was aware of a likely motivation for settlement – the client's impending retirement – he did not directly discuss this motivation with the client. Had this issue been raised and discussed between them, without judgment, the lawyer may have been better able to understand the decision to settle. The client was a sophisticated individual who had presumably made a sound business decision. If the client had shared with his counsel more of his reasoning and calculations regarding the settlement – which may require the lawyer to ask him directly, or at least to indicate that this would be important information for him to have – the lawyer would have been better placed to offer an appraisal of the complete picture.

The lawyer's reaction to the settlement also suggests that he should examine his personal investment in a particular outcome. Despite his client's needs being met, the lawyer was dissatisfied. While counsel's goals and his client's goals are not necessarily synonymous – and cannot be expected to be[123] – it is important for the new lawyer to be aware of what personal values are affecting his response to his client and to the case. Why did he feel so strongly that the client should not settle? How much of this was due to the entrenchment of the key beliefs, and how much a well-founded fear of the client "selling himself short" in the settlement stakes?

The family case turns on similar issues, but in this case the client is a vulnerable woman negotiating a divorce and who has the continuing responsibility for her three children. Her decisions will have significant repercussions for her own future and for that of her children. It was vital that A's lawyer feel comfortable that A had explored all of her options, including holding out for a better deal. Interviewed after the settlement was finalized, A's lawyer justified the outcome in relation to the pension divison, stating that "her focus was on the present, not the future (the pension), and she needed a good deal for the present." She went on to say, "I suspect that so much will happen in the next twenty years that this will probably not be important to her by then."[124] Trained as a collaborative lawyer, she was conscious of the need not to insist on a conventional legal distribution of the assets when her client preferred another approach. She also wanted to enable his client, who on the face of it was very vulnerable and relatively powerless, to act as powerfully as possible based on her own judgment.

However, in the process, perhaps this lawyer underestimated the extent of the pressure being placed on his client, or was even unaware of its source. It is unclear whether A and her lawyer really examined all of the relevant information – including the behaviour of B, the husband, who for economic reasons was still living in the matrimonial home at the time of the negotiations, before A made her final decision. Both A and her lawyer recognized the practical reality that the settlement had to be concluded before B would be able to leave the matrimonial home. A did not have the resources to conduct protracted negotiation or litigation. Unfortunately, these circumstances created a series of inevitable pressures on A to accept the offer. There may have been space for A's lawyer to sit down with her client and discuss how they could enhance her BATNA (best alternative to a negotiated agreement), in a way that would allow her to reach a decision under less pressure. For example, perhaps there could have been a short interim agreement in which B moved out of the house at their shared expense. This would have been worthwhile for A if it relieved her from intense pressure to accept B's last offer. While the new lawyer must work with the realities of the client's situation, she should work hard to enhance them where at all possible.

While A's lawyer reasonably believed that it was important to put the information about A's son's problems at school on the table in a four-way meeting, in order to foster a collaborative dialogue (and better enable the parties to co-parent in the future), this incident demonstrates the risk of applying collaborative principles without regard for context. Disclosing this information compromised the safety and security of A and her son.

A commitment to openness – an important value for collaborative law – cannot be allowed to trump other considerations, especially when the client is vulnerable. Like any principle, aspiring to openness does not mean that this or any other collaborative value should be promoted regardless of context.

The story also reveals the potential of having both lawyers work together on a single issue. For example, A said she felt that having both lawyers talk to her husband on the topic of her pension rights was helpful. A similar discussion between all parties might also have been helpful in recognizing the problem of A making decisions under pressure. This story also suggests that it may have been helpful for the husband's lawyer to have been more in the picture regarding the intimidation being experienced by A. Perhaps A's lawyer underestimated the signficance of this or perhaps felt that he could deal with it without revealing this behaviour to the other side. In hindsight, this may have been a misjudgment.

Both these stories illustrate the fact that when clients directly participate in negotiations, their decision-making role is hands-on and often shortens the time frame between proposal and resolution. Lawyer and client need to fully understand each other's assessments and motivations going into such meetings. Both stories also serve as a reminder that in a new working partnership, the client makes the final decision. If the lawyer is satisfied that the client is making an informed choice, he gives up the power of standing or entitlement to complain that the outcome does not appear "just" from his perspective.

In different ways and to different degrees, these two stories demonstrate the capacity of clients, both business and personal, to make decisions that diverge from traditional notions of justice and fairness. Of course, this reality was part of the experience of the old lawyer also. Many commercial lawyers readily acknowledge that justice is often an abstract quality in business disputes. Many family lawyers would agree that cases often settle based on what is feasible and practical for the family, within the ballpark of legal entitlements rather than according to the strict letter of the law.

The situations and the dilemmas are the same, but what is different for the new lawyer is that he may more easily and comfortably accept client decisions, provided they are appropriately informed and are not coerced. Fighting is not his only advocacy role. For the old lawyer, no matter how many times this situation has occurred, his traditional beliefs and values do not help him in identifying a practical basis for resolving the tension between rights and settlement. In contrast, the new lawyer approaches his role in a way that ensures that he gathers from the client the additional information (information about motivations, goals, and needs that goes beyond what relates to making the rights-based case) he needs in order that they can jointly assess any settlement offer. In bridging the gap between formal rights-based justice and informal, client-chosen "justice," the new lawyer must above all ensure that his client is fully informed, aware of all possible options, and understands their choices. A new working partnership with his client enables the new lawyer to develop, practise, and rationalize this approach without compromising his commitment to the client's goals and interests.

7
The Role of the Law and Legal Advice

> When you practise long enough, you'll understand there are some brilliant legal arguments that are not worth making.[1]

The successful use of consensus-building processes to resolve disputes depends on more than polished legal arguments. It requires the new lawyer to be an effective negotiator, a good communicator, an assertive advocate, and a partner with her client in the business of conflict resolution. What then is the role of law and legal advice within consensus building and how do lawyers utilize their specialist legal knowledge in their modified professional role? To what extent does the growth of settlement processes presage the emergence of a new role identity for lawyers in relation to their expert and specialist knowledge of the law?

Advocates for mediation and collaborative processes sometimes appear to suggest that there is no role for legal expertise in these fora. This discussion may include assertions about "paradigm change" and hints that lawyers, not unlike recovering alcoholics, must completely forswear the use of law as a tool to resolve conflict. In this chapter, I shall argue that this notion of paradigm change misunderstands and mischaracterizes the evolution of the new lawyer's role and, more generally, the movement toward consensus building and settlement processes in law. Paradigm change is not required or necessary here – it is neither intellectually sustainable nor practically desirable. Instead, what is needed to complement the changes we are seeing in legal disputing processes is a careful reformulation of the place and role of traditional legal advice. This is a shift in emphasis rather than a rejection of technical legal advice and its substitution with something else. This shift entails harnessing the predictive power of law and a deeper understanding of the relationship between informal norms as well as recognized rules and standards in the resolution of conflict.

The Integration of Legal Expertise

Where does legal advice fit into the practice of the new lawyer? We have already seen that the new lawyer spends a large proportion of her time preparing for and conducting negotiations or collaborative dialogue with the other side in a dispute. Negotiation skills occupy an explicit and central role within the skill set of the new lawyer and are more highly valued than they were by the old lawyer. Negotiation skills for the new lawyer are also deeper and more complex than what is required to state and restate a positional legal argument. Nonetheless, the use of the law to predict alternatives to negotiation remains a critical dimension of skillful negotiation. In legal negotiations, the law provides the most important benchmark against which to appraise options and measure outcomes. Used in this way, the law is far more than a threat to go to trial – a threat that is rarely carried out and therefore has limited impact. Instead, it is a means of agreeing on an external standard or norm or agreeing to substitute another standard or norm that the parties find more appropriate and acceptable.

Second, we have also seen that in conflict resolution advocacy, communication becomes the primary vehicle not only for the making of arguments but also for the resolution of conflict, whether via negotiation, mediation, or another settlement process. A heightened emphasis on communication skills does not diminish the need for legal intelligence, but it does affect the ways in which such knowledge is integrated into discussion between the parties. Legal expertise is no more neutral in terms of communication values than any other frame of knowledge. Lawyers often present legal opinion (especially to the opposing counsel or party) as "just the way it is," without recognizing that legal advice always represents some form of interpretation and that the manner of the message affects the way in which it is heard. Instead of being presented as an immutable position, a threat, or an "unfortunate reality," predictive legal opinions in negotiation should be presented with as much sensitivity for the communication frame as any other negotiating tactic. For example, communication theorists point out that the continuous use of arguments that attack the goals of the other side (for example, by unequivocally stating a legal position) tend to lead to an impasse, whereas arguments that explore, and even attack, underlying problems and causes open up problem-solving discussions. This scholarship further suggests that the most credible messages are those that are direct and clearly outline consequences, rather than overstatements, ambiguity, or vagueness, which are likely to be less believable and have far less impact.[2] In short, legal arguments are still an important part of legal negotiations, but their delivery should be tactical – that is, they must recognize and respect the context of consensus building – rather than presented as unassailable and "given."

Third, the new lawyer strives to create a problem-solving partnership with her client, to the extent that that is feasible and desirable (for the client) in any one case. An enhanced mutuality of both purpose and action between lawyer and client requires that the client offer further and better explanation of some issues to the lawyer, and that the lawyer offer the same to the client. As we saw in the last chapter, a partnership requires a greater sharing of motivations and goals by the client and a more complete explanation of legal and other issues by the lawyer. In this approach, the client deserves no less commitment and skill in legal research and advice giving than the traditional paradigm, and may in fact require more discussion of the legal implications of the particular case in terms accessible to the client. However, it is also the responsibility of the new lawyer to ensure her client understands that law is just one way of approaching a principled basis for resolution. It is her obligation to be clear and transparent about the uncertainty involved in predicting legal outcomes, but a prediction is part of her professional responsibilities. Lawyers are sometimes guilty of over-anticipating legal outcomes by talking them up and/or neglecting to mention their uncertainty. Instead, a middle course that sensibly recognizes the impact of law as well as its limitations should be the goal for the new lawyer.

The role of law and legal advice in a model of conflict resolution advocacy is perhaps the most complex, contentious, and challenging dimension of the practice of the new lawyer. Like the changing nature of the lawyer-client relationship, it is a topic that we are just on the verge of exploring and understanding. There are no simple answers here. Suggesting that lawyers eschew the use of legal argument in a negotiation or not offer their clients specialist legal advice grossly underestimates the complexity of this topic. It confuses the symptoms of overzealous legal advice – for example, case inflation and positional bargaining – with the per se possession of legal expertise. Neglecting the use and application of legal knowledge to dispute resolution is not only a disincentive for some lawyers who might otherwise be willing to think harder and more seriously about conflict resolution advocacy, it is also a wholly inaccurate characterization of the integration of law and legal principles into the practice of the new lawyer.

What Is the Significance of Law in Consensus-Building Processes?
Despite the many new demands and the changes envisaged in the role of the new lawyer and the increasing importance of negotiation and communication skills, her legal expertise remains her primary professional qualification. The relationship between authoritative norms and principles, often in the form of laws, and conflict resolution advocacy does not

have the same seductive clarity as the role of law in the traditional paradigm. Yet it is a relationship that is critically important to the practice of the new lawyer.

The Social Role of Legal Norms

In order to settle disputes in a manner that feels just to the parties, reference to norms and principles, which are often legal norms and principles, is always important. Mediation theory has suggested a range of approaches in which parties determine what norms they adopt in order to resolve their conflict, whether these are "given" (by reference to societal standards or legal obligations) or created or "legislated" by the parties themselves.[3] Where the possibility for appeal to an adjudicator lies in the background, as it does in legal disputes, we should expect the role of formal norms to be even more pronounced. If the alternative to settlement is adjudication, and even where this possibility is, in practice, a statistically small one, it is important that the parties understand what the outcome might be if the matter were to be resolved according to legal principles (or, at least, according to a realistic "best guess" of what this might look like). This evaluation will doubtlessly affect the disputants' appraisal of the offers on the table. At the same time, counsel should ensure that their clients understand the infrequency of adjudication and the likelihood that settlement will occur at some point short of trial – a difficult balance to strike. The so-called "shadow" of the law[4] is an important predictive tool for when resort to law or a continuation to trial is a possible consequence of failure to settle.[5]

The relationship between legal rules and social norms is much debated. Legal rules and social norms are clearly not perfectly commensurate, otherwise every dispute, with sufficient resources available for adjudication, could presumably be resolved by an appeal to law. Even those who argue for increased adjudication and the wider application of laws to disputing would concede that not every legal solution meets each disputant's particular moral, cultural, and economic needs.[6] At the same time, discarding any reference to legal rules because of their potential to establish the interests of the dominant class or because of complaints that the legal system is oppressive to those outside that dominant group or class ignores the meaning that legal rules are given by communities that endorse them, albeit indirectly, via democratic processes.

Given the multicultural nature of modern Western societies, there is in fact remarkably little public debate over the appropriateness of laws, with some notable exceptions such as (currently) gun control, the legalization of marijuana, and abortion rights, for example. Whether this reflects a moral consensus or a lack of power on the part of dissenters is far from clear. Certainly not all laws have universal support, but in the West formal legal systems are a remarkably stable and consistent source of public values. Even when there is evidence of alienation or dissent from particular laws, law as an entity continues to have meaning for conflict resolution as a source of norms and values. In some cases, it may be the most important source on which disputants can agree.

The explanation for the remarkable support enjoyed by the legal system from large sectors of the community, including those who appear relatively disempowered or powerless to alter its form, may lie less in its substantive content and more in its symbolic significance as a source of social and moral stability. In other words, the use of law by disputants as a source of norms may represent an acceptance of its authority as much or more than actual agreement with its substantive content. This dynamic is evident when, for example, disputants seem willing to accept the authority of the law in the absence of personal knowledge (and therefore assessment) of the precise nature of these rules. Susan Silbey and Patricia Ewick have explored the relationship between "ordinary people" caught up in legal conflicts and the rules they assume or believe exist.[7] They find a widespread need to believe in a system of authoritative norms that frames credible, acceptable outcomes. Law is understood as being remote from everyday problems and yet crucially authoritative or, as Silbey and Ewick put it, "reified."[8] Thus, a belief in law takes on a value that is independent from the substantive merits of particular laws and, instead, is a belief in a system of law. Faith in the legal system and in its rules to create just outcomes appears to be highly normative among lay people who regard law as an impartial, objective, external norm that is separate and removed from everyday life (and therefore not subject to picky objections or trifling criticisms).

In this way, the law can "get away with" making demands that might not otherwise be acceptable. For example, Silbey and Ewick say that the number of references in their research group to waiting and time wasted in relation to the operation of the legal system "defies reproduction," yet this inefficiency is widely accepted without serious complaint.[9] As a result of its normative status, law influences behaviour and cultural tolerances for particular dispute resolution processes and outcomes among those without legal knowledge. In so doing, law plays a crucial role in dispute resolution beyond its use by lawyers to predict outcomes in a lawsuit.

Informal systems of norms besides law – for example, established social norms or widely practised customs – are also important in disputing and dispute resolution. Some consensus-building models explicitly promote the discussion of such norms – for example, where neighbours are invited to propose community tolerances for late night noise and partying or where business disputants draw on established industry practices and conventions. We know that the use of the legal system lies on the margins of real-life disputing, with just 10-20 percent of disputes involving more than $1,000 using a lawyer.[10] The influence of informal norms is especially significant in a culture in which "lumping it" or using self-help to resolve conflicts is highly normative. Informal but shared systems, which are often ignorant of or isolated from the "actual" law, are evident in many communities where they are crucial to practicalities of coexistence and cooperation. Robert Ellickson's study of cattle ranchers in Shasta County describes ranchers as settling their disputes not so much "in the shadow of the law" but, rather, "beyond the shadow of the law," with an entrenched norm against seeking monetary relief using litigation.[11] The ranchers have their own, sophisticated system of values and beliefs about justice and due process, which they use as an almost complete substitute for the legal system but which shares many of its features. For example, Ellickson provides an example of one widely followed convention that establishes just how much evidence a person must have about another's alleged wrongdoing before they can make public accusations against them.[12] He describes another norm that allows for a "freighted warning" (usually including the expression "or else"), after which an extraordinary remedy beyond damages would be necessary (in the legal system, the equivalent would be an injunction).[13]

Norms and values, often unarticulated, surround every dispute. Each conflict is framed at some level as an appeal to what the disputant argues are the dominant (most reasonable, widely recognized, and longest established) norms and the subsequent behavioral expectations (of response or redress). For this reason, we should expect to see a claiming of authority for a particular rule-based system in every negotiation, whether it is formalized as law or a community or industry value.

Law is one source of such norms, and it is a very important one, especially in legal disputing. An appeal to law, even in the absence of legal expertise, often has important persuasive force because of the "reified" status of formal law. When disputants take the further step of retaining lawyers, they expect a certain formalizing of arguments about norms as legal rights. Law and legal principles are a part of the normative framing that lawyers bring to a negotiation. When lawyers are invited to participate in conflict resolution, they must be permitted to use their legal knowledge to appraise the potential legal outcome. This type of assessment is an important aspect of how lawyers assist their clients in appraising their best alternative to a negotiated agreement (see the further discussion later in this chapter).[14]

To expect lawyers to effectively negotiate or mediate without reference to law is illogical and implies that law is somehow antithetical to effective collaboration. Moreover, such constraints deny clients a legitimate source of power that they are paying for by retaining a lawyer. Ultimately, legal advice is important in lawyer-managed dispute resolution because law is a critical part of the normative and procedural context for the negotiation.

At the same time, the new lawyer understands that legal norms are just one part of the normative structure that should be considered when evaluating settlement options and that it is for the client to then determine just how dominant these should be in negotiation and resolution.

Legal Frameworks Can Protect Vulnerable and Less Powerful Parties
Reference to legal principles in developing consensus takes on a special significance when such principles are necessary to protect otherwise vulnerable and marginalized parties. This function of law is a counterbalance to the criticism that law often protects the interests of the most powerful members of society. While dominant interests often seek to use the law to their advantage – and sometimes succeed – it is important to remember that lawyers can and do also use the law to protect the fundamental equality rights of less powerful parties.

There may be a misconception that negotiation and collaboration actively require parties to give up their rights. In fact, there is no reason why mediation and negotiation should not assume and uphold basic rights concepts. The use of rights principles in informal negotiations and similar processes is an example of the potential for the integration and complementarity of a rights- and interest-based approach to conflict resolution. Rights precedents, as well as widely accepted social norms of fairness, can and should be referenced when one party proposes an unfair, oppressive, or coercive outcome. Individuals buying legal services should expect the basic protection of the law, and more powerful commercial parties should not be able to take advantage of them simply because they are better resourced. Racial, gender, and socio-economic characteristics should not disadvantage any party in conflict, either in unfair or unbalanced procedures or in a prejudicial or biased outcome. Lawyers should ensure that any emerging consensus in negotiation or mediation upholds basic standards of equality and fairness. These need not be identical to legal protections, but they should not violate principles of equality, anti-discrimination, or oppression.

An explicit commitment to these principles may be an important first step for lawyers in setting the parameters and reference points of any one particular consensus-building process. Ellen Waldman proposes a model of "norm-advocating" mediation in which either counsel or a third party may insist that relevant legal (and perhaps ethical) norms are incorporated into any possible agreement.[15] For example, it is commonplace for jurisdictional regulations or guidelines on child support payments to be used as a general guideline in family mediation. A norm-advocating approach will not be appropriate for all clients since it may constrict the range of possible outcomes, a factor that should also be weighed in the balance. However, such an approach should be seriously considered, and explicitly set out, at the start of any negotiation when counsel believes there is a risk that her client may be pressured to accept an unfair or oppressive agreement, and/or when significant long-term rights and entitlements are at stake. Counsel has a clear responsibility to ensure that her client is not bullied or intimidated into accepting a prejudicial agreement, compromising important rights entitlements that she does not voluntarily cede and that have potentially long-term impact on the client or others. There may be a useful parallel here with the approach taken by many codes of conduct developed for mediators, which commonly require their members to withdraw rather than abet an oppressive agreement. For example, the Code of Professional Conduct of Family Mediation Canada includes a provision that the mediator should withdraw if they believe an agreement that is being reached is "unconscionable."[16] Similarly, lawyers should ensure that any emerging consensus in negotiation or mediation upholds basic standards of equality and fairness. These need not be identical to legal protections, but they should not violate principles of equality, anti-discrimination, or oppression.

Many of the concerns articulated about informal processes, especially by feminist and critical theory scholars, relate to a fear that informal processes will not protect basic rights and that the development of private agreements will undermine formal protections for those individuals otherwise disadvantaged in terms of resources, social status, and political power. Coercion behind closed doors can persuade less powerful parties to give up entitlements that seek to adjust the balance between their lack of power and the advantage of institutional actors and those privileged by gender, race, or class. The story of the divorce negotiation told at the end of Chapter 6 may be cited as an example of such dangers. Since it is in the nature of informal processes to develop their own norms, and sometimes waive strict legal entitlements, there are additional fears that the agenda of the mediator may skew the process and the outcome.[17] Feminists point to a well-founded concern that mediators may adopt ideological agendas and impose them on the parties. For example, in the field of family law, mediators may push the notion of family preservation and hold a bias toward joint custody.[18] Another theme in this critique is the risk that emphasizing the "emotional" and "personal" elements of a conflict delegitimizes the role of the law and rights entitlements and may distance the outcomes from these basic norms.[19] There are further concerns that informal processes are a form of second-class justice, assuming that those with power and resources will always prefer rights-based adjudicative processes. Informal processes may be more widely used by those who cannot afford the resources to access formal justice models, rendering them a source of systemic discrimination.[20] And where courts promote informal settlement processes, there is a further fear that this promotion represents an extension of state control, since outcomes that are not countenanced by law – and that are sometimes highly intrusive – become binding on the parties.[21]

In responding to this forceful and important critique, the new lawyer must be open and able to use rights arguments when appropriate in defending basic rights in negotiation and mediation, and especially when her client is vulnerable or susceptible to undue pressure from the other side. Critics are right to highlight the dangers for such a client of an informal process in which there is no adjudicator to impose rights-based outcomes, and in which the parties may often be considering some degree of deviation or waiver from legal entitlements. The new lawyer must work with her client to find the appropriate balance in each negotiation between party self-determination and rights protections. As we have seen, this dilemma is not a new one for lawyers, and already arises every time legal agents are involved in private ordering and settlement. Unlike her predecessors, the new lawyer has some new conceptual frameworks and assessment tools with which to manage this dilemma within the context of the new lawyer-client partnership.[22] Conceptually, the new lawyer accepts that in practice, parties will sometimes agree to outcomes that in some form or fashion diverge from their formal legal entitlements. Commercial lawyers can supply numerous examples of this practice (for example, see the story of the business settlement at the end of Chapter 6). Divorce negotiations also offer many practical illustrations, some of which have become so common, they are regularly raised by parties and/or their lawyers. Diverging from or modifying the relevant legal rule may amount to a restructuring of benefits (for example, an undertaking to pay the costs of returning to school in exchange for a lump-sum payment; or an agreement to delay sale of the matrimonial home or another asset where continued joint management benefits all parties). Alternatively, one party may decide in the course of negotiations to leave benefits to which they are entitled "on the table" – for example, a share of a particular asset legally classified as "joint," or entitlement to an unlimited period of spousal support.

Practically, any such divergence from a legal entitlement should be carefully evaluated, in light of as much relevant information – both legal and non-legal – as possible to ensure informed consent and the absence of coercion. Lawyers should be especially careful to ensure that clients do not waive rights as a result of oppression, intimidation, lack of knowledge, or lack of power. Both stories at the end of Chapter 6 suggest some of the challenges and complexities of this evaluation.

The critique of informal processes raises an important question to which we have, as yet, limited answers. To what extent do parties in consensus-building processes who are represented by lawyers waive or diminish their legal entitlements? Are waivers of rights mostly balanced – such as, for instance, in the example above of exchanging a lump-sum payment for college tuition – and how often are they apparently one-sided, such as in the story of the divorce negotiation at the end of Chapter 6? It is extremely difficult to answer this question empirically given the confidentiality of many agreements. It is also very difficult to quantify, other than monetarily, what is received in exchange for a reduction of a legal demand. The data available (on financial outcomes in family support negotiations) suggest that informal agreements may in fact achieve outcomes that are somewhat better than legal entitlements (in the sense of higher monetary settlements).[23] The answers to this question may also depend on the issue and forum. Neil Vidmar's study of small claims mediation found that accommodations in those cases reduced potential awards.[24] At the same time, it is probably true that we may feel less concern about small claims court litigants waiving "rights" in relation to final awards than we do about women waiving rights to support in order to secure agreement to, for example, their sole custody from their ex-spouses.

Within the small sample of the Collaborative Lawyering Research project,[25] there appeared to be little difference between the actual outcomes and the likely legal outcomes. When asked at the end of the case to compare the negotiated outcome to the likely legal outcome, all of the collaborative lawyers interviewed said that the substance of the outcome in collaborative family lawyering was no different or had very little difference from what they might have expected in a traditional litigation-negotiation process, especially in relation to financial support. When less predictable issues were involved, such as in mobility cases when custody was in contention, the negotiations proceeded on the reasonable assumption that while any number of arguments could be made, there was no clear legal outcome. As one lawyer put it:

> How different is this outcome from a litigated one? Not much at all. What is different is how they got there and what they are feeling about it.[26]

It is very important that informal processes continue to be monitored for signs of abusive or oppressive use against less powerful parties. However, fears over party exploitation and the waiver of legal rights may suggest that there is no place for rights advocacy within informal processes. On the contrary, formal laws and social norms are an important means of measuring fairness in informal processes. Law can and should be used as a means of monitoring and, where necessary, adjusting privately negotiated outcomes, by virtue of its moral strength and its authoritative nature. Where it takes the side of those who might otherwise be unfairly treated by more powerful parties or institutions, law has an especially important role to play in ensuring fair bargaining processes and equitable outcomes in informal dispute resolution. Lawyers are the guardians of these protections and carry the responsibility of ensuring that the law plays out its role even when negotiation and mediation takes place in informal, unmonitored settings.

Legal Assessment Is a Strategic Tool in Consensus Building

Legal research and evaluation have an important strategic and practical function in relation to deal making and settlement appraisal. I have already argued here that within a consensus-seeking model, the specialist legal advice lawyers can and should offer their clients offers a set of possible norms for resolution and sometimes provides important benchmarks for legal rights and protections. In addition, law and the legal advice that clients receive from their lawyers enables an appraisal of the risks and rewards of the options on the table at any one time. It is key to the development of intentional, realistic, and complete scenarios for what will happen if settlement cannot be reached. In this sense, predictive legal advice is an element of advocacy in negotiation and mediation.

The appraisal of risks and rewards inherent in potential resolutions is often described in conflict resolution literature as the best alternative to a negotiated agreement (BATNA).[27] The concept of BATNA has been popularized by Roger Fisher, Bill Ury, and Bruce Patton as a tool to assess the risk of continuing with a dispute. It suggests the identification of a hypothetical best case scenario if negotiation does not result in settlement before adjudication.[28] Examining a hypothetical "best alternative" to a negotiated solution, which usually implies, at minimum, increased costs, mounting levels of stress, and continuing personal and/or commercial uncertainty, provides disputants with a benchmark (often a "reality check") against which to judge the relative benefits and downsides of settlement. Research shows that general legal knowledge among one-shot litigants is very low, and thus the development of negotiation alternatives, both best and worst case, is crucial for some clients who need a reality check and who may otherwise overestimate the certainty and likelihood of their chances of success.[29]

Counsel's use of law in the development of an alternative to negotiation should be careful and not overstate the case, however tempting. Ideally, counsel should be able to stand back and review all contested legal arguments in an objective appraisal, which is then delivered to the client. Lawyers sometimes chide their clients for holding on to unrealistic ideas about what they might achieve by using the legal system. However, just as often, it seems, lawyers are themselves the source of those overblown expectations. Sometimes clients are initially painted an overly optimistic picture by their lawyer, only to be told to "face reality" further down the line when they are given a settlement offer. In developing an alternative to negotiation, counsel should be careful to be consistent and to carefully note the potential variables (which include the growing pressure the client may feel to settle the matter as time goes by).

Law is also a vital tool for identifying and determining important parameters and constraints that may sometimes be important for the parties to understand in reaching their own agreement. Legal advice often provides important information about the legal consequences of negotiated outcomes that would be otherwise unanticipated by the parties. For example, advice on the tax consequences of particular settlement options, as well as advice on any other regulatory framework that may impact the potential agreement, is often relevant for commercial parties. Finally, using legal evaluation as a strategic tool may supply enough pressure to bring the other side to the table to negotiate in the first place and perhaps to keep them there when bargaining bogs down.

For the new lawyer, legal advice does not and cannot stand alone, and it should be woven into other considerations including, for example, costs, timing, business consequences, and possible non-legal solutions. The concept of BATNA is incomplete if it is understood only as an assessment of likely legal outcome. The most complete and useful sense of "best alternative" is one that integrates anticipated legal outcomes with other consequences of not settling the dispute at that time. Legal advice should not be separated from other types of advice giving. A legal appraisal should be woven into the ongoing assessment and development of a strategy that aims to achieve the best possible result for the client, which is furthered by selecting a particular dispute resolution process, mediator, approach to bargaining, and, perhaps ultimately, a proposal for settlement. In the same way, delivering explicitly "therapeutic" advice (which most lawyers are not qualified to provide in any professional sense) without consideration of other relevant circumstances, including law, is an incomplete approach. Clients want advice given in context, and this context includes the law.

The use of BATNA as a strategic tool is not unknown to more conventional positional forms of bargaining, but its application takes on some additional aspects where it is used by the new lawyer to explore a range of settlement options in a consensus-building process. For example, counsel should discuss with their client not only their own likely legal outome but also the best case that can be made for the other side. This discussion will help counsel better explain a proposal that is within the likely range of legal alternatives envisaged by both sides. As well, the new lawyer should include in a discussion of BATNA an analysis of the integrative potential – a range of outcomes that offer benefits to both sides, or that cede to each side some of their stated priorities – that will be lost by an essentially distributive outcome based on likely legal outcomes (sharing out one fixed benefit based on the relative strength of the legal arguments). This analysis will offer the client a more rounded evaluation of the conflict and its possible solutions than a BATNA that simply focuses on the strengths and weaknesses of one's own arguments.

Legal Advice Is a Professional Responsibility

Finally, legal advice is a critical dimension of what clients contract with their lawyers to provide, whether in the context of negotiation or adjudication. Clients come to lawyers expecting legal advice, and this is a reasonable expectation. Yet, as the profession remakes itself in a new culture (and market) of conflict resolution, it is not always being met.

Those clients who express frustration with their lawyers' unwillingness to give them legal advice specific to their case complain further that some of their lawyers are unilaterally substituting another, different type of expertise, placing themselves instead in the role of therapist or counsellor:

I don't want to pay my lawyer to do therapy. I want my lawyer to give legal advice, [so that I] know my rights.[30]

I can do this [receive counselling] with a counsellor for way less. I don't expect to get the counselling aspect from the lawyer, but the nitty-gritty of the law – what is fair for each to demand. Those are the questions you expect the lawyer to answer.[31]

The current understanding of "legal services" includes legal advice specific to the client's case which requires at least some original research based on these facts and circumstances. Any other approach to the role of legal advice in consensus building – for example, "general" legal advice – demands transparency in the contract for professional services and may even raise questions about the appropriate designation of this as a lawyer-client relationship. Without an explicit, independently informed waiver, all clients are entitled to legal research and subsequent advice as a critical part of the exchange transaction between lawyer and client. Practically speaking, lawyers who avoid or even refuse to provide legal advice specific to their client's case, as opposed to a "macro" overview of the law in this area, may be failing to provide legal services in any widely understood sense. This approach raises problems not only for individual clients – some of whom are already dissatisfied with this method – but also for bar associations and provincial legal aid plans that might otherwise consider funding innovative collaborative processes that continue to use formal legal norms as a benchmark.

This emphasis on the provision of legal advice does not preclude, and in fact can enhance, the possibility of counselling the client on other sources of norms that may be more appropriate and effective for this particular case. It is important that clients understand that there are choices of norms. Lawyers are well placed to explain to their clients that norms other than legal rules, such as those described earlier, are often important in negotiations. There may be more willingness on the part of a client to recognize other sources of norms, whether or not they choose to rely on these, if they have first been given legal advice. The new lawyer may find her client more open to alternate, and perhaps more appropriate and useful, norms if she first attends to her responsibility to provide traditional legal advice.

The Limits of the Law in Consensus-Building Processes

Recognizing the importance of law in creating lasting agreements through negotiation does not mean that it does not also have limits, both practical and conceptual. Private ordering using informal negotiation processes, sometimes referenced to legal norms and sometimes not, is pervasive in all societies. Private ordering is one of the ways in which individuals exercise self-determination in a democratic society, and is itself an assumption of many liberal legal theories, for example, doctrines such as *caveat emptor*. People cannot be forced to contract into rights, they can only be offered them. Even before the sharp decline in cases reaching trial (the so-called "vanishing trial"), we already knew that the vast majority of conflicts are resolved privately rather than in court. This means that law will often be peripheral to dispute resolution.

The following sections address some of the practical ways in which dispute resolution within a system of laws is inevitably constrained and helps explain the widespread use of private ordering. They also point to some of the ways in which the new lawyer can be instrumental in facilitating fair agreements that substitute alternate substantive and process norms.

The Limits of Legal Remedies

The remedies made available to disputants via the legal system are behavioural. That is, they generally require certain actions to be done or ended (on pain of punishment, although such punishment is usually minimally effective). By far the most common remedy is an award of damages, which monetarizes the harm done or the value of the right infringed. This focus on monetary remedies means that the options generally in play in a negotiation where legal argument dominates tend to conform to these same monetary models. Inevitably, this has the impact of limiting the potential creativity of both lawyers and clients and, perhaps worse, means that any other proposed solution is difficult to compare with a legal (strictly monetary) outcome.

The only time legal remedies go beyond monetary outcomes is when they require certain acts to cease (injunctive relief) or, in rare circumstances, the specific performance of an obligation.[32] The direct impact of legal sanctions is therefore, at best, that they affect behaviour, whether by requiring a payment in compensation or proscribing certain actions. Yet resolving a conflict often requires closure in a number of ways that go beyond the completion or cessation of certain behaviours. Bernard Mayer suggests that people have conflict resolution needs along three dimensions, of which behaviour is just one – the other two dimensions are cognitive and emotional.[33] When there is emotional resolution, a disputant can feel less intensely about a conflict, stop emotionally depleting themselves by brooding on the conflict, and feel as if it is now a thing of the past. While divorce has a legal ending point (the final decree), many people who go through the procedure say that there is a moment at which they finally "feel" divorced, regardless of the stage of legal (or behavioural) resolution. Cognitive resolution occurs when a person's beliefs and perceptions about a conflict are changed – for example, when they recognize a range of reasons for the injury they have suffered rather than holding fast to the rigid assumption that the other side deliberately and maliciously harmed them. This example illustrates just how complex and difficult it is to achieve cognitive change, which may occur long after there has been behavioural and even emotional resolution. Yet, ultimately, all three dimensions tend to develop in tandem and to support one another.

Legal remedies generally do not provide for cognitive and emotional resolution, and few lawyers or clients would suggest that they do. Sometimes – for example, when a judgment cannot be collected – legal remedies do not provide for behavioural resolution either. There may be a sense of satisfaction of being "done" when legal proceedings or negotiations are completed, but there may also be a pervasive sense that a focus on purely legal arguments and remedies somehow misses the "real" problem. Some clients continue to feel a lack of closure, even when they have won their case.[34] To be fair, most lawyers would not encourage their clients to believe that they could expect to obtain emotional or cognitive resolution using legal procedures for dispute resolution. Changing one's perceptions of the other side almost certainly requires setting aside a positional rights-based argument, and emotional progress or closure seems less likely when the parties remain at arm's length and deal exclusively through agents. In contrast, mediation and other dialogue processes open up these possibilities, with or without legal (behavioural) resolution. Clients in mediation speak about the satisfaction of talking face to face, whether or not they achieve a legal resolution. For example,

"David," a corporate client involved in a contract dispute, said that he was able to gain more information than he would have in any other process, because the discussion was not constrained by the law. Mediation helped the parties reach an agreement, although the resolution was not finalized for two or three months after the session. He assigned importance to being able to speak honestly, without fear of legal repercussions: "It helped me to offload where I couldn't before"; "I felt I had something to say and to contribute to the process."[35]

For some clients, this chance to talk face to face leaves them feeling better about the dispute. An individual involved in a debt collection with a large organizational plaintiff described his experience as follows:

[The process] gave me a chance to express my complaints ... I felt quite at ease and was able to express what I wanted to express, and the [other party] was able to express their concerns. We were both listening and talking. It had a good feeling in that respect.[36]

Achieving a measure of cognitive or emotional resolution does not exclude a legal remedy, of course. However, it often requires an intentionally constructed process, which probably includes face-to-face discussion between the disputants, making space for the discussion of issues beyond the securing of legal remedies. In mediation it is sometimes the case that despite the willingness of one party to provide a remedy similar or even identical to what is demanded, the other side is still not willing to agree. This can be extremely disorienting for counsel who may be unable to understand this resistance to a substantively satisfactory offer as anything other than stubbornness on the part of her client. However, the real reason for this situation is almost always the existence of an unmet need in resolution, beyond what the legal remedy may offer. The new lawyer should recognize a refusal to accept an apparently reasonable offer as an important clue to resolution. As well as the behavioural resolution, it may be that an apology or an acknowledgment is needed, or that a gesture of taking responsibility needs to be made by the other side. Or it may be that a procedural adjustment is required in order that the party to whom the "reasonable offer" is being made can feel fairly treated and really listened to.

Securing a legal remedy, by which we virtually always mean financial compensation, is by no means always the answer to a hard-to-settle case. In most cases, the client will settle only when he feels that his reasonable expectations (from his perspective) have been met. For sophisticated and one-shot clients alike, these expectations sometimes require both a process and an outcome that recognizes the need for cognitive and/or emotional resolution *as well as* a behavioural outcome. The sources of individual expectations are both complex and highly diverse. They reflect our past experiences and the values that we have formed as a result. Since expectations are highly personal, they are often implicit rather than explicit and are felt rather than known, and they may or may not be capable of rational articulation. Yet the individual expectations of the parties – both the expectations that brought them into open conflict in the first place and those they now hold for the outcome of the dispute – are a critical element in the internal dynamic of disputing.[37] In a litigation model, the expectations and aspirations individuals bring to their disputes are often hidden or obscured by the need to fit their personal accounts into a series of generic legal definitions of both injury and redress (the "stock stories" of legal pleadings).[38] Limiting the consideration of possible solutions in collaboration to legal remedies has numerous drawbacks for negotiators. This approach is unlikely to leave the parties feeling satisfied no matter what the outcome and will unnecessarily limit the range of options that have been examined and discussed. It may also be a symptom of a wider issue: that the problem itself has been misidentified or under-diagnosed.

An Exclusively Legal Analysis May Miss a Larger Problem

Framing a negotiation issue only in terms of legal principles will always exclude practical options that may be acceptable to the parties. This is true no matter what the context and no matter who the parties are to the dispute – whether they are business parties seeking a practical commercial solution, family members trying to resolve conflict among themselves, or larger organizations dealing with their own employees or third parties. Legal principles are one, albeit critical, frame for understanding the causes of conflict and possible routes to resolution: they work best when the parties see minimal or no integrative potential and require a short-term fix. They are rarely sufficient to establish a future relationship because they rarely impact the origins of the conflict.

For example, relying on a wholly legal framework is unlikely to resolve long-term problems such as poor relations between trading or investment partners, co-parenting between acrimonious spouses, or workplace culture or productivity within a corporation. This is not only because a legal remedy is incomplete as a durable and long-term solution to the conflict but also because it obscures or overlooks other issues that may not admit clear legal arguments and redress. A legalistic approach to the problem is unlikely to enable resolution of the deeper underlying issues that caused the problem in the first place – for example, different parenting styles, poor workplace morale leading to high absenteeism, systemic discrimination or harassment issues, or ineffective or inadequate communication systems. A narrow legal approach to understanding the issues may even suppress some of the most important elements of the conflict – for example, articulating differences in parenting styles and the impact on the children themselves; poor leadership within the corporation or perhaps the transition from one management culture to another; or inadequate conflict monitoring and early resolution systems.

The element of the conflict that is often lost if the dispute is framed in purely legal terms relates to the parties' implicit and frequently unarticulated expectations about the standards of fairness appropriate behaviour "manners," reciprocity, apology and forgiveness, and so on. The application of legal rules and arguments to a conflict may narrow or even obscure an underlying issue that is critical to resolution.[39] I once worked with two parties disputing over a monetary hold-back on a private residential property sale. The reason given for the hold-back by the purchasers, the new owners of the property, was that they had found water leaking into the basement after they took possession. At the time of the mediation, an offer had been made by the new owners to the vendors (a couple) that represented most, although not all, of the hold-back. However, the vendors would not even consider this (apparently reasonable) offer. In private caucus, the female vendor revealed a key event in the development of the dispute that had not been mentioned in the pleadings for either side or in the earlier joint session. This event was the destruction and removal by the new owners of a child's playhouse that had stood in the backyard of the property. Evidently, it had been agreed between the parties at the time of the sale that the vendors would return for the playhouse a few days after the transfer of ownership.

The playhouse had great sentimental value for the female vendor. Her expectation was that the purchasers of her old home would appreciate that the playhouse was important to her and would allow her to return to collect it, despite their disappointment with the state of the basement. When they did not follow through with their undertaking to allow her to remove the playhouse, it became a significant part of her grievance against them, and she felt unable to discuss settlement of the hold-back issue without first raising this issue. Once the issue of the playhouse was formally added to the agenda, the substantive matter of the hold-back settled quickly. The female vendor explained to the new owners the basis for her expectation and received a simple but genuine apology, which acknowledged the sentimental value of this playhouse for her. The new owners – a childless couple – were also able to explain that they were unaware of the full significance of the playhouse and that their expectation had been that the dispute was simply a monetary negotiation over the hold-back. The reduction of individual expectations in this case to form pleadings had obscured what was for the female vendor a central part of her reality and a key issue in the conflict for her. The pleadings had not disclosed this issue and neither had the lawyer been told of it, but it represented a critical obstacle to settlement.[40] The result was that settlement was promoted by the discovery of a brand-new "issue" that had not been previously set on the table for discussion because it had not formed a part of the legal framing of the dispute.

Legal Principles Are "Culture Blind"

Legal principles inevitably reflect dominant cultural values and may not identify the particular cultural norms of the parties. However, in order to assert an authoritative and universal status that rests on fairness and justice, legal norms must claim to be equally applicable to all persons of all cultures: in effect, that they are "culture blind." This fiction must be assumed if the core values of the legal system and its procedural rules are to be acceptable and meaningful to all persons of all cultures.

This is an obvious over-simplification upon which a growing body of scholarship casts serious doubt. The cultural background of the disputants, primarily their ethnicity or gender, is often a significant factor in preferring certain processes over others and in setting particular goals (for example, community harmony or individual recognition and reward).[41] Generalizable conflict orientations and bargaining styles have been described for certain groups, once again primarily distinguishable in terms of ethnicity and gender.[42] Some work has also attempted to relate conflict style to socio-economic status, measured according to income and education.[43]

Despite the cultural specificity with which individuals and communities approach conflict resolution, an appeal to the law and legality is sometimes an expression of an identity claim: "People turn to legality to assert values, rights (their own or others), or even some conception of justice."[44] Appeal to law sometimes seems to endow a claim with an extra level of moral authority (notwithstanding that this "reified" notion of law and legality usually does not relate to any actual or specific knowledge of the law). In reality, the underlying cultural values of the law that governs the situation may be quite alien to the values of the individual who assumes its force.

Meaning making in conflict – how people make sense of and understand their experiences – draws on a complex and highly diverse web of influences. Culture in the context of conflict needs to be understood as more particularized and pervasive than broadly drawn distinctions, such as ethnicity and gender or contextual or institutional norms. "Personal culture" in the disputing world includes all of the values and beliefs that affect how each individual understands his or her experiences of conflict, whether these are derived from family upbringing, religious affiliation, industry or sector experience, and so on.[45] The behaviours that our cultural norms direct us toward, and guide us to expect from others, represent the beginning of our theory of any conflict we find ourselves in and the assumptions that will guide our future responses and behaviours. Once made, these assumptions will drive our interpretations of future events and our responses to them – months or even years into a lawsuit – and as time goes on they become harder than ever to shake.

Cultural variables are present in every conflict. As one writer describes it, culture is not a variable but, rather, "the law of variation" in conflict analysis.[46] This means that the universalism claimed by the legal model is neither realistic nor effective in recognizing the impact of cultural variables on disputing and dispute resolution. The misapprehension that the law is culturally neutral – in its language, procedures, and rules – obscures the significance of cultural expectations and assumptions in disputing, and limits the potential of the law to consensually resolve conflicts in a number of ways. Disputants may become disillusioned when they find their expectations of the law disappointed – that it is not in fact supportive of their actions or that it uses processes they find intimidating, inconvenient, or otherwise discomforting. They may feel that the law cannot help them or address their problems and so they become a part of the silent majority who simply "lump it" when they find themselves in conflict. Second, its claim to universalism means that law has few if any mechanisms for identifying personal cultural norms or cultural misunderstandings between disputants and even fewer for addressing these in process or in outcomes.

I once worked with a First Nations community where two lawsuits had been brought by band members against the Band Council, one involving an employment matter and the other a construction dispute. Each plaintiff had hired a Caucasian lawyer from outside the community, and the Band Council had gone to their lawyers (also non-Aboriginal) for advice. Each case followed the same pattern. In each case, a settlement had been proposed by the plaintiffs' lawyers and then considered by the lawyer for the Band Council. In each, the defence lawyer recommended that the chief and council reject the settlement offer, advising them that the plaintiffs were unlikely to do as well in court. I was asked to co-mediate both disputes along with a band member. The parties in each lawsuit decided in advance of mediation that they did not want their legal representatives present nor did they wish to review any settlement proposals that emerged from mediation with their counsel before making a decision. Since my own cultural norms suggested that for a party to entirely dispense with legal advice might be prejudicial to their interests, I spent some time checking with each side that this was indeed their wish, and going over the implications with them of making a binding agreement in mediation. My co-mediator, a respected band member and a lawyer herself, assured me that the parties were comfortable with this arrangement. In fact, they would not agree to mediation on any other basis. Everyone was clear that an agreement reached in mediation would be a matter of honour, agreed fairness, and a decision for the community, and that they would not seek legal advice on any such agreement.

Both disputes settled in mediation. In each case, the amount agreed in settlement, plus a series of non-monetary undertakings, was considerably higher than the sum that the Band Council's lawyers had advised them to reject in the earlier settlement offer. Each settlement was taken to the full Band Council for review. No one there suggested that the fact that the settlement sums were higher than the earlier offers the council had been advised to reject by their lawyers was a relevant consideration. Instead, discussions were limited to the perceived fairness, appropriateness, and practicality of the settlement in each case. Once satisfied, the Band Council members ratified the settlements, and the suits were discontinued.[47]

These cases and their outcomes (extraordinary to the mediator and to counsel but evidently normative for the disputants and their Band Council) illustrate the limits of legal principles in resolving disputes within cultures that do not "own" or recognize these same principles. The law is only minimally efficient in resolving disputes that have a significant cultural (personal, institutional, ethnic) element, at best providing a touchstone for how one particular culture (not their own) would deal with this dispute. Addressing cultural variations is an important part of the work of negotiators and mediators – and, hence, also of lawyers – in developing processes and outcomes that are responsive to these types of differences.

Each of these limits on the use of law in consensus-building processes should alert the new lawyer to an additional important reality: that client decision making regarding the settlement of lawsuits is not always based on those rational, objective, and tangible factors that are the product of a discourse between lawyer and client regarding the application of the law. For a minority of disputants, predictive data regarding legal and other consequences will be sufficient by itself for them to decide whether or not to continue with a dispute. Characteristically, these are clients who are distanced from the conflict – both its origins and its ramifications – and who feel little or no personal investment in the outcome. While such disputants do exist, they are a very limited group, even in the corporate context, and it is quite unusual to find a corporate decision maker who regards the dispute as both someone else's fight and of no personal consequence. Rational decision making based solely on predictive legal advice is rare, and may say more about the relationship of trust that exists in such cases between lawyer and client than it does about the power of the law to meet both the objective and the personal elements of conflict resolution.

Instead, the new lawyer should assume that her predictive legal advice will represent just one – although perhaps the most important – factor in the client's decision over continuing or settling a dispute. She may also anticipate that where her legal advice conflicts with the clients' other instincts, both conscious and unconscious, it will probably be overridden. The new lawyer should be aware that conventional legal risk appraisal alone, especially when offered at an early stage in the file, often feels remote from the disputant's construction of the conflict,[48] and may undermine the potential for settlement. It may even lead to entrenchment. Disputants tend to override expert advice when the assessment of experts feels irrelevant to the disputant's actual experience of the conflict. Alternatively, expert advice may be accepted because of its authoritative source, but the disputant's continuing ambiguity will resurface in other ways (commonly in last-minute roadblocks to settlement or in non-compliance with the terms of settlement). These types of dynamics are symptomatic of an over-reliance on legal models of analysis and redress, without appreciating the other influences that affect judgment over resolution and sometimes relegate law to the sidelines.

Misapprehensions about the Impact of Law on Consensus Building

> I give as little legal advice as possible, because there is so much contamination and you are trying to get them focused back on life issues.[49]

This quote illustrates an attitude expressed by some lawyers whose commitment to collaborative processes appears to amount to a rejection of law as a tool in these negotiations. Some collaborative lawyers feel that giving legal advice is no longer appropriate in their new role. For example, as one lawyer expresses, "I don't give any legal advice and am very careful not to even be too directed towards idea suggestion."[50] Other collaborative lawyers say that they are unlikely to do much legal research specific to a client's case and provide clients with only "general" legal advice. As one lawyer explains, "I don't give clients [specific] legal advice in the briefing or in the initial interview – I macro it."[51] Clients of collaborative lawyers sometimes complain that they have not received legal advice specific to their case but, instead, have only received vague generalities.[52] Their lawyers appear to believe that providing them with legal advice will only harden their positions. Glimpses of this same assumption that law is "contaminating" also appear less frequently in discussions among mediators, both lawyers and non-lawyers.

These lawyers express a concern that speaking about the law may unnecessarily and prematurely close down the consideration of a range of options for resolving the dispute. For example, one lawyer states:

> You know, we're very rights-based and we're very based on what our legislation, our province says and all that kind of thing. And we've really put that aside to a large degree. I mean, again, we have an obligation to make sure that people know what the court might do, which is, I think, as we get older, increasingly hard to figure out. But instead [we] favour options, what are the options ... So what we try to avoid is saying: "You have the right to do this and these are your rights, these are your legal rights," overtly.[53]

While this lawyer articulates a legitimate concern that clients may grab onto a legal appraisal and then refuse to consider other options, the rejection of law as a tool to resolve conflict is both an overreaction (the notion that any mention of law will doom a collaborative negotiation) and an oversimplification of the relationship between law and conflict resolution. As this chapter has sought to demonstrate, law inevitably provides some of the norms that can be called into aid in a conflict. Ignoring or minimizing its role fails to recognize the usefulness and power of law as a social system of norms. Where a matter is already part of the litigation system, adjudication on the basis of legal principles is the context within which negotiation will take place, however unlikely it is that a trial will result. Moreover, as this chapter has argued, a sense of "law" is rarely irrelevant to the outcome of a dispute, whether that is occurring inside or outside formal litigation. What disputants think about the law – what they think it is and what they think all of it means – is a critical aspect of almost every dispute handled by a lawyer.

There is also a whiff of paternalism in the way some collaborative lawyers describe the need to keep the law "away" from their clients. For example:

> The black letter law impacts too harshly, and the clients think too black and white – this way, the clients come up with more creative solutions.[54]

The new lawyer should assume that her clients are capable (with her coaching) of discriminating between legal principles that may be used strategically to drive or enhance an outcome and those that risk escalating the conflict by oversimplifying the issues. A failure or refusal to provide specific legal advice, however it may be rationalized, is also a breach of the professional responsibilities a lawyer owes her client, absent an explicit waiver. In the partnership between the new lawyer and her client, detailed and specific legal advice is one of the tools the client is offered to deal with the conflict. How this information is used in bargaining is for lawyer and client to determine, but first it has to be provided. A unilateral determination by the lawyer that legal advice is not "appropriate" or "relevant" or may be "contaminating" is not an acceptable professional choice. Lawyers can and should always point out to clients that the legal outcome is uncertain, unpredictable, or may be affected by factors beyond their control (for example, which judge sits on the case). They can also, if they wish, advise clients that a better and more lasting solution would invoke the shared norms of the parties (whether or not these have a strictly formal legal basis). Lawyers should trust their clients to manage this information and not withhold legal advice because of fears that it will destroy the possibility for consensus.

How Conflict Resolution Advocates Can and Should Use the Law

Participating with one's client in processes exploring resolution and settlement does not negate the use and application of legal knowledge any more than it negates the role of advocacy on the clients' behalf. Conflict resolution advocacy requires a thorough appraisal of the impact the law can and may have on the outcome, and what other means may be available for determining an outcome that is acceptable to the parties. It challenges counsel to understand and know both when law can be effective in moving toward just resolution and when it impedes, constrains, or obscures possibilities. Combining legal expertise and consensus building does not eliminate the relevance or use of legal knowledge or render it somehow redundant for the new lawyer. Instead, the process of consensus building changes the context in which advice is provided and expands its practical and strategic applications. It requires that the new lawyer pay attention to the usefulness and appropriateness of legal norms in this particular negotiation, rather than promoting the law as a general and often unidimensional approach to dispute resolution.

Raising legal issues in consensus building is one means of framing the process of dialogue in a particular way, by incorporating legal norms and alternatives to agreement. As this chapter has argued, raising and promoting rights issues is especially important where there is a danger of an unfair agreement between notably unequal parties. In this way, both interests and rights dialogues are integrated into a dialogue that emphasizes persuasion over compulsion. Neither one substitutes for or overrides the other, and ideally each complements the other in order to produce the best possible outcome for the client. One way of imagining this integration is that counsel must maintain bottom lines (for which a predictive legal outcome is often important and useful) and work to get the best possible deal for his client, but that in practice this will only happen if the other side can be persuaded of the fairness and value of the same bargain.[55]

The relationship between law and dispute resolution is similar to the relationship between rights and interests, positions and interests, or distributive and integrative models of bargaining. Each is less the opposite or a contradiction of the other than the other side of the same coin, reflected in a difference in "depth of analysis and style of presentation."[56] Interests are not the antithesis of positions, but they are the uncovering of the motivations behind the purpose stated in the position. In self-interested bargaining, the position implicates the interests, and the interests sustain the position. Similarly, the legal principles involved in any one dispute are not the antithesis or the contradiction of other possible solutions the parties may agree on, but another dimension of the resolution of the same conflict, representing another choice for the parties. Some aspects of the dispute may be best resolved using legal principles (for example, the distributive elements), and others may require creative problem solving that reflects the strengths and weaknesses of each side's legal alternatives. Understanding the relationship between law and informal dispute resolution in this way avoids the conceptual and practical mischaracterization of collaborative negotiation as "paradigm change," which is both highly misleading and ultimately ineffectual in promoting change.

The new lawyer should use her legal expertise to further her clients' chances of an outcome that meets their needs and is durable and feasible. She will employ her legal knowledge to develop a realistic alternative to negotiation and to use this to test potential solutions and, perhaps, to reality-test entrenched or inflated expectations. Legal principles can provide a beginning point for a discussion over acceptable principles, and where the law is relatively clear and predictable, or where the legal guidelines are widely recognized, it may be sufficient to resolve one or more specific issues. She will offer her client as clear a picture as possible of her rights entitlements and, where appropriate, either promote these explicitly or ensure that any bargain meets this standard in some form or fashion. What the new lawyer should not expect from the law is that its principles will necessarily always be sufficient to meet the needs and values of the parties or that it can offer the type of tailor-made, nuanced solution often appealing to domestic and commercial parties alike. Counsel should also be cautious about the potential for legal theories to present a conflict as a series of selective particular frames, none of which represent the real "core" of the conflict and that impede a whole problem analysis that may sometimes be the key to settlement.

Legal expertise in isolation from problem solving has never been an effective strategy for counsel, and this is increasingly the case in a new era of mandatory and institutional settlement procedures. In combination with effective negotiation, conflict resolution advocacy, and partnership in problem solving with the client, law is a key norm, resource, and strategic tool.

8
Ethical Challenges Facing the New Lawyer

> Legal ethics is the applied philosophy of lawyering; it goes to
> the heart of what it means to be a lawyer.[1]

The evolving nature of legal practice creates new professional and ethical challenges for the legal profession, as well as new versions of old dilemmas. Some of the new ethical questions relate to the changing conceptions of advocacy described in this book and, in particular, the balance between client interests, commitment to new forms of conflict resolution processes, and the lawyer's personal beliefs and values about dispute resolution. When is it time to fight, and when is it time to settle? And how to engage the client in these choices and decisions? These and other issues also reflect the changing relationship between lawyer and client, which creates a host of questions about boundaries and shared responsibilities. The role opened up to the client in some processes – for example, mediation and collaborative law – takes counsel beyond the parameters of her traditional relationship with her client. As a result, many age-old dilemmas take on a new twist for the new lawyer – for example, how to enable client autonomy in decision making, how to give advice on accepting an offer from the side, and how much pressure to place on the client to adopt a particular course.

Ethics and Behaviour in Informal Dispute Resolution Processes

Other ethical issues arise specifically in the context of negotiation, collaboration, and mediation. These are informal and unregulated environments and, as such, encounter and deal with problems behind closed doors and often with minimal sharing of experiences among practitioners. There are many questions about what types of behaviour should be deemed ethical in these settings. The nature of private and unscrutinized dispute resolution processes means that issues that typically arise – for example, advantage-taking in negotiation, involuntary or false disclosure, and issues of good faith – are not resolvable by reference to a third party (like a judge or master) or a rulebook (like the *Rules of Civil Procedure*). In the absence of clearly articulated and shared standards, counsel must learn to monitor and respond initially to such occurrences on a largely intuitive level, until such time as widely accepted principles emerge. We are only just at the beginning of discovering what new ethical challenges will emerge when lawyers work with their clients in a wider range of conflict resolution processes and at an even earlier stage of clarifying what behaviours are and are not acceptable.

One of the benefits of the zealous advocacy model is that it ensures relative clarity over certain ethical aspects of lawyering practice. The practical and philosophical separation of the roles of lawyer and client, for example, tends to mask many potential questions about decision making and control; in this case, authority often defaults to the lawyer. The focus on rights-based strategies allows lawyers to narrowly understand due diligence in terms of providing legal advice, whether or not this advice is followed. Some important aspects of socially expected behaviour and response – for instance, behaviour in court – are governed by appropriate procedural rules. The norms of professional behaviour between "gentlemen" adversaries outside court, although unwritten, are also fairly clearly established via internal collegial values and enforced via peer pressure.[2] This is not to suggest that issues of professional behaviours and ethical practice do not arise within traditional zealous advocacy – the most obvious quandary is what types of aggressive strategic behaviours (for example, delays, pressure or intimidating behaviour, and the withholding of information) can be justified as acceptable forms of client advocacy. Descriptions of advocacy given in professional codes generally emphasize an image of resolute and fearless advocacy, which is then often tempered by warnings about what might be regarded as "sharp practice."[3] There is an uneasy tension between exhortations to be resolute and fearless and cautions about inappropriate behaviours, and the lines between appropriate and inappropriate behaviour are often unclear to young lawyers. Some of the tensions within the zealous advocacy model, and their ethical dimensions, are explored in more detail in Chapter 5.

These issues arise in relation to an adjudicative frame for dispute resolution and, hence, predictably they tend to be addressed using rights-based thinking and decision-making processes. A common result is a focus on rules of conduct rather than on ambiguity, novel situations, or the use of discretion and contextual judgment. For example, in the literature on lying, a central concern is with breach of professional conduct rules and the subsequent impact on the future of litigation as well as with whether a lie is later discoverable, rather than, for example, with the risk of building an agreement on deception or the effect of truth telling or lying on the future of the bargaining relationship. As many writers have pointed out, a rule-based approach cannot adequately deal with the myriad situations that arise in negotiation.[4]

Nor does a rule-based approach address the establishment of unwritten but dominant norms. One of these norms in the traditional model is that negotiation is widely regarded as a corollary to litigation and adjudication, perhaps to be used for advantage. In a model of conflict resolution advocacy, negotiation, mediation, and other collaborative settlement processes represent a commitment to advocating for a good solution rather than simply an adjunct to the process of litigation. Approaching negotiation and other settlement-oriented processes in this way allows the new lawyer to anticipate potential ethical dilemmas characteristic of informal and unregulated environments, which assume both an openness toward a range of possible outcomes and a closer working partnership with the client. The commitment to using negotiation to genuinely explore settlement rather than to press a position or as a tactical ploy also enables an analysis of these dilemmas from the perspective of consensus building rather than in relation to other rights-based processes. In other words, where the norm of usage and function has changed for negotiation, what does this mean about the types of issues we might anticipate and how might we wish to address these? This is a far cry from "how much lying/evasion/aggresion can I get away with under the Rules?"

Ethics and Professional Identity

It is useful to first locate this discussion of ethics within the broader context of the contemporary debate over professionalism and ethics. This debate, which is currently taking place in bar associations all over North America, reveals growing concern within the profession over the maintenance of ethical standards and appropriate professional behaviours in jurisdictions where the legal profession is prospering as a business, but its public image is increasingly negative. Professionalism in this sense relates to a constellation of professional values such as high ethical standards, competence, civility, collegiality, and commitment to public service. The relationship between professionalism and ethical behaviours is often unclear because a notion of professionalism seems to transcend the rule-bound sense of ethical conduct widely taught in courses on professional responsibility. Anthony Kronman highlights this as the difference between learning the grammatical rules of a language and being able to actually converse in this language.[5]

Professionalism incorporates rules of ethical conduct and much more. It comprises not only the profession's regulatory framework but also its culture and mores – in other words, the profession's identity and self-image. According to Andrew Abbott, professional identity includes not only substantive knowledge but also a highly developed abstract knowledge system that guides social practices.[6] It is within this abstract knowledge system that professions develop models of appropriate professional and ethical behaviours, which are less explicit but just as or even more important than formal, substantive rules of conduct. This includes behaviour toward the other side in negotiations, interactions with opposite counsel in social and professional settings, the tone of professional correspondence, and relationships with members of the bench. While we should expect significant diversity in social practices reflecting the many different contexts for legal practice – large urban firms, sole practice, government, in-house counsel work, and so on – a core sense of professionalism requires a corresponding core of shared norms to sustain it.

A renewed sense of professionalism in law envisages the voluntary development of high standards of conduct, striving after excellence and a commitment to wider public and/or community values. The discussion presently taking place within the profession suggests an inchoate and evolving role identity. It is no coincidence that debate over a renewed vision of professionalism is taking place at the same time the role identity of lawyers, and the work that they do for clients, is going through a process of substantial change.

A Decline in Professionalism?

For many years, two themes have been constant in literature about the legal profession: the decline of professionalism and ethical standards and the low repute of the profession among the general public. There is a widespread sense that the commitment to professionalism, informed by a spirit of vocation, has been lost. Despite these concerns, the formal teaching of professional responsibility has remained the "orphan" of legal education. While in the United States professional responsibility is a required course for American Bar Association schools, in Canada, it is an optional course taken by a minority of law students.[7] More significantly, professional ethical issues hardly ever come up and are addressed at best tangentially in the rush to cover material in substantive law courses. Writers in Canada and the United States have sharply criticized both professional bodies and the law schools for their neglect of the teaching of professional responsibility.[8] In the last ten years, many professional bodies have started to look for ways to revitalize the debate over professionalism and ethics by instituting task forces and think tanks, commissioning research and holding conferences and other fora. It is an issue, evidently, on which many practising lawyers hold an opinion. Numerous articles on this topic have appeared in bar journals and professional publications in the past fifteen years.[9]

With the growing realization that the legal profession is in a state of change comes a fear that the profession is no longer tethered to the fundamental ideals of a vocation or calling and, as a consequence, has "lost its way." A number of important books written within the last ten years have raised this fear, describing a trend away from law as a vocation that encompassed a range of social roles and purposes and toward law as a business. In *The Lost Lawyer: Failing Ideals of the Legal Profession,* Kronman describes how a narrowed focus on lawyers as specialist technicians (often the servants of corporate interests) has swamped the moral purpose of lawyering in which the lawyer saw himself as engaged in a lifelong endeavour to work for the public good.[10] The term Kronman uses to describe this earlier vision – the lawyer-statesman – is taken up by Walter Bennett in *The Lawyer's Myth: Reviving the Ideals of the Legal Profession.*[11] Bennett describes the moral impotence he sees assumed by his law students in which they believe themselves powerless in a world of practice that dismisses idealism and high moral purpose as irrelevant. Bennett's assertion that law students often give up on the goals and visions with which they came to law school is supported by numerous studies of the impact of law school on idealism and goals.[12] Both Kronman and Bennett conclude that the apparent rejection of the purposive moral aspects of lawyering result in a void of professional identity, which is too often filled by crude adversarialism and a general decline in the norms of civility and ethical practice. Both authors see this not only as a crisis that implicates the work, profitability, and reputation of the profession but also as a loss of professional ideals and dignity. As Kronman starkly puts it, the legal profession is "in danger of losing its soul."[13]

The lament for the decline in professionalism is permeated with nostalgia for older, disappearing forms of practice. This sentiment is extremely problematic given the forms of gender, racial, ethnic, religious, and economic exclusions that have permitted the complacent collegiality of traditional professionalism. In some quarters, the yearning for the ideals of traditional practice may be less about turning away from adversarialism and more about returning to the "good old days" of an elitist and exclusionary bar. Many do not share Kronman's "before-and-after" picture of the legal profession.[14] The broadened demographic of the profession inevitably presents new challenges to old practices and loss of core ideals may be explained by the welcome inclusion of a wider and more diverse population of lawyers.

It is more difficult to argue with Kronman's contention that role identities are inevitably tied to hierarchies of skills and values and thus to the skills and motivations of individuals attracted to and remaining in this profession. This means that as we change the role identity of the lawyer, we also change what we value about lawyers. In *The Lost Lawyer,* Kronman looks back at a "nostalgic" model of small-town legal practice and compares it with contemporary, urban, "mega-firm" practice. There are differences in skills and abilities associated with the different models. Kron-man's small-town lawyer-statesman needed excellent personal judgment in advising and dealing with clients – his personal judgment was a critical aspect of what clients came to him for and valued about him. In contrast, today's big-firm lawyers are valued for their technical expertise. They probably have greater specialist knowledge than their predecessors and, in taking instructions from the client, rarely question, contradict, or refuse to follow their wishes.[15] Similarly, as we develop a more complete picture of the skills and qualities of the new lawyer, the knowledge and attributes that were once appropriate to a profession constantly "on its feet" in court, making legal arguments, become less relevant to a profession that specializes in conflict resolution advocacy. Eventually, this adjustment may mean that the types of individuals who are drawn to the profession, and their aspirations and motivations for practice, may also change. The contrast between the skills and attitudes of the contemporary big-firm lawyer and those associated with conflict resolution advocacy suggest further confusion and even contradiction of direction within contemporary models of legal expertise.

Law is not the only profession experiencing changes in its professional role and identity with the result a sense of "drifting" and uncertainty. A similar phenomenon has been noted in the medical profession, particularly in the shift in some types of general practice responsibility from doctors to nurses, who are now qualified as nurse practitioners. This change has unsettled the role identity and status of doctors as they adjust to the inclusion of other professionals within hospitals and general practices who share some, but not all, of their skills and qualifications. The redrawing of professional roles and identities leads to uncertainty, stress, and sometimes to conflict.

The disappearance of clear and obvious role models and mentors during a period of change is further demoralizing.[16] For young lawyers, who are their role models? Atticus Finch, the champion of causes, or Gandhi, the paragon of virtue, may feel very distant to today's lawyers. As the profession moves toward an expanded role as the skillful resolver of conflict, who will be there, in either the public eye or in a media role, to represent the skillful negotiator and problem solver? As we saw in Chapter 2, the role of mentors and role models is critical in developing a sense of professional identity for young lawyers.

Where do the changes set out in Chapter 1 and described throughout this book leave legal professionalism? One possibility is that we are seeing significant changes in the social practices of lawyering – resulting in changes to what Abbott describes as the profession's abstract knowledge system – which are a reflection of changes in the professional identity of the lawyer. The extent and pace of change and transition offer a possible explanation

for the diminishing of professional civility and habits of professional cour-
tesies noted by some writers.[17] Another way of understanding the status
quo is that there is no longer a choate core of professional values, and that,
instead, the changes the legal profession is facing have produced a range
of social practices within different groups, including large firms, small
country practice, local bars associations, and courts, none of which are as
cohesive as these were when the profession was less diverse.

Within the wider context of uncertainty and questions over professionalism, the new lawyer must be prepared to confront and respond to
challenges and dilemmas arising from her increasing use of informal dispute resolution and settlement processes. The first debate – and a critical
one for a profession facing so much change – is over just what type of
dilemmas and situations constitute "ethical" behaviour and implicate professional values in the first place. I shall argue that the importance of individual discretionary judgment in the conduct of private, informal dispute
resolution processes significantly expands the range of dilemmas and situations that raise ethical questions for counsel.

What Do We Mean by "Ethics" in Informal Dispute Resolution Processes?

The shape that "ethical" decisions take in informal dispute resolution processes is quite different from problems that arise in formally regulated
processes, which are more likely to be anticipated and accounted for in
written codes of civil procedure and professional conduct.[18] In order to
comprehend the issues that arise in informal dispute resolution processes,
both conceptual and practical, we must first broaden our understanding
of "ethics" for the purposes of this discussion. If we limit what we mean
by "ethics" to situations in which there appears to be an applicable rule
of professional conduct such as conflict of interest or privilege and confidentiality, we shall miss the heart of the professional challenge for the
new lawyer in using informal processes.

Instead, I want to propose that we understand ethical behaviours as
potentially implicated by any *value-based* choice between alternate courses
of action (which may be a conscious choice or one that is intuitive and
unconscious). This includes choice of a dispute resolution forum, choice
of strategy, decisions about information exchange, decisions about client
role and participation, decisions about whether or not to negotiate, decisions about whether or not to settle, and so on. Of course, not all of these
issues always, or even usually, raise value dilemmas serious and weighty
enough to impact ethics and professionalism. For instance, deciding on which
end of the negotiation table your client will sit, whether the negotiation should be in your offices or the offices of the other side, or, perhaps,

whether your client will come to a meeting with the other side at this stage in the process are hardly issues that should concern ethical or behavioural standards. However, many aspects of planning and participating in informal dispute resolution processes do raise choices that implicate values and may also sometimes raise questions about appropriate professional behaviours. Decisions over whether to engage in negotiation often implicate values, and a persistent refusal to negotiate may raise ethical and professional issues. So might refusing to cooperate with information exchange or coming to mediation with no intention of discussing settlement, although these are more contentious examples.[19] Whatever our conclusions, if we understand any value-based choice between alternatives as potentially raising ethical and/or professional issues, ethics immediately becomes a much larger and broader topic. In informal and largely unregulated processes such as mediation and collaborative law, such choices arise far more frequently than they do in a more structured litigation process.

Some of the issues regarding appropriate ethical behaviour in dispute resolution are relatively predictable and well documented – for example, avoiding conflicts of interest when acting as a lawyer-mediator. Some of these issues have been codified to some extent – for example, both the American Bar Association and the Law Society of Upper Canada now have a provision that applies to lawyers who act as mediators.[20] However, as our experience of new dispute resolution processes grows, so does our awareness of potential and previously unanticipated ethical issues – issues that are no less (and possibly more) important because they are not addressed by any existing professional codes. For example, how do we recognize a client's informed consent to enter a new and unfamiliar process or to accept an offer made in this process? What type of pressure is acceptable for a lawyer to place on her client to settle? A more specific example is how much pressure is appropriate for a collaborative lawyer to place on her client to remain in the process and not institute litigation (and, hence, disqualify this lawyer from continuing to provide legal services)? What ethical issues arise when a lawyer fails to convey a settlement offer to a client or when a lawyer immediately rejects an offer made in her client's presence in mediation without first consulting her client? How does an explicit commitment to share all information with the other side in a settlement process relate to solicitor-client privilege?

A broadened understanding of ethics in informal dispute resolution also encourages us to elaborate on our notion of "professionalism" for the new lawyer by considering the underlying values implied by different choices and actions. In contrast with more traditional notions of professionalism, ethical and professional behaviour in this environment may be more fluid and contextual, admitting no one "right" answer. This lack of certainty is the result of the dynamics of the process of informal dispute resolution itself, which is always fluid and contextual, and in which personal judgment will often be critical in the absence of applicable rules and principles.

These qualities make it especially important that we think hard and creatively about the *process* of how we determine a "right" (implying "appropriately professional") approach to dilemmas in formal dispute resolution. The concept of "discursive ethics" is useful in this case.[21] Discursive ethics attempts to understand the moral reasoning behind any decision or action by examining the assumptions within the situation – for example, the use of language, the assumed power or weakness of the participants, the preferred outcomes, and so on. Our effort is thus directed not toward the "rightness" or "wrongness" of the decision or action itself but, rather, toward uncovering and critiquing the basis for an ethical choice in any given situation. This epistemological approach to ethical decision making reflects feminist theories of knowledge that understand "truth" as contextual and therefore forever fluid – "situated and provisional rather than absolute and final."[22] Such a methodology enables the development of a process in which individual and experiential "truths" can be identified, deconstructed, and shared. This process seems particularly appropriate for use in cases where choices are made by counsel faced with situations for which there are no "rules" or even, as yet, a convention or culture of fair process. Such an approach also enables a direct engagement and dialogue between lawyer and client over these issues, and it has the potential to allow a shared understanding of ethical behaviours and responses to emerge from the discussion.

Uncovering the assumptions and moral reasoning behind our intuitive approach to new or extended ethical dilemmas is a critical step in the development of a professional ethical identity for the new lawyer. Four emerging ethical issues relevant to the practice of the new lawyer will be highlighted in the next sections. Some of these issues also appear in a somewhat different guise in more traditional legal practice, which provides a starting point for their analysis and discussion. The four issues highlighted here are by no means intended as a comprehensive or exhaustive review of the potential for difficult choices raised by informal dispute resolution processes. However, they do illustrate the complexity of the dilemmas presented and the range of developing responses.

Informed Consent
Informed consent – ensuring that a client understands the consequences of a decision or action and has been appropriately advised of both the potential risks and rewards – is a perennial dilemma, and raises hard questions of ethical and professional practices in the traditional practice paradigm. Obtaining informed consent to a litigation strategy, to forward an offer

to the other side, to a drafted legal document such as a contract or a will, or to a settlement is a delicate negotiation and may be especially difficult when the client is distressed, stubborn, or simply confused. Counsel must decide with how much force he presents his advice and how much room is given to client autonomy. There must be space for the client to reject the lawyer's advice and yet he must, at the same time, be "informed" – he has simply reached a different conclusion than his lawyer. In practice, this difference may be difficult for the lawyer to accommodate.

The more choices faced by the client, the more professional advice they require and the more decisions they will face that require informed consent. Clients using lawyers as advisors in both contentious and non-contentious matters have many more choices available to them today than was the case thirty years ago. In non-contentious matters, where the primary focus of the lawyer's work is likely to be the drafting of documents, expanding legal and technological frameworks for the planning and regulation of commercial and personal relationships offer more complex options and choices.

In litigation, the single-track litigation model has been replaced by numerous alternatives, some required and some voluntary and all potentially tainted in the absence of informed consent. Before the advent of extensive case management and court-initiated settlement processes, clients were asked to formally consent to filing or defending a suit, but thereafter there was little call for lengthy client consultations over procedure. When a case is on a standard litigation track, in the absence of procedural interventions such as case management or mediation, which require client consultation, there is relatively little for lawyer and client to debate outside how much money to spend, and over how long a period. Of course, some lawyers have always made a practice of checking in regularly with their clients to ensure that they consent to the "next steps" – for example, bringing a motion or embarking on discoveries. However, the initiation of legal action, or even the retaining of a lawyer, has traditionally been widely understood as a handing over of authority by the client to the lawyer, and a general consent to accepting the lawyer's best judgment in pursuing a strategy to win the case. This arrangement was comfortable for counsel, and certainly for some, although not all, clients, because it gave the lawyer significant autonomy in decision making.

In today's dispute resolution environment, there are many more choices and decisions that counsel and client need to discuss at the outset of all but the most routine matters. Ontario has recognized this reality in a new rule of professional conduct requiring lawyers to discuss process options with their clients, and other jurisdictions have similar provisions.[23] In order to comply with this rule conscientiously, lawyers may need to know more than they presently do about the available options, and they certainly need to spend more time on this conversation. When lawyers propose new and unfamiliar dispute resolution processes to their clients – processes that may result in those clients compromising their asserted legal entitlements in order to settle – they are obligated to ensure that clients provide "informed consent" to whatever strategy, or combination of strategies, is adopted.

Obtaining "informed consent" to a process choice means more than simply describing a single option and asking the client to agree to this approach. Promoting a single process – collaborative law, mediation, or litigation – risks unreasonably limiting the client's options. Informed consent requires that the client understand that they are choosing this process as an *alternative* to other possibilities. An informed decision includes understanding the particular characteristics of this process and what its potential advantages and drawbacks might be. Some collaborative lawyers tell potential clients that they can only be retained on a collaborative basis. While counsel is probably entitled to limit her practice in this way (no bar has yet ruled this a breach of professional responsibilities), and she may have sincere reasons for believing that this course is best for her client, this approach leaves some clients (for example, a long-term client of this lawyer or a new client who has determined that they really want to be represented by this lawyer) with little real alternative to collaborative law. A lawyer committed to taking only collaborative cases may indicate that she is not available if the client prefers another route, but she should not shrink from describing what those alternatives might look like. For example, collaborative law clients should know that mediation may be an alternative for them, and they should understand the pros and cons of each process. In practice, it appears that some collaborative lawyers are often reluctant to describe "rival" procedures like mediation.[24]

Ensuring that a client has informed consent regarding whether or not to use mediation or collaborative law requires both the provision of accurate and sufficient information about mediation and alternative processes like collaborative law and the presentation of this information in an unbiased way that is accessible to the client. The second requirement is a demanding one, but some counsel appear to be not even meeting their responsibilities to the first. For example, some collaborative law clients who participated in the Collaborative Lawyering Research project appeared to know little or nothing at all about the possibility of mediation as an alternative to collaborative law. Worse, a few appeared to have formed the view that their collaborative lawyers were in effect "mediating" the case:

Question: Did you think about mediation as an alternative?
Answer: No. They [the lawyers] talk about it very briefly but it was sort of like: "We're meeting and we're going through these issues, but we're

mediating, we're here ... as facilitators to help and to give you individual advice."[25]

The unbiased presentation of information about dispute resolution choices takes on a special significance when one reviews research on the relationship between client opinions of the value of dispute resolution alternatives and those of their lawyers.[26] Unsurprisingly, counsel is extremely influential in his views on various process options. It is clear that for many collaborative law clients their impressions of family mediation are entirely or primarily formed by the information given them by their lawyers. This problem is one of attitude rather than process. Any number of forms or rules requiring lawyers to discuss a range of options with their clients will not lead to a comprehensive analysis of the relative merits of process options unless lawyers themselves buy into the idea of offering their clients a variety of processes and the ability to choose among them, with the lawyer's advice. This does not preclude counsel from stating his preference and the reasons for it, but requires that other options are fairly canvassed. This is no different from the general standard we set for professional advice giving: that the advice is not slanted in such a way to make only one choice attractive.

Aside from ensuring that clients receive information, and in a relatively unbiased form, another critical aspect of informed consent is the accurate setting of expectations. An additional challenge here is the relative inexperience of lawyers with many of the new dispute resolution processes that they may propose to their clients. For practical purposes they may be simply unable, rather than unwilling, to give their client sufficient information to ensure that they form realistic and accurate expectations and that future surprises are minimized (although not eliminated since this is probably impossible with either formal or informal dispute resolution procedures). For example, most if not all collaborative lawyers inform their clients of the impact of choosing a collaborative lawyer and walk them through a participation agreement that sets out, among other terms, a clause disqualifying the lawyer from representing them in the event that they decide to litigate, to commit to full and voluntary disclosure, to embark on a collaborative "team" approach, and so on. However, these are fairly abstract definitions that may not be meaningful to the client, and the problem may be compounded where counsel can offer only limited experience of context, including the practical implications of participating in an extra-legal, voluntary negotiation process. The challenge is how collaborative lawyers can create a real understanding for a naïve, possibly first-time client of the practical meaning and substance of the formal language of the participation agreement.

In contrast, experienced collaborative lawyers are much better able to set realistic expectations. They do this by cautioning their clients at the outset that the collaborative process, like any voluntary negotiation process, tends to move at the speed of the slowest party and by warning the client that, despite the best intentions, the unexpected disclosure of unwelcome information by the other side may make collaboration more difficult, at least in the immediate aftermath. Experienced collaborative lawyers are also far more likely to warn the client that the process may sometimes reach an impasse and that there may be occasions when they feel like giving up on collaboration in favour of litigation.

Research shows a correlation between inadequate or incomplete client consent at the stage of contracting into collaborative law and client complaints about the process during or after. Such complaints cover a broad range of process issues, including disclosure requirements (like access to private discussions with one's lawyer and lawyer-client privilege), the pace at which the negotiations are proceeding, compliance (that is, the limits on overseeing interim agreements or undertakings given in four-way meetings), and the calculation of fees, especially when there are other professionals involved. Each of these complaints reflects an incomplete understanding and inaccurate expectations at the beginning of the collaborative process regarding this issue and raises ethical concerns about informed consent in new and unfamiliar settings like collaborative law. Sometimes the problem is less the work of the lawyer and more the unbridled optimism of the client, but in every case the lawyer has a professional responsibility to ensure that the client is provided with as complete, accurate, and realistic a picture of what they are contracting into as possible.

Similar issues appear in private mediation cases, although the reasons behind lack of informed consent may vary. Few lawyers insist that their clients use mediation with quite the same degree of zeal that presently characterizes collaborative lawyers. One area in which the problem of informed consent remerges is where mediation is not mandatory but court personnel or judges place pressure on the parties to agree to mediation. This situation gives the impression, perhaps accurately, that participating in mediation is a way of buying favour with the judge, especially if lawyer and client anticipate a future hearing before him or her.[27] Sometimes the degree of pressure a judge places on a disputant who is uninformed about mediation may result in a confusion or conflation of mediation with adjudication in the disputant's mind.[28] In such cases, counsel must take the time to explain the process ramifications to their client, including the fact that their choice may be influenced by many factors but is not mandated, and obtain an informed consent before proceeding with mediation.

Even more disturbing is the consistency with which research data suggests that clients in mandatory processes such as case management, court-connected mediation, and settlement conferences often come to these sessions with little or no idea of what to expect. The fact that these processes are manda-tory does not relieve or reduce counsel's obligation to inform his client and ensure that she has a sufficient understanding of the process. The efforts of court programs to convey explanatory literature to parties is often frustrated by the failure of lawyers to pass on this information to their clients.[29] In the Ontario court-connected pilot, an evaluation in 1995 found that 79 percent of clients said they had been briefed by the lawyer "just before" the mediation session. Fifty-eight percent described themselves as being "not at all familiar" with mediation before the session.[30] The fol-lowing quote from an interview is typical of the general confusion and lack of clarity that seemed to surround the mediation process for clients at that time:

> I didn't find out [about the mediation session] until my lawyer informed me on the way down to Toronto [for the session]. Until then I thought that we were going to trial.[31]

The obligation to ensure informed consent to mediation or collabora-tion should be especially strictly adhered to when there is a potential for harm to a vulnerable client. The necessity of carefully screening potential mediation and collaborative law clients for a history of violence and intimidation has come to the fore in the last twenty years, but complaints continue that some counsel (and mediators) do not take these issues seri-ously enough and sometimes place their clients at risk.[32] If the new lawyer works with at-risk clients, she should understand that these clients will often avoid or be less than truthful in answering questions about family vio-lence. They may feel embarrassed and ill at ease being asked such ques-tions by their lawyer. Screening is more than a matter of putting questions to the client – they must be asked clearly and sensitively. Ideally, counsel should also be trained to recognize signs and cues that suggest a history of violence.

Following full information and advice, the choice of process is ulti-mately the client's, no matter what the advice of their lawyer. Some of these clients – for example, a woman separating from a violent or bully-ing partner – prefer to try a consensus-building approach and sometimes function very effectively with support in a highly structured and con-trolled dialogue. When the lawyer feels that such a choice is prejudicial or even dangerous, what should she do? Some lawyers may prefer not to work with clients when they feel they are "out of their depth" – for exam-ple, in high-conflict cases in which there is a history of intimidation. A lawyer who continues with a potentially vulnerable client into collabora-tion or mediation must understand the possible impact of this vulnera-bility on the quality of communication in the bargaining process and the additional risks and stresses for her client. She must help the client recognize and appraise the impact of these factors. For example, the client must understand and accept that there will (generally) be face-to-face communication if mediation or collaboration is used, and this places some responsibility on counsel to ensure that the client feels able to function effectively in a face-to-face meeting. This discussion between lawyer and client – which should touch on comfort, safety, and assertiveness – should continue throughout a collaborative or mediative process. Informed consent to a process lasts only as long as each meeting and needs to be regularly revisited when there are special concerns. When the circumstances are so extreme that counsel feels a face-to-face meeting is unsafe, client autonomy remains the overriding value, but the lawyer always has the option to withdraw.

This section has focused on issues of informed consent at the point of choosing or entering into a process. Issues of informed consent also arise when it becomes apparent only during bargaining that a client is being pressured into accepting an unfair or inadequate settlement (see the discussion later in this chapter under the heading "Pressure to Settle") or is somehow constrained from fully comprehending the ramifications of a proposed settlement sufficient to give informed consent to all of its terms. Counsel has an ethical responsibility to ensure that her client has provided an informed consent to any agreed outcome, even when the mooted solution appears to be "obviously" in the clients' interests.[33] It is vital that in giving consent the client recognizes and understands any concerns her lawyer points out, whether or not she accepts these. Once again, the new lawyer is faced with striking a delicate and complex balance, here between the principle of client self-determination and counsel's professional obligation to ensure informed consent.

In the Service of Whom?

> If lawyers were to see their social and legal role less as
> "zealously representing" clients' interests and more as solving
> clients' ... problems, what legal ethics would follow?[34]

Committing to a problem-solving approach to conflict resolution blurs the sharp lines of battle drawn by adversarial advocacy between one's own client and the other parties to the dispute. Adversarial advocacy offers the seductive clarity of remaining inside a "bubble" of positional argument and justification. Consensus building bursts this bubble since the other side takes on far greater strategic and practical significance in attempting to resolve conflict rather than in fighting.

Caring – practically speaking rather than emotionally or ideologically – about the other side's interests also gives rise to many implications for appropriate professional and ethical behaviours toward one's own client. One of the recurrent doubts raised about resort to collaborative problem-solving processes is whether counsel will sufficiently protect and stand up for their clients' rights when they are working to accommodate opposing interests. There is a lingering suspicion that bringing a client to mediation implies that the lawyer cannot, or is not prepared to, make a strong case for his client. This attitude presupposes that advocacy can only take place within the context of positional argument and oversimplifies the complexity of the advocacy role. Advocacy means advancing one's clients' best and most important interests. As one collaborative lawyer put it, "This is not litigation-lite."[35] Chapter 5 discusses in detail the ways in which lawyers should and can continue to act as advocates for their clients within consensus-building processes.

Nonetheless, a certain amount of tension between a commitment to advancing one's clients' interests while remaining responsive to what the other side needs and wants is inevitable. This is the classic Prisoner's Dilemma game – in other words, how to protect one's own or one's clients' interests while recognizing that, short of a pre-emptive and decisive strike, achieving this goal is largely dependent upon satisfying the interests of the other party. How can counsel claim value for her own client while maximizing mutual gains for all parties in the conflict? Is some element of loyalty and commitment to one's client lost in the process? This tension may be most familiar to family practitioners who often understand their professional responsibility to include a consideration of the implications of divorce for the whole family, especially when children are involved. Working with an explicit agenda of collaboration and accommodation – in family mediation or collaborative family law – raises these tensions to a conscious level. It faces counsel with a question that is both practical and ethical – just who is my "client" and what special relationship do I have with them that I do not have with the other parties, with whom I am seeking to make an agreement?

A small minority of collaborative lawyers articulate the view that they no longer relate to a particular "client" in the same way they did in traditional practice. For example, two lawyers explain, "As an advocate, I am looking more at the family as a unit"[36] and "I never saw myself as being [the client's] advocate, I was primarily [the collaborative team's] guide to their own capacity for having their internal behaviours be the right behaviours, vis-à-vis one another."[37] This last lawyer goes on to describe his role as being identical in relation to each member of the collaborative "team." This approach believes that "success ... is based on the strength of my relationships with colleagues."[38] In the same vein, a few collaborative lawyers suggest that there is a case for lawyers even switching clients for a while and spending some time alone with the other client and building rapport.[39] Some collaborative lawyers understand this as a new approach to contracting with their client: "A contract with the client to find a solution which is in the interests of the whole family."[40]

It is less clear if collaborative law clients understand this apparent change in the status quo and its ramifications for their relationship with their lawyer. The other difficulty with this perspective is that counsel is not working privately with each member of the "whole family," nor is he taking instructions from them collectively. Therefore, these lawyers risk substituting their own judgment for those of other family members. Motivated by their desire to participate in the formulation of healthy family solutions to the challenges of separation and divorce, these lawyers may conflate collaboration with resiling from some of their advocacy responsibilities to their own client.

It is important to recognize that these views represent only a small number of collaborative lawyers, the majority of whom still perceive that their primary responsibility is to the client. In fact, most collaborative lawyers are clear that their relationship with their client is as an advocate and not as an impartial, neutral "team" member. The following remark is typical of this approach and the importance attached to this distinction:

> I absolutely think I have a special responsibility to my client. I mean I am their attorney. I am her attorney or his attorney and there is no question in my mind that that is my primary duty. I mean, that's what my job is, that's what I'm being retained for and if that's not the case, there can be a mediation with two mediators who are neutrals.[41]

An appropriate balance appears possible when counsel acknowledges her primary attachment to her client while recognizing the inevitable interrelationship of all family members if the goal is to resolve the conflict with a realistic, durable, and widely accepted outcome:

> What is good for the client is that she or he has a divorce that she or he can live with – one that is less destructive and less costly ... In acting for the client you have to take account of the interests of the whole family.[42]

There is to date less debate and perhaps less concern that lawyers representing clients in mediation will give up their special advocacy role on behalf of their own client (and become a "potted plant").[43] On the contrary, a cause of greater concern is that lawyers who bring their clients to mandatory mediation are likely to be overly positional and aggressive and use the process in "bad faith" (see the discussion later in this chapter).

However, the question of "service to whom" sometimes arises in a different way in mediation, in cases in which a relationship develops between a particular mediator and the lawyers who work with him on a regular basis. Mediators have a distinct incentive to develop positive relationships with "repeat-player" lawyers (and, less often, "repeat player" clients) since their livelihood usually depends on the market's assessment of their work. From the perspective of counsel, a "special" relationship with a particular mediator might conceivably encroach on client loyalty. As John Lande points out, "Mediators and lawyers may find that they share an interest in pressuring principals to settle."[44] For example, counsel may use a particular ("muscle") mediator to "reality check" (or arm-twist) his client when he is concerned that the client's expectations are unrealistic. While resorting to a "muscle mediator" may be a carefully chosen and appropriate strategy in some cases, it is important for lawyers representing clients in mediation to be clear that their primary relationship and commitment is to their client and not to the mediator.

Another challenging dimension of client loyalty in conflict resolution advocacy is how the new lawyer should relate to counsel representing the other side. In traditional lawyer-to-lawyer relationships, a distance and detachment is maintained in professional settings, and it is normative to be assertive, even aggressive, with counsel for the other side. Clients rarely feel that their lawyer is more attached to counsel for the other side than to their interests. In fact, clients are far more likely to complain about the level of animosity between opposing lawyers that may further escalate the conflict.

This assumption is challenged when lawyers regularly work together in settlement processes. When lawyers, especially those working in smaller communities but also members of tight networks developed within larger bar associations, work consistently with others who share their values about conflict resolution processes, they develop relationships that are personal as well as professional. These relationships can and sometimes do generate their own internal incentives for successful outcomes, which are quite independent of the client's interests. The lawyers like working together, feel like they are a "team," and want to continue to maintain this close working relationship. They may feel accountable to one another as well as to their individual clients. Lawyers working in collaborative processes must take care not to create professional relationships that threaten their (both actual or perceived) commitment to their client.

It is revealing that while most collaborative lawyers see only a positive impact of having a better relationship among counsel – and certainly it is hard to argue with the contention that a professional and trusting working relationship is better than one characterized by competitiveness and animosity – their clients see more downsides to such a relationship. The hurt and dissatisfaction that may be created by an overtly amicable approach, especially when this has not been discussed as an intentional strategy with the client in advance, is exemplified by one collaborative client who comments that her lawyer "wanted to chat up my husband and bond with him ... I felt abandoned."[45] Nonetheless, most lawyers practising collaborative law regard their work with the other members of the collaborative team as secondary to their loyalty to their client. One lawyer explained this to her clients by telling them, "Even if I am nice to the other side, I am *your* lawyer."[46]

The new lawyer must be cognizant of the implications and the risks of the closer and perhaps more amicable relationships they will develop with opposing counsel if they regularly meet them in negotiation or other collaborative processes. This rapport will be important to developing good outcomes, but some manifestations may alarm the client. The new lawyer should be aware of the consequences of close professional ties – for example, membership in the same professional network or formal practice group – to other lawyers (or mediators) as well as of the necessity of being transparent in discussions about these ties with her client. She should be ready to set limits to this relationship that are comfortable for herself and her client.

When considering the question of being "in the service of whom," there is a final, albeit less obvious, contender for counsel's attention and loyalty in seeking settlement with the other side. This is loyalty to the chosen dispute resolution process itself. The Collaborative Lawyering Research project found that a very small number of collaborative lawyers, described as "team players," felt that they owed loyalty to the process of collaboration and, hence, to their professional colleagues in the process over and above their loyalty to their client (one is quoted earlier in this section). Such is their belief and investment in collaborative law processes that these lawyers see that maintaining the integrity of the process as being more important than the actual results, a view not shared by their clients. They appear to believe that demonstrating a commitment to collaboration even in the face of insuperable odds is part of their professional responsibility in building the field of collaborative law. These lawyers express complete faith that the collaborative law process will eventually produce an acceptable outcome and expect the same measure of faith from clients (although such trust, unsurprisingly, is not always forthcoming). Failed cases that do not reach settlement are explained as failures to use the process properly. At its most extreme, this attitude can be articulated in the following way:

I don't really care about whether the outcome is optimal in terms of dollars and cents, but that [my client] and I live up to our collaborative principles.[47]

These same lawyers tend to be skeptical of giving the client specific legal advice (see the discussion in Chapter 7). They are more focused on the process than on substantive issues and outcomes, illustrated by the way they prepare their clients for bargaining:

> *Question:* So your preparation with the client would be a preparation for the process, rather than actually doing an analysis of their case with them? *Answer:* That's right.[48]

Somewhat similar views and attitudes about mediation are expressed by a small number of lawyers in the Culture Change project. The so-called true believer has made a strong personal commitment to the usefulness of the mediation process, which goes further than simply reorienting their practice strategies to new client expectations and requirements. In common with the small group of collaborative lawyers described earlier, the true believer uses quasi-religious metaphors such as "converted" (for example, "I'm a person who has now converted and I admit to being a believer in mediation"[49] and "I got religion"[50]) to describe this process of personal and professional change. However, the true believer does not appear to invest the process with the same almost reified powers and capacities as the small group of collaborative lawyers described above, and instead will recognize some (albeit a small number of) cases as unsuited for mediation.

It is important that whatever the strength of her commitment to a particular dispute resolution process, the new lawyer does not allow this loyalty and faith in a process to supersede her loyalty to her individual client. Each case and every client require an assessment of suitable dispute resolution processes without an assumption that one particular approach will always work. This assessment relates to counsel's obligation to ensure her client's informed consent (discussed earlier in this chapter), having offered him a broad spectrum of dispute resolution options rather than simply directing him to the lawyer's preferred process. Overzealous commitment to one particular dispute resolution model raises a danger that commitment to the process itself overrides this particular client's interests.

The primary loyalty of the new lawyer, just like the old lawyer, is to her client. This does not mean that process beliefs – akin to the old lawyer's belief in "justice as process" – and good working relationships with other counsel are inappropriate. Far from it. These elements can inform and often enhance client service. However, they are a dimension of and not a substitute for meeting professional responsibilities toward the client.

Bargaining in Good Faith

Complaints that the other side came to mediation unprepared to seriously discuss settlement, intending to use the process instrumentally, or lacking "good faith" in some other way, are common.[51] Naturally, the cause of the problem is always laid at the feet of the other side. Blaming the other side is always a useful way of answering a client's questions about why settlement was not achieved in mediation, but to be fair to these lawyers, there is plenty of evidence to show that some counsel deploy tactics deliberately intended to undermine the purpose and possible outcomes of mediation. These include unnecessary delays, using mediation to intimidate the other side into reducing their expectations, and using mediation as a "fishing expedition" for information without any serious intent of settling.[52] The following statement, which was made by a commercial litigator speaking about mandatory mediation, is a frank example of the potential for abuse of the mediation process, and of disregard for any notion of good faith, however defined:

> If I act for the Big Bad Wolf against Little Red Riding Hood and I don't want this dispute resolved, I want to tie it up as long as I possibly can, and mandatory mediation is custom made. I can waste more time, I can string it along, I can make sure this thing never gets resolved because you've already figured out that I know the language. I know how to make it look like I'm heading in that direction. I make it look like I can make all the right noises in the world, like this is a wonderful thing to be involved in when I have no intention of ever resolving this. I have the intention of making this the most expensive, longest process but is it going to feel good. It's going to feel so nice, we're going to be here and we're going to talk the talk but we're not going to walk the walk.[53]

While the strategy described in this quotation seems to be an unqualified example of "bad faith," there is also a range of well-documented and widely observed practices in mediation that could be more accurately described as "lacking in good faith." These include failing to prepare adequately, failing to bring the necessary personnel to the mediation session, failing to exchange relevant information in advance or to bring it to the mediation, and so on. These lapses may have more to do with a lack of familiarity with the mediation process than with intentional bad faith, but the cumulative effect is much the same – mediation is generally frustrated by these types of behaviours. In an evaluation of the Saskatchewan Queen's Bench mediation program in 2003, a number of lawyers expressed high levels of frustration about the likelihood that they would prepare conscientiously for mediation, bring their client, only to be confronted by a lawyer on the other side who was not willing to bargain openly or in good faith. The following comments are typical:

> Some lawyers make only pathetic efforts to prepare in [sic] mediation.

Some lawyers – they are living in the dark ages – tell their clients not to say anything, and this makes mediation a waste of time for myself and my client.

It can be embarrassing where you prep and bring your client, and then the other side walks [out] after ten minutes.[54]

Some jurisdictions in North America have adopted a rule that enables the mediator to impose sanctions if she believes that one party or the other has not come in good faith, adequately prepared, and ready to bargain seriously.[55] There is enormous difficulty in defining bad faith, and it is even more difficult to pin down an "absence of good faith." For example, is the refusal to disclose a particular piece of information prior to mediation justifiable client advocacy or is it a breach of good faith? If one side asks for an adjournment of mediation, which reasons are to be classified as "good faith" and which are to be treated as "bad faith"? Is perpetual optimism a necessary component of good faith (and surely it is time limited)? Is the delivery of a patently insincere apology, such as the one described by a client as being a statement that "only a moron would think [that] was coming from the heart,"[56] a matter of bad faith or simply poor stage management? And most controversially of all, is a failure to deliver a "reasonable" offer in mediation a sign of bad faith or simply a carefully considered conclusion not to offer settlement at this time?

The difficulty of drawing these lines has produced a debate in the United States over the feasibility of good faith rules policed by the mediator.[57] Concerns are centred on the definitional questions and the need to involve the court in making these decisions (thereby perhaps intruding on confidentiality). Some have also suggested that legislating a good faith rule encourages bad faith conduct because it provides a benchmark that some lawyers will then find a way to get around – for example, by giving untruthful responses to questions about settlement authority and readiness to negotiate. There are also concerns that a good faith rule with strict sanctions may be used to intimidate weaker parties and may even interfere with counsel's right to refuse to settle if it is not in his client's interests.[58] In Canada, these concerns appear to have stalled – for the time being at least – any further debate over good faith regulations in mandatory mediation programs. However, with or without regulation, the question remains as to what types of behaviour the new lawyer should adhere to in order to demonstrate good faith, and what standards she can reasonably expect of others.

Some legal cultures appear to be developing their own norms of good faith bargaining behaviours before and during settlement meetings, in much the same as they may have previously developed protocols in other areas of informal bargaining, for example, lawyer-to-lawyer negotiations, plea bargaining with the local crown councils, or in-chambers discussions with a particular judge or master. Smaller and more cohesive communities are often successful in setting and largely maintaining widely accepted standards and conventions. In mediation, these types of conventions usually include conventions for the adequate preparation for mediation (sometimes including a style of mediation brief), documentary exchange (for example, beginning with the voluntary exchange of the affidavit of documents), and sometimes a frank discussion between counsel to avoid unnecessary energy being expended by either side if one or the other believes mediation to be inappropriate or premature. One lawyer in the community of Prince Albert, Saskatchewan (population 40,000), explained:

> Prince Albert has a collegial culture, and negotiation and collaboration is part of that culture. This is as easy a place to talk rationally about a file as anywhere, and this program [mandatory mediation] has worked well here because that was already the mindset.[59]

This attitude helps to explain the reaction expressed by some lawyers in the course of a review of mandatory mediation programs in Ontario (1999-2000) and Saskatchewan (2002-03). Lawyers in these jurisdictions asserted that even if the program were to be discontinued they would continue to use mediation because it is widely accepted within their legal communities.[60] For these lawyers, and within their (smaller) communities, good faith bargaining had become an established norm complete with social sanctions for breach. It is noteworthy that, once accepted, these changed norms represent both community values and a personal commitment, demonstrated by the investment that many lawyers in smaller communities put into maintaining mediation programs either formally or informally. Under these circumstances, a good faith rule may be unnecessary – peer pressure does the job much more effectively.

In other legal communities – often larger, more competitive, and sometimes (by dint of numbers) anonymous environments – it is still normative and even assumed that counsel will often use mediation and other collaborative processes instrumentally and sometimes in bad faith.[61] This difference is so well established that among some lawyers practising in smaller communities with a stronger good faith ethos there is recognition that they should expect a different attitude from lawyers from larger and less collegial communities. The following comment is typical:

> I see a real difference of attitude in Toronto lawyers compared to Ottawa lawyers about mediation. They have not accepted it and they still hold back. They don't go in there with the intention of disclosing, bearing your

soul ... it's not working in Toronto the way it should work ... there's a really different attitude ... I've tried to persuade some Toronto counsel to go to mediation or to even just sit down and talk when the case is not one of the ones in the [mandatory mediation] system, and you just don't get that type of cooperation. In Toronto ... there's still the ambush mentality ... There's always been a difference in how they practice law in Toronto – just read a discovery transcript.[62]

Faced with what feels like "bad faith" in negotiation, mediation, or collaboration, what is the appropriate professional and ethical response for the new lawyer? A few lawyers take on the task of educating their peers with almost missionary zeal.[63] This may make a difference over the long term but rarely answers an immediate practical problem in an ongoing negotiation. A more common reaction to perceived bad faith is to respond in kind – the so-called tit-for-tat strategy that Robert Axelrod's gaming experiments argued was the most effective approach.[64] For example, if the other side fails to disclose requested information, your side does the same; if the other side refuses to put an offer on the table, you do too. However, outside a laboratory, the tit-for-tat strategy carries many dangers. Mimicking bad faith behaviour undermines the integrity of the process and, quite possibly, the lawyer's own reputation. It also inevitably escalates the process and may result in an impasse. There is a difficult balance to be struck between withdrawing from a process that seems to have limited usefulness in advancing the clients' goals and directly calling and addressing the bad faith behaviour in an effort to salvage the negotiation. Continuing to disclose information in the face of an obdurate silence from the other side, or working on offers when there seems little chance that the other side is ready or willing to reciprocate, is unlikely to be in the client's interest.

The new lawyer should practise talking directly and explicitly to the other side about issues of bad faith and, based on those discussions, advise their client whether or not to continue. Another possible approach in mediation is to place greater responsibility for facing down bad faith on the shoulders of the mediator. Data from clients suggest that some would like to see the mediator play a more proactive role in managing recalcitrant and obstructive behaviour on the part of counsel.[65] Some lawyers agree: "[In this case], the mediator made all the difference despite the lawyer telling the client not to speak. The mediators should be willing to get their hands dirty" – that is, by being interventionist when counsel is being obstructive to the process.[66] One limitation is that not all mediators are willing to play such a proactive role, whether because of concerns over alienating future customers if they lean too heavily on individual counsel or because of a lack of personal confidence and experience. How they might handle such an issue may be an important question for counsel to raise with a potential mediator before retaining them, especially when they are concerned about the possibility of bad faith bargaining.

The new lawyer and her client must jointly determine whether to continue to negotiate when there are signs of bad faith. There are many different degrees here, for example, whether the problematic behaviour is simply unhelpful or downright obstructive, or whether there is a failure to disclose information or actual obfuscation or deception. In deciding how to respond to either bad faith or the absence of good faith, counsel must responsibly evaluate what interests his client has in continuing to bargain, whether the process is salvageable or if trust has been irreparably damaged, and what alternatives exist.

A final issue is what the new lawyer should do when faced with bad faith behaviour by her own client. Many clients who are repeat users of mediation and other settlement processes recognize the potential benefits of using mediation and other settlement processes to gather information about the other side, and regard them as a serious attempt at resolution. However, this good faith is not universal. Clients may sometimes be tempted to suggest elements of an agreement that they cannot deliver, or present information in a way that obfuscates its real meaning or omits important details. Counsel should discourage this type of bad faith on the part of her client just as strongly as she would if it emanated from the other side. However powerful the client, the new lawyer should be willing to point out the practical risks of a purely instrumental use of opportunities for negotiation and mediation, such as impeding any possibility of early settlement and/or risking the durability of any agreement reached. Moreover, and especially if good faith bargaining is to become an established norm, counsel should also be willing to point out the ethical implications of exploiting the good faith of the other side without reciprocation. As she develops a stronger and more coherent sense of her own professional ethical responsibilities in relation to good faith bargaining, the new lawyer will be able to more confidently tackle this conversation with her client.

Pressure to Settle in the Process

In earlier chapters of this book, I have worked through several examples of situations in which the new lawyer has to find the appropriate balance between advising his client on a settlement offer and allowing him to make the final, informed decision. This next and final example of a new or reconfigured ethical issue derives from the same situation, but casts the problem a little differently. How much pressure is legitimate pressure for counsel to place on his client to accept a settlement offer he considers fair and reasonable?

When clients accompany their lawyers to meetings designed to explore resolution, they immediately change the dynamics of decision making around settlement.[67] When lawyers more conventionally negotiate with one another, usually at arm's length, they exchange proposals between themselves and ultimately convey a recommendation to their client for their instructions. While this latter practice is sometimes represented as shared or even client-driven decision making, it often amounts to lawyers simply telling their clients what they should do. When clients participate in negotiation, this agency role is bypassed, and clients hear for themselves what is being offered (or denied). There is no sugar-coating of the offer by their lawyer – equally, there may be something in the offer the client hears that counsel would not have recognized the importance of alone. The possibility of settlement becomes at once concrete and immediate.

A potential downside is that clients may sometimes feel pressured to agree to a settlement at the end of such a meeting, without adequate time to reflect and consider. The incentive to get the matter "done today" affects both counsel and client and may rush a solution that is later regretted. The following comment about the dynamics of mediation could apply equally to collaborative four-way meetings or settlement conferencing:

> There becomes an intense pressure to settle because you want to be successful at the mediation. So the mediation creates an expectation. And I think some people try to use that to force the other side to give up more than they should because everyone wants so desperately for it to work. So there does become this quite intense pressure by the end of the day to get to yes.[68]

The question of how much pressure counsel might legitimately place on her client to accept what she understands to be a good outcome, and at what point this pressure becomes coercive, is closely related to the earlier discussion of client autonomy and decision making.[69] However, when clients attend negotiation, such decisions may be reached more rapidly and in an intense climate. The new lawyer may be able to do little to diminish the impact of the natural tendency to want to try to achieve closure, but she should pay close attention to the potential of a dynamic driving agreement that may later give rise to buyer's remorse or other regret or misgivings on the client's behalf. Counsel should anticipate the possibility of a momentum moving toward settlement that might "railroad" her client into an agreement in much the same way that she would anticipate any other known, internal pressures to settle, such as a financial crisis making settlement imperative, an unfavourable legal or factual opinion that diminishes the best alternative to a negotiated agreement, or simply a stated desire on the part of the client to be done with the conflict. In other words, the new lawyer should be aware of psychological pressures and incentives that may move her client toward settlement, and deal openly with these.

The collaborative law process sets up some particularly unique pressures to settle, which need to be carefully anticipated by collaborative lawyers if they are to avoid the potential for a dynamic of coercion. This pressure on lawyer and client is exacerbated by the structure of collaborative law, which requires that counsel withdraw if the client commences litigation (the so-called disqualification clause). The sense in collaborative files is often that "just one more meeting" will enable the clients to arrive at a settlement. Like any settlement process, the pressure on the client to reach an agreement increases as the number of meetings and the time and money expended rises. The personal investment of some collaborative lawyers in the collaborative process may present a problem for their clients who need to make a practical determination at some point whether or not to continue in collaboration or resort to litigation. One collaborative client commented that given the investment of the lawyers, the rhetoric ("you may choose to withdraw at any time") and the reality are not always lined up:

> I think the lawyers can't be objective because they want this process to work. [My lawyer] said I could step out of the process anytime I wanted to. In fact, that wasn't very helpful![70]

While the disqualification clause is often justified as a mutual incentive to work at settlement, it also means that the greater the client's investment in a collaborative process – in the form of time, money, emotional energy, and the working relationship developed with the collaborative attorney – the greater the sense of entrapment, which may discourage clients from withdrawing. As one client put it:

> Now that we're this far, it's hard to leave. I have already spent around [$X] and all of this time.[71]

Some collaborative lawyers take active steps to avoid a sense of entrapment by scheduling regular discussions with their clients about whether or not to continue in the collaborative process. This is an excellent practice and one that should be widely adopted by the new lawyer, whatever settlement mechanism he is utilizing in any given case. Counsel may need to encourage his client to hang in just a little longer in order to see results, as every negotiation meets roadblocks on the way to settlement. However, commitment to exploring settlement is rarely open-ended or, outside collaborative law, exclusive – the parties may need to proceed with litigation and then return to bargaining at a later stage. The effectiveness of negotiation and settlement processes needs constant evaluation. The new lawyer has a responsibility to continuously reappraise the situation and be genuinely open to a change of strategy.

The structure of third-party-led settlement processes means that counsel is not the only character who may apply pressure to the client – there is also the possibility that such pressure may come from the mediator, judge, or other third-party actor. Third parties, especially authoritative ones, are provided with many opportunities to pressure disputants. The three highly coercive mediator styles memorably named "hashers, bashers, and trashers" by James Alfini more than fifteen years ago are just as prevalent today.[72] There is a sense among some professional mediators that part of the "value-added" service they offer is their ability to twist the arms of parties in order to push them toward settlement.

This perception of the need for strong-arm tactics is in part the consequence of a mediator's reputation often being tied to her volume of settlements. In one notorious case, a mediator told the parties that he would lose his 100 percent settlement record if they refused to sign the agreement.[73] Research suggests that lawyers prefer mediators who settle and often pick mediators based on this record alone.[74] Other widespread strategies, which are especially common in aggressive cultures such as labour-management negotiations but are also seen in court mediation programs, include using fatigue and hunger as levers to persuade the parties to agree. In Ontario's 1995 pilot civil mediation program, as many as 30 percent of clients interviewed said they experienced some pressure to settle.[75] Comments from one client group included: "I agreed just to get it over with" and "I felt bulldozed by the mediator" as well as the following reference to the physical conditions:

> I felt that we settled under duress. No food, no restaurants in the area, the coffee was awful, no one had change for the machine. I felt hurried and pressured at times.[76]

The new lawyer has a professional and ethical responsibility to ensure that her client is protected from mediator strategies to pressure them into agreement and that, if necessary, the mediation can be suspended or even terminated. This is one of the many important ways in which strong client advocacy within mediation is critical to maintaining the procedural fairness of the process. However, lawyers themselves are sometimes acquiescent in mediator pressure. They may seek out "hashers, bashers, and trashers" (or "muscle mediators") for clients who they feel need some strong "reality checking."[77] While it may be appropriate to sometimes use an authoritative third party to convince an otherwise unpersuaded client that, for example, she faces a poor outcome at trial, counsel must be careful not to allow or encourage undue pressure, especially from a third party who has no decision-making role.

Between 1999 and 2004, a small but growing number of cases were brought to US federal and state courts requesting the overturning of mediated settlements on the basis of duress by either the mediator (seventeen cases in total) or the lawyer (eighty-two cases).[78] These cases are using traditional contract arguments, such as duress, mistake, and undue influence. A debate is emerging over the use of "cooling off periods" in mediated agreements to ensure that parties and counsel are fully comfortable with their shared understandings, and to avoid litigation over enforceability.[79] These figures show that lawyers, and not third parties, remain the most common focus of client complaints about pressure in settlement processes. In relatively rare circumstances, this pressure from counsel is blatant – for example, when a lawyer is abusive to the client or threatens to withdraw if they do not accept an offer.

The new lawyer is committed to a working partnership, and such behaviour is obviously clearly inconsistent with professional responsibilities and values. But what should the new lawyer do when she witnesses this type of behaviour on the part of another counsel? Ethically, there is a strong case for the negotiation to be immediately suspended or terminated. Aside from the ethical ramifications, there can be no practical advantage in obtaining an agreement for one's own client that has been extracted under duress from the other side.

More frequently, of course, the type of pressure exerted by counsel on her client is less explicit and more subtle. A common example of behaviour that I have seen in mediation is when the lawyers dominate exchanges and then fail to consult with their clients or even to make eye contact with them before making an on-the-spot decision over rejecting an offer. Again, this behaviour is obviously inconsistent with the values and responsibilities of the new lawyer, who is committed to working jointly with her client. For any lawyer, such behaviour appears to undermine the principle of informed client consent. Yet if the new lawyer observes the other side excluding her client from decision making in subtle but significant ways, her quandary is more difficult. While there is no direct responsibility for the informed consent of the other side, a lack of consent could invalidate the agreement at a later point or simply render it ineffectual. I would argue that in order to maintain the integrity of informal bargaining processes, the exclusion of any client from active decision making should be treated very seriously and should always be confronted and addressed by counsel. Reaching a point at which such behaviour is widely regarded as unprofessional and unethical may take time – in adjusting to the participation of clients in negotiation, we see that lawyers are cautious and sometimes resistant about relinquishing control.

A final source of potential pressure to settle in the process comes from an increasingly activist bench and the rising use of judicial dispute resolution, including settlement conferences and judicial mediation. This trend is a reflection of a wider interest in settlement throughout the civil court system, as well as the social power of a judge to persuade a party that they should settle. The following is a skeptical but typical comment on this phenomenon from a litigator:

> One of the things you worry about in the kind of settlement philosophy that pervades our system these days is that people are in effect forced into settlement – they are forced into settlements by either judges who put pressure on them or by the realities of litigation and the cost of litigation.[80]

Whatever the source of the pressure to settle, the key ethical and professional issue for the new lawyer is the line between reasonable and legitimate pressure and coercion. A measure of investment and subsequent entrapment is inevitable in any dispute resolution process. Pressure is inherent in any lawsuit – to settle, to continue – and often parties succumb to it. There is a natural desire in most cases to close the conflict and move on, and this may be heightened in the moment and in the negotiation process itself. As well, as the above quote reminds us, the most significant factor in producing pressure to settle in litigation is cost. The goal of cost reduction almost always influences reluctant parties to at least consider settlement. In making explicit the search for a cost-efficient solution, informal dispute resolution processes are recognizing the reality of cost pressures, but how far should this information be pressed on the parties? For example, how often is it appropriate for counsel (or a third party) to remind the parties of the costs associated with continuing their conflict, or is there no limit to how regularly counsel should revisit costs as a component of assessing his client's best alternative to a negotiated agreement? How far should a collaborative lawyer go in persuading a disillusioned party to stay with the process a little longer in order to (perhaps) see some return on their investment in negotiations? And when is the use of pressure – perhaps pressure from a third party selected by counsel for this purpose – appropriate to check the unrealistic expectations of a client?

These questions are only just being raised and will take time and experience to answer. The bottom line for the new lawyer is that she is committed to a joint decision-making process with her client and to ensuring that all decisions made about settlement are made with informed consent. This means that she should deliver her own advice clearly and directly but without arm-twisting or threats. As a conflict resolution advocate, she must ensure that her client continues to feel she is "on her side," even if her advice is contrary to what the client prefers. This requires a realistic appraisal and up-front discussion of other pressures to settle, including costs, stress, and simply the rush of the moment in negotiation. Counsel may sometimes need to encourage the client to make a decision when that indecision is hurting him or he has become comfortable in a stalled negotiation. The new lawyer should also see it as her responsibility to protect the client from undue pressure from other sources, such as opposing counsel, mediators, or judges. The new lawyer and her client are building a space in which they can work together on the resolution of the conflict, with all of the information available to them, which includes a recognition of all the sources, both legitimate and illegitimate, of pressure to settle.

Conclusions

The new lawyer takes on all the traditional professional responsibilities of counsel as well as some additional ones. These include the responsibility to educate the client on a range of alternate process options, to establish a constructive relationship with the other side that does not undermine her loyalty to her client, to commit to the good faith use of appropriate conflict resolution processes and to model good faith bargaining attitudes, to anticipate pressures to settle, and to advocate strongly for a consensus solution that meets, above all, the needs of her client. It is in relation to these additional responsibilities that the new lawyer faces the greatest challenges in developing an appropriate professional response to new (or reconfigured) ethical dilemmas.

Ethical issues often arise in informal dispute resolution in situations that are difficult to predict. Frequently, the appropriate professional and ethical response is unclear. Rules of professional conduct for lawyers have historically not been directed at these types of fora, and instead anticipate procedures that are both more public (and, hence, scrutinized) and rule-driven. In this area perhaps more than any other area of legal practice, counsel must struggle in the absence of rules or even clear guidance to develop behaviours and practices that are, first, acceptable within their own ethical framework and, second, acceptable within their community of practice.

The great majority of lawyers do not turn to their professional code of conduct for guidance on ethical and professional issues but, instead, seek help from colleagues, mentors, and personal advisors (spiritual or secular).[81] Ideally, a sense of what is and what is not appropriate behaviour emerges from a combination of experience, dialogue, and reflection, a "discursive ethics" in which issues such as those addressed in this chapter are openly raised and discussed. The methodology of debate promoted by discursive ethics demands a commitment to a transparent professional culture of ethical behaviours that is not yet instinctual for the legal profession. Acknowledging that the new lawyer is searching for "good practice" in processes that are often new and unfamiliar, and in which "right" answers are elusive, is the first step in translating the experiences of counsel and clients into acceptable ethical standards for settlement processes.

9
Where the Action Is: Sites of Change

The developments of the last thirty years – including the escalating costs of litigation, the emergence of the mega-firm, the broadening demographic base of the profession, and civil justice reforms – are momentous in their capacity to change the way that legal services are delivered and the ways in which lawyers understand their professional role. Such is the scale of change that we are only just beginning to recognize its many diverse consequences. To construct a complete picture of the many ways in which legal practice is changing, it is necessary to include many disparate elements: structural, economic, demographic, procedural, and cultural. These elements do not fit seamlessly together to form a single, consistent theory of change. Nor do they provide us with a clear prediction of what the legal profession will look like twenty years from now. This is not surprising, since each of the elements of change has evolved piecemeal, often without a considered relationship to the other elements and largely in response to market conditions. There was no intentional "grand strategy" to modernize legal services but, rather, pressure from multiple sources for a different professional and economic structure, diverse areas of expertise, changing professional mores, a different model of client service, and, ultimately, a changing professional identity for lawyers. Questions about what that new professional identity, or choices among multiple identities, will look like are a long way from being answered – in fact, the questions themselves are only just being asked. This book is an effort to ignite and advance this debate.

Three critical sources of influence and leadership help frame both our questions and our choices about professional identity for lawyers in the twenty-first century. These are described in this chapter as "sites of change" because of their potential to bring forward and promote initiatives and innovations that will play an important part in the evolution of the new lawyer. One of these "sites" is legal education, which has been touched on in earlier chapters in this book, but which deserves a more complete examination in recognition of the role it might play in shaping the future of the legal profession. A second fulcrum of influence and power that stands outside but alongside the profession is the judiciary. The role of judges in the adjudicative system is undergoing significant change in ways that are complementary to changes in the role of lawyers. As a result of the widespread introduction of judicial case management and judicial mediation, which are often pushed forward by judges themselves and are never effective without their support, many judges are reconsidering the part they play in dispute resolution. The significance of the attitude of the bench toward change cannot be underestimated – their professional leadership will be key to the future.

Finally, this chapter will also briefly consider the relationship of law to other related professional disciplines and innovations in inter-professional collaboration. As the professional function and identity of lawyers adjusts and evolves, their place in the constellation of professional services must change as well. The extent to which lawyers and law firms see themselves as being a part of, rather than independent from or more important than this constellation of professional collaboration will also be highly significant for the future of legal services.

Legal Education

In Chapter 2, legal education was recognized as critical to both the creation and reinforcement of the dominant norms and values of the legal profession. In that chapter, I argued that legal education remains in thrall to the traditional models of lawyering that are beginning to lose their place in the delivery of legal services – for instance, the image of the lawyer as trial lawyer; the values of adversarial advocacy; the assumption that technical expertise translates into authority in client relationships; and, more generally, the social and economic elitism that characterized an overwhelmingly white, male, legal profession until recently. Change within the core of legal education has been glacial in pace. Elective courses such as skills courses or "critical theory" courses, while important inclusions, often fail to challenge the central assumptions of what "success" in legal practice looks like, or what are the most important skills of the lawyer. Instead, these courses tend to focus on developing a more critical theoretical perspective on law and lawyering, rather than directly questioning the practice assumptions and mores of the profession.

Some of my colleagues in the academy would argue that it is not the place of legal education to confront the deficiencies of legal practice. Many legal educators pridefully understand their role as limited to learning about the law rather than learning to practise law. There is a feeling that law school should somehow "rise above" debates over the nitty-gritty of practice and client service. I cannot agree. Ultimately, the question is:

How do we understand the relationship between legal practice and legal education?

First, it seems fair to assume that for legal education to stay relevant, changes in legal practice must resonate in the academy. After all, professional education generally assumes some sort of measurable relationship between success in education and competence in practice. In fact, any empirical evidence for this assumption is strikingly absent in law, and the one study that has been completed finds no such relationship.[1] What is far easier to show is that in today's highly competitive market for articling or entry-level positions, "success" at law school (in the form of good or very good grades) generally leads to success in securing employment. The gatekeepers of the profession do not consider people – they consider their grades, whether at the stage of law school admission or at the point of recruitment into first positions in law firms.[2] This means that the assessment processes of legal education are critical in establishing who proceeds to what type of position and in the absence of which alternative forms of assessment reporting – for example, narratives rather than grades or personal interviews for all candidates regardless of presenting grades – "There is no way of telling how many of those excluded might, in fact, have proved very suitable for the profession."[3]

Even if we are comfortable with the internal validity of these gatekeeping processes – and I personally am not – we should still be concerned by the remoteness of so much of what takes place in law school from the realities of legal practice. Law school focuses on conflict resolution exclusively via adjudication using the study of appellate judgments. It presents a picture of legal practice, as litigation and especially as trial work, that is out-of-date and unrealistic. It virtually ignores transactions and non-contentious work. It neglects to integrate clients – presented only as plaintiffs or defendants who represent a vehicle for making a legal argument – into this picture. The existence of clients as real people, with motivations and interests, is rarely, if ever, alluded to in law school classrooms, let alone their stories, their needs and goals, or their expectations for effective dispute resolution services.

Practical skills, and the conceptual frameworks for developing and modifying such skills, are taught in limited elective courses or sometimes in legal clinics. These courses and programs are often considered intellectually "soft" options and are often taught by practitioners "outside" the elite circle of full-time faculty. They and the students that they teach occupy a subculture within the law school.

Generally, law school offers students and faculty an alternative reality to practice. The actual work and changing tasks of lawyers are either not discussed at all or are presented as comprised of constant trial work and heroic fights against oppression and wrongdoers. Few, if any, law school classes allude to the realities of the changes in legal practice described in this book, such as less courtroom advocacy, fewer trials, increasingly dissatisfied and often demanding clients, and sometimes routine, mundane, and boring work with marginal professional autonomy. Beyond the intrusion of job fairs and career days, law school exists in a zone that is both conceptually and practically isolated from legal practice. This isolation is apparent despite the fact that the most important topic on the minds of upper-year law students is obtaining a position in a reputable firm. Lawyers in practice tend to look back on their days at law school with wry hindsight that amounts to "that was fun, and sometimes interesting, but completely removed from what I do now." It is little wonder that some law graduates are disappointed by what they find in practice, as well being ill prepared.

For the most part, law schools do not see themselves as teaching students about how to be a lawyer, what that might be like, what choices and challenges they might face in practice, but rather, how to "think like a lawyer." This bifurcation between "thinking" and "doing" is reflected in an apparently interminable and seemingly inconclusive debate over the extent to which the law curriculum should be driven by the exigencies of legal practice – that is, how far law school should teach practical professional skills along with conceptual tools for analysis and reflection. The problem with this debate – and perhaps the reason it never seems to advance – is the tendency to assume that a choice must be made between two dichotomous goals for legal education vocational training and intellectual development.[4] The fallacy of this dichotomy is immediately obvious if one recognizes that the law always draws its meaning from the context in which it is applied.[5] Any level of legal studies, whether it is basic or advanced, theoretical or applied, jurisprudential or interdisciplinary, must reflect the ways in which law is understood, used, and practised in the real world, notwithstanding the program's focus on academic analysis or vocational applications.[6] The intellectual understanding of law is embedded in its practical applications, and practical applications require legal knowledge and comprehension. In this way, the conceptual and practical dimensions of learning about the law are inextricably linked. As one lawyer comments, "Law schools teach law as stripes – but legal practice is really plaid."[7]

If the debate over learning about law is reframed within a realization of the interconnectedness of theory and practice, it becomes obvious that we have been asking, or understanding, the wrong question all along. The real issue is not whether legal education should take a special place for itself in developing the intellectual capacities of future legal practitioners – the answer to this is obviously yes. At no other point in their careers are lawyers going to be afforded the opportunity to study feminist legal theory, critical race theory, or legal history, all of which have the potential to significantly deepen and enrich their understanding of the role of law and lawyers. No one disputes the fact that law school is the place where future lawyers must learn to read, analyze, and dissect appellate cases for arguments that they can apply to their own files. The real question is the extent to which legal education understands its intellectual mission to include an appreciation of the realities of legal practice and the choices (ethical and practical) that exist, the skills that are required, and the centrality of human conflict and dispute resolution in all of their many forms to the mission of legal services. A simple dichotomy between practical and abstract knowledge is misleading and unhelpful in fulfilling this mission.

It is also true that legal education has choices over just how far to intentionally integrate practice into theory, and vice versa. Some measure of integration between theory and practice seems critical to fulfilling the mission of legal education, both pedagogically and practically; any one law school may choose to emphasize more or less practical context and teach more or less theory in developing an integrated curriculum. A few schools have developed extensive clinical programming in a conscious effort to extend the reach of applied and practical knowledge into the curriculum. However, even in these schools, the clinical curriculum is largely separate from the remainder in terms of personnel (clinical faculty versus academic faculty), location (clinics are often off-campus storefronts), and substance (the discourse of a clinical program is usually entirely different in content and tone from any other academic course). There is a further sense of separation between students who select clinical courses and those who do not.

Law schools also face choices about just what types of practical context and applications they might integrate into their curriculum. For example, almost every North American law school has a mooting program. Should the law schools continue to invest in skills training in appellate advocacy to the extent that they do and to the exclusion of other, perhaps more relevant and useful, professional skills? This question becomes more urgent in light of the changes occurring within the profession and the persistence in law school of outdated and inaccurate stereotypes about legal practice. The emphasis on mooting is an example of attachment to an area of skills development that is far less relevant now than when mooting programs were first introduced into many law schools in the 1970s. Yet the virtual disappearance of trial advocacy from many sectors of practice seems to have no impact on continuing investment in mooting programs, both new and old.

Concerns about the relevance of legal education and the subsequent competence of those individuals admitted to practice have been voiced in various different guises for over twenty years. During the late 1980s, there was vocal criticism of law school and professional education as being too remote from the realities and practicalities of legal practice (in particular, in the United Kingdom, the United States, Australia, and New Zealand).[8] This criticism was followed by the development of skills-based professional courses in some jurisdictions (for example, in British Columbia, Canada, and at the Institute of Professional Legal Studies in New Zealand), which taught and assessed the basics of client interviewing, negotiation, legal drafting, and trial advocacy. Contemporary concepts of "competency" for lawyers include not only these more traditional skills but also those skills and capacities necessary for offering effective client service in the new environment of fewer trials, more diverse dispute resolution processes, and changing client expectations of value and service.

A report by the Canadian Bar Association in 1999 recognizes this crossroads, arguing that an increasingly pluralist legal system demands a different core of lawyering skills and preparation for practice. Among its many recommendations, the report urges law schools to begin to take seriously training students in a more multidisciplinary body of skills and knowledge, including communication, psychology, and human relations skills.[9] Professional regulators are also beginning to recognize the need for further adjustment – following the first "skills wave" of the 1980s – in order to respond to changes in practice, such as the phenomenon of the vanishing trial and the expansion of institutionalized settlement processes in the courts.

A colleague and I assisted the Law Society of Upper Canada (LSUC) in conducting a "skills audit" of lawyers in the province in 2004.[10] It concluded:

> The data from our skills audit suggest that lawyers need to develop skills which are much broader than those used in trial advocacy. Lawyers still need those skills but they need to broaden the range of skills they can offer clients. While they are still client advocates they have to engage in new forms of advocacy in different fora. A significant component of their advocacy is expressed in writing – in pleadings, in motions, in pre-trial conference and mediation briefs. Moreoever much of this advocacy is designed to help clients accomplish goals – obtain a licence, register a patent, end a relationship, etc. – which may never require a trial in the traditional sense.[11]

As a result of these findings, which indicated a significant shift away from trial practice and an increased focus on settlement advocacy, the LSUC overhauled its professional qualifying program and adjusted its emphasis from trial advocacy to settlement advocacy.[12] This decision reflects a growing consensus that teaching law as an adversarial strategy developed via appellate trial decisions is incomplete as a preparation for legal practice in the twenty-first century. The present focus on one particular disputing model – adjudication – and a single approach to dispute analysis – based on rights – produces an epistemology that assumes that all disputing is normative with a "right" and a "wrong" (or technically less strong) position. In this model, the function of knowledge is to enhance the power to win, hence, the highly competitive culture of law school and the obsession with the "magic bullet," which is the appellate decision that will clinch the argument in the hypothetical trial. The law curriculum seems to unselfconsciously reinforce a model of conflict that has been largely unchanged for decades and is increasingly out of step with process innovations and an emerging culture of practical conflict resolution. The following statements from litigators looking back on their legal education sum up the message that this curriculum conveys and what it leaves out:

When I came out of law school all I wanted to do was trials.[13]

They never talked about settling in law school.[14]

By focusing almost exclusively on a single, rights-based approach to conflict resolution, which is so removed from the reality of most legal disputing, legal education does worse than simply not educate future lawyers about how to use new dispute resolution processes effectively in their clients' interests. It also fails to foster the capacity for creative problem solving and reflexivity that is widely recognized as critical to twenty-first-century legal practice.[15] As one of the many Task Forces struck by professional regulators over the past twenty years to consider the future of legal education expressed it:

No program of legal education would be sufficient if it did not also engender a capacity, openness and willingness to change and be a career long student.[16]

Reconceptualizing the complexity and necessity of a meaningful relationship between legal practice and legal education requires us to think very hard about how to move the teaching of law from "stripes" to "plaid." We need to develop courses that look at the actual, rather than the glamourized, business of legal practice: dealing with clients, resolving matters by negotiation, using written advocacy. We also need pedagogies that enable the integration of theory and practice in a simple yet meaningful way. "Reflective practice," which comprises a responsiveness to change, flexibility, and an emphasis on professional self-growth, is increasingly talked about as an appropriate contemporary goal for educators and practitioners alike.[17] A reflective practice model, used widely in medical and nursing education,[18] focuses on teaching future professionals to analyze and learn from their experiences, emphasizing self-awareness, self-critique, and constant analysis and review. The next generation of lawyers cannot possibly master the ever-changing and expanding substance of legal regulation and precedent. Instead, they require effective problem-solving skills and the ability to learn from their experiences. However, the emphasis on information transmission and knowledge testing in law school does little or nothing to teach and promote reflective practice and the related capacity for problem solving. Information transmission via lectures that deal extensively with legal rules but ignore dispute resolution, client service, and professional attitudes promotes neither reflective practice nor problem solving. Whereas reflective practice and problem solving require adaptability, flexibility, and an openness to change, law school teaches adherence to rules, regulations, and existing legal, pedagogic, and cultural norms. In short, if we are serious about accepting responsibility to relate legal education to legal practice, and about using "reflective practice" as a central concept and tool for teaching and learning in legal education, we must be ready to challenge the entrenched values and pedagogic assumptions of legal education and consider radical redesign.

So far, this discussion has concentrated on how legal education might be brought into closer alignment with legal practice in order to ensure that it teaches the qualities needed for effective lawyering in the twenty-first century. A further question we should be asking when contemplating the future of the profession is whether legal education can and should go further in playing a proactive role in the future of the profession. While academics have introduced important new courses into the law school curriculum over the last twenty years (for example, on feminist theory, race and critical theory, and international human rights), they have historically been less than proactive in relation to issues that affect professional identity and practice habits. It is noteworthy that changes in legal education relating to legal practice contexts and capacities – for example, the development of an expanded skills-based curriculum in the United Kingdom and Australia in the 1980s – have been the result of innovations trickling down from the profession to academe, rather than pre-emptive strikes by the academy.[19] The law schools and the profession also seem to have difficulty taking direction from one another in anything other than the most disinterested fashion. Witness the contemporary debate over "professionalism," which illustrates the limited ability of the academy and the profession to work together on an issue without one accusing the other of being responsible for the problem and doing nothing to fix it.

While it may seem natural for changes in the profession to (eventually) trickle down to the law schools, this one-way movement of ideas severely limits the influence of the law schools in shaping the future of the profession. Imagine, instead, a scenario in which the law schools take on a leadership role in response to changes in legal practices and curriculum change. This role would include both anticipating change and critically responding to it. Legal educators could make an independent judgment to anticipate the ways in which the curriculum needs to adjust to better prepare students for the realities of legal practice in the twenty-first century. Such preparation would include envisioning many different types of legal practice for law graduates, including commercial/corporate work (with a preventive law dimension), administrative law (including hearings advocacy), counsel to corporations and government departments, settlement specialists, personal legal services for wealthier and poorer communities, and so on. Despite their diversity, all of these avenues share common needs for education and training, including the importance of problem solving using a wide range of conflict resolution skills, and for some sectors, client relations and communication skills.

Changes in teaching content and practice to meet these needs would be both conceptual, such as diversifying the models of conflict analysis and resolution that law schools promote via the informal curriculum, and practical, such as the skills and knowledge about how to use the tool of the law that is taught via the formal curriculum. The reflective practice model is an important foundation for teaching students with as yet limited experiences not only how to learn from those experiences but also how to become a lifelong learner in their future practice.

Being proactive about anticipating and tracking change does not mean that change would or should be reflected uncritically in the law school curriculum. On the contrary, this is an important opportunity for law faculty and students, and perhaps invited practitioners, to work together on emerging issues of professional identity in a critical, constructive, and reflective environment. Individual law schools could choose to go further still by making their own individual determination of what norms and values will be important to the lawyers of the future, including professional attitudes and approaches to managing client relations, and then teaching these explicitly and transparently in their curriculum. The significance of the years spent in law school in the moral and professional development of the law student is well established. It is at law school that the values of future practitioners are critically shaped and sometimes reshaped. Legal education has a critical role to play in a regeneration of professional attitudes and mores.

This effort will take more than simply the introduction of more courses teaching the formal rules of professional conduct. Law students need to be challenged to think about the relationship between their personal values and those of the profession and the system that they will serve. In the spirit of reflective practice, they need to be confronted with practical dilemmas to negotiate and evaluate in an environment that is open, questioning, and constantly aware of the real human stories behind the face of legal practice. Far from demeaning themselves to the level of "trade schools," law schools would be able to capture, rather than squander, the intellectual capital embedded in teaching and learning about practice if they were to take on the challenge of being proactive in response to questions of professional norms and values, and exploring and conceptualizing the professional identity of the twenty-first-century lawyer.

If legal education is to remain relevant to the delivery of legal services in the twenty-first century, the law curriculum needs to be reoriented and refocused. If law school is to maintain its power and prestige in the development and training of young lawyers, it must realign legal education with the realities of legal practice, yet not uncritically. The types of changes in curriculum focus and emphasis outlined in this section seem likely to occur over time, whether law schools step up to a proactive role or, as historically seems more likely, simply follow and adopt the developments in practice. Legal education's long-time assumption of legal centralism, in which rights-based legal processes are the primary and preferred means of dispute resolution, is no longer either self-evident or realistic. "Process pluralism,"[20] which is characterized by "the availability and acceptability of a wide range of goals, norms, procedures, results, professional roles, skills and styles in handling disputes involving legal issues" is here to stay.[21] This fact is beginning to be recognized in individual initiatives.[22] More, much more, must follow.

The New Judge

The role of the judge in the civil courts is changing as the institutionalization of case management and settlement processes place judges in an increasingly supervisory and managerial role.[23] A wide range of processes are being developed and tested, including early case management (agreeing on a schedule for the production of documents, a timetable for discoveries, and the resolution of threshold issues), judicial mediation (when the judge is charged with bringing the parties to settlement), as well as more traditional pre-trial processes (where judges play an evaluative role). In some jurisdictions, judges play a crucial role in deciding whether or not to require parties to attend mediation (for example, with an outside mediator) and in such cases judicial support and understanding of the process being offered is key to the effectiveness of the program.[24] The timing of such interventions is diverse, as are the requirements (if any) for briefs or documents filed in advance, the attendance of clients, and so on.

Styles and philosophies also vary widely. In some courts, judges understand their role as purely facilitative, while in others they assume a more evaluative stance, whatever the formal process. In some, judges encourage or even demand the participation of clients, while in others they deal only with their counsel. With rapid yet uncoordinated development across courts and jurisdictions, the need for research on process and style variations is increasingly urgent. Such research would illuminate the scope and diversity of innovations in courts across North America.

In the criminal courts also, the introduction of juvenile diversion and alternative measures regimes is impacting the role of the criminal court judge. In some matters, criminal judges are required to consider alternative measures to incarceration,[25] and sometimes they become involved in aspects of diversion into community processes such as victim-offender mediation and community panels. There is also a small but growing interest among judges working in criminal justice and mental health areas in the ideas of therapeutic jurisprudence, which cast the judge in a dynamic, interactive dialogue with the offender or patient rather than as a remote figure passing down judgment from the bench.[26] Judges who have been instrumental in establishing alternative forms of criminal courts – for example, Judge Alex Calabrese of the Red Hook Community Justice Center in New York – are motivated by a sense that these alternative approaches to crime are changing the ability of the community to police and take care of itself. As Judge Calabrese comments in an interview:

> I feel that I can accomplish much more at the Justice Center. The options that I had at the Criminal Court were basically jail and no jail, with very limited drug treatment. At the Justice Center, I have a full range of services where I can release a defendant on the condition that he or she take advantage of all these services. So you have a real chance at getting to the problem and preventing the defendant from coming back to the justice system.[27]

The move toward specialist family courts staffed by specialist judges and the integration of a range of supportive family services into these courts, such as parent education programs, mediation, and counselling, is also changing the way these judges understand their role. Working in tandem with other professionals, including social workers, mental health workers, and child welfare specialists, judges in the most innovative family service centres see themselves as members of a team and their own intervention as just one element in managing family conflict. Referral to complementary services both enlarges the judge's sense of what is available and possible and gives her an insight into the impact of such programming on the lives of those with whom they are dealing in family court.

All of these procedural innovations are beginning to have a significant impact on the way some judges understand their role in the criminal, civil, and family courts. Other important factors have also contributed to this evolving sense of identity for our judiciary. One is the widespread recognition that faith in justice systems is declining, along with access, as many who would use the courts find that they cannot afford a lawyer, or simply prefer self-help for a range of reasons.[28] This means that judges are seeing a very significant increase in numbers of self-represented litigants over the past ten years.[29] The growth in numbers of *pro se* litigants is at least partially related to the decline in civil and family legal aid.[30] This phenomenon is profoundly changing the way many judges do their work, especially in civil and family court. In the absence of counsel, judges are left to assess the individual litigant's ability to make self-interested decisions (for example, not proceeding with an unrealistic view of the possible legal outcomes). One consequence is that more judges regard communication and conflict management skills as critical for their day-to-day courtroom hearings. They are no longer always, or almost always, dealing with lawyers but are often dealing directly with members of the public, some of whom may be distressed, confused, or even belligerent.

Subtle but significant changes in the judicial role, and the new skills that these changes imply, show up clearly in a survey I conducted for the Canadian National Judicial Institute in 2002.[31] When judges were asked: "What abilities and skills do you personally consider to be most important for a judge?" what they said and what they did not say was noteworthy. The most consistent characterizations of pre-eminent abilities and skills related to communication skills (including listening, explaining in clear language, managing people, and managing difficult courtroom interaction) and personal attributes (for example, open-mindedness, empathy, patience, and respect for litigants). Formal legal knowledge was usually mentioned as an aside or as an assumed basis of the judicial function. Furthermore, when respondents did allude to legal knowledge, it was almost always in combination or integrated with communication skills and/or personal attributes. Typical is the comment of one respondent, who, after listing communication and people management qualities, ended by stating: "And if [a judge] knows the law, so much the better."

When asked to identify areas of new skills and practice in which they felt the need for more skills development, 45 percent of judicial respondents stated that enhancing settlement conferencing skills was a personal priority for them.[32] This result seems to reflect a real appetite among some sectors of the bench for casting themselves as settlement specialists.[33] Of course, it also suggests that for a significant number of judges, settlement work is not seen as being a priority and perhaps reflects some ambivalence about the appropriate judicial role in steering cases toward settlement. It seems likely that, just as we are seeing within the profession, the judiciary will divide into those who enthusiastically embrace dispute settlement as a new and exciting aspect of their role and others who feel less comfortable or even opposed to this extension of their professional function and responsibilities.

Members of the bench wield significant influence in pressing for and then supporting professional and procedural change. Judges have demonstrated that they can play a significant role in effecting changes in legal culture.[34] A critical element of changing attitudes toward any innovation or change is the credibility imparted to the process by the support of professional leaders, and none are more significant than members of the judiciary in any one jurisdiction or region. In the process of collecting data for the Culture Change project (1999-2000), every one of the lawyers in the Ottawa sample made unprompted remarks about the exceptional leadership role played by Justice James Chadwick and Master Robert Beaudoin in building support for mandatory mediation in Ottawa. In Toronto, there are some professional leaders committed to mediation, but these are fewer and less powerful than their compatriots in Ottawa. These differences were clearly reflected in different peer group norms regarding recourse to mandatory mediation between Ottawa and Toronto.[35]

Procedural changes in the courts, efforts to promote the early resolution of civil and family disputes, and the rehabilitative emphasis of restorative justice initiatives in the criminal courts are changing the relationship between the judiciary and disputing systems and, consequently, the way that judges imagine their role and the skills they require. The National Judicial Institute survey suggests that judges themselves are highly aware of these issues, and many are eager to participate in new approaches to principled settlement. Despite this openness to change, there remain many contentious issues at the heart of this debate that require further and better examination. There are signs that a discussion over the appropriate role of the judge in dispute settlement is beginning to take place. Just as we have seen in relation to lawyer's practices, it is possible that each jurisdiction and every region will develop somewhat different approaches and cultures of judicial dispute settlement. The contentious issues, however, are likely to be the same everywhere. A threshold question is whether those individuals who are appointed as decision makers in an adjudicative system can also be responsible for accommodation and settlement within that same system. All settlement programs, including pre-trials, are careful to ensure that the same judge never presides over both a settlement and a trial of the same matter. Nonetheless, the question persists as a matter of role definition and public policy. To what extent should those appointed as authoritative decision makers within a system of justice be involved in facilitating resolution that may draw on principles chosen by the disputants themselves rather than the rules for which judges are responsible? And since a judge is the ultimate "knower of rules" within an adjudicative model, what does this mean for the facilitation of an agreement by an authoritative decision maker either before or outside this adjudicative system? Can judges ever be perceived as neutral settlers of cases? What about their innate authority and ability to "persuade"? How are courts monitoring the outcomes of judicial settlement programs? Will such evaluations consider the impact on using judges in settlement on public perceptions of the legitimacy and fairness of the justice system?[36]

The fact that questions such as these about the judicial role in dispute resolution are being raised at all is indicative of the degree to which judicial practice has already been affected by changes in legal practice and the landscape of legal disputing. This issue will have truly "come of age" when debate begins over revisiting the qualities sought in prospective judges to reflect the nuances of a settlement as well as an adjudicative role. In other words, do we need new judges to work with new lawyers?

Inter-Professional Collaboration

No book on the future of the legal profession is complete without considering the challenges to the traditionally solitary nature of professional legal advice and representation from related professions, and the possibilities of inter-professional collaboration. Where models of legal service are themselves changing, the relationship between the lawyer's role and other types of professional assistance is also affected. Further, movement toward a more holistic vision of client advocacy, which is not limited to providing legal expertise, is changing the way legal services are conceptualized and delivered by some lawyers, and may provide an impetus for closer working relationships with other professionals. As we have seen with other changes, clients themselves are demanding different services and are sometimes dissatisfied with anything other than a comprehensive and integrated professional service, whether it is in relation to a business matter (law, accountancy, tax advice, or financial planning) or a family conflict (law, child welfare specialists, counselling, or social work).

Unchallenged in their dominance in legal services for centuries, lawyers have faced over the past thirty years the growing incursion of paralegals into areas that were once considered the "bread and butter" of small-town lawyers (real estate, wills, small claims, and family). The legal profession has invested significant energy into driving this challenge away – described by Richard Abel as "repelling the barbarians"[37] – using various strategies, including price fixing, lobbying for restrictions on representation, and even imposing insurance penalties on lawyers who break ranks and work with the "barbarians."[38] The profession has also heavily relied on the classic arguments advanced by specialists resisting competition: that only lawyers can meet the highest professional practice and ethical standards. Inevitably, the paralegal community has responded with efforts to regulate themselves and present themselves as professionals. The contemporary reality is that the legal profession is forced to accept paralegals on terms they hope will be of their choosing, including agreements on restrictions on the unauthorized practice of law that define the area of work that can only be conducted by a licensed practitioner.[39]

A related, but different, challenge has come from other professionals offering advice to individuals and businesses in times of stability (in the form of planning) and crisis (in the form of interventions). There are many examples of this "incursion" in both corporate and personal sectors of legal services. Business clients obviously benefit from and increasingly demand the combined services of lawyers, accountants, financial planners, investment advisors, merger and acquisition specialists, tax specialists, human resource and organizational development specialists, and labour relations specialists. In the family area, family clients can benefit from the combined expertise of lawyers, therapists, child and family counsellors, child welfare specialists, and financial planners. In each case, the added value for clients who can afford a range of integrated services is that they are able to build comprehensive, long-term solutions to planning for uncertainties, crises, or conflicts instead of purchasing piecemeal advice, which may overlook opportunities for creative solutions, or which may ultimately conflict or collide with advice from other professional consultants. Concerns over the participation of lawyers in multidisciplinary teams centre on fee arrangements and the difficulty of properly identifying which part of a professional fee is for legal advice. There are also other practical issues, including the proper protection of lawyer-client privilege when lawyers work alongside other professionals who do not have similar obligations, as well as the potential of an increased volume of conflicts of interest that could result when a multidisciplinary firm "shares" clients.

One response to the growing client interest in comprehensive business services has been the development of specialist financial services within law firms, which prefer this approach to the risk of being "taken over" by the accountancy profession. Another has been the gradual development of multidisciplinary practices (or MDPs), which usually pair law firms with accountancy firms and house a range of business services. Currently, most Canadian provinces and US states do not allow fee sharing among lawyers and professionals from other disciplines (the District of Columbia and Ontario are two exceptions), although many others have initiated a process of review and debate.[40] In other common law countries, law societies and bars associations are beginning to develop regulations permitting MDPs, but there are continuing battles over the form these associations will take and the business models they will adopt. In some jurisdictions, MDPs are permitted only if lawyers remain in overall control of the enterprise. In these models, lawyers are only allowed to associate with other regulated professionals, and MDPs can only offer services that either qualify as legal services or support the practice of law.[41]

These debates demonstrate the nervousness of lawyers about forming professional associations with other professions and the loss of autonomy and status this may imply. They also illustrate the widespread concern among larger firms serving business clients over losing business to comprehensive financial services firms. Furthermore, these new structures for delivering services pose "unresolved ethical, regulatory and disciplinary questions, in respect of which legal norms provide little guidance."[42]

Similar developments can be seen within the family law area. In a few cases family law practices have begun to include on-site counselling and specialist services, sometimes sharing office space with other professionals. One format that has emerged is the "collaborative divorce team," where lawyers committed to the collaborative law model partner with other professionals, including mental health practitioners, therapists, child welfare specialists and financial advisors, who are likely to be involved in the management and resolution of a divorce file.[43] The emergence of the "team" model provides an interesting example of what inter-professional collaboration might look like as well as its special challenges. Despite an apparent difference in motivation between the formation of MDPs, which are generally regarded by commercial lawyers as a sound business move rather than an ideological choice, and the development of collaborative divorce teams, which are usually inspired by a belief that combining professional expertise brings better results to family clients, many of the same issues and dilemmas arise in each context. A primary stumbling block for the collaborative divorce team model is similar to the issue that has bedeviled the development of MDPs: just who is in charge? In a collaborative divorce team, the lawyer appears to almost always be the primary referral "hub" – in other words, clients come first to a lawyer and are then introduced to the other professionals. In theory, of course, another family professional, such as a therapist or child specialist, might make the initial referral to a lawyer and then remain as part of the collaborative team. This type of referral process does occasionally happen, but it is rare. The focus on the lawyer as the referral "hub" causes significant controversy among other collaborative professionals, especially therapists, who argue that there is no reason why control over referrals should default to the lawyer in the team.

> Therapists should not be dependent on lawyers for referrals. I could see therapists referring to lawyers and not just lawyers referring to therapists.[44]

The referral hub controversy illustrates the dilemma that flows from lawyers working with others in professions that have historically less status and generally charge a lower hourly fee than counsel. Who directs the "traffic" and brings professionals "on board" in a collaborative team is just one of a raft of issues that arise in relation to control and hierarchy within the team.

This problem becomes even more pointed when the distinctive role of the lawyer, who continues to bill at a higher rate than other collaborative professionals within the team, begins to depart from traditional expectations. As we have seen, a minority of collaborative lawyers see their role as being less one of providing specialist legal advice and more one of "friend" and "supporter" in the collaborative process. Even if they do not conform to this stereotype, collaborative lawyers drawn to the team model tend to be those who feel comfortable with a closer and less traditionally expertise-based relationship with their client. In other words, some of these lawyers prefer a quasi-therapeutic role for themselves. This raises questions about the nature of the boundaries around the role of the client therapist or coach and the role of the collaborative lawyer. Therapists sense a risk of encroachment on their therapeutic role by lawyers who have reconceived their role as quasi-therapeutic. In some teams this convergence of working modes may be welcomed, but in others it may cause conflict, especially when the lawyer neglects to provide the specialist legal advice that has historically justified her higher fee:

> I question the fact that they [lawyers] are charging huge lawyer's fees for doing a process that is not legal. Their legal expertise does not come into this very much, and the clients are being charged as if they are getting legal expertise.[45]

Aside from fee disparities, there is also the vexed question of staying within one's professional competencies, which may be highlighted by the composition of a multidisciplinary team. Unlike therapists, lawyers are not professionally trained and qualified to on a therapeutic relationship with the client. They may assume they know more than they do. Operating from within their own professional frame of reference, which is historically isolated from other professionals, and inevitably affected by the elitism of the profession toward the other professionals with whom they now find themselves collaborating, it may be difficult for lawyers to imagine just how much more there is to know before wading in. As this therapist explains:

> Lawyers are not accountable about how they understand family systems theory, they can just wing it any way they want it. Therapists are supervised and tested in student papers and practica.[46]

Some therapists raise concerns that lawyers may be encouraging their clients to deal with emotional issues in four-way sessions without being able to really understand and manage the ensuing dynamics. The reflections of some collaborative clients bear out this concern. The following comment from a client about the experience of participating in a four-way meeting with her husband and the lawyers is typical:

> I think this part of the process has a Pollyanna quality to it. Everybody is being nice to each other, everybody is told they should be open and honest and completely up front and everybody should be sharing. And, you know, that's nice, except that this is by nature an antagonistic process. There's no way around that ... My lawyer took me out of the four-way and told me: "You mustn't be so hostile." The lawyers are trying to be so even about it but, damn it, I feel angry in there. What do they expect?[47]

A different but equally hard to manage strain may be placed on inter-professional collaboration when a collaborative client finds that she prefers working with her therapist over her lawyer, because legal expertise and the skills offered by her lawyer are not the real focus of what she needs and wants. When clients prefer to use therapists to resolve their conflicts and work out a basic agreement, which is then presented to the lawyers to be formally memorialized, the lawyers may feel excluded and unsure of what their real function is in relation to the clients.[48] They are uncomfortable that so much of the bargaining and decision making has gone before them without their input. Similar struggles over "shares" of the client, and resulting issues of overall control and direction of the file, can be envisaged in MDPs and business partnerships.

Aside from issues of control and role parameters, there are also obvious differences in practice methodology and underlying philosophy between different professions. There is a tendency for each profession to value its particular expertise above others. This is a familiar problem, for example, in multi-professional health care settings where doctors, nurses, nurse-practitioners, social workers, public health workers, and others often clash over appropriate forms of treatment for a patient and just whose expertise should prevail in the case of conflict. It is especially problematic for lawyers who have so little experience in working with other professionals and then only at arm's length. Further, each profession has its own distinctive approach to core questions of client service, which may be managed slightly differently in different professions. One example already seen in the as yet limited history of collaboration between family lawyers and mental health professionals is the different approach to client confidentiality norms and rules that are taken by each. Whereas lawyers can ask their clients to voluntarily waive their entitlement to solicitor-client privilege, leaving them free to share information with the other side, many therapists feel uncomfortable even broaching this topic with their clients. The need to maintain the commitment to protect client confidences is a core value for therapists that comes with a strong sense of moral, as well as practical, obligation. Therapists working in collaborative divorce teams have addressed this issue by obtaining client consent, but even then their paradigm of client service makes this adjustment awkward and counter-intuitive.

There are also noticeable differences in the way lawyers and mental health professionals approach problem solving, which reflect different training and traditions of analysis. For example, lawyers often find open brainstorming – putting any and all ideas on the table without evaluation or censor – extremely difficult. Lawyers are unaccustomed to this type of creative problem solving, and are trained to assume that even the most tentative proposal means letting information "out of the bag." As well, lawyers find it difficult to problem solve without almost immediately coming up with a suggestion as to how to solve the problem. Therapists embrace creative option generation much more naturally, since it does not contradict any innate principles of their training. There are also differences between lawyers and therapists in relation to conceptions of advocacy. One lawyer described the way that different approaches to client advocacy might cause confusion within a collaborative divorce team:

> Coaches are more inclined to look at this as problem solving for the family – they are less aware of how something they might say might shift the whole negotiation in the room. Lawyers are more aware of what might affect their own client – and lawyers and coaches are sometimes on different wavelengths about this.[49]

Behind the awkward and sometimes ethically complicated mechanics of organizing an MDP, a multi-professional family services firm, or any other form of inter-professional collaboration, lie fascinating conceptual issues about the relationship between legal advice and other professional services. Unlike the traditional zealous advocate model, which does not assume any responsibility for dealing with anything other than the clients' legal problems, conflict resolution advocacy means that client problems are framed more broadly and holistically, and draw the lawyer into other approaches to problem solving. These approaches may require or suggest new professional partners.

In seeking new partners in inter-professional collaboration, lawyers must identify a clear (and indispensable) role for themselves. The absence of a clear and choate professional identity may be slowing the pace at which lawyers are presently exploring and developing the potential for inter-professional collaboration. In order to work collaboratively and constructively with other professionals, lawyers must ask themselves a number of searching questions, including: What do I bring to my clients as their lawyer that other professionals do not? What are the core functions of the lawyer's role? Where do the boundaries lie between my work and the work of other professionals? What is my work worth to the individual client, compared with the input of other professionals? When does my client need the advice and input of another professional? How well am I able to recognize client needs that I cannot meet and refer that client to an appropriate specialist? Are there cases I cannot begin to assist in unless and until other types of professional assistance are first provided? For example, some family lawyers believe that some of their divorce clients cannot begin to negotiate a settlement until they have greater clarity about financial planning issues or therapeutic support. Similarly, commercial lawyers may sometimes feel unable to advise their clients until they have the input of a specialist, such as tax, industry, accountancy, public relations, and labour relations.

These are difficult and complex questions the legal profession has only just begun to consider. Moreover, it is a debate that includes others who are themselves well-educated professionals with strong opinions. It is not simply a matter of lawyers deciding, as they are accustomed to doing, what the rules of the new game of inter-professional collaboration should be. Lawyers may find themselves having to adjust their expectations of control and autonomy in relation to not only their own clients but also other professionals. The bottom line is whether lawyers can sufficiently expand both their imaginations and their collegial instincts in order to work effectively and productively in collaboration with other professionals. These challenges and issues do not suggest that inter-professional collaboration is impossible. What these tensions illustrate is that for the new lawyer to successfully negotiate these collaborative quagmires, she must establish a choate and realistic professional identity, both internalized and externalized in relation to the expertise of other professionals.

Epilogue

This book has described what has changed about the practice of law over the past thirty years. I have tried to identify the most significant developments that have affected the way in which law is practised, and the resulting changes in models of client service and advocacy. At the same time, I have highlighted here what has not changed, including legal education, the key beliefs of legal practice, and many practice norms and habits.

In the process of making this evaluation, I have addressed the many fault lines that are opening up in these deeply cherished beliefs and norms of behaviour. In some of these areas, the legal profession gives the impression that it has its eyes tightly closed and is just hoping that when it opens them again everything will have gone back to "normal." This resistance to change is natural and is likely to be especially prevalent where the stakes are high and law is an elite profession. However, the landscape of legal disputing has changed dramatically and this is our present reality. As William Felstiner points out, "Change and resistance are inextricably tied together in an oppositional tension where the weight shifts gradually from one to the other, even shifts backwards at times, but in the long run runs in the direction of change."[1] In closing, I want to suggest that the profession get ready for the pace of change to speed up. What has changed already will not change back. And there is much more change on the horizon as the basis for resistance is increasingly eroded.

The compound effect of the economic and structural changes described in Chapter 1 has been to greatly increase the likelihood of young lawyers practising in larger firms, in a specialist area, and for corporate clients. This effect, in turn, has turned up the competitive heat in the larger bar associations, with increasingly adversarial approaches to advocacy becoming associated with big firm commercial practice. These changes are significant for how young lawyers, in particular, understand the core values and goals of the profession that they are entering. Since large-firm corporate/commercial practice generally garners the largest fees, the highest salaries, and, most prestige, these highly adversarial lawyers have become role models for many young lawyers. Ask a class of law students whom they regard as a role model and what they associate with "success" in legal practice, and, a few dissenters aside, you will hear a discussion focused generally on aggressively self-confident personalities, self-promotion, adversarial behaviour, high salaries, and high-profile cases and clients.

Yet the rise of adversarialism and an increasing focus on competitive big-firm practice is entirely at odds with many of the other significant changes described in Chapter 1 and elaborated throughout this book – namely, the unmistakable shift away from trials and toward settlement processes that rest on less adversarial norms. These processes require the development of both skills and a mindset that, while building on traditional approaches to lawyering, have many distinctive and novel qualities. The most successful lawyers of the next century will be practical problem solvers, creative and strategic thinkers, excellent communicators, who are persuasive and skillful negotiators, thoroughly prepared advocates for good settlements, who are able and willing to work in a new type of professional partnership with their clients, and aware of the need to constantly update their knowledge of conflict management processes and techniques as well as substantive law. This is the lawyer as conflict resolution advocate, and whom this book calls the new lawyer.

There will not be just one type of new lawyer. In fact, diversity rather than conformity is embedded in the concept of the new lawyer. There is a need for diversity of lawyers and lawyer styles to meet different client needs. There is also the realization that no one process of dispute resolution can be appropriate for all conflicts and that many different options should be contemplated and assessed by lawyer and client together. There will also, of course, continue to be many different arenas of professional practice for lawyers, but each practice setting will need a plan for the future that embraces change and anticipates more to come. While some lawyers may choose to prefer, for example, collaborative family law practice on Main Street over corporate commercial work on Bay Street (and vice versa), neither of these worlds can escape the impact of the other, and both are a part of the future of legal practice. Mandatory mediation and case management apply similarly to commercial litigation as they do to small claims or family matters. Corporate and institutional clients have reasons to prefer settlement that are as pressing as a personal client on a limited budget. Equally, both Bay Street and Main Street firms need a business model that enables them to stay competitive in an era of paralegals, in-house counsel, and other specialists. Every member of the legal profession is affected by negative public attitudes toward lawyers and justice systems, and they must be ready to take on this challenge by listening to clients, making changes, and promoting the values of professionalism and integrity.

There is an unresolved normative tension between economic and broader cultural (procedural and social) changes facing the legal profession. This tension demands a debate over the values and norms of the profession that opens up entrenched, even sacred, beliefs in order to develop new – appropriate, contemporary, and responsive – models of professional identity. There are expressions of ambivalence, dissatisfaction, and incompleteness everywhere among young lawyers entering the profession as well as old hands. This is especially apparent in relation to key aspects of the lawyering role that have historically enjoyed fairly stable norms and patterns of behaviour – for example, in relation to client advocacy, lawyer-client relationships, and appropriate ethical behaviours – and that are now adjusting to new conditions and expectations.

A coherent professional identity for lawyers requires an integration of these changes into their values, behaviours, and goals for their future careers. Satisfied and fulfilled professionals are those who possess a clear sense of professional identity and purpose. This is a worthy goal for both new and older members of the profession in these times of change. The emerging model of the new lawyer offers present and future members of the profession the philosophical and practical framework for a renewed sense of focus, commitment, and satisfaction.

Notes

Chapter 1: Changes in the Legal Profession and the Emergence of the New Lawyer

1 M. Galanter, "The Vanishing Trial: An Examination of Trials and Related Matters in Federal and State Courts" (2004) 1 Journal of Empirical Legal Studies 459.

2 Unpublished data from the Culture Change project. Between 2000 and 2001, I conducted in-depth interviews with a sample of commercial litigators in both Toronto and Ottawa who regularly participated in the court-connected mediation programs in each city. J. Macfarlane, "Culture Change? A Tale of Two Cities and Mandatory Court-Connected Mediation" (2002) 2 Journal of Dispute Resolution 241.

3 See, for example, the Ipsos-Reid 2004 survey "Canadian Bar Association Futures Initiative Survey," Canadian Bar Association, http://www.cba.org.

4 Microsoft recently hired a new chief counsel whose interview presentation consisted of a single PowerPoint slide: "let's stop fighting" (meaning "let's stop spending money on fighting").

5 John Lande points out the contrast between the values of business, which are often reflected by in-house counsel, and those of traditional legal practice (for example, an emphasis on precedent and a lack of creativity). See J. Lande, "Failing Faith in Litigation? A Survey of Business Lawyers' and Executives' Opinions" (1998) 3(1) Harvard Negotiation Law Review 1.

6 William Ury describes access to knowledge as the most important tool of the twenty-first century, and such knowledge is now available as never before to non-lawyers. W. Ury, *The Third Side: Why We Fight and How We Can Stop* (New York: Penguin, 2000).

7 J. Heinz and E. Laumann, *Chicago Lawyers: The Social Structure of the Bar* (Chicago: American Bar Foundation, 1982) at 213.

8 D. Landon, *Country Lawyers: The Impact of Context on Professional Practice* (New York: Praeger, 1990) at 5.

9 R. Abel, *American Lawyers* (Oxford: Oxford University Press, 1989). This is demonstrated in Canada and the United States by the proliferation of continuing legal education courses on alternative dispute resolution, which, although often superficial, have become a "must-have" for legal practitioners.

10 See, for example, B. McAdoo, *The Impact of Rule 114 on Civil Litigation Practice in Minnesota* (Minneapolis, MN: Supreme Court Office of Continuing Education, 1997); B. McAdoo and A. Hinshaw, *Attorney Perspectives on the Effect of Rule 17 on Civil Litigation in Missouri* (Colombia, MO: University of Missouri-Columbia School of Law, May 2002); and R. Wissler, "Court-Connected Mediation in General Civil Cases: What We Know from Empirical Research" (2002) 17 Ohio State Journal on Dispute Resolution 641 (reporting on data from Ohio's mediation programs).

11 Geert Hofstede, "Management Scientists Are Human" (1994) 40(1) Management Science 4. National (cultural) environment leads to norms and values. There are distinct cultural differences that are related to differences in national environments.

12 B. Curran and C. Carson, *The Lawyer Statistical Report: The US Legal Profession in the 1990s* (Chicago: American Bar Foundation, 1994).

13 Canadian Bar Association, *Crystal Clear: New Perspectives for the Canadian Bar Association,* Report of the Canadian Bar Association Future Committee (Ottawa: Canadian Bar Association, 2006) at 13.

14 J. Heinz et al., "Diversity, Representation and Leadership in an Urban Bar: A First Report on a Survey of the Chicago Bar" (1976) 1(3)American Bar Foundation Research Journal 717.

15 See J. Heinz, R. Nelson, and E. Laumann, *Summary of Chicago Lawyers II* (Chicago: American Bar Foundation, 1995), http://www.abf-sociolegal.org/1998rep/legalprof.html.

16 J. Hagan and F. Kay, "Social Mobility and Hierarchical Structure in Canadian Law Practice," in W. Felstiner, ed., *Reorganisation and Resistance* (Oxford: Hart Publishing, 2005) 281 at 282.

17 R. Daniels, "The Law Firm as an Efficient Community" (1992) 37 McGill Law Journal 807; and J. Hagan and F. Kay, *Gender in Practice: A Study of Lawyers' Lives* (New York: Oxford University Press, 1995), which draws on a 1990 survey of Ontario lawyers.

18 Ross has estimated that while associate salaries have risen by 1,000 percent in the preceding thirty years, billing rates have risen by "only" 400 percent. William G. Ross, *The Honest Hour: The Ethics of Time-Based Billing by Attorneys* (Durham: Carolina Academic Press, 1996).

19 Patrick Schiltz, formerly a partner in a large law firm, argues persuasively that this gap can only be bridged by requiring ever-increasing numbers of billable hours from associates and then selling those hours to clients at a far higher rate than the associates are paid. See P. Schiltz, "On Being a Happy, Healthy and Ethical Member of an Unhappy, Unhealthy and Unethical Profession" (1991) 52 Vanderbilt Law Review 872.

20 Hagan and Kay, see note 16 above, 281 at 282.

21 See R. Nelson and R. Sandefur, "From Professional Dominance to Organisational Dominance," in Felstiner, ed., see note 16 above at 313.

22 R. Nelson, "The Futures of American Lawyers: A Demographic Profile of a Changing Profession in a Changing Society," in R. Abel, ed., *Lawyers: A Critical Reader* (New York: New Press, 1997) 20 at 21.

23 Association of Corporate Counsel, http://www.acca.com.

24 Canadian Corporate Counsel Association, http://www.cancorpcounsel.org.

25 Hagan and Kay, see note 17 above.

26 Nelson, see note 22 above, 20 at 26.

27 Hagan and Kay, see note 16 above at 281.

28 B. Wilson, Chair, *Touchstones for Change: Equality Diversity and Accountability* (Ottawa: Canadian Bar Association, 1995).

29 F. Kay, "Flight from Law: A Competing Risks Model of Departures from Law Firms" (1997) 31(2) Law and Society Review 301.

30 F. Kay, C. Masuch, and P. Curry, *Diversity and Change: The Contemporary Legal Profession in Ontario* (Toronto: Law Society of Upper Canada, 2004) at 27.

31 Felix N. Weekes and A. Elliot Spears, *Survey of Black Lawyers, Black Articling Students and Recently Called Black Lawyers* (Toronto: Law Society of Upper Canada, 1992). See also Michael B. St. Patrick, "Black Bay Street Lawyers and Other Oxymora" (1998) 30 Canadian Business Law Journal 267.

32 Kay, Masuch, and Curry, see note 30 above at 41.

33 The most recent (2002) study shows that just 1.8 percent of filings in the US Federal Court go to a full trial, down from 11.5 percent in 1962. Galanter, see note 1 above.

34 Ministry of the Attorney General, *Ontario Civil Justice Review: First Report,* March 1995, http://www.attorneygeneral.jus.gov.on.ca/english/about/pubs/cjr/firstreport/cost.asp at chapter 11. Today, this figure would be closer to $50,000 (all figures in Canadian dollars).

35   Galanter, see note 1 above.
36   J. Twohig, C. Baar, A. Meyers, and A.M. Predko, "Empirical Analyses of Civil Cases Commenced and Cases Tried in Toronto 1973-94," in Ontario Law Reform Commission, *Rethinking Civil Justice: Research Studies for the Civil Justice Review*, volume 1 (Toronto: Ontario Law Reform Commission, 1996) at 77.
37   See J. Macfarlane, "What Does the Changing Culture of Legal Practice Mean for Legal Education?" (2001) 20 Windsor Yearbook of Access to Justice 191; and J. Macfarlane and J. Manwaring, "Reconciling Professional Legal Education with the Evolving (Trial-less) Reality of Legal Practice" (2006) 1 Journal of Dispute Resolution 253.
38   See, for example, G. Hadfield, "Where Have All the Trials Gone? Settlements, Nontrial Adjudications and Statistical Artifacts in the Changing Disposition of Federal Civil Cases" (2004) 1(3) Journal of Empirical Legal Studies 705.
39   *Civil Justice Review 1995-96*, first report, chapter 4, http://www.attorneygeneral.jus.gov.on.ca/english/about/pubs/cjr/firstreport/courts.asp.
40   Twohig, Baar, Meyers, and Predko, see note 36 above.
41   The Canadian minister of justice speaking to the House of Commons Standing Committee on Justice and Legal Affairs. *Minutes of Proceedings and Evidence*, Issue No. 62, 17 November 1994.
42   See Human Rights Watch Backgrounder, April 2003, http://www.hrw.org/backgrounder/usa/incarceration/.
43   Section 718.2(e) of the Canadian *Criminal Code*, R.S.C. 1985, c. C-46, s. 264, states that "all available sanctions other than imprisonment that are reasonable in the circumstances should be considered for all offenders, with particular attention to the circumstances of aboriginal offenders."
44   *Youth Criminal Justice Act*, S.C. 2002, c. 1.
45   The relationship between criminal and civil matters and appropriate processes to deal with each is examined at length in Law Commission of Canada, *Transforming Relationships through Participatory Justice* (Ottawa: Law Commission of Canada, 2004).
46   Especially in relation to case flow and settlement timelines and in terms of client satisfaction. See Roselle L. Wissler, "The Effectiveness of Court-Connected Dispute Resolution in Civil Cases" (2004) 22 Conflict Resolution Quarterly 55.
47   See the assessment offered in Law Commission of Canada, *Transforming Relationships through Participatory Justice* (Ottawa: Law Commission of Canada, 2004) at 15-87.
48   These terms occur frequently in the data collected for the Culture Change project, see note 2 above. For other studies that suggest a relationship between experience with mediation and positive attitudes toward its use, see Roselle L. Wissler, "When Does Familiarity Breed Content? A Study of the Role of Different Forms of ADR Education and Experience in Attorneys' ADR Recommendations" (2002) 2(2) Pepperdine Dispute Resolution Law Journal 199; C. McEwen, N.H. Rogers, and R.J. Mainman, "Bring in the Lawyers: Challenging the Dominant Approaches to Ensuring Fairness in Divorce Mediation" (1995) 33 Maine Law Review 237; J. Lande, "Getting the Faith: Why Business Lawyers and Executives Believe in Mediation" (2000) 5 Harvard Negotiation Law Review 137 at 199; M. Medley and J. Schellenberg, "Attitudes of Attorneys toward Mediation" (1994) 12(2) Mediation Quarterly 185 at 195-96; and Macfarlane, see note 2 above at 299-301.
49   Unpublished data from a 2002-03 evaluation of the court-connected mediation program in the Saskatchewan Court of Queen's Bench. The evaluators (J. Macfarlane and M. Keet) conducted interviews and focus groups with both lawyers and their clients [*Learning from Experience*].
50   Macfarlane, see note 2 above at 317.
51   Unpublished data from *Learning from Experience*, see note 49.
52   See, for example, N. Welsh, "Making Deals in Court-Connected Mediation: What's Justice Got to Do with It?" (2001) 79 Washington University Law Quarterly 788 at 795-804; K. Kovach and L. Love, "Mapping Mediation: The Risks of Riskin's Grid" (1998) 3 Harvard Negotiation Law Review 71 at 96; and Macfarlane, see note 2 above at 268-77.
53   Although it is important to recognize the voluntary commitment to finding a new and

different way to practise law demonstrated by, for example, the collaborative family lawyers groups and the holistic lawyers movement.

54 See B. McAdoo, "A Report to the Minnesota Supreme Court: The Impact of Rule 114 on Civil Litigation Practice in Minnesota" (2002) 25 Hamline Law Review 401 at 417-19; and the "Dismissers" from Macfarlane, see note 2 above at 257-58.

55 Macfarlane, see note 2 above at 302.

56 Unpublished data from the Culture Change project.

57 See A. Schneider, "Shattering Negotiation Myths: Empirical Evidence on the Effectiveness of Negotiation Style" (2002) 7. Harvard Negotiation Law Review 143 at 187-90. Schneider finds that the adversarial negotiators have become more extreme and "nastier" over the past twenty-five years (the original Williams study was undertaken in 1976). See G. Williams, *Legal Negotiation and Settlement* (St. Paul: West Publishing, 1983); and Macfarlane, see note 2 above at 302 and 306.

58 Ronald J. Gilson and Robert H. Mnookin, "Disputing through Agents: Cooperation and Conflict between Lawyers in Litigation" (1994) 94 Columbia Law Review 509 at 535; and John L. Barkai and Gene Kassebaum, "Using Court-Annexed Arbitration to Reduce Litigant Costs and to Increase the Pace of Litigation" (1989) 16(S5) Pepperdine Law Review 43 at 47.

59 Chief Justice Committee Ontario, "Chief Justice of Ontario's Advisory Committee on Professionalism," http://www.ocaa.ca/CJOColloquia.asp. While much ink has been spilled on this topic recently, it has been a pervasive concern for more than a decade. For substantive rather than nostalgic approaches, see, for example, F. Zacharias, "Reconciling Professionalism and Client Interests" (1995) 36 William and Mary Law Review 1303; and J. Sammons, "The Professionalism Movement: The Problems Defined" (1993) 29 Georgia Law Review 1035.

60 See, for example, in the United States, R. MacCrate, *Legal Education and Professional Development: An Educational Continuum,* Report of the Task Force on Law Schools and the Profession: Narrowing the Gap (Chicago: American Bar Association, 1992).

61 L. Riskin, "Mediation and Lawyers" (1982) 42 Ohio State Law Journal 41 at 43-48.

62 Consultative Group on Research and Education in Law, *Law and Learning* (Ottawa: Social Science and Humanities Research Council of Canada, 1983) (also known as the Arthur's Report).

63 W.B. Cotter, *Professional Responsibility Instruction in Canada: A Coordinated Curriculum for Legal Education* (Montreal: Conceptcom, 1992).

64 Robert C. Post, "On the Popular Image of the Lawyer: Reflections in a Dark Glass" (1987) 75 California Law Review 379 at 380; and Bill Ong Hing, "In the Interest of Racial Harmony: Revisiting the Lawyer's Duty to Work for the Common Good" (1994-95) 47 Stanford Law Review 901 at 927.

65 J. Nolan-Haley, "Lawyers, Clients and Mediation" (1998) 73 Notre Dame Law Review 1369 at 1372.

66 See the many stories in S. Silbey and P. Ewick, *The Common Place of Law: Stories from Everyday Life* (Chicago: University of Chicago Press, 1998).

67 M. Galanter, "Why the 'Haves' Come Out Ahead: Speculations on the Limits of Legal Change" (1974) 9 Law and Society Review 95.

68 M. Heumann and J. Hyman, "Negotiation Methods and Litigation Settlement Methods in New Jersey: You Can't Always Get What You Want" (1997) 12 Ohio State Journal of Dispute Resolution 253 at 295-305.

69 Thomas Kuhn's concept of "paradigm shift" means the actual replacement or substitution of the old with a new paradigm. T. Kuhn, *The Structure of Scientific Revolution* (Chicago: University of Chicago Press, 1962).

70 Macfarlane, see note 2 above at 306 [emphasis added].

71 For example, J. Cooley, *Mediation Advocacy* (Louisville, CO: National Institute for Trial Advocacy, 1996); and C. Noble, L. Dizgun, and P. Emond, *Mediation Advocacy* (Toronto: Emond Montgomery, 1998).

72 Macfarlane, see note 2 above at 306.

73 Abel, see note 9 above.

74 *Ibid.*

75 Macfarlane, see note 2 above at 316.

76 This point may also apply to the development of voluntary networks. For example, in Medicine Hat, Alberta (population 51,000) the two most prominent members of the Family Bar (totalling eighteen lawyers) attended training for collaborative law in the late 1990s. They returned inspired and began a collaborative lawyering group for family lawyers. Within a year, all but one of the members of the Family Bar had joined up. Not practising collaboratively is now considered counter-culture in Medicine Hat.

77 See R. Wissler, "Barriers to Attorneys Discussion and Use of ADR" (2004) 19(2) Ohio State Journal on Dispute Resolution 459 at 488-89.

78 Kuhn, see note 69 above.

79 J. Macfarlane, *The Emerging Phenomenon of Collaborative Family Law (CFL): A Qualitative Study of CFL Cases* (Ottawa: Department of Justice, 2005), http://www.canada.justice.gc.ca/en/ps/pad/reports/2005-FCY-1 at 37.

80 Geert Hofstede's work on how organizations and national cultures change emphasizes the interaction of environmental factors with behaviours and norms. See, for example, G. Hofstede, *Culture's Consequences: International Differences in Work-Related Values* (Beverly Hills, CA: Sage, 1980). This book describes Hofstede's survey of workplace cultures in forty countries and identifies some of the factors that lead to cultural differences.

81 See, for example, the papers in C. Bell and D. Kahane, eds., *Intercultural Dispute Resolution in Aboriginal Contexts: Canadian and International Perspectives* (Vancouver: UBC Press, 2004), especially D. Kahane, "Dispute Resolution and the Politics of Cultural Generalisation."

82 See N. Welsh, "Making Deals in Court-Connected Mediation: What's Justice Got to Do With It?" (2001) 79 Washington University Law Quarterly 788; and N. Welsh, "The Thinning Vision of Self-Determination in Court-Connected Mediation: The Inevitable Price of Institutionalisation?" (2001) 6 Harvard Negotiation Law Review 101.

83 Macfarlane, see note 2 above at 259.

84 The classic argument set out in Owen M. Fiss, "Against Settlement" (1984) 93 Yale Law Journal 1073.

85 Macfarlane, see note 2 above at 313 [emphasis added].

86 D. Goldman, *Emotional Intelligence: Why It Can Matter More Than IQ* (New York: Bantam Books, 1994).

87 Unpublished data from the Culture Change project.

Chapter 2: Constructing Professional Identity

1 Leonard E. Gross, "The Public Hates Lawyers: Why Should We Care?" (2000) 29 Seton Hall Law Review 1405; M. Galanter, *Lowering the Bar: Lawyer Jokes and Legal Culture* (Madison, WI: University of Wisconsin Press, 2005); and Walter K. Olsen, *The Rule of Lawyers: How the New Litigation Elite Threatens America's Rule of Law* (New York: St. Martin's Press, 2003).

2 Robert C. Post, "On the Popular Image of the Lawyer: Reflections in a Dark Glass" (1987) 75 California Law Review 379 at 380; and Bill Ong Hing, "In the Interest of Racial Harmony: Revisiting the Lawyer's Duty to Work for the Common Good" (1994-95) 47 Stanford Law Review 901 at 927.

3 The subject of dedicated websites (for example, http://www.lawyer-jokes.us/ and http://www.ahajokes.com/lawyer_joke_of_the_day.shtml) and texts (for example, Andrew McMeel, *Lawyers Quotes, Jokes and Anecdotes* (Kansas City: Andrew McMeel Publishing, 2001); and Beth Tripmacher, *The Best Lawyer Jokes Ever* (New York: Metrobooks, 2002).

4 J. Elkins, "Reading/Teaching Lawyer Films" (2004) 28(4) Vermont Law Review 813 at 830.

5 See, for example, D. Kellner, *Media Culture: Cultural Studies, Identity and Politics between the Modern and the Post Modern* (London: Routledge, 1995).

6 Known as the "cultivation theory." See, for example, George Gerbner et al., "Growing Up with Television: The Cultivation Perspective," in Jennings Byrant and Dolf Zillman, eds., *Media Effects: Advances in Theory and Research* (Hillsdale, NJ: Lawrence Erlbaum Associates, 1994) at 17.

7 Gerbner et al., see note 6 above at 23-25.

8 "To Kill a Mockingbird," starring Gregory Peck, directed by Robert Mulligan (Universal Studios, 1962).
9 "Clarence Darrow," starring Henry Fonda, directed by John Rich (Kultur Video, 1974), based on the life and trials of the real-life lawyer.
10 "Inherit the Wind," starring Spencer Tracy, directed by Stanley Kramer (United Artists, 1960), based on the 1925 Scopes trial. The Spencer Tracy character was based on Clarence Darrow.
11 See, for example, M. Asimow, "Bad Lawyers in the Movies" (2000) 24(2) Nova Law Review 533.
12 Elkins, see note 4 above; and Post, see note 2 above at 380; and Hing, see note 2 above.
13 "In the Name of the Father," starring Emma Thompson, directed by Jim Sheridan (Universal Pictures, 1993).
14 "Erin Brockovich," starring Julia Roberts, directed by Steven Soderbergh (Universal Pictures, 2000).
15 See the discussion in J. Grant, "Lawyers As Superheroes: The Firm, The Client, and The Pelican Brief" (1996) 30 University of San Francisco Law Review 1111.
16 For a meta-analysis of the qualities associated with pre-law students, success at law school, and professional practice, see S. Daicoff, "Lawyer, Know Thyself: A Review of Empirical Research on Attorney Attributes Bearing on Professionalism" (1997) 46 American University Law Review 1337.
17 For a classic statement of the role of norms, see T. Parsons, *The Structure of Social Action* (New York: McGraw Hill, 1937). Parsons' original view of the universality of values and norms has been substantially refined by the literature of social constructivism and interpretivism (for example, see E. Durkheim, *Suicide: A Study in Religion* (first published in French, London: Routledge and Kegan Paul, 1970); and H. Garfinkel, *Studies in Ethnomethodology* (Englewood Cliffs, NJ: Prentice Hall, 1967), to recognize cultural and other contextual factors).
18 D.M. Schneider, "Notes toward a Theory of Culture," in K.H. Basso and H.A. Selby, eds., *Meaning in Anthropology* (Albuquerque: University of New Mexico Press, 1976) 197 at 203.
19 Chief Justice Committee Ontario, "Chief Justice of Ontario's Advisory Committee on Professionalism," http://www.ocaa.ca/CJOColloquia.asp. The debate over professionalism is discussed in more detail in chapter 8 in this book.
20 See, for example, Lawerence Silver, "Anxiety and the First Semester of Law School" (1968) 4 Wisconsin Law Review 1201; Suzanne C. Segerstrom, "Perceptions of Stress and Control in the First Semester of Law School" (1996) 32 Willamette Law Review 593; and Howard S. Erlanger and Douglas A. Klegon, "Socialization Effects of Professional School: The Law School Experience and Student Orientation to Public Interest Concerns" (1978) 13 Law and Society Review 11.
21 See, for example, Daicoff, note 16 above.
22 Deborah Rhode, "Ethics by the Pervasive Method" (1992) 42 Journal of Legal Education 31 at 41.
23 See note 19 above.
24 For an extended discussion of the challenges of teaching ethics to prospective lawyers and the extent to which the law schools fall short, see, for example, Beverly Balos, "The Bounds of Professionalism: Challenging Our Students; Challenging Ourselves" (1997) 4 Clinical Law Review 129; Paul Brest, "The Responsibility of Law Schools: Educating Lawyers as Counselors and Problem Solvers" (1995) 58 Law and Contemporary Problems 5; Sammons, see note 19 above; and David B. Wilkins, "Redefining the 'Professional' in Professional Ethics: An Interdisciplinary Approach to Teaching Professionalism" (1995) 58 Law and Contemporary Problems 241.
25 The bell curve is an example of a "competitive" grading policy, in contrast with an "individualistic" or a "co-operative" model.
26 A. Hochschild, "Inside the Clockwork of Male Careers," in F. Howe, ed., *Women and the Power to Change* (New York: McGraw-Hill Book Company, 1975) 47 at 64. In law school, this is often manifested by one's ability to assimilate and converse in the "special language" of law.

27 See J. Macfarlane, "Teacher Power in the Law School Classroom" (1996) 19 Dalhousie Law Journal 71 at 82.

28 See, for example, the critique of "relevancy" made by Mary Jane Mossman in "Feminism and Legal Method: The Difference It Makes" (1986) 30 Australian Journal of Law and Society 30 especially at 44-45.

29 J. Moulton, "A Paradigm of Philosophy: The Adversary Method," cited in L. Code, *What Can She Know? Feminist Theory and the Construction of Knowledge* (Ithaca, NY: Cornell University Press, 1991) at 23-24. "The adversary method is most effective," Moulton claims, "in structuring isolated disagreements about specific theses and arguments. Hence it depends for its success n the artificial isolation of such claims and arguments from the contexts that occasion their articulations" (at 23).

30 L. Riskin, "Mediation and Lawyers" (1982) 42 Ohio State Law Journal 29 at 41-43.

31 See Macfarlane, see note 27 above at 81-84.

32 W. Conklin, "Teaching Critically within a Modern Legal Genre" (1993) 8(2) Canadian Journal of Law and Society 33 at 41.

33 See, for example, Silver, see note 20 above; and Segerstrom, see note 20 above.

34 Law Society of Upper Canada, "Placement Report 2003-2004 of Students Enrolled in the Forty-Sixth BAC 2003," http://education.lsuc.on.ca/Assets/PDF/apo/repPlacementReport 2003-04.pdf. In the 2003-04 year, 66.4 percent of students indicated that they had secured employment at the time of their call to the bar. This is an increase from 62.5 percent at this time last year. The hire-back rate of students returning to the firm they articled with remains steady at 49.7 percent.

35 L. Mather, C. McEwen, and R. Maiman, *Divorce Lawyers at Work: Varieties of Professionalism in Practice* (Oxford: Oxford University Press, 2001) at 41-63.

36 See, for example, H. Kritzer and F. Zemans, "Local Legal Culture and the Control of Litigation" (1993) 27 Law and Society Review 535 (where a change in the rules of civil procedure that made lawyers more accountable for frivolous actions was differentially applied across several jurisdictions); T. Church, "Examining Local Legal Culture" (1985) 3 American Bar Foundation Research Journal 449; and, most recently, "Toward an Understanding of 'Local Legal Culture'" (1981) 6 Justice System Journal 200 (arguing that local legal culture can be used to explain differences in case processing timelines and delays and backlogs between different courts).

37 Mather, McEwen, and Maiman, see note 35 above.

38 *Ibid.* at 61.

39 See the established conventions described in the smaller community of Prince Albert, Saskatchewan, in J. Macfarlane and M. Keet, *Learning from Experience: An Evaluation of the Saskatchewan Queen's Bench Mediation Program* (Regina: Saskatchewan Justice, April 2003) at 18 [*Learning from Experience*].

40 For example, in Toronto, some litigators now routinely exchange affidavits of documents in advance of mediation. See J. Macfarlane, "Culture Change? A Tale of Two Cities and Mandatory Court-Connected Mediation" (2002) 2 Journal of Dispute Resolution 241 at 262.

41 Unpublished data from the Culture Change project.

42 *Ibid.*

43 Mather, McEwen, and Maiman, see note 35 above at 91.

44 An example given by several lawyers participating in the Culture Change project was the Canadian Medical Association, which is evidently highly resistant to any form of mediated compromise. Other insurance carriers were also identified as taking a similar approach, and some were more open to settlement discussion.

45 Unpublished data from the Culture Change project.

46 Macfarlane, see note 40 above at 279.

47 Sometimes described as a social constructionist perspective. See, for example, Peter Berger and Thomas Luckmann, *The Social Construction of Reality: A Treatise in the Sociology of Knowledge* (New York: Doubleday, 1966).

48 J. Macfarlane, *The Emerging Phenomenon of Collaborative Family Law (CFL): A Qualitative Study of CFL Cases* (Ottawa: Department of Justice, 2005), http://www.canada.justice.gc. ca/en/ps/pad/reports/2005-FCY-1 at 26.

49 That is, behaviour is not determinative of attitudes and vice versa. See, for example, Michael J. Saks and Edward Krupat, *Social Psychology and Its Applications* (New York: Harper and Row, 1988) at 197-98. However, dissonance theory also suggests that we try to reduce the dissonance between our behaviour and our attitudes in order to avoid the discomfort this produces.

50 For a policy proposal on the appropriate use of mandatory processes to encourage consensus building and settlement, see Law Commission of Canada, *Transforming Relationships through Participatory Justice* (Ottawa: Law Commission of Canada, 2004).

51 In Ontario, *Courts of Justice Act,* R.R.O. 1990, Reg. 194, amended to O. Reg. 260/05, Rule 24.1. In Saskatchewan, *Queen's Bench Rules,* Rule 641. In Florida, *Florida Statutes,* chapter 44. In California, *California Code of Civil Procedure,* tit. 11.6, ss. 1775-1775.15.

52 For relevant research on this point, see, for example, Roselle, L. Wissler, "When Does Familiarity Breed Content? A Study of the Role of Different Forms of ADR Education and Experience in Attorneys' ADR Recommendations" (2002) 2(2) Pepperdine Dispute Resolution Law Journal 1999; and C. McEwen, N.H. Rogers, and R.J. Mainman, "Bring in the Lawyers: Challenging the Dominant Approaches to Ensuring Fairness in Divorce Mediation" (1995) 33 Maine Law Review 237.

53 Unpublished data from *Learning from Experience,* see note 39 above.

54 Unpublished data from the Culture Change project.

55 See N. Welsh, "The Thinning Vision of Self-Determination in Court-Connected Mediation: The Inevitable Price of Institutionalisation?" (2001) 6 Harvard Negotiation Law Review 101.

56 Macfarlane, see note 40 above. See also further discussion in Chapter 6, pp. 144-50.

57 W. Bennett, *The Lawyer's Myth: Reviving the Ideals of the Legal Profession* (Chicago: University of Chicago Press, 2001) at 28-50.

58 A. Dershowitz, *Letter to a Young Lawyer* (New York: Basic Books, 2001).

59 In a class exercise, most of the students were unable to identify a satisfactory role model from inside the legal profession. Of those chosen from outside the profession, Oprah Winfrey and Wayne Gretzy topped the list.

60 See, for example, the story told by *Women Lawyers: Rewriting the Rules* (New York: Penguin, 1985) at 86-86.

61 See the concerns articulated in B. Wilson, Chair, *Touchstones for Change: Equality, Diversity and Accountability* (Ottawa: Canadian Bar Association, 1995).

62 Since alcohol consumption is a prevalent part of many social professional settings, observant Muslims and others who do not drink alcohol may feel excluded or that they must exclude themselves.

63 D. Wilkins and Gulati G. Mitu, "Why Are There So Few Black Lawyers in Corporate Law Firms? An Institutional Analysis," in R. Abel, ed., *Lawyers: A Critical Reader* (New York: New Press, 1997) 101 at 102.

64 See, for example, the *Solicitors' Practice Rules* (1990); and the Law Society of Upper Canada's *Code of Advocacy* (last amended 13 January 2003), both available at http://www.law society.org.uk/professional/conduct.law.

65 Law Society of Upper Canada, *Rules of Professional Conduct* (2000), Rule 4.01, http://www.lsuc.on.ca/regulation/a/profconduct/.

66 American Bar Association (ABA), *Canons of Professional Ethics,* first adopted 27 August 1908, Canon 7, http://www.abanet.org/cpr/mrpc/Canons_Ethics.pdfModel.

67 *Rules of Professional Conduct,* see note 65 above, Commentary on Rule 4.01.

68 ABA, *Model Rules of Professional Conduct,* 2007 version, Rule 3.1, http://www.abanet.org/cpr/mrpc/model_rules.html.

69 Law Society of British Colombia, *Canon of Legal Ethics,* 1992, http://www.lawsociety.bc.ca/publications_forms/handbook/chapter-01.html, Rule 3(5).

70 This distinction is discussed in A. Zariski, "Disputing Culture: Lawyers and ADR" (2000) 7 Murdoch University Electronic Journal of Law 1 at 2; and, on the relationship between material and immaterial elements of culture generally, see C. Geertz, "Thick Description: Toward an Interpretive Theory of Culture," in *The Interpretation of Cultures* (New York: Basic Books, 1973) 3 at 3-30.

71 In contrast, see the *Code of Ethics* of the American Association of Psychologists (1992) at

http://www.apa.org/ethics/code. The preamble ends with these words: "Each psychologist supplements, but does not violate, the Ethics Code's values and rules on the basis of guidance drawn from personal values, culture and experience."

72 This is the distinction between "espoused theory" and "theory-in-action" drawn by Donald Schon. See, for example, D. Schon, "Educating the Reflective Practitioner" (1995) Clinical Law Review 231; and D. Schon, *The Reflective Practitioner* (San Francisco: Jossey-Bass, 1983).

73 See M.A. Wilkinson, C. Walker, and P. Mercer, "Do Codes of Ethics Actually Shape Legal Practice?" (2000) 45 McGill Law Journal 645.

Chapter 3: Three Key Professional Beliefs

1 R. Nelson and D. Trubek, "Arenas of Professionalism: The Professional Ideologies of Lawyers in Context," in R. Nelson, D. Trubek, and R. Solomon, eds., *Lawyers Ideals/ Lawyers Practices* (Ithaca, NY: Cornell University Press, 1992) 177 at 177.

2 See T. Church, "Examining Local Legal Culture" (1985) 3 American Bar Foundation Research Journal 449; and M. Heumann, *Plea Bargaining: The Experience of Prosecutors, Judges and Defense Attorneys* (Chicago: University of Chicago Press, 1978).

3 Church, see note 2 above at 506.

4 The Royal Charter establishing the Law Society of England and Wales was established in 1845.

5 R. Kidder, "The End of the Road? Problems in the Analysis of Disputes" (1980-81) 15 Law and Society Review 717 at 719 and 723.

6 C. Simmel, *Conflict* (New York: Free Press, 1955).

7 Kidder, see note 5 above at 723.

8 V. Aubert, "Competition and Dissensus: Two Types of Conflict and Conflict Resolution" (1963) 7 Journal of Conflict Resolution 26.

9 Unpublished data from the Culture Change project.

10 R. Bell, *Understanding African Philosophy: A Cross-Cultural Approach to Classical and Contemporary Issues* (New York: Routledge, 2002) at 77.

11 Unpublished data from the Culture Change project.

12 *Ibid.*

13 *Ibid.*

14 J. Macfarlane, "Culture Change? A Tale of Two Cities and Mandatory Court-Connected Mediation" (2002) 2 Journal of Dispute Resolution 241 at 282.

15 C. Moore, *The Mediation Process* (San Francisco: Jossey-Bass, 1996) at 60-61.

16 See, for example, D. Lax and J. Sebenius, *The Manager as Negotiator: Bargaining for Competitive Gain* (New York: Free Press, 1986); and C. Menkel-Meadow, "Towards Another View of Legal Negotiations: The Structure of Problem-Solving" (1984) 31 University of California Los Angeles Law Review 754.

17 In other words, those conflicts are the appropriate subject of public discourse because of their wide implications for standards of fairness and justice throughout society. See, for example, Owen M. Fiss, "Against Settlement" (1984) 93 Yale Law Journal 1073; and David Luban, "Settlements and the Erosion of the Public Realm" (1995) 83 Georgetown Law Journal 2619.

18 Unpublished data from the Culture Change project.

19 *Ibid.*

20 *Ibid.*

21 See, for example, the discussion between lawyer and client recorded and analyzed in A. Sarat and W. Felstiner, "Law and Strategy in the Divorce Lawyer's Office," in R. Abel, ed., *Lawyers: A Critical Reader* (New York: New Press, 1997) 44 at 47.

22 Sarat and Felstiner, see note 21 at 48.

23 Unpublished data from the Culture Change project.

24 Macfarlane, see note 14 above at 22.

25 Unpublished data from the Culture Change project.

26 J. Thibaut, L. Walker, S. LaTour, and S. Houlden, "Procedural Justice as Fairness" (1974) 26 Stanford Law Review 1271; and J. Thibaut and L. Walker, *Procedural Justice: A Psychological Analysis* (New York: Erlbaum, 1975).

27 Similar results are reported from a study asking citizens for their appraisal of (1) the fairness of government policy and (2) their personal benefits (specifically regarding taxation and benefits). See T. Tyler, K. Rasinski, and K. McGraw, "The Influence of Perceived Injustices on Support for Political Authority" (1985) 15 Journal of Applied Psychology 700. It has been further suggested that preference for procedural fairness, as well as the identification of the factors that make up procedural fairness is fairly consistent across a range of cultural contexts. See, for example, K. Leung and E.A. Lind, "Procedural Justice and Culture: Effects of Culture, Gender and Investigator Status on Procedural Preferences" (1986) 50 Journal of Personality and Social Psychology 1134; E.A. Lind, Y.J. Huo, and T. Tyler, "... And Justice for All: Ethnicity, Gender and Preferences for Dispute Resolution Procedures" (1994) 18 Law and Human Behaviour 269; and E.A. Lind and T. Tyler, *The Social Psychology of Procedural Justice* (London: Plenum Press, 1998) at 107-11.
28 T. Tyler, "The Role of Perceived Injustice in Defendants' Evaluations of their Courtroom Experience" (1984) 18 Law and Society Review 51.
29 See T. Tyler, "Conditions Leading to Value Expressive Judgments of Procedural Justice: A Test of Four Models" (1987) 52 Journal of Personality and Social Psychology 333. See generally Lind and Tyler, see note 27 above at 104-6.
30 See A. Lind, "Procedural Justice, Disputing and Reactions to Legal Authorities," in A. Sarat, ed., *Everyday Practices and Trouble Cases* (Evanston: Northwestern University Press, 1998) 177, especially the discussion of litigants' reactions to settlement conferences at 188.
31 Unpublished data from the Culture Change project.
32 D. Rosenthal, *Lawyer and Client: Who's in Charge?* (New York: Russell Sage Foundation, 1974). See also C. Hosticka, "We Don't Care about What Happened, We Only Care about What Is Going to Happen: Lawyer-Client Negotiations of Reality" (1979) 26 Social Problems 559 (examining relationships between legal clinic lawyers and their clients). However, see the doubts cast on this unproblematized view of power by W. Felstiner and A. Sarat in "Enactments of Power: Negotiating Reality and Responsibility in Lawyer/Client Interactions" (1992) 77 Cornell Law Review 1447.
33 See, for example, E. Spangler, *Lawyers for Hire: Salaried Professionals at Work* (New Haven: Yale University Press, 1986). However, this may be changing.
34 See R. Gilson and R. Mnookin, "Disputing through Agents: Cooperation and Conflict between Lawyers in Litigation" (1994) 94 Columbia Law Review 509.
35 M. Galanter, "Why the 'Haves' Come Out Ahead: Speculations on the Limits of Legal Change" (1974) 9 Law and Society Review 95.
36 See D. Schon, *The Reflective Practitioner* (San Francisco: Jossey-Bass, 1983). See the further discussion in J. Macfarlane, "Look before You Leap: Knowledge and Learning in Legal Skills Education" (1992) 19 Journal of Law and Society 291.
37 See L. Riskin, "Mediation and Lawyers" (1982) 43 Ohio State Law Journal 29 at 43-48. This is what Anthony Kronman describes as "thin advice." A. Kronman, *The Lost Lawyer: Failing Ideals of the Legal Profession* (Cambridge, MA: Harvard University Press, 1993).
38 Kronman, see note 37 above at 121-28.
39 J. Heinz et al., "Diversity, Representation and Leadership in an Urban Bar: A First Report on a Survey of the Chicago Bar" (1976) American Bar Foundation Research Journal 717.
40 R. Nelson, "Ideology, Practice and Professional Autonomy: Social Values and Client Relationships in the Large Law Firm," in Abel, ed., see note 21 above, 70 at 73.
41 See R. Nelson and R. Sandefur, "From Professional Dominance to Organisational Dominance," in W. Felstiner, ed., *Reorganisation and Resistance: Legal Professions Confront a Changing World* (London: Hart Publishing, 2006).
42 L. Riskin, "Mediation and Lawyers" (1982) 43 Ohio State Law Journal 29 at 43-48.
43 *Ibid.* at 96.
44 L. Mather and B. Yngvesson, "Language, Audience, and the Transformation of Disputes" (1980-81) 15(3-4) Law and Society 775. On further aspects of this problem, see J. Macfarlane, "The Mediation Alternative," in J. Macfarlane, ed., *Rethinking Disputes: The Mediation Alternative* (Toronto: Emond Montgomery and Cavendish Publishing, 1997) at 4-7.
45 Nelson and Trubek, see note 1 above at 177.

46 W. Simon, "The Ideology of Advocacy: Procedural Justice and Professional Ethics" (1978) Wisconsin Law Review 29 at 53-54.

47 Highly problematic for actually absorbing and practising an ethos of ethical professionalism. See Schon, note 36 above; and the further discussion in Chapter 8.

48 What David Luban describes as the principle of moral non-accountability. See D. Luban, "The Adversary System Excuse," in David Luban, ed., *The Good Lawyer: Lawyers' Roles and Lawyers' Ethics* (Totowa, NJ: Rowman and Allenheld, 1983) 83; see also M. Schwartz, "The Professionalism and Accountability of Lawyers" (1978) 66 California Law Review 669. See also the further discussion in Chapter 5 in this book.

49 Macfarlane, see note 44 above at 17-19.

50 Unpublished data from the Collaborative Lawyering Research Project.

51 Macfarlane, see note 44 above at 18.

52 See P. Schiltz, "On Being a Happy, Healthy and Ethical Member of an Unhappy, Unhealthy and Unethical Profession" (1991) 52 Vanderbilt Law Review 871 especially at 874-87. Schiltz cites a number of studies that suggest lawyers suffer from low career satisfaction. Note, however, that others contest just how widespread this discontent is. See Nelson and Sandefur, note 41 above at 336.

53 There are growing signs of an effort to take the highly theoretical ideas developed by therapeutic jurisprudence and turn them into a practical theory of lawyering (and judging). See, for example, D. Stolle, D. Wexler, B. Winick, and E. Dauer, "Integrating Preventive Law and Therapeutic Jurisprudence: A Law and Psychology-Based Approach to Lawyering" (1997) 34 California Western Law Review 15; and B. Winick, "Therapeutic Jurisprudence and the Role of Counsel in Litigation," in D. Stolle, D. Wexler, and B. Winick, eds., *Practicing Therapeutic Jurisprudence* (Durham: Carolina Academic Press, 2000) at 309.

54 See, for example, E. Martin, P. Seligman, Paul R. Verkuil, and Terry H. Kang, "Why Lawyers Are Unhappy" (2005) 10 Deakin Law Review 49 at 50; and John P. Heinz, Kathleen E. Hull, and Ava A. Harter, "Lawyers and Their Discontents: Findings from a Survey of the Chicago Bar" (1999) 74 Indiana Law Journal 735. This article cites statistics from a number of surveys, each of which reveals that a majority of the lawyers questioned would not, if they had their time over again, join the legal profession.

55 See, for example, F. Zacharias, "Reconciling Professionalism and Client Interests" (1995) 36 William and Mary Law Review 1303; A. Kronman, *The Lost Lawyer: Failing Ideals of the Legal Profession* (Cambridge, MA: Harvard University Press, 1993); and A. Kronman, "Professionalism" (1999) 2 Journal of the Institute for the Study of Legal Ethics 89.

Chapter 4: Translating the Beliefs into Practice

1 See, for example, M. Heumann and J. Hyman, "Negotiation Methods and Litigation Settlement Methods in New Jersey: You Can't Always Get What You Want" (1997) 12 Ohio State Journal on Dispute Resolution 253; and C. Menkel-Meadow, "The Transformation of Disputes by Lawyers: What the Dispute Paradigm Does and Does Not Tell Us" (1985) Missouri Journal on Dispute Resolution 25.

2 M. Galanter, "The Vanishing Trial: An Examination of Trials and Related Matters in Federal and State Courts" (2004) 1 Journal of Empirical Legal Studies 459.

3 *Ibid.*

4 See H. Kritzer, *Let's Make a Deal: Understanding the Negotiation Process in Ordinary Litigation* (Madison, WI: University of Wisconsin Press, 1991) at 130-34. H. Genn, *Hard Bargaining* (Oxford: Oxford University Press, 1987) at 30-36.

5 Kritzer, see note 4 above at 130-34.

6 See the classic description in Steven H. Clarke, E.D. Ellen, and K. McCormick, *Court-Ordered Civil Case Mediation in North Carolina: Court Efficiency and Litigant Satisfaction* (Chapel Hill, NC: Institute of Government, University of North Carolina, 1995).

7 A classic and publicly documented example of this common phenomenon occurred in Canada following the general election of 2000. The then leader of the opposition, Stockwell Day, was sued by lawyer Lorne Goddard over a letter that Day had written while a minister in the Alberta government to a newspaper in Alberta in which he accused Goddard

of supporting child pornography because he had acted for a client accused of possessing child pornography. When Goddard sued for defamation, asking for damages of $600,000, the Alberta government covered Day's legal bills. In December, government lawyers settled out of court for $60,000, but the case cost taxpayers a further $732,000 in legal costs for both Day and Goddard. It was disclosed that an original offer of settlement had been made at an early stage by Goddard's representatives for the sum of $70,000 – just $10,000 more than the final settlement to Goddard – *including* costs. "Day's Lawsuit Cost Taxpayers Close to $800,000," CBC News, 17 January 2001.

8 J. Macfarlane, "Culture Change? A Tale of Two Cities and Mandatory Court-Connected Mediation" (2002) 2 Journal of Dispute Resolution 241 at 292.

9 Kritzer, see note 4 above at 130-34; and Genn, see note 4 above at 30-36.

10 Unpublished data from the Culture Change project.

11 Macfarlane, see note 8 above at 291.

12 *Ibid.* at 291-92; and B. McAdoo, "A Report to the Minnesota Supreme Court: The Impact of Rule 114 on Civil Litigation Practice in Minnesota" (2002) 25 Hamline Law Review 401 at 432-37.

13 Macfarlane, see note 8 above at 292.

14 *Ibid.* at 292.

15 J. Macfarlane, *Court-Based Mediation in Civil Cases: An Evaluation of the Toronto General Division ADR Centre* (Ottawa: Queen's Printer, 1995).

16 See R. Hann, C. Barr, and Associates, *Evaluation of the Ontario Mandatory Mediation Program (Rule 24.1) Final Report: The First 23 Months* (Ottawa: Queen's Printer, 2001).

17 See, for example, J. Macfarlane and M. Keet, "Civil Justice Reform and Mandatory Civil Mediation in Saskatchewan: Lessons from a Maturing Program" (2004) 42(3) Alberta Law Review 677 at 688-90.

18 Macfarlane, see note 8 above at 303.

19 W. Felstiner and A. Sarat, "Enactments of Power: Negotiating Reality and Responsibility in Lawyer/Client Interactions" (1992) 77 Cornell Law Review 1447.

20 Macfarlane, see note 8 above at 275.

21 D. Binder and S. Price, *Legal Interviewing and Counseling: A Client-Centred Approach* (St. Paul: West Publishing, 1977).

22 Ronald J. Gilson and Robert H. Mnookin, "Disputing through Agents: Cooperation and Conflict between Lawyers in Litigation" (1994) 94 Columbia Law Review 509 at 537-41.

23 Jeffrey Z. Rubin and Frank E.A. Sander, "When Should We Use Agents? Direct versus Representative Negotiation" (1998) 4 Negotiation Journal 395 at 398.

24 Macfarlane, see note 8 above at 268-70.

25 *Ibid.* at 269.

26 *Ibid.*

27 *Ibid.* at 270.

28 See N. Welsh, "The Thinning Vision of Self-Determination in Court-Connected Mediation: The Inevitable Price of Institutionalisation?" (2001) 6 Harvard Negotiation Law Review 101. For some alternative perspectives and a deeper examination of this topic, see the discussion in Chapter 6.

29 Judges themselves are identifying the development of new skills in order to manage these fora as a new priority for judicial education. See B. McAdoo, "All Rise, the Court Is in Session: What Judges Say About Court-Connected Mediation" (2007) 22(2) Ohio State Journal on Dispute Resolution 377 especially at 397-402; and see the discussion of the new judge in Chapter 9.

30 Genn, see note 4 above.

31 J. Baldwin and M. McConville, *Negotiated Justice* (London: Martin Robertson, 1977).

32 See L. Mather, C. McEwen, and R. Mainman, *Divorce Lawyers at Work: Varieties of Professionalism in Practice* (Oxford: Oxford University Press, 2001) at 113-14.

33 See A. Schneider and N. Mills, "What Family Lawyers Are Really Doing When They Negotiate" (2006) 44(4) Family Court Review 612 at 616-19. Schneider and Mills explain their finding by pointing to the emotional and vengeful context of family law.

34 Unpublished data from the Collaborative Lawyering Research project.
35 See, for example, C. Menkel-Meadow, "Lawyer Negotiations: Theories and Realities – What We Learn from Mediation" (1993) 56 Modern Law Review 361; Clarke, Ellen, and McCormick, see note 6 above; and Genn, see note 4 above.
36 See the discussion in Chapter 3.
37 See B. Mayer, *The Dynamics of Conflict Resolution: A Practitioner's Guide* (San Francisco: Jossey-Bass, 2000) at 151-55.
38 "Pareto optimality" refers to the point at which all possible benefits to each side have been examined, and no additional benefit can be added at the expense of one side over the other. Mayer, see note 37 above at 158-60.
39 Macfarlane, see note 8 above at 306.
40 Unpublished data from the Culture Change project.
41 *Ibid.*
42 R. Axelrod, *The Evolution of Co-operation* (New York: Basic Books, 1984).
43 See the discussion in Gilson and Mnookin, see note 22 above.
44 G. Chornenki, "Mediating Commercial Disputes: Exchanging 'Power Over' for 'Power With,'" in J. Macfarlane, ed., *Rethinking Disputes: The Mediation Alternative* (Toronto: Emond Montgomery and Cavendish Publishing, 1997) 159 especially at 162-65.
45 W. Simon, *The Practice of Justice* (Cambridge, MA: Harvard University Press, 1998) at 64-65; and see J. Macfarlane, "The New Advocacy: Implications for Legal Education and Teaching Practice" in R. Burridge et al., ed., *Effective Teaching and Learning in Law* (London: Kogan Page, 2002) 164 at 173-77; and J. Macfarlane, "What Does the Changing Culture of Legal Practice Mean for Legal Education?" (2001) 20 Windsor Yearbook of Access to Justice 191 at 200-5.
46 Genn, see note 4 above.
47 Unpublished data from the Culture Change project.
48 Unpublished data from the Collaborative Lawyering Research project.
49 J. Macfarlane, *The Emerging Phenomenon of Collaborative Family Law (CFL): A Qualitative Study of CFL Cases* (Ottawa: Department of Justice, 2005), http://www.canada.justice.gc.ca/en/ps/pad/reports/2005-FCY-1 at 43.
50 Unpublished data from the Culture Change project.
51 Unpublished data from the Collaborative Lawyering Research project.
52 Macfarlane, see note 49 above at 30.
53 Macfarlane, see note 8 above at 302.
54 Douglas Litowitz, *The Destruction of Young Lawyers: Beyond One L* (Akron, OH: University of Akron Press, 2005).
55 The qualities associated with adversarial bargaining in Schneider's study include some fairly extreme characteristics such as arrogance, manipulation, and evasion. See A. Schneider, "Shattering Negotiation Myths: Empirical Evidence on the Effectiveness of Negotiation Style" (2002) 7 Harvard Negotiation Law Review 143, Appendix A at 210.
56 *Ibid.* Gerald Williams' original survey is reported in G. Williams, *Legal Negotiation and Settlement* (St. Paul: West Publishing, 1983).
57 Schneider, see note 55 above at 146.
58 D. Tannen, *The Argument Culture* (New York: Random House, 1998) at 7-10.
59 G. Lakoff and M. Johnson, *Metaphors We Live By* (Chicago: University of Chicago Press, 1980) at 4-5.
60 Tannen, see note 58 above at 8.
61 See the discussion in Macfarlane, see note 8 above at 293-95.
62 C. McEwen, "Managing Corporate Disputing: Overcoming Barriers to the Effective Use of Mediation for Reducing the Cost and Time of Litigation" (1998) 14 Ohio State Journal on Dispute Resolution 1.
63 Unpublished data from the Culture Change project.
64 See, for example, John L. Barkai and Gene Kassebaum, "Using Court-Annexed Arbitration to Reduce Litigant Costs and to Increase the Pace of Litigation" (1989) 16(S5) Pepperdine Law Review 43 at 47; and Weinstock, Osborne and Company Students at Law, "Let's Play Twister, Let's Play Risk, Yeah Yeah Yeah: An Analysis of Discovery Abuse in

Civil Litigation" (March 2001), http://www.cfcj-fcjc.org/full-text/2001_dra/weinstock.htm.
65 Heumann and Hyman, see note 1 above.
66 Macfarlane, see note 8 above at 307-8.
67 *Ibid.* at 282.
68 *Ibid.* at 311.
69 *Ibid.* at 282.
70 L. Riskin, "The Contemplative Lawyer" (2002) 7 Harvard Negotiation Law Review 1, referring to his earlier work on the "philosophical map" in L. Riskin, "Mediation and Lawyers"
   (1982) 42 Ohio State Law Journal 41 at 41-43.
71 See the website of the International Association of Holistic Lawyers at http://www.iahl.org.
72 The International Institute for Conflict Prevention and Resolution (CPR) offers members
   a corporate pledge that undertakes to "seriously explore negotiation, mediation or other
   ADR processes in conflicts arising with other signatories before pursuing full-scale litigation." The CPR claims 4,000 corporate signatories and 1,500 law firm signatories. See
   http://www.cpradr.org. A similar scheme exists in the United Kingdom, sponsored by the
   Centre for Effective Dispute Resolution (http://www.cedr.co.uk), which also provides model
   alternative dispute resolution contract clauses drafted by lawyers from leading commercial
   law firms.
73 R. Fisher, "What about Negotiation as a Specialty?" (1983) 69 American Bar Association
   Journal 1220.
74 For a brief description and rationale, see J. McCauley, "The Role of Specialised Settlement
   Counsel," http://www.mediate.com./mccauley.
75 W. Coyne, "The Case for Settlement Counsel" (1999) 14 Ohio State Journal on Dispute
   Resolution 367.
76 For a description of the work that would need to be done in order to create a broader
   alternative dispute resolution culture within a law firm, see the materials produced by
   the CPR at http://www.cpradr.org.
77 Axelrod, see note 42 above.
78 Some lawyers who practise co-operative law also practise "collaborative law" when their
   clients are willing to sign a formal retainer agreement to this effect. For a description of
   the rationale and possible mechanisms of co-operative lawyering, see J. Lande, "Negotiation: Evading Evasion – How Protocols Can Improve Civil Case Results" (2003) 21 Alternatives to the High Cost of Litigation 149.
79 The so-called disqualification clause.
80 T. Sholar, "Collaborative Law: A Method for the Madness" (1993) 23 Memphis State University Law Review 667.
81 R. Rack, "Settle or Withdraw: Collaborative Lawyering Provides Incentive to Avoid Costs
   of Litigation" (Summer 1998) 8 Dispute Resolution Magazine at American Bar Association Dispute Resolution Section, http://www.collaborativelaw.com.
82 *Ibid.* The need for a Disqualification Agreement is still hotly debated. See, for example,
   Lande, see note 78 above at 149.
83 J. Macfarlane, "Experiences of Collaborative Law: Preliminary Results from the Collaborative Lawyering Research Project" (2004) 1 Journal of Dispute Resolution 179 at 197.
84 See, for example, the discussion in J. Lande and G. Herman, "Fitting the Forum to the
   Family Fuss: Choosing Mediation, Collaborative Law, or Cooperative Law for Negotiating Divorce Cases" (2004) 42 Family Court Review 280.
85 Macfarlane, see note 83 above at 197.
86 *Ibid.* at 197-98.
87 In their study of divorce lawyers, Mather, McEwen, and Mainman describe the "communities of practice" – geographic, client-based, and substantive – that anchor individual divorce lawyers to a set of informal norms and etiquettes. See Mather, McEwen, and
   Mainman, see note 32 above at 41-48.
88 Macfarlane, see note 49 above at 198.
89 For example, where there is real concern over the behaviour of a group member who
   continues to practise in a highly adversarial manner, discussions are starting to take place

within collaborative law groups over developing expulsion (or discretionary renewal) procedures. Ironically, this approach to discipline has the potential to adopt some of the characteristics of a zero-sum approach.

90 See Gilson and Mnookin, see note 22 above at 564; and C. Tinsley, J. Cambria, and A. Schneider, "Reputations in Negotiation," in C. Honeyman and A. Schneider, eds., *The Negotiators Fieldbook* (Chicago: American Bar Association) 203 at 205.

91 R. Abel, *American Lawyers* (Oxford: Oxford University Press, 1989).

92 Virtually all collaborative cases thus far have been in the family law area. Some instances of the use of collaborative retainers have been reported in employment cases (in Cincinnati, at the Collaborative Law Center, 8 West Ninth Street, Cincinnati, OH) and estates cases (in Medicine Hat, Association of Collaborative Family Lawyers of Medicine Hat, c/o Pritchard and Company LLP 204, 430 6th Avenue SE (Box 100) Medicine Hat, AB).

93 For a detailed discussion of this issue, see J. Macfarlane "Will Changing the Process Change the Outcome? The Relationship between Procedural and Systemic Change" (2005) 65 Louisiana Law Review 1487.

94 See, for example, Roselle L. Wissler, "When Does Familiarity Breed Content? A Study of the Role of Different Forms of ADR Education and Experience in Attorneys' ADR Recommendations" (2002) 2(2) Pepperdine Dispute Resolution Law Journal 1999; John Lande, "Getting the Faith: Why Business Lawyers and Executives Believe in Mediation" (2000) 5 Harvard Negotiation Law Review 137 at 199; and Morris L. Medley and James A. Schellenberg, "Attitudes of Attorneys Toward Mediation" (1994) 12 Mediation Quarterly 185 at 195-96.

95 This remains the strongest argument in support of mandatory mediation processes, even if they are instituted in a limited manner. For a policy proposal on the appropriate use of mandatory processes to encourage consensus building and settlement, see Law Commission of Canada, *Transforming Relationships through Participatory Justice* (Ottawa: Law Commission of Canada, 2004) at 161. See also discussion *infra* Part 4(c).

96 The relationship between rights- and interests-based approaches to the resolution of conflicts is considered further in Chapter 7, which analyzes the impact of the shadow of the law (rights-based evaluation) on consensus building. For an excellent discussion of the relationship between rights and interests and distributive and integrative bargaining, see Mayer, see note 37 above at 145-60.

Chapter 5: The New Advocacy

1 B. Mayer, *Beyond Neutrality* (San Francisco: Jossey-Bass, 2004).

2 James Coleman, *Community Conflict* (New York: Free Press, 1957); J. Laue, *Third Men in New Arenas of Conflict: An Assessment of the Work of the National Center for Dispute Settlement* (1970) (unpublished paper on file with the author); and J. Laue and G. Cormick, "The Ethics of Intervention in Community Disputes," in G. Bermant, H. Kelman, and D. Warwick, eds., *The Ethics of Social Intervention* (Washington, DC: Halstead Press, 1978) at 205-32.

3 See, for example, the work of Donald Landon on country lawyers. D. Landon, *Country Lawyers: The Impact of Context on Professional Practice* (New York: Praeger, 1990).

4 See, for example, A. Kronman, *The Lost Lawyer: Failing Ideals of the Legal Profession* (Cambridge, MA: Harvard University Press, 1993); William H. Simon, "The Ideology of Advocacy: Procedural Justice and Professional Ethics" (1978) 29 Wisconsin Law Review 34; and W. Simon, *The Practice of Justice* (Cambridge, MA: Harvard University Press, 1998).

5 See the American Bar Association's *Model Code of Professional Responsibility* (1969), Canon 7, http://www.abanet.org/cpr/mrpc/mcpr.pdf, and the *Model Rules of Professional Conduct* (1983) (revised 2002), preamble, http://www.abanet.org/cpr/mrpc/preamble.html. See note in Chapter 2.

6 Simon, see note 4 above at 8. Simon also describes the "public interest view," which measures appropriate advocacy according to its contribution to the public good, and the "contextual view," which assumes that each situation must be judged on its special circumstances rather than assuming any one dominant approach.

7 Note Simon's alternative "public interview view." Simon, see note 4 above. See Kronman, see note 4 above at 146-48. On the problem of "cognitive dissonance," see Simon again at 68-69.

8 In practice, of course, the zealous advocacy principle and the adversarial spirit that is associated with it demands this type of unquestioning commitment to all clients, not only to those who appear "deserving."

9 Unpublished data from the Culture Change project.

10 Although as Lynn Mather, Craig McEwen, and Richard Maiman argue, the norms of some communities of practices is not adversarialism but "reasonableness." L. Mather, C. McEwen, and R. Maiman, *Divorce Lawyers at Work: Varieties of Professionalism in Practice* (Oxford: Oxford University Press, 2001) at 48-56.

11 J. Macfarlane, "Culture Change? A Tale of Two Cities and Mandatory Court-Connected Mediation" (2002) 2 Journal of Dispute Resolution 241 at 302.

12 Unpublished data from the Culture Change project. Instead, those who tried to articulate some type of justice concept substituted justice as process for substantive justice. See the further discussion in Chapter 3 of this book.

13 D. Luban, "The Fundamental Dilemma of Lawyering: The Ethics of the Hired Gun," in R. Abel, *Lawyers: A Critical Reader* (New York: New Press, 1997) 3 at 6.

14 Lord Henry Brougham, quoted in Luban, see note 13 above at 4 [emphasis added].

15 For a critique of the impact of the elevation of technical rationality on professional education, see D. Schon, *The Reflective Practitioner* (San Francisco: Jossey-Bass, 1983).

16 Note that Lord Henry Brougham is also famously quoted as saying, "A lawyer is a gentlemen that rescues your estate from your enemies and then keeps it to himself." Lord Henry Brougham, quoted in Luban, see note 13 above at 3.

17 See B. Abel-Smith and R. Stevens, *In Search of Justice: Society and the Legal System* (London: Allen Lane, 1968); and see the discussion in H. Kritzer, *The Justice Broker* (Oxford: Oxford University Press, 1990) at 7-8.

18 A. Schneider, "Shattering Negotiation Myths: Empirical Evidence on the Effectiveness of Negotiation Style" (2002) 7 Harvard Negotiation Law Review 143 at 146.

19 Macfarlane, see note 11 above at 297 [emphasis added].

20 *Ibid.* at 302.

21 *Ibid.* at 297.

22 J. Heinz and E. Laumann, *Chicago Lawyers: The Social Structure of the Bar* (New York: Russell Sage, 1982).

23 R. Nelson, "Ideology, Practice and Professional Autonomy: Social Values and Client Relations in the Large Law Firm," in Abel, see note 13 above, 70 at 73. See also the discussion in Chapter 3 in this book.

24 See the story and subsequent analysis in W. Simon, "Lawyer Advice and Client Autonomy: Mrs Jones Case," in D. Rhodes, ed., *Ethics in Practice: Lawyers Roles Responsibilities and Regulation* (Oxford: Oxford University Press, 2000).

25 Macfarlane, see note 11 above at 304.

26 M. Schwartz, "The Professionalism and Accountability of Lawyers" (1978) 66 California Law Review 669.

27 Patrick Schiltz notes that it is "common for the top partners in the biggest firms to earn upwards of $2 million per year." P. Schiltz, "On Being a Happy, Healthy and Ethical Member of an Unhappy, Unhealthy and Unethical Profession" (1991) 52 Vanderbilt Law Review 871 at 900.

28 J. Macfarlane, "Experiences of Collaborative Law: Preliminary Results from the Collaborative Lawyering Research Project" (2004) 1 Journal on Dispute Resolution 179 at 203.

29 Unpublished data from the Collaborative Lawyering Research project.

30 See, for example, Landon, note 3 above.

31 Kronman, see note 4 above.

32 *Ibid.* at 41-43 and 128-34.

33 Other writers have argued that this is nostalgia for a profession that never was. See R. Abel, "Theories of the Legal Profession," in Abel, see note 13 above, 117 at 131.

34 M. Galanter, "The Vanishing Trial: An Examination of Trials and Related Matters in Federal and State Courts" (2004) 1 Journal of Empirical Legal Studies 459.

35 Macfarlane, see note 28 above at 204.

36 Macfarlane, see note 28 above at 204.
37 Macfarlane, see note 11 above at 256.
38 See the detailed discussion in J. Macfarlane, "Why Do People Settle?" (2001) 45 McGill Law Journal 663.
39 See H. Kritzer, *Let's Make a Deal: Understanding the Negotiation Process in Ordinary Litigation* (Madison, WI: University of Wisconsin Press, 1991) at 130-34. See also the discussion in Chapter 3 in this book.
40 Macfarlane, see note 11 above at 298.
41 *Ibid.* at 298 [emphasis added].
42 C. Guittard, "Preparing for Mediation and Negotiation" (1991) 37 Practical Lawyer 65.
43 Unpublished data from the Collaborative Lawyering Research project.
44 For example, the strategic importance of considering the interests of the other side is identified by Mather, McEwen, and Maiman as a convention in divorce advocacy. Mather, McEwen, and Maiman, see note 10 above at 115.
45 W. Ury, R. Fisher, and B. Patton, *Getting to Yes,* 2nd edition (New York: Penguin, 1991).
46 Macfarlane, see note 11 above at 298.
47 Law Society of Upper Canada, *Rules of Professional Conduct* (2000), http://www.lsuc.on.ca/media/rpc.pdf; Rule 24.1, http://www.e-laws.gov.on.ca/DBLaws/Regs/English/900194a_e.htm; and *Queen's Bench Act,* S.S. 1998, c. Q-1.01, s. 42.
48 Macfarlane, see note 11 above at 262; and J. Macfarlane and M. Keet, "Civil Justice Reform and Mandatory Civil Mediation in Saskatchewan: Lessons from a Maturing Program" (2005) 42(3) Alberta Law Review 677 at 689-90.
49 As one lawyer put it, "You don't allow the process to overwhelm your strategy." Unpublished data from the Culture Change project.
50 J. Macfarlane, *Court-Based Mediation in Civil Cases: An Evaluation of the Toronto General Division ADR Centre* (Ottawa: Queen's Printer, 1995) at 22.
51 On preventive law and its relationship with therapeutic jurisprudence, see, for example, Dennis P. Stolle, David B. Wexler, Bruce J. Winick, and Edward A. Dauer, "Integrating Preventive Law and Therapeutic Jurisprudence: A Law and Psychology Based Approach to Lawyering," in Dennis P. Stolle, David B. Wexler, and Bruce J. Winick, eds., *Practicing Therapeutic Jurisprudence: Law as a Helping Profession* (Durham: Carolina Academic Press, 2000).
52 Unpublished data from the Culture Change project.
53 *Ibid.*
54 *Ibid.*
55 Macfarlane, see note 11 above at 302.
56 Unpublished data from the Culture Change project.
57 See quote that begins, "First and foremost our training is in rights-based advocacy ...," p. 104.
58 Unpublished data from the Culture Change project.
59 *Ibid.*
60 Kronman, see note 4 above at 62-74.
61 Unpublished data from the Collaborative Lawyering Research project.
62 Simon, see note 24 above, 200 at 165.
63 The concept of representing the client as his or her "highest functioning self" has been developed by Pauline Tesler and described in P. Tesler, *Collaborative Law: Achieving Effective Resolution in Divorce without Litigation* (Chicago: American Bar Association Family Section, 2001) at 30-32.
64 Macfarlane, see note 28 above at 206.
65 J. Macfarlane, *The Emerging Phenomenon of Collaborative Family Law (CFL): A Qualitative Study of CFL Cases* (Ottawa: Department of Justice, 2005), http://www.canada.justice.gc.ca/en/ps/pad/reports/2005-FCY-1 at 25-28.

Chapter 6: The Lawyer-Client Relationship
1 Unpublished data from the Collaborative Lawyering Research project.
2 Lucie White makes this point in "The Transformative Potential of Clinical Legal Education"

(1997) 35 Osgoode Hall Law Journal 603 at 610, and cites the definition to the *Oxford English Dictionary*, 2nd edition, volume 3 (Oxford: Clarendon, 1989) at 320.

3 The classic model of lawyer dominance is described by Z. Bankowski and G. Mungham, *Images of Law* (London: Routledge and Kegan Paul, 1976).

4 C. McEwen, "Pursuing Problem-Solving or Predictive Settlement" (1991) 19 Florida State University Law Review 77 at 81.

5 See the work of Howard Becker, *Education for the Professions* (Chicago: University of Chicago Press, 1962), on the traditional conceptions of professionalism that have dominated professional/client relationships for most of the twentieth century. See also the extended discussion of the historical origins of the lawyers' professional norms in Chapter 2.

6 D. Rosenthal, *Lawyer and Client: Who's in Charge?* (New York: Russell Sage Foundation, 1974) at 7.

7 See *ibid*. See also C. Hosticka, "'We Don't Care About What Happened, We Only Care about What Is Going to Happen': Lawyer-Client Negotiations of Reality" (1979) 26 Social Problems 559 (examining relationships between legal clinic lawyers and their clients). However, see the doubts cast on this unproblematized view of power by W. Felstiner and A. Sarat, "Enactments of Power: Negotiating Reality and Responsibility in Lawyer/Client Interactions" (1992) 77 Cornell Law Review 1447.

8 See R. Nelson and R. Sandefur, "From Professional Dominance to Organisational Dominance," in W. Felstiner, ed., *Reorganisation and Resistance: Legal Professions Confront a Changing World* (London: Hart Publishing, 2006). At the same time, it is important to recognize that conflicts between lawyers and their clients are relatively rare and that many lawyers adopt a highly influential and even controlling role, but without explicit conflict or challenge. See R. Nelson, "Ideology, Practice and Professional Autonomy: Social Values and Client Relationships in the Large Law Firm" in R. Abel, ed., *Lawyers: A Critical Reader* (New York: New Press, 1997) 70.

9 J. Macfarlane, "Culture Change? A Tale of Two Cities and Mandatory Court-Connected Mediation" (2002) 2 Journal of Dispute Resolution 241 at 293.

10 L. Mather, C. McEwen, and R. Maiman, *Divorce Lawyers at Work: Varieties of Professionalism in Practice* (Oxford: Oxford University Press, 2001) at 90 and see generally 87-110.

11 W. Simon, "Lawyer Advice and Client Autonomy: Mrs Jones Case," in D. Rhodes, ed., *Ethics in Practice: Lawyers Roles Responsibilities and Regulation* (Oxford: Oxford University Press, 2000).

12 A. Sarat and W. Felstiner, "Law and Strategy in the Divorce Lawyer's Office," in R. Abel, ed., see note 8 above, 44 at 49.

13 J. Macfarlane, *The Emerging Phenomenon of Collaborative Family Law (CFL): A Qualitative Study of CFL Cases* (Ottawa: Department of Justice, 2005), http://www.canada.justice.gc.ca/en/ps/pad/reports/2005-FCY-1 at 42 [emphasis added].

14 C. Menkel-Meadow, "The Transformation of Disputes by Lawyers: What the Dispute Paradigm Does and Does Not Tell Us" (1985) Missouri Journal of Dispute Resolution 25 at 31.

15 Lynn Mather and Barbara Yngvesson, "Language, Audience, and the Transformation of Disputes" (1980-81) 15 Law and Society Review 775.

16 M.J. Mossman, "Feminism and Legal Method: The Difference it Makes" (1986) 3 Australian Journal of Law and Society 30.

17 Rosenthal borrows the contrast between "problems" and "difficulties" from the political philosopher T.H. Weldon, *The Vocabulary of Politics* (London: Penguin Books, 1953) at 75-83.

18 Unpublished data from the Culture Change project.

19 H.S.Becker, *Education for the Professions* (Chicago: National Society for the Study of Education, 1962) at 38. In this book, Becker is writing about professions in general, but the point is highly pertinent to the legal profession.

20 This material is on file with the author.

21 See, for example, S. Henshall, "The Consumer Manifesto: Empowering Communities of Consumers through the Internet," http://www.firstmonday.org/issues/issue5_5/henshall/index.html, at issue 5.

22 W. Ury, *The Third Side* (New York: Penguin 2000) at 95 and 97.
23 For the origins of a functionalist theory of the doctor-patient relationship, see Talcott Parsons, *The Social System* (Glencoe, IL: Free Press, 1951); see Mary Sengstock, "Parson's Analysis of the Doctor-Patient Relationship" (2004), http://hometown.aol.com/mcsengstoc/parsons.htm.
24 J. Hughes, "Organization and Information at the Bed-Side: The Experience of the Medical Division of Labor by University Hospitals' Inpatients" (Ph.D. dissertation, University of Chicago, 1994), chapter 1, http://www.changesurfer.com/Hlth/DPReview.html.
25 T. Szasz and M. Hollender, "A Contribution to the Philosophy of Medicine: The Basic Models of the Doctor-Patient Relationship" (1956) 97 Archives of Internal Medicine 585.
26 See, for example, Lawopinion.com Incorporated, http://www.lawopinion.com.
27 L. White, "Subordination, Rhetorical Survival Skills: Notes on the Hearing of Mrs G.," in Abel, ed., see note 8 above, 300 at 300-1.
28 Illustrated by the increasing use of "public involvement projects" in resource management and environmental decision making, see, for example, Lawrence Susskind and Denise Madigan, "New Approaches to Resolving Disputes in the Public Sector" (1984) 9(2) Justice System Journal 179; and Frank Dukes, "Public Conflict Resolution: A Transformative Approach" (1993) 9 Negotiation Journal 45.
29 See R. Gibson and R. Mnookin, "Disputing through Agents: Cooperation and Conflict between Lawyers in Litigation" (1994) 94 Columbia Law Review 509.
30 Unpublished data from the Culture Change project.
31 Macfarlane, see note 9 above at 293-95.
32 *Ibid.* at 295.
33 Unpublished data from the Culture Change project.
34 Macfarlane, see note 9 above at 255.
35 See the discussion in Chapter 1.
36 C. McEwen, "Managing Corporate Disputing: Overcoming Barriers to the Effective Use of Mediation for Reducing the Cost and Time of Litigation" (1998) 14 Ohio State Journal on Dispute Resolution 1.
37 A story told to me by a colleague who was privy to the details of this interview, shortly after the interview took place in 2006.
38 J. Lande, "Failing Faith in Litigation? A Survey of Business Lawyers' and Executives' Opinions" (1998) 3(1) Harvard Negotiation Law Review 1 at 20-21.
39 *Ibid.* at 18-19.
40 For example, *Ontario Rules of Civil Procedure,* R.R.O. 1990, Reg. 194, amended to O.Reg 260/05, Rule 24.1; *Ontario Rules of Civil Procedure,* R.R.O. 1990, Reg. 194, Rule 76.10 (simplified procedure); and *Intake and Case Flow Management Rules,* Alta. Reg. 163/2001, s. 3(1).
41 Unpublished data from the Collaborative Lawyering Research project.
42 Macfarlane, see note 13 above at 43.
43 *Ibid.* at 36.
44 *Ibid.*
45 Unpublished data from the Collaborative Lawyering Research project.
46 See further discussion later in this chapter under the section "Decision Making and Control."
47 See the meta-analysis in Roselle L. Wissler, "Court-Connected Mediation in General Civil Cases: What We Know from Empirical Research" (2002) 17(3) Ohio State Journal on Dispute Resolution 641 at 650-51.
48 See Roselle L. Wissler, "The Effectiveness of Court-Connected Dispute Resolution in Civil Cases" (2004) 22 Conflict Resolution Quarterly 55 at 69; and Wissler, see note 47 above, 641 at 682.
49 J. Macfarlane and M. Keet, "Civil Justice Reform and Mandatory Civil Mediation in Saskatchewan: Lessons from a Maturing Program" (2004) 42(3) Alberta Law Review 677 at 691.
50 Unpublished data from J. Macfarlane and M. Keet, *Learning from Experience: An Evaluation of the Saskatchewan Queen's Bench Mediation Program* (Regina: Saskatchewan Justice, April 2003).

51 *Ibid.*
52 See, for example, David A. Binder, Paul Bergman, Susan C. Price, and Paul R. Tremblay, *Lawyers as Counsellors: A Client-Centred Approach,* 2nd edition (St. Paul: West Publishing, 2004).
53 See, for example, A. Alfieri, "Reconstructing Poverty Law Practice: Learning Lessons of Client Narratives" (1991) 100 Yale Law Journal 2107; and L. White, "Mobilising on the Margins of Litigation: Making Space for Clients to Speak" (1987-88) 16 New York University Review of Law and Social Change 535.
54 On mental health patients, see, for example, B. Winick, "Coercion and Mental Health Patients" (1997) 74 Denver University Law Review 1145 (reporting that where patients are listened to and involved in making decisions about their confinement they are less likely to experience coercion, even if committed against their will). On poverty law clients and on criminal clients, see D. Wexler, "Relapse Prevention Planning Principles for Criminal Law Practice," in D. Stolle, D. Wexler, and B. Winick, eds., *Practicing Therapeutic Jurisprudence* (Durham: Carolina Academic Press, 2000) at 237 (arguing that preventive planning that involves the offender in identifying the problematic behaviour, possible trigger points, and how to prevent it in the future leads to improved recidivism rates).
55 Binder, Bergman, Price, and Tremblay, see note 52 above at 12.
56 M. Patry, D. Stolle, D. Wexler, and A. Tompkins, "Better Legal Counseling through Empirical Research: Identifying Psycholegal Soft Spots and Strategies," in Stolle, Wexler, and Winick, see note 54 above, 69 at 73-39.
57 I take this expression from Linda Mills, in her essay "Affective Lawyering: Emotional Dimensions of the Lawyer-Client Relationship, in Stolle, Wexler, and Winick, see note 54 above, 419. She writes, "I learned in my legal practice to rely on my psychological skills to improve my effectiveness as a lawyer" (at 421).
58 Unpublished data from the Collaborative Lawyering Research project.
59 Macfarlane, see note 13 above at 43.
60 Unpublished data from the Culture Change project.
61 See, for example, J. Macfarlane, *Court-Based Mediation in Civil Cases: An Evaluation of the Toronto General Division ADR Centre* (Ottawa: Queen's Printer, 1995) at 8-9 (showing that 15 percent of cases referred to mandatory mediation settled before mediation).
62 Unpublished data from the Culture Change project.
63 *Ibid.*
64 White, see note 2 above at 610.
65 Macfarlane, see note 13 above at 30.
66 Unpublished data from the Collaborative Lawyering Research project.
67 Macfarlane, see note 13 above at 43.
68 *Ibid.* at 55.
69 *Ibid.* at 54.
70 Unpublished data from the Collaborative Lawyering Research project.
71 Macfarlane and Keet, see note 50 above at 24-25.
72 See also the discussion in Chapter 5.
73 See William Simon's cautionary tale earlier in Simon, note 11 above.
74 This is reminiscent of the claims of transformative mediation. R.B. Bush and J. Folger, *The Promise of Mediation* (San Francisco: Jossey-Bass, 1994). Transformative mediation argues that "real" conflict resolution and its benefits come only from the exchange of acknowledgment and recognition between the disputants (at 84-95).
75 R. Freeman, "Parenting after Divorce: Using Research to Inform Decision-Making about Children" (1998) 15 Canadian Journal of Family Law 79.
76 J. Macfarlane, "Experiences of Collaborative Law: Preliminary Results from the Collaborative Lawyering Research Project" (2004) 1 Journal of Dispute Resolution 179 at 210.
77 Unpublished data from the Collaborative Lawyering Research project.
78 *Ibid.*
79 J. Nolan-Haley, "Lawyers, Clients and Mediation" (1998) 73 Notre Dame Law Review 1369 at 1379.

80 See, for example, N. Welsh, "The Thinning Vision of Self-Determination in Court-Connected Mediation: The Inevitable Price of Institutionalisation?" (2001) 6 Harvard Negotiation Law Review 101, and the further discussion later in this chapter.
81 Macfarlane, see note 9 above at 272.
82 Unpublished data from the Culture Change project.
83 One client in the original Toronto alternative dispute resolution pilot told the evaluators that the first time his lawyer told him they were going to a mediation meeting that day and not, as he expected, to a hearing before a judge was when they were driving into the city that morning. Macfarlane, see note 61 above at 41.
84 Macfarlane, see note 9 above at 275.
85 *Ibid.*
86 *Ibid.*
87 Welsh, see note 80 above at 125. Welsh argues that this is the price that has been paid for the legitimacy bought with the institutionalization of mediation within the court system.
88 N. Welsh, "Disputants' Decision Control in Court-Connected Mediation: A Hollow Promise without Procedural Justice" (2002) 1 Journal of Dispute Resolution 179 at 184-86.
89 Macfarlane and Keet, see note 49 above at 692.
90 Alternative Dispute Resolution Centre clients, quoted in Macfarlane, see note 61 above at 55. Many similar comments were made by clients in the evaluation of the Saskatchewan Queen's Bench mandatory mediation program, reported in Macfarlane and Keet, see note 50 above at 24-26. There are also signs that lawyers who represent corporate clients increasingly recognize that some types of settlement discussion actually work better without the lawyers being present to "chill" the climate or, worse, to increase the tension and hostility.
91 Macfarlane, see note 9 above at 274.
92 *Ibid.*
93 See, for example, Macfarlane and Keet, see note 50 above at 12-14; Wissler, see note 48 above; and Bobbi McAdoo, "A Report to the Minnesota Supreme Court: The Impact of Rule 114 on Civil Litigation Practice in Minnesota," Supreme Court Office of Continuing Education (2002) 25 Hamline Law Review 401.
94 Unpublished data from the Collaborative Lawyering Research project.
95 See, for example, D. Stolle, D. Wexler, B. Winick, and E. Dauer, "Integrating Preventive Law and Therapeutic Jurisprudence: A Law and Psychology Based Approach," in Stolle, Wexler, and Winick, eds., see note 54 above, 357 at 5-44; A. Watson, *Psychiatry for Lawyers* (New York: International Universities Press, 1978); and Andrew S. Watson, "The Lawyer in the Interviewing and Counselling Process" (Indianapolis: Bobbs-Merrill, 1976).
96 M. Silver, "Love, Hate and Other Emotional Interference in the Lawyer/Client Relationship," in Stolle, Wexler, and Winick, eds., see note 54 above, 357 at 360.
97 For example, by counter-transference in which the lawyer takes on (often misplaced) emotions on the client's behalf. *Ibid.*, 357 at 370-74.
98 William Brennan, "Reason, Passion and the Progress of Law" (1988) 10 Cardozo Law Journal 3 at 4, who continues "dispensing the correct rule prescribed for each legal problem presented."
99 A poignant example is the description of the lawyer-client interaction in Sarat and Felstiner, see note 12 at 47.
100 Mills, see note 57 above at 422.
101 Unpublished data from the Collaborative Lawyering Research project.
102 Macfarlane, see note 13 above at 9.
103 *Ibid.*
104 D. Landon, *Country Lawyers: The Impact of Context on Professional Practice* (New York: Praeger, 1990) at 122.
105 *Ibid.* at 128.
106 *Ibid.* at 127-31.
107 Charles Fried, "The Lawyer as Friend: The Moral Foundations of the Lawyer-Client

Relation" (1976) 85 Yale Law Journal 1060 (justifying the role of zealous advocacy as a form of loyalty).

108 See S. Morris, "The Lawyer as Friend: An Aristotelian Inquiry" (2001) 26 Journal of the Legal Profession 55 at 58-61, who locates this idea within Aristotle's writings on friendship. See Aristotle, *Nicomachean Ethics,* translated by Martin Ostwald (Englewood Cliffs, NJ: Prentice Hall, 1962).

109 Thomas L. Shaffer and Robert F. Cochran, "Lawyers as Strangers and Friends: A Reply to Professor Sammons" 18 University of Arkansas Little Rock Law Journal 69. Their text, which sparked the debate, is T. Shaffer and R. Cochran, *Lawyers Clients and Moral Responsibility* (St. Paul: West Publishing Company, 1994).

110 J. Sammons, "Rank Strangers to Me: Shaffer and Cochran's Friendship Model of Moral Counselling in the Law Office" (1995) 18 University of Arkansas Little Rock Law Journal 1.

111 Macfarlane, see note 76 above at 203-4.

112 Macfarlane, see note 13 above at 53.

113 *Ibid.* at 34-35.

114 *Ibid.* at 53.

115 Silver, see note 96 above at 361-64.

116 *Ibid.* at 34.

117 Unpublished data from the Culture Change project.

118 Shaffer and Cochran, see note 109 above at 83.

119 Unpublished data from the Collaborative Lawyering Research project.

120 Unpublished data from the Culture Change project.

121 Unpublished data from the Collaborative Lawyering Research project.

122 *Ibid.*

123 See the discussion to this effect in J. Sternlight, "Lawyers' Representation of Clients in Mediation: Using Economics and Psychology to Structure Advocacy in a Nonadversarial Setting" (1999) 14 Ohio State Journal on Dispute Resolution 269 at 297-348.

124 Unpublished data from the Collaborative Lawyering Research project.

Chapter 7: The Role of the Law and Legal Advice

1 J. Macfarlane and M. Keet, *Learning from Experience: An Evaluation of the Saskatchewan Queen's Bench Mediation Program* (Regina: Saskatchewan Justice, April 2003) at 28.

2 For example, L. Putnam, "Communication and Interaction Patterns," in C. Honeyman and A. Schneider, eds., *The Negotiator's Fieldbook* (Chicago: American Bar Association, 2006) 385 at 389.

3 See, for example, E. Waldman, "Identifying the Role of Social Norms in Mediation: A Multiple Model Approach" (1997) 48 Hastings Law Journal 703. Waldman sets out a model of "norm-generating" mediation, in which parties are encouraged to brainstorm their own values and principles to resolve their dispute rather than appealing to perceived entitlements or norms (at 710-23); and "norm-educating" mediation – commonly used in divorce mediation – which encourages the parties to identify appropriate social norms including, but not limited to, legal principles with which to resolve their dispute (at 727-42). Waldman also describes a further model, the norm-advocating model, which is discussed in the following section.

4 R. Mnookin and C. Kornhauser, "Bargaining in the Shadow of the Law: The Case of Divorce" (1979) 88 Yale Law Journal 950.

5 There is much debate among mediators about the proper place of law in mediation. For one approach that explicitly endorses the inclusion but not the dominance of law and lawyers in mediation, see the website of the Center for Mediation in Law, http://www.mediationinlaw.org/about.html.

6 Owen M. Fiss, "Against Settlement" (1984) 93 Yale Law Journal 1073; and David Luban, "Settlements and the Erosion of the Public Realm" (1995) 83 Georgetown Law Journal 2619.

7 P. Ewick and S. Silbey, *The Common Place of the Law: Stories from Everyday Life* (Chicago: University of Chicago Press, 1998).

8 *Ibid.* at 77-82.

9 *Ibid.* at 97.
10 See the results of the Civil Litigation Research project, in Joel B. Grossman, Herbert M. Kritizer, Austin Sarat, William L.F. Felstiner, and David M. Trubek, "The Costs of Ordinary Litigation" (1983) 31(1) University of California Los Angeles Law Review 73.
11 R. Ellickson, *Order without Law: How Neighbours Settle Disputes* (Cambridge, MA: Harvard University Press, 1991) at 60.
12 *Ibid.* at 133.
13 *Ibid.* at 212.
14 R. Fisher, W. Ury, and B. Patton, *Getting to Yes: Negotiating Agreement without Giving In,* 2nd edition (New York: Penguin Books, 1991) at 97-106.
15 Waldman, see note 3 above at 742-56.
16 Family Mediation Canada, *Code of Professional Conduct,* http://www.fmc.ca/pdf/CodeProfessionalConduct.pdf, Article 13(4).
17 See, for example, Annette Townley, "The Invisible-ism: Heterosexism and the Implications for Mediation" (1992) 9(4) Mediation Quarterly 397.
18 Martha J. Bailey, "Unpacking the Rational Alternative: A Critical Review of Family Mediation Movement Claims" (1989) 8 Canadian Journal of Family Law 61 at 76-86.
19 See *ibid.* at 70-72; and Penelope Bryan, "Collaborative Divorce: Meaningful Reform or Another Quick Fix?" (1999) 5 Psychology, Public Policy and Law 1001.
20 See Richard Delgado, C. Dunn, and D. Hubbert, "Fairness and Formality: Minimizing the Risk of Prejudice in Alternative Dispute Resolution" (1985) 6 Wisconsin Law Review 1391.
21 R. Hofrichter, "Neighborhood Justice and the Social Control Problems of American Capitalism: A Perspective," in R. Abel, ed., *The Politics of Informal Justice* (New York: Academic Press, 1982).
22 See the discussion in Chapter 6.
23 See, for example, *Custody Access and Child/Spousal Support: A Pilot Project* (Ottawa: Ellis Research Associates, Department of Justice, 1995), http://www.justice.gc.ca/en/ps/rs/rep/1996/tr96-12a.html. As well, the results of the small sample in the Collaborative Lawyering Research project suggest that parties to consensual agreements are often willing to "leave money on the table" or exceed their legal obligations. See J. Macfarlane, *The Emerging Phenomenon of Collaborative Family Law (CFL): A Qualitative Study of CFL Cases* (Department of Justice, 2005), http://www.canada.justice.gc.ca/en/ps/pad/reports/2005-FCY-1 at 57-59.
24 N. Vidmar, "Assessing the Effects of Case Characteristics and Settlement Forum on Dispute Outcomes and Compliance" (1987) 21(1) Law and Society Review 155.
25 Macfarlane, see note 23 above at 57-60.
26 *Ibid.* at 57.
27 Fisher, Ury, and Patton, see note 14 above.
28 *Ibid.* at 97-106. Others have argued that the more realistic measure would be "worst case scenario." Yet others propose the "most likely" outcome as the pragmatic choice. Each assessment requires the same basic data elements set out earlier in the chapter.
29 See, for example, M. Williams and J. Hall, "Knowledge of the Law in Texas: Socioeconomic and Ethnic Differences" (1972) 7 Law and Society Review 99; M. Galanter, "Reading the Landscape of Disputes: What We Know and Don't Know (and Think We Know) about Our Allegedly Contentious and Litigious Society" (1983) 31(1) University of California Los Angeles Law Review 4.
30 Macfarlane, see note 23 above at 38.
31 *Ibid.*
32 J. Cassels, *Remedies: The Law of Damages* (Toronto: Irwin Law, 2000).
33 B. Mayer, *The Dynamics of Conflict Resolution: A Practitioner's Guide* (San Francisco: Jossey-Bass, 2000) at 97-108.
34 A 1995 study, which matched a control group of litigants participating in (an advanced stage of) traditional litigation with those offered mediation, found that only 8.5 percent of control group litigants described themselves as completely satisfied with the outcome of their case (either settled between the lawyers or adjudicated). The most frequently

given reason for a negative or partly negative assessment of outcome in the remaining 91.5 percent (including some litigants who won their cases at trial) was the length of time and emotional energy consumed by the process. J. Macfarlane, *Court-Based Mediation in Civil Cases: An Evaluation of the Toronto General Division ADR Centre* (Ottawa: Queen's Printer, 1995) at 22.

35 J. Macfarlane and M. Keet, "Civil Justice Reform and Mandatory Civil Mediation in Saskatchewan: Lessons from a Maturing Program" (2004) 42(3) Alberta Law Review 677 at 690.

36 Unpublished data from J. Macfarlane and M. Keet, *Learning from Experience: An Evaluation of the Saskatchewan Queen's Bench Mediation Program* (Regina: Saskatchewan Justice, April 2003).

37 See the further discussion of the role of expectations in settlement in J. Macfarlane, "Why Do People Settle?" (2001) 45 McGill Law Journal 663 at 678-89.

38 See Lynn Mather and Barbara Yngvesson, "Language, Audience, and the Transformation of Disputes" (1980-81) 15 Law and Society 775; and Carrie Menkel-Meadow, "The Transformation of Disputes by Lawyers: What the Dispute Paradigm Does and Does Not Tell Us" (1985) Missouri Journal of Dispute Resolution 25.

39 Mather and Yngvesson, see note 38 above at 777-79.

40 Macfarlane, see note 37 above at 678-79.

41 Michelle LeBaron, "Intercultural Disputes – Mediation, Conflict Resolution, and Multicultural Reality: Culturally Competent Practice," in E. Kruk, ed., *Mediation and Conflict Resolution in Social Work and the Human Sciences* (Chicago: Nelson Hall, 1997) at 321.

42 Important work on conflict orientation and bargaining style related to gender and ethnicity includes Deborah M. Kolb, "Her Place at the Table: Gender and Negotiation," in L. Hall, ed., *Negotiation: Strategies for Mutual Gain* (London: Sage Publications, 1993) at 138; C. Rose, "Bargaining and Gender" (1995) 18 Harvard Journal of Law and Policy 547; Paula Trubisky, Stella Ting-Toomey, and Sung-Ling Lin, "The Influence of Individualism-Collectivism and Self-Monitoring on Conflict Styles" (1991) 15 International Journal of Intercultural Relations 65; and J. Rubin and F. Sander, "Culture, Negotiation and the Eye of the Beholder" (1991) 7 Negotiation Journal 249.

43 Richard Miller and Austin Sarat, "Grievances, Claims and Disputes: Assessing the Adversary Culture" (1980-81) 15 Law and Society Review 525 at 551.

44 Ewick and Silbey, see note 7 above at 133.

45 Cultural consciousness inevitably shapes communication and is integral to the making of meaning. This constructionist perspective is articulated by early sociologists such as Peter Berger and Thomas Luckman, *The Social Construction of Reality: A Treatise in the Sociology of Knowledge* (New York: Doubleday, 1966), and later by Sally Merry, *Getting Justice and Getting Even: Legal Consciousness among Working Class Americans* (Chicago: University of Chicago Press, 1990), and Susan Silbey, with Patricia Ewick, *The Common Place of Law* (Chicago: University of Chicago Press, 1998), and exemplified in dispute resolution scholarship by the work of John Paul Lederach, *Preparing for Peace: Conflict Transformation across Cultures* (New York: Syracuse University Press, 1995).

46 G.O. Faure, "Conflict Formulation: Going beyond Culture-Bound Views of Conflict," in Rubin Bunker and Associates, eds., *Conflict, Co-operation and Justice: Essays Inspired by the Work of Morton Deutsch* (San Francisco: Jossey-Bass, 1995) 39 at 53.

47 This story is also described and discussed at greater length in J. Macfarlane, "When Cultures Collide," in C. Bell and D. Kahane, eds., *Intercultural Dispute Resolution in Aboriginal Contexts: Canadian and International Perspectives* (Vancouver: UBC Press, 2004) 94 at 100-1.

48 The prevalence of "stock stories" (Mather and Yngvesson, see note 38 above), combined with what William Simon calls "ritualist advocacy" (see W. Simon, 'The Ideology of Advocacy: Procedural Justice and Professional Ethics" (1978) 29 Wisconsin Law Review 29 at 54) often produces a feeling of detachment for clients. "The burning issue which originally belonged to the disputants, both intellectually and emotionally, becomes detached from them on both levels when it is placed in the hands of the legal system." J. Macfarlane,

"The Mediation Alternative," in J. Macfarlane, ed., *Rethinking Disputes: The Mediation Alternative* (Toronto: Emond Montgomery, 1997).

49 Macfarlane, see note 23 above at 37.

50 Unpublished data from the Collaborative Lawyering Research project.

51 *Ibid.*

52 Macfarlane, see note 23 above at 37-38. This fits with the assertions of some collaborative lawyers that they provide only "generalist" legal advice.

53 *Ibid.* at 10.

54 *Ibid.* at 37.

55 See the discussion in Chapter 5 at pp. 110-11.

56 Mayer, see note 33 above at 157.

Chapter 8: Ethical Challenges Facing the New Lawyer

1 A. Dodek, "Canadian Legal Ethics: A Subject in Search of Scholarship," review essay (2000) 50 University of Toronto Law Journal 115.

2 Lawyers work in collegial contexts – described by Mather, McEwen, and Maiman as "communities of practice" – which have their own internal norms of socially acceptable behaviours enforced via peer pressure. See L. Mather, C. McEwen, and R. Maiman, *Divorce Lawyers at Work: Varieties of Professionalism in Practice* (Oxford and New York: Oxford University Press, 2001) 41-48.

3 See the further discussion on advocacy definitions in Codes in Chapter 3.

4 See, for example, Gerald B. Wetlaufer, "The Ethics of Lying in Negotiations" (1990) 75 Iowa Law Review 1219 for an exposition and a critique of the rule-based approach.

5 A. Kronman, "The Law as a Profession," in D. Rhodes, ed., *Ethics in Practice: Lawyers' Roles, Responsibilities and Regulation* (Oxford: Oxford University Press, 2000) 29 at 30.

6 A. Abbot, *The System of Professions: An Essay on the Division of Expert Labor* (Chicago: University of Chicago Press, 1988).

7 W.B. Cotter, *Professional Responsibility Instruction in Canada: A Coordinated Curriculum for Legal Education* (Montreal: Conceptcom, 1992).

8 H.W. Arthurs, "Why Canadian Law Schools Do Not Teach Legal Ethics," in K. Economides, ed., *Ethical Challenges to Legal Education and Conduct* (Oxford: Hart Publishing, 1998); A. Dodek, "Canadian Legal Ethics: A Subject in Search of Scholarship" (2000) 50 University of Toronto Law Journal 115; S.M. Bundy, "Ethics Education in the First Year: An Experiment" (1995) 58 Law and Contemporary Problems 19; and E.B. Spaeth Jr., J.G. Perry, and P.B. Wachs, "Teaching Legal Ethics: Exploring the Continuum" (1995) 58 Law and Contemporary Problems 153.

9 See, for example, F. Zacharias, "Reconciling Professionalism and Client Interests" (1995) 36 William and Mary Law Review 1303; D. Wilkins, "Redefining the 'Professional' in Professional Ethics: An Interdisciplinary Approach to Teaching Professionalism" (1996) 58 Law and Contemporary Problems 241; A. Kronman, "Professionalism" (1999) 2 Journal of the Institute for the Study of Legal Ethics 8; J. Sammons, "The Professionalism Movement: The Problems Defined" (1993) 29 Georgia Law Review 1035; D. Tanovich, "The Reconstruction of a Distinctly Canadian Role Morality 'In the Interests of Justice' and Its Implications for Reform" (presented at the Fourth Chief Justice of Ontario's Coloquia on the Legal Profession, University of Windsor, 3 March 2005); J.O. Calmore, "'Chasing the Wind': Pursuing Social Justice, Overcoming Legal Mis-Education, and Engaging in Professional Re-Socialization" (2004) 37 Loyala of Los Angeles Law Review 1167; and S. Hartwell, "Moral Growth or Moral Angst? A Clinical Approach" (2004) 11 Clinical Law Review 115.

10 A. Kronman, *The Lost Lawyer: Failing Ideals of the Legal Profession* (Cambridge, MA: Harvard University Press, 1993).

11 W. Bennett, *The Lawyer's Myth: Reviving the Ideals of the Legal Profession* (Chicago: University of Chicago Press, 2001).

12 See, for example, James R. Elkins, "Rites de Passage: Law Students 'Telling Their Lives'" (1985) 35 Journal of Legal Education 27.

13 Kronman, see note 10 at 113-16.

14 Fred Zacharias, see note 9 above at 1307, states, "No term in the legal lexicon has been more abused than 'professionalism.'"

15 R. Nelson, "Ideology, Practice and Professional Autonomy: Social Values and Client Relationships in the Large Law Firm," in R. Abel, ed., *Lawyers: A Critical Reader* (New York: New Press, 1997) 70 at 72.

16 A point made effectively by Walter Bennett, see note 11 above.

17 B.D. Bills, "To Be or Not to Be: The Civility of the Young Lawyer" (2005) 5 Connecticut Public International Law Journal 31; M.E. Aspen, "Overcoming Barriers to Civility in Litigation" (1999) 69 Mississippi Law Journal 1049; and T.A. Baker, "A Survey of Professionalism and Civility" (2005) 38 Indiana Law Review 1305.

18 See also J. Macfarlane, "Mediating Ethically: The Limits of Codes of Conduct and the Potential of a Reflective Practice Model" (2002) 39(4) Osgoode Hall Law Journal 49.

19 There is a growing literature on the issue of "good faith" in bargaining. See, for example, K. Kovach, "Good Faith in Mediation: Requested, Recommended or Required? A New Ethic" (1997) 38 South Texas Law Review 575. Most jurisdictions are understandably hesitant about legislating such a requirement, although some have attempted such a rule. See J. Lande, "Using Dispute System Decision Methods to Promote Good-Faith Participation in Court-Connected Mediation Program" (2002) 50 University of California Los Angeles Law Review 69; and the discussion later in this chapter.

20 Law Society of Upper Canada, *Rules of Professional Conduct* (2000), http://www.fmc.ca/pdf/CodeProfessionalConduct.pdf, Rule 4.07. See also Canadian Bar Association, *Alternative Dispute Resolution Section Model Code of Conduct for Mediators* (1998), http://www.attorneygeneral.jus.gov.on.ca/english/courts/manmed/codeofconduct.asp, Rule 5; and American Bar Association, *Model Rules of Professional Conduct* (1983) (revised 2002), http://www.abanet.org/cpr/mrpc/mrpc_toc.html, Rule 1.12.

21 L. Cooks and C. Hale, "The Construction of Ethics in Mediation" (1994) 2(1) Mediation Quarterly 55 at 72. The original notion of discourse ethics comes from the work of Jürgen Habermas, in particular, his *Theory of Communicative Action* (Frankfurt: Suhrkamp, 1981).

22 K. Barnett, "Feminist Legal Methods" (1990) 102 Harvard Law Review 829 at 881.

23 Law Society of Upper Canada, *Rules of Professional Conduct,* see note 20 above, Rule 2.20(3): "A lawyer should consider the use of alternative dispute resolution (ADR) for every dispute and, if appropriate, the lawyer shall inform the client of ADR options and if so instructed, take steps to pursue those options." Other codes have a similar provision, see, for example, American Bar Association, *Model Rules of Professional Conduct* (1983) (revised 2002), see note 20 above, Rule 1.4; Virginia State Bar, *Rules of Professional Conduct* (2006), http://www.vsb.org/docs/rules-pc_2006-07pg.pdf, Rule 1.2; and Colorado Bar Association, *Colorado Rules of Professional Conduct* (1992) (revised 2007), http://www.cobar.org/group/index.cfm?category=384&EntityID=CETH, Rule 2.1.

24 J. Macfarlane, "Experiences of Collaborative Law: Preliminary Results from the Collaborative Lawyering Research Project" (2004) 1 Journal of Dispute Resolution 179 at 212-16; and J. Macfarlane, *The Emerging Phenomenon of Collaborative Family Law (CFL): A Qualitative Study of CFL Cases* (Ottawa: Department of Justice, 2005), http://www.canada.justice.gc.ca/en/ps/pad/reports/2005-FCY-1 at 71-76.

25 Macfarlane, "Experiences of Collaborative Law," see note 24 above at 213.

26 See, for example, J. Macfarlane and M. Keet, "Civil Justice Reform and Mandatory Civil Mediation in Saskatchewan: Lessons from a Maturing Program" (2004) 42(3) Alberta Law Review 677 at 691-93.

27 See, for example, J. Nolan-Haley, "Court Mediation and the Search for Justice through Law" (1996) 74 Washington University Law Quarterly 47.

28 On this point, see the discussion in T. Hedeen and P.G. Coy, "Community Mediation and the Court System: The Ties That Bind" (2000) 17 Mediation Quarterly 351.

29 See, for example, the accounts in J. Macfarlane and M. Keet, *Learning from Experience: An Evaluation of the Saskatchewan Queen's Bench Mediation Program* (Regina: Saskatchewan

Justice, April 2003) at 29-30; and J. Macfarlane, *Court-Based Mediation in Civil Cases: An Evaluation of the Toronto General Division ADR Centre* (Ottawa: Queen's Printer, 1995) at 41-42. When asked if they had sent information about the mediation session on to their clients, 49 percent of lawyers responded in the affirmative, but only 37 percent of their clients said they had received the materials (based on questionnaire data, n=707).

30 Macfarlane, *Court-Based Mediation,* see note 29 above at 42.

31 *Ibid.* at 41.

32 See, for example, E. Kruk, "Power Imbalance and Spouse Abuse in Divorce Disputes: Deconstructing Mediation Practice via the 'Simulated Client' Technique" (1998) 12 International Journal of Law, Policy and Family 1; and T. Grillo, "The Mediation Alternative: Process Dangers for Women" (1991) 100 Yale Law Journal 1545 especially at 1590-93.

33 See Anthony's story in Macfarlane, see note 18 above at 74-81.

34 C. Menekel-Meadow, "The Limits of Adversarial Ethics," in D. Rhodes, ed., *Ethics in Practice: Lawyer's Roles, Responsibilities and Regulations* (Oxford: Oxford University Press, 2000), 123 at 135.

35 Unpublished data from the Collaborative Lawyering Research project.

36 Macfarlane, *Court-Based Mediation,* see note 29 above at 46.

37 *Ibid.* at 47.

38 *Ibid.* at 23.

39 Unpublished data from the Collaborative Lawyering Research project.

40 *Ibid.* at 46-47.

41 Macfarlane, *Court-Based Mediation,* see note 29 above at 48.

42 *Ibid.* at 46.

43 This expression, which refers to a lawyer who sits in silence and does not participate in the mediation, appears to originate in C. Guittard, "Preparing for Mediation and Negotiation," parts 1 and 2 (1991) 37 Practical Lawyer 77 and 65.

44 J. Lande, "How Will Lawyering and Mediation Practices Transform Each Other?" (1997) 24 Florida State University Law Review 839 at 885.

45 Unpublished data from the Collaborative Lawyering Research project.

46 *Ibid.* [emphasis added].

47 Macfarlane, *Court-Based Mediation,* see note 29 above at 23.

48 *Ibid.* at 23.

49 Unpublished data from the Culture Change project.

50 *Ibid.*

51 See, for example, Macfarlane and Keet, note 29 above at 55-56.

52 J. Macfarlane, "Culture Change? A Tale of Two Cities and Mandatory Court-Connected Mediation" (2002) 2 Journal of Dispute Resolution 241 at 257.

53 *Ibid.* at 267.

54 Unpublished data from Macfarlane and Keet, see note 29 above.

55 According to J. Lande, "Why a Good-Faith Requirement is a Bad Idea for Mediation" (2005) 23(1) Alternatives to the High Cost of Litigation 1, at least twenty-two US states now have statutes requiring good faith participation in mediation along with twenty-one federal district courts and seventeen state courts.

56 Macfarlane and Keet, see note 29 above at 19.

57 See the broad general rule proposed by Kimberlee Kovach in "Good Faith in Mediation: Requested, Recommended or Required A New Ethic?" (1997) 38 South Texas Law Review 575 at 622-23. For a different approach, see J. Lande, see note 19 above. Lande argues that consensus building is more effective than a rule.

58 See Lande, see note 55 above at 9.

59 Unpublished data from Macfarlane and Keet, see note 29 above.

60 Macfarlane, see note 52 above at 316; and Macfarlane and Keet, see note 29 above at 30.

61 For example, data collected among Toronto litigators compared with the Ottawa bar. See Macfarlane, see note 52 above at 313-16.

62 Unpublished data from the Culture Change project.

63 *Ibid.*

64 R. Axelrod, *The Evolution of Co-operation* (New York: Basic Books, 1984).

65 Macfarlane and Keet, see note 26 above at 692-93.

66 Unpublished data, from Macfarlane and Keet, see note 29 above; see also Macfarlane and Keet, note 26 above at 694-97.

67 See also the discussion in Chapter 6 under "Client Participation."

68 Unpublished data from the Culture Change project.

69 See, in particular, the discussion in Chapter 6.

70 Unpublished data from the Collaborative Lawyering Research project.

71 Macfarlane, see note 29 above at 6.

72 J. Alfini, "Trashing, Bashing and Hashing It Out: Is This the End of 'Good Mediation'?" (1991) 19 Florida State University Law Review 47.

73 *In re Patterson*, 969 P.2d 1106 (Wash Ct App., 1999), cited in P. Thompson, "Enforcing Rights Generated in Court-Connected Mediation: Tension between the Aspirations of a Private Facilitative Process and the Reality of Public Adversarial Justice" (2004) 19 Ohio State Law on Dispute Resolution 509 at 558. Generally, see F. Sander, "The Obsession with Settlement Rates" (1995) 11 Negotiation Journal 329.

74 B. McAdoo, "A Report to the Minnesota Supreme Court: The Impact of Rule 114 on Civil Litigation in Minnesota" (2002) 25 Hamline Law Review 401 at 428-29.

75 However, it was not clear whether this was pressure from the mediator and/or pressure from counsel on either side, unless the comment specifically indicated the source.

76 Macfarlane, see note 29 above at 43.

77 Lande, see note 44 above at 885.

78 A database of all US federal and state cases that review questions relating to mediation is being maintained at the Hamline University Law School. See J. Coben and N. Thompson, "Disputing Irony: A Systematic Look at Litigation about Mediation" (2006) 11 Harvard Negotiation Law Review 43.

79 N. Welsh, "The Thinning Vision of Self-Determination in Court-Connected Mediation: The Inevitable Price of Institutionalisation?" (2001) 6 Harvard Negotiation Law Review 1 at 87.

80 Unpublished data from the Culture Change project.

81 M.A. Wilkinson, C. Walker, and P. Mercer, "Do Codes of Ethics Actually Shape Legal Practice" (2000) 45 McGill Law Journal 645.

Chapter 9: Where the Action Is

1 Even an interest in conducting such research seems to be lacking. The only study I am aware of is L. Volk, "Legal Preparation Tested by Success in Legal Practice" (1919) 33 Harvard Law Review 168.

2 Described as "prevailing negativism," this is the model that governs most education/practice transitions. See C.A. Dailey, *Assessment of Lives* (San Francisco: Jossey-Bass, 1971).

3 R. Harrison, "Overview of Accreditation, Validation, Evaluation and Assessment in Professional Education," in S. Goodland, ed., *Education for the Professions: Quis Custodiet?* (Guildford: SRHE-NFER-Nelson, 1984) at 151.

4 For the class statement of this position in Canada, see Consultative Group on Research and Education in Law, *Law and Learning* (Ottawa: Social Science and Humanities Research Council of Canada, 1983) (also known as the Arthur's Report).

5 J. Macfarlane, "Look before You Leap: Knowledge and Learning in Legal Skills Education" (1992) 19 Journal of Law and Society 291 at 294-97.

6 See the classic discussion in W. Twining, "Legal Skills and Legal Education" (1988) 22 Law Teacher 4.

7 Mary Hanna, quoted in E. Myers, "Teaching Good and Teaching Well: Integrating Values with Theory and Practice" (1997) 47 Journal of Legal Education 401.

8 See, for example, R. MacCrate, *Legal Education and Professional Development: An Educational Continuum,* Report of the Task Force on Law Schools and the Profession: Narrowing the Gap (Chicago: American Bar Association, 1992); Marre Committee, *A Time for Change: Report of the Committee on the Future of the Legal Profession* (London: General

Council of the Bar/Law Society of Upper Canada, 1988); and Australian Law Reform Commission, *Managing Justice: A Review of the Federal Justice System,* Report No. 89 (Sydney: Australian Law Reform Commission, 1999) at chapters 2 and 3, www.austlii.edu.au/au/other/alrc/publications/reports/89.

9 Canadian Bar Association, *Attitudes, Skills, Knowledge: Proposals for Legal Education to Assist in Implementing a Multi-Option Civil Justice System in the Twenty-First Century,* Joint Committee Report on Legal Education (Ottawa: Canadian Bar Association, 1999).

10 J. Macfarlane and J. Manwaring, for the Law Society of Upper Canada, *Taxonomy of Professional Skills* (2005), unpublished, on file with the author.

11 J. Macfarlane and J. Manwaring, "Reconciling Professional Legal Education with the Evolving (Trial-less) Reality of Legal Practice" (2006) 1 Journal of Dispute Resolution 253 at 262.

12 For a detailed discussion of the results of a skills audit and the subsequent development of the new curriculum, see Macfarlane and Manwaring, see *ibid.*

13 Unpublished data from the Culture Change project.

14 *Ibid.*

15 See, for example, A. Lerner, "Law and Lawyering in the Workplace: Building Better Lawyers by Teaching Students to Exercise Critical Judgment as Creative Problem-Solvers" (1999) 32 Akron Law Review 107; Janet Reno, "Lawyers as Problem-Solvers," keynote address to the American Association of Law Schools (1999) 49 Journal of Legal Education 5.

16 The Bar Admission Course Review Working Group (chaired by Philip Epstein QC), "Discussion Paper" Report to Convocation, 27 February 1998 at 5. Similar statements about the overarching need for professional legal education to develop the capacity for lifelong learning appear in (for example) MacCrate, see note 8 above; Marre Committee, see note 8 above; and Australian Law Reform Commission, see note 8 above.

17 The source of the concept of "reflective practice" is generally attributed to the work of Donald Schon and Chris Argyris. See D. Schon, *The Reflective Practitioner* (San Francisco: Jossey-Bass, 1983); D. Schon, *Educating the Reflective Practitioner* (San Francisco: Jossey-Bass, 1987); and D. Schon and C. Argyris, *Theory in Practice: Increasing Professional Effectiveness* (San Francisco: Jossey-Bass, 1980). In relation to legal practice, see D. Schon, "Educating the Reflective Legal Practitioner" (1995) 2 Clinical Law Review 231; and the first *Report of the Lord Chancellor's Advisory Committee on Legal Education and Conduct* (London: Lord Chancellor's Department, 1996).

18 See, for example, Christopher Johns and Dawn Freshwater, eds., *Transforming Nursing Through Reflective Practice,* 2nd edition (London: Blackwell, 2006); and Silvia Mamede and Henk G. Schmidt, "The Structure of Reflective Practice in Medicine" (2004) 38(12) Medical Education 1302.

19 See also J. Macfarlane, "The Challenge of ADR and Alternative Paradigms of Dispute Resolution: How Should the Law Schools Respond?" (1997) 31 Law Teacher 13 at 19-20.

20 Sally Engle Merry, "Legal Pluralism" (1988) 22(5) Law and Society Review 869.

21 J. Lande, "Getting the Faith: Why Business Lawyers and Executives Believe in Mediation" (2000) 5 Harvard Negotiation Law Review 137.

22 For example, the introduction of negotiation and mediation courses into growing numbers of law schools as elective components (for a review, see J. Watson-Hamilton, "The Significance of Mediation for Legal Education" (1999) 17 Windsor Yearbook of Access to Justice 280); the introduction of mandatory dispute resolution courses in some law schools, such as the University of Ottawa (see E. Zweibel, "Where Does ADR Fit into the Mainstream Law Curriculum?" (1999) 17 Windsor Yearbook of Access to Justice 295); and, at the professional stage, the Law Society of Upper Canada's new Skills and Professional Responsibility Program, which commences in 2006 and is discussed earlier in this book.

23 Judith Resnick, "Managerial Judges" (1982) 96 Harvard Law Review 374; H. Baer Jr., "History, Process, and a Role for Judges in Mediating Their Own Cases" (2001) 28 New York University Annual Survey of American Law 143; E.V. Ludwig, "The Changing Role of the Trial Judge" (2002) 85 Judicature 216; and T. Farrow, "Thinking about Dispute Resolution" (2003) 41 Alberta Law Review 559.

24 See the data presented by Bobbi McAdoo in B. McAdoo, "All Rise, the Court Is in Session: What Judges Say about Court-Connected Mediation" (2007) 22(2) Ohio State Journal on Dispute Resolution 377 at 430.

25 See, for example, section 718.2(e) of the *Criminal Code*, R.S.C. 1985, c. C-46, s. 264; and sections 38(2)(d) and 39(2) of the *Youth Criminal Justice Act*, S.C. 2002, c. 1.

26 See, for example, D. Wexler and B. Winick, eds., *Law in a Therapeutic Key: Developments in Therapeutic Jurisprudence* (Durham: Carolina Academic Press, 1996).

27 Interview with Judge Alex Calabrese, Red Hook Community Justice Center, http://www. courtinnovation.org.

28 See M. Galanter, "Reading the Landscape of Disputes: What We Know and Don't Know (And Think We Know) about Our Allegedly Contentious and Litigious Society" (1983) 31(1) University of California Los Angeles Law Review 4.

29 There is little precise statistical evidence available with respect to the number of unrepresented litigants. However, professionals within the court system observe that the numbers of such litigants in the system are increasing. Some estimate that over 50 percent of proceedings involve one or more unrepresented litigants. Special Committee on Self-Represented Litigants, *Report on Self-Represented Litigants, Background and General Recommendations* (Toronto: Ontario Court of Justice, 1999). However, it is estimated that 15-25 percent of unrepresented litigants are ones who might be able to afford a lawyer, but do not want one or cannot keep one. D.A. Rollie Thompson, "The Judge as Counsel" (Spring 2005) 8 Canadian Forum on Civil Justice 3; D.A. Rollie Thompson and Lynn Reierson, "A Practicing Lawyer's Field Guide to the Self-Represented" (2002) 19 Canadian Family Law Quarterly 529 at 530. The Ontario Superior Court reported that between 1995 and 1999 the number of self-represented litigants in Ontario's Unified Family Court rose by 500 percent. Lynne Cohen, "Unrepresented Justice" (2001) 25 Canadian Law 40. This dramatic increase has also been noted in more recent years. The Judge as Counsel, Rollie Thompson, see note 27 above; and Ministry of the Attorney General, "2003/04-2005/06 Service Plan," http://www.bcbudget.gov.bc.ca/2003/sp/ag/ag_strategic.htm.

30 In Canada, from 1993-94 to 2002-03, the number of approved civil legal aid applications (the large majority being for family law) dropped from 386,617 to 247,536, a 36 percent decrease. See Canadian Centre for Justice Statistics, *Legal Aid in Canada, Resource and Caseload Tables 1997-98*, Catalogue No. 85F0028XIE (Ottawa: Statistics Canada, 1999) at Table 10; and Canadian Centre for Justice Statistics, *Legal Aid in Canada, Resource and Caseload Statistics 2002-03*, Catalogue No. 85F0015XIE (Ottawa: Statistics Canada, 2004) at Table 12. The *Ontario Legal Aid Review* reported that "in 1996-97 the Plan issued only 14,063 family law certificates ... The contrast with previous years is striking. In the fiscal year 1993-94, 65,691 family law certificates were issued in the province. The number of family certificates has dropped to levels not seen since 1970." See *Ontario Legal Aid Review, A Blueprint for Publicly Funded Legal Services*, volume 1 (Toronto: Government of Ontario, 1997).

31 The methodology adopted in this survey was a modified Delphi approach. The Delphi method circulates text among panels of experts for their input and generally continues this process for a number of rounds until a consensus emerges. In this case, two Delphi rounds were conducted using a survey including both closed and open questions. The survey asked judges to identify judicial skills and abilities, new areas of need for training and further education, and incrementally developed an inventory of judges' skills and abilities. Three Delphi panels were formed, one representing judges who had served up to five years on the bench, a second for mid-career judges (six to fifteen years since appointment); and a final panel representing senior judges (more than fifteen years on the bench). The panels were fairly evenly divided between federal and provincial appointments and men and women.

32 Complete results from the Delphi survey are available from the National Judicial Institute, http://www.nji.org.

33 Perhaps this also reflects a growing interest in judges in providing private mediation and arbitration services after retirement.

34 See R. Wissler, "Barriers to Attorneys Discussion and Use of ADR" (2004) 19(2) Ohio State Journal on Dispute Resolution 459 at 488-89.
35 Culture Change project, in Macfarlane, see note 13 above at 315-16.
36 A point noted by McAdoo, see note 24 above at 430.
37 R. Abel, "The Professional as Political: English Lawyers through the 1989 Green Papers through the Access to Justice Act 1999," in W. Felstiner, ed., *Reorganisation and Resistance* (Oxford: Hart Publishing, 2005) 13 at 22.
38 *Ibid.* at 22-24.
39 See Law Society of Upper Canada, *Task Force on Paralegal Regulation* (Toronto: Law Society of Upper Canada, 23 September 2004); Bill 14, *Access to Justice Act,* S.O. 2006, c. 21 (assented to 19 October 2006, 2d Sess., 38th Leg., Ontario).
40 A good example of the controversy stirred by multidisciplinary practices (MDPs) is provided by the history of this debate in British Columbia. A two-year debate culminated in a 2001 report by the Multi-Disciplinary Practice Working Group, which recommended that the recognition of MDPs be rejected by the benchers (see http://www.law society.bc.ca/publications_forms/bulletin/2000-01/01-12-14_MDP.html).
41 See, for example, *New South Wales Legal Practice Rules* (1987; amended 1997), Rule 40, section 48G. For a more relaxed and unrestricted approach, see the recommendations of the Canadian Bar Association, *Report of the International Practice of Law Committee on Multi-Disciplinary Practices and the Legal Profession* (Ottawa: Canadian Bar Association, 1999) at 31.
42 M. Thornton, "The Australian Legal Profession: Towards a National Identity," in Felstiner, see note 37 above, 134 at 138.
43 See the description of the team model in N. Cameron, *Collaborative Practice: Deepening the Dialogue* (Vancouver: Continuing Legal Education Society of British Columbia, 2004) at 106-15.
44 J. Macfarlane, *The Emerging Phenomenon of Collaborative Family Law (CFL): A Qualitative Study of CFL Cases* (Ottawa: Department of Justice, 2005), http://www.canada.justice.gc. ca/en/ps/pad/reports/2005-FCY-1 at 55.
45 *Ibid.*
46 *Ibid.* at 54.
47 *Ibid.* at 34-35.
48 *Ibid.* at 55.
49 *Ibid.*

Epilogue

1 W. Felstiner, "Reorganisation and Resistance," in W. Felstiner, ed., *Reorganisation and Resistance* (Oxford: Hart Publishing, 2005) 1 at 8.

Index

LAW AND
SOCIETY

Lori G. Beaman
Defining Harm: Religious Freedom and the Limits of the Law (2007)

Stephen Tierney (ed.)
Multiculturalism and the Canadian Constitution (2007)

Kimberley White
Negotiating Responsibility: Law, Murder, and States of Mind (2007)

Dawn Moore
Criminal Artefacts: Governing Drugs and Users (2007)

Hamar Foster, Heather Raven, and Jeremy Webber (eds.)
Let Right Be Done: Aboriginal Title, the Calder Case, and the Future of Indigenous Rights (2007)

Dorothy E. Chunn, Susan B. Boyd, and Hester Lessard (eds.)
Reaction and Resistance: Feminism, Law, and Social Change (2007)

Margot Young, Susan B. Boyd, Gwen Brodsky, and Shelagh Day (eds.)
Poverty: Rights, Social Citizenship, and Legal Activism (2007)

Rosanna L. Langer
Defining Rights and Wrongs: Bureaucracy, Human Rights, and Public Accountability (2007)

C.L. Ostberg and Matthew E. Wetstein
Attitudinal Decision Making in the Supreme Court of Canada (2007)

Chris Clarkson
Domestic Reforms: Political Visions and Family Regulation in British Columbia, 1862-1940 (2007)

Jean McKenzie Leiper
Bar Codes: Women in the Legal Profession (2006)

Gerald Baier
Courts and Federalism: Judicial Doctrine in the United States, Australia, and Canada (2006)

Avigail Eisenberg (ed.)
Diversity and Equality: The Changing Framework of Freedom in Canada (2006)

Randy K. Lippert
Sanctuary, Sovereignty, Sacrifice: Canadian Sanctuary Incidents, Power, and Law (2005)

James B. Kelly
Governing with the Charter: Legislative and Judicial Activism and Framers' Intent (2005)

Dianne Pothier and Richard Devlin (eds.)
Critical Disability Theory: Essays in Philosophy, Politics, Policy, and Law (2005)

Susan G. Drummond
Mapping Marriage Law in Spanish Gitano Communities (2005)

Louis A. Knafla and Jonathan Swainger (eds.)
Laws and Societies in the Canadian Prairie West, 1670-1940 (2005)

Ikechi Mgbeoji
Global Biopiracy: Patents, Plants, and Indigenous Knowledge (2005)

Florian Sauvageau, David Schneiderman, and David Taras, with Ruth Klinkhammer and Pierre Trudel
The Last Word: Media Coverage of the Supreme Court of Canada (2005)

Gerald Kernerman
Multicultural Nationalism: Civilizing Difference, Constituting Community (2005)

Pamela A. Jordan
Defending Rights in Russia: Lawyers, the State, and Legal Reform in the Post-Soviet Era (2005)

Anna Pratt
Securing Borders: Detention and Deportation in Canada (2005)

Kirsten Johnson Kramar
Unwilling Mothers, Unwanted Babies: Infanticide in Canada (2005)

W.A. Bogart
Good Government? Good Citizens? Courts, Politics, and Markets in a Changing Canada (2005)

Catherine Dauvergne
Humanitarianism, Identity, and Nation: Migration Laws in Canada and Australia (2005)

Michael Lee Ross
First Nations Sacred Sites in Canada's Courts (2005)

Andrew Woolford
Between Justice and Certainty: Treaty Making in British Columbia (2005)

John McLaren, Andrew Buck, and Nancy Wright (eds.)
Despotic Dominion: Property Rights in British Settler Societies (2004)

Georges Campeau
From UI to EI: Waging War on the Welfare State (2004)

Alvin J. Esau
The Courts and the Colonies: The Litigation of Hutterite Church Disputes (2004)

Christopher N. Kendall
Gay Male Pornography: An Issue of Sex Discrimination (2004)

Roy B. Flemming
Tournament of Appeals: Granting Judicial Review in Canada (2004)

Constance Backhouse and Nancy L. Backhouse
The Heiress vs the Establishment: Mrs. Campbell's Campaign for Legal Justice (2004)

Christopher P. Manfredi
Feminist Activism in the Supreme Court: Legal Mobilization and the Women's Legal Education and Action Fund (2004)

Annalise Acorn
Compulsory Compassion: A Critique of Restorative Justice (2004)

Jonathan Swainger and Constance Backhouse (eds.)
People and Place: Historical Influences on Legal Culture (2003)

Jim Phillips and Rosemary Gartner
Murdering Holiness: The Trials of Franz Creffield and George Mitchell (2003)

David R. Boyd
Unnatural Law: Rethinking Canadian Environmental Law and Policy (2003)

Ikechi Mgbeoji
Collective Insecurity: The Liberian Crisis, Unilateralism, and Global Order (2003)

Rebecca Johnson
Taxing Choices: The Intersection of Class, Gender, Parenthood, and the Law (2002)

John McLaren, Robert Menzies, and Dorothy E. Chunn (eds.)
Regulating Lives: Historical Essays on the State, Society, the Individual, and the Law (2002)

Joan Brockman
Gender in the Legal Profession: Fitting or Breaking the Mould (2001)

Printed and bound in Canada by Friesens

Set in Stone by Robert Kroeger

Copy editor: Stacy Belden

Proofreader: Stephanie VanderMeulen

Indexer: Christine Jacobs